I0885807

Praise for *Truth Before Reconciliation*

"This incredibly urgent collection defines and analyzes Indian residential school denialism, explains why it is on the rise, maps its techniques and networks, and offers practical, legal, archival, pedagogical, and public history responses. Truth Before Reconciliation *rises to the monumental task of helping Canadians differentiate between rage bait and fact."*

—Pam Palmater, Toronto Metropolitan University

"This first book-length study of denialism will be a seminal book in the field. It is an excellent and clear refutation of the key talking points of many denialists and their mistaken assumptions and desire to deceive. Truth Before Reconciliation *should be in every school, university, and public library."*

—David B. MacDonald, University of Guelph

"Residential school denialism rarely takes the form of outright claims that the system never existed. More often, it appears through subtle but powerful moves that minimize, cherry-pick, or decontextualize the historical record, softening the devastating impacts of residential schools and colonial violence on Indigenous peoples and their communities. In Truth Before Reconciliation, *Sean Carleton and Niigaan Sinclair carefully expose these patterns and demonstrate why they matter. By situating denialism within broader struggles over historical literacy and public education, the authors show how incomplete or distorted understandings of the past continue to shape relationships in the present. At a time when debates about truth, reconciliation, and public memory are often hotly contested, this book offers an essential and timely intervention—guiding readers back to the historical record while challenging denialist myths through careful analysis and the lived experiences of those working on the front lines of residential school history and truth-telling. This book offers everyone a clear direction forward."*

—Janice Forsyth, University of British Columbia

"This timely book offers crucial insight into the rise of residential school denialism, and through nuanced examination of the people and strategies behind it, provides the knowledge and understanding we need to resist and defuse it."

—Carey Newman, University of Victoria

"It is so important we continue to teach truth amidst the hurtful noise of denialism and the creep it is making into Canadian society, from mainstream media to classrooms and to the House of Commons. This foundational book, edited by Niigaan Sinclair and Sean Carleton, contains true voices, lived experience, and undeniable facts about settler colonialism in Canada. Truth Before Reconciliation *is strong, essential reading for every Canadian looking to understand Indian Residential School denialism, how harmful it is and how unjust it is. Canada has a complex relationship with Indigenous Peoples, and this book examines why and how the country can work to turn things around. It is an important written arsenal in the fight against denialism and hate."*

—Tanya Talaga, author of *The Knowing*

"It took such immense courage for Survivors to share their lived experience of residential schooling with the TRC, and the world at large. It's time for us to lift the burden of confronting denialists' manipulation of historical record from the shoulders of Survivors and intergenerational Survivors. This multi-voiced volume provides the arguments and the evidence necessary to stand up for the truth. Thank you Drs. Sinclair and Carleton for creating and curating this essential and timely book."

—Shelagh Rogers OC, Honorary Witness,
Truth and Reconciliation Commission of Canada
Chancellor, Queen's University

TRUTH

BEFORE RECONCILIATION

Truth Before Reconciliation: Confronting Residential School Denialism

30 29 28 27 26 1 2 3 4 5

University of Manitoba Press
Winnipeg, Manitoba, Canada
Treaty 1 Territory
uofmpress.ca

For EU product safety concerns please contact Mare Nostrum Group B.V., Mauritskade 21D, 1091 GC Amsterdam, The Netherlands, gpsr@mare-nostrum.co.uk.

Cataloguing data available from Library and Archives Canada
ISBN 978-177284-162-6 (PAPER)
ISBN 978-177284-164-0 (PDF)
ISBN 978-177284-165-7 (EPUB)
ISBN 978-177284-163-3 (BOUND)

Cover design by Vincent Design Inc.
Cover image: National Reconciliation Day, 30 September 2022, The Canadian Press/John Woods
Interior design by Karen Armstrong

Printed in Canada

The University of Manitoba Press acknowledges the financial support for its publication program provided by the Government of Canada through the Canada Book Fund, the Canada Council for the Arts, the Manitoba Department of Sport, Culture, and Heritage, the Manitoba Arts Council, and the Manitoba Book Publishing Tax Credit.

Proceeds from the sale of this book will be donated to Indian Residential School Survivors Society (www.irsss.ca).

Funded by the Government of Canada | Canada

CERTIFIED CANADIAN PUBLISHER

TRUTH
BEFORE RECONCILIATION

CONFRONTING RESIDENTIAL SCHOOL DENIALISM

EDITED BY
SEAN CARLETON AND NIIGAAN SINCLAIR

University of Manitoba Press

"Without truth, justice is not served, healing cannot happen, and there can be no genuine reconciliation."

—Truth and Reconciliation Commission of Canada

The following content concerns Canada's Indian Residential School System and includes references to child abuse, sexual abuse, death, genocide, and intergenerational trauma, which may be distressing to readers. It also discusses the actions of those who seek to deny, downplay, distort, and minimize harms related to residential schooling, which may be triggering.

If you need support, please take care and access the following resources available:

- National Indian Residential School Crisis Line: 1-866-925-4419
- Indian Residential School Survivors Society: 1-800-721-0066
- Hope for Wellness Helpline: 1-855-242-3310

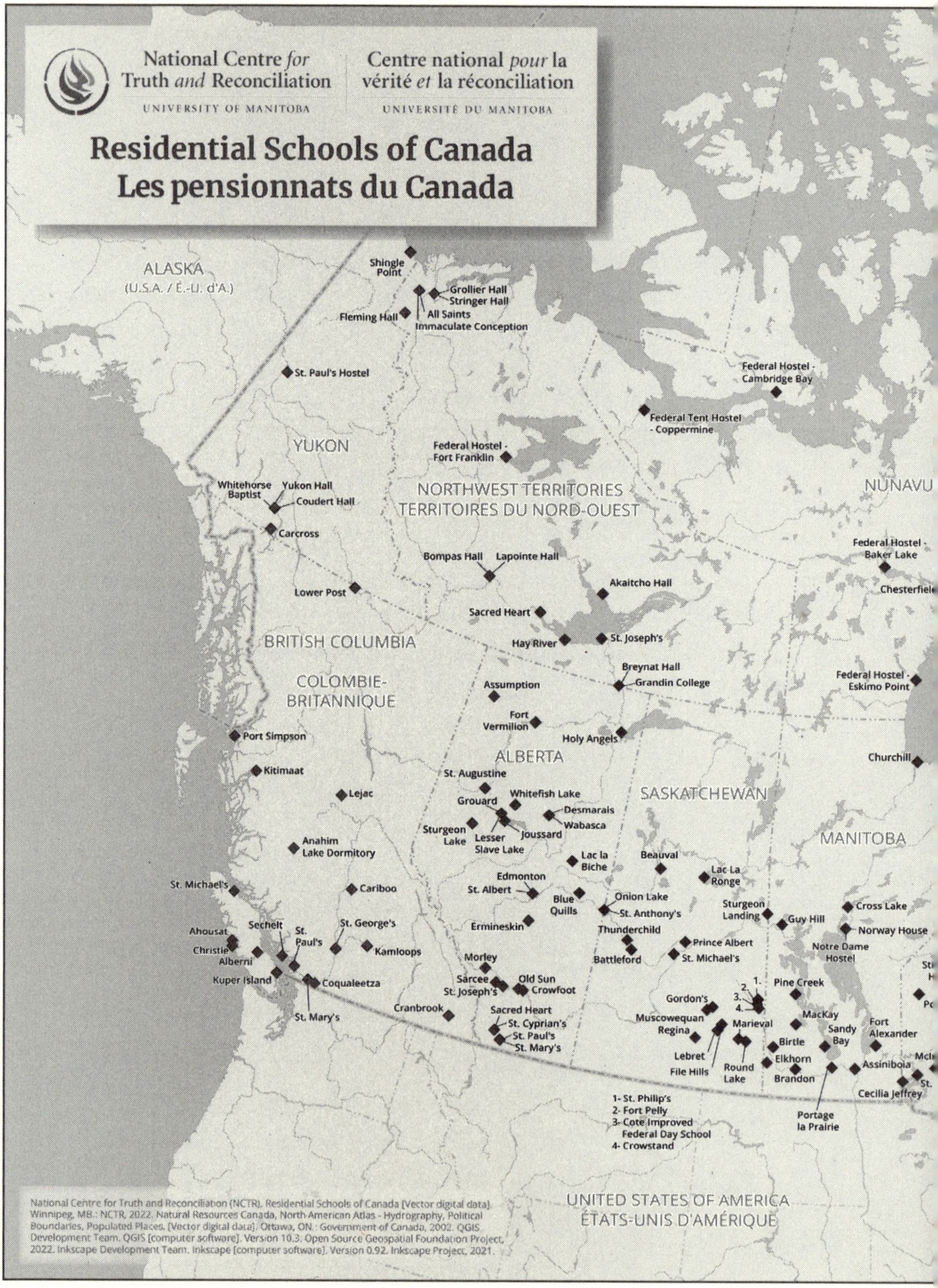

Map 1. Residential Schools of Canada. National Centre for Truth and Reconciliation.

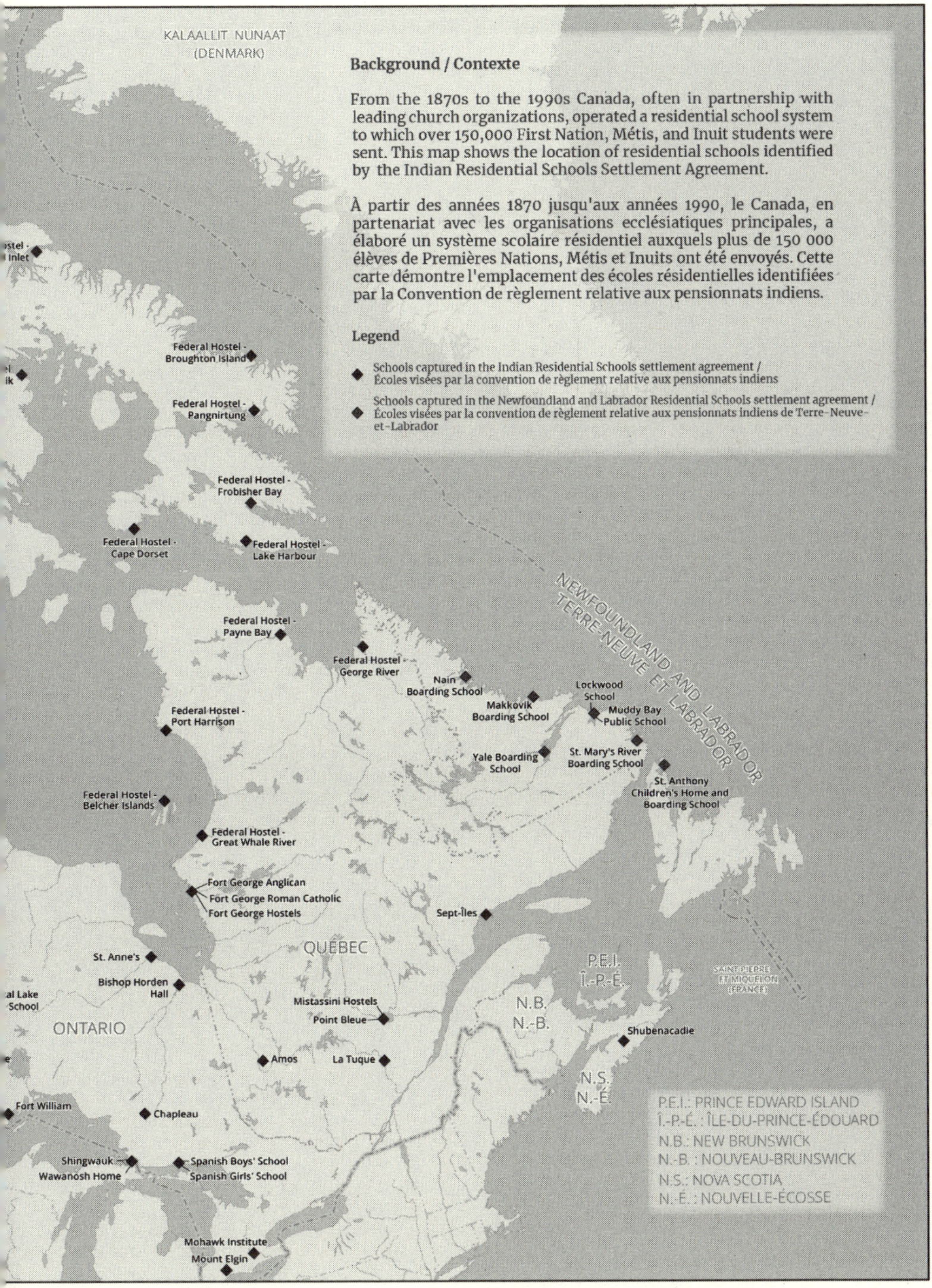

Background / Contexte

From the 1870s to the 1990s Canada, often in partnership with leading church organizations, operated a residential school system to which over 150,000 First Nation, Métis, and Inuit students were sent. This map shows the location of residential schools identified by the Indian Residential Schools Settlement Agreement.

À partir des années 1870 jusqu'aux années 1990, le Canada, en partenariat avec les organisations ecclésiatiques principales, a élaboré un système scolaire résidentiel auxquels plus de 150 000 élèves de Premières Nations, Métis et Inuits ont été envoyés. Cette carte démontre l'emplacement des écoles résidentielles identifiées par la Convention de règlement relative aux pensionnats indiens.

Legend

◆ Schools captured in the Indian Residential Schools settlement agreement / Écoles visées par la convention de règlement relative aux pensionnats indiens

◆ Schools captured in the Newfoundland and Labrador Residential Schools settlement agreement / Écoles visées par la convention de règlement relative aux pensionnats indiens de Terre-Neuve-et-Labrador

CONTENTS

ILLUSTRATIONS

Map

Figures

Tables

ABBREVIATIONS

ACC	Anglican Church of Canada
AIRS	Alberni Indian Residential School
APTN	Aboriginal Peoples Television Network
BCA	British Columbia Archives
CBC	Canadian Broadcasting Corporation
CCM	Welcoming Winnipeg Initiative Committee of Community Members
CHA	Canadian Historical Association
DIA	Department of Indian Affairs
EM	Electromagnetic
GPR	Ground-Penetrating Radar
GSC	Geological Survey of Canada
IAB	Indian Affairs Branch
IAP	Independent Assessment Process
ICA	International Council on Archives
ICC	International Criminal Court
IDS	Indian Day Schools
IRS	Indian Residential Schools
IRSSA	Indian Residential School Settlement Agreement
IRSS	Indian Residential School System
IRSSS	Indian Residential School Survivors Society
KIRS	Kamloops Indian Residential School

LAC	Library and Archives Canada
LiDAR	Light Detection and Ranging
MEC	Muskowekwan Education Centre
MITHP	Manitoba Indigenous Tuberculosis History Project
NAC	National Advisory Committee on Residential Schools Missing Children and Unmarked Burials
NCTR	National Centre for Truth and Reconciliation
NDTR	National Day for Truth and Reconciliation
OMI	The Missionary Oblates of Mary Immaculate
OSI	Office of the Independent Special Interlocutor for Missing Children and Unmarked Graves associated with Indian Residential Schools
RCC	Roman Catholic Church
RCMP	Royal Canadian Mounted Police
RSD	Residential School Denialism
TMU	Toronto Metropolitan University
TRC	Truth and Reconciliation Commission of Canada
UBC	University of British Columbia
UCC	United Church of Canada
UNDRIP	United Nations Declaration on the Rights of Indigenous Peoples
UNGC	United Nations Genocide Convention

CONTRIBUTORS

Sean Carleton is a settler historian and an Associate Professor of History and Indigenous Studies at the University of Manitoba. He is the author of *Lessons in Legitimacy: Colonialism, Capitalism, and the Rise of State Schooling in British Columbia*. He is also a member of the Royal Society of Canada College New Scholars, Artists, and Scientists.

Crystal Gail Fraser is a Gwichyà Gwich'in historian and Indigenous Studies scholar at the University of Alberta. She is the author of *By Strength, We Are Still Here: Indigenous Peoples and Indian Residential Schooling in Inuvik, Northwest Territories*, co-author of the national bestseller *Talk Treaty to Me: Understanding the Basics of Treaties and Land in Canada*, and recipient of a 2025 Governor General's Award for Scholarly Excellence.

Raymond Frogner is the Senior Director of Research and Head of Archives for the National Centre for Truth and Reconciliation (NCTR). His mother was sent to Shaftsbury Mission in northern Alberta, and he has family relations in Duncan's First Nation. He holds an MA in History from the University of Victoria and a Master of Archival Studies degree from the University of British Columbia. He is a Fellow of the Association of Canadian Archivists (ACA) and Co-Chair of the International Council of Archives Special Committee on Indigenous Matters. He has twice won the ACA's W. Kaye Lamb Award for best article in the journal *Archivaria*, and in 2025 he won the Society of American Archivists' Archival History Article Award for best article. He continues to speak and write on issues of Indigenous rights and identity.

Leah Gazan is the Member of Parliament for Winnipeg Centre and a member of the Wood Mountain Lakota Nation in Treaty 4 Territory. Her motions to recognize the Indian Residential School program as genocide and to recognize the crisis of MMIWG2S+ as a nation-wide emergency received unanimous consent in the House of Commons, and she has recently proposed legislation to add to the criminal code residential school denialism as a form of inciting hate.

Reid Gerbrandt is a PhD student in the Department of Sociology at York University. His main research areas focus on genocide studies, denialism, and settler colonialism. His current dissertation research examines residential school denialist talking points within various Canadian media outlets, along with social media platforms.

Lindsay Gibson is Associate Professor of Social Studies Education in the Department of Curriculum and Pedagogy at the University of British Columbia. He is the Teaching and Learning Cluster Co-Lead of the *Thinking Historically for Canada's Future* SSHRC Partnership Grant and has written a variety of publications about various history education topics.

Michelle Good is a writer of Cree ancestry and a member of the Red Pheasant Cree Nation in Saskatchewan. After decades of working with Indigenous communities and organizations, she obtained her law degree. She earned her MFA in creative writing while practising law. Good's bestselling book *Truth Telling: Seven Conversations about Indigenous Life* in Canada was shortlisted for the Basillie Prize for Public Policy. Her debut novel, *Five Little Indians*, won the Governor General's Literary Award for Fiction, the Amazon Canada First Novel Award, the Kobo Emerging Writer's Prize, and CBC's Canada Reads, and was shortlisted for the Atwood Gibson Writers' Trust Fiction Prize and longlisted for the Giller Prize. Michelle's poems, short stories and essays have been published in magazines and anthologies across Canada.

Skylee-Storm Hogan-Stacey identifies with Kanien:keha'ka and settler heritage, with their father's family from Kahnawà:ke Mohawk Territory and their mother's family as settlers in what is now Newfoundland. She holds a BA (Hons.) in Law and Justice from Algoma University and an MA in History from the University of Western Ontario, and draws on these diverse experiences in her work with the Data Sovereignty Research Collaborative at the First Nations Information Governance Centre.

Alan Lester is Professor of Historical Geography at the University of Sussex, UK and the author of several books on imperial governance, humanitarianism and settler colonialism. Most recently he is editor of *The Truth About Empire: Real Histories of British Colonialism.*

Andrew Martindale is Professor in the Department of Anthropology at the University of British Columbia. His research focuses on the history of British Columbia via archaeology and in partnership with First Nations.

Mary Jane Logan McCallum is Professor of History and Canada Research Chair in Indigenous History, People and Archives at the University of Winnipeg. She is a band member of the Munsee Delaware Nation and researches and writes about modern Indigenous histories of education, health, and labour.

Krista McCracken is a public historian and archivist who has worked at the Shingwauk Residential Schools Centre since 2010.

James Miles is Assistant Professor of Social Studies Education in the Faculty of Education at the University of Alberta. He previously was a social studies and history teacher.

Erin Millions is Assistant Professor of History at the University of Winnipeg. Her work centers community-engagement and Indigenous perspectives in exploring 19th- and 20th-century interactions between Indigenous peoples and British/Canadian colonialism. As a settler scholar, her public-engaged history work includes the Manitoba Indigenous Tuberculosis History Project, Indigenous Afternoons in the Archives, community-centered commemoration of the Indian Residential School System with Parks Canada, Welcoming Winnipeg Initiative Committee of Community Members, *Canadian Geographic* Paths to Reconciliation Project, and historical research for the Canadian Museum for Human Rights and the BBC.

Kimberly Murray is Queen's University's National Scholar in Indigenous Legal Studies in the Faculty of Law. She is the former Executive Director of the Truth and Reconciliation Commission of Canada and was the federally appointed Independent Special Interlocutor for Missing Children and Unmarked Graves and Burial

Sites Associated with Indian Residential Schools. Kimberly is a member of Kanehsatà:ke Mohawk Nation, holds an LLM and LLB from Osgoode Hall Law School, and has been bestowed several Honorary LL.Ds.

Neegaunibinessikwe is an IRS survivor from Long Plain First Nation, Mai'iingan Clan (Wolf) and is currently a member of the National Centre for Truth and Reconciliation's Survivors Circle.

Adele Perry, FRSC, is a settler historian of colonialism and gender. She is Distinguished Professor in History and Women's and Gender Studies and Director of the Center for Human Rights Research at the University of Manitoba.

Jackson Pind is a mixed settler-Anishinaabe historian with Indigenous ancestry from Alderville First Nation. He is currently Assistant Professor of Indigenous Methodologies at the Chanie Wenjack School of Indigenous Studies at Trent University.

Niigaan Sinclair is Anishinaabe (St. Peter's/Little Peguis) and Professor of Indigenous Studies at the University of Manitoba. He is an award-winning writer, editor, author, and activist who was named to the "Power List" in 2022 by *Mclean's* magazine as one of the most influential individuals in Canada.

Kisha Supernant (Métis/British) is Director of the Institute of Prairie and Indigenous Archaeology and Professor in the Department of Anthropology at the University of Alberta. Her research interests include the use of digital technologies in archaeology, Indigenous archaeology, community-driven research, and heart-centered archaeological practice. Over the past several years, she has been helping Indigenous communities in western Canada use technology to locate and protect unmarked graves.

Omeasoo Wahpasiw (nehiyaw iskwew, Saddle Lake) works on the unceded territory of the Anishinaabe and Algonquin Nations at Carleton University. She is cross-appointed in the Institute of Interdisciplinary Studies and Azrieli School of Architecture and Urbanism. Omeasoo contributes thoughtful insight and criticism, creativity and wit through news media, chapters and articles the cover Canadian law and policy, ideas of place and space rooted in nehiyaw epistemologies, and the tangible physical expressions of Indigenous life and sovereignty across Turtle Island.

Phyllis Webstad is Northern Secwépemc (Shuswap) from the Stswecem'c Xget'tem First Nation (Canoe Creek Indian Band), and she currently resides in Williams Lake, British Columbia with her husband. She has one son, five grandchildren, and one step-son. Phyllis is the Founding Member of Orange Shirt Day—Every Child Matters and Founding Member and CEO for Orange Shirt Society. When she was just six years old in 1973/1974, Phyllis attended St. Joseph's Mission Indian Residential School, aka The Mission, near Williams Lake, British Columbia. Her grandmother bought her an orange shirt to wear on her first day of school, but upon arrival, her shirt was removed. No matter how much she cried or protested, her special new shirt was never returned. The Orange Shirt Society was created in 2019 as a legacy to Phyllis's Orange Shirt Story. Orange Shirt Day—Every Child Matters: National Day for Truth and Reconciliation, recognized annually on 30 September, is a day to honour residential school Survivors and their families and to remember those that never made it home. It is a day for people to reflect, educate themselves and commit to Truth and Reconciliation. A published author, Phyllis has eight books that share her story in her own words: *The Orange Shirt Story*; *Phyllis's Orange Shirt*; *Beyond the Orange Shirt Story; With Our Orange Hearts; Every Child Matters; Today is Orange Shirt Day; Decolonization and Me;* and *w7ec n7elye ey (We Are Still Here).*

Andrew Woolford is Professor of Sociology and Criminology at the University of Manitoba, former president of the International Association of Genocide Scholars, and secretary of the Assiniboia Residential School Legacy Group. He is author of *Genocide in Canada* and *This Benevolent Experiment: Indigenous Boarding Schools, Genocide and Redress in the United States and Canada.*

ACKNOWLEDGEMENTS

First and foremost, we thank all Survivors and former students of Canada's Indian Residential School System for their courage in sharing the truth about their experiences. Truth-telling is an important part of what Survivors, such as Theodore Niizhotay Fontaine (*Broken Circle*) and Bev Sellars (*They Called Me Number One*), have described as the process of breaking the silence. This collection honours the strength of Survivors, and it asks readers to take up the challenge of defending the truth about Indian Residential Schools for the generations to come. As part of our commitment to supporting Survivors, we have directed the University of Manitoba Press to send royalties from this book to the Indian Residential School Survivors Society (www.irsss.ca).

This book is a collective effort. It would not be possible if not for the hard work and dedication of the incredibly talented team of contributors and collaborators, and we thank them for all their good work. We also thank Adele Perry, Pauline Tennent, and the Centre for Human Rights Research at the University of Manitoba for their generous support. Hannah Belec conducted key research that greatly assisted the completion of the collection. As well, we thank our colleagues and students in the Department of Indigenous Studies at the University of Manitoba for their inspiration and encouragement.

Many residential school denialists self-publish books and articles and engage in pseudo-scholarship to give their unethical work the appearance of academic credibility and legitimacy. As such, we felt strongly that this book needed to be subjected to the rigours of the formal peer-review process to maximize quality, accuracy, and authority. Undergoing anonymous peer-review always means more work, but the reward is putting forward the best possible scholarship. We thank the three expert reviewers for their detailed and constructive feedback that has made this book stronger.

Personally, Sean wishes to thank his community partners, colleagues, students, and family for their unwavering support. Being a public figure pushing back on residential school denialism is not easy, and the challenges are not shouldered alone. Niigaan thanks his family and the many relations who attended residential schools and bravely shared their stories. Let this collection be a testament to the fact our generation heard you, believed you, and are making sure that something like this will never happen again. Niigaan also thanks his colleagues at CBC, APTN, the *Winnipeg Free Press*, and media platforms around the world for providing a space for the truth of residential schools to be made known.

The University of Manitoba Press (UMP) has established itself as *the* publisher of truth and reconciliation titles, and for good reason. From design and copyediting to final production and promotion, everyone at UMP has been a dream to work with. We thank David Larsen, Kyla Neufeld, Stephanie Paddey, Anoja Muthucumaru-Barham, and Sasha Bouché. In particular, Jill McConkey—recently honoured with the Canadian Historical Association's Lifetime Achievement Award for her contributions to Canadian and Indigenous History—has supported this book from the beginning and prioritized its publication. UMP understands the importance of standing up for the truth about Indian Residential Schools. We are grateful for UMP's support.

Lastly, we want to acknowledge all the people who have, in various ways, shared in the work of identifying and confronting residential school denialism in recent years but who are not included in this book as contributors. We tried to have many different voices and perspectives, including references to additional work in the Notes and Selected Bibliography, as possible; however, it is impossible to include everyone and everything. This book is just one tool, one part of the larger movement to confront residential school denialism and put truth before reconciliation. We hope that it will encourage more people to stand up for the truth. Indeed, being a witness to history does not mean simply understanding the past. Witnessing comes with responsibility. Being a witness is an active rather than passive process; it is something everyone can do to support truth and reconciliation and build a better future.

Murray Sinclair, Mazina Giizhik-iban, once said that, in the work of truth and reconciliation "there are three kinds of people out there—those that are never going to be on our side, those that are already on our side, and . . . the middle, which is the majority of Canadians." While this book is for the latter two groups, it is an invitation to *everyone* to see the transformative potential of understanding the truth about the past and working together to build a better future. Coming from a place of love, compassion, and solidarity, *Truth Before Reconciliation* is a call to action to join this important and timely work.

INTRODUCTION

by Sean Carleton and Niigaan Sinclair

On 7 March 2017, Lynn Beyak delivered a controversial speech in the Senate defending Canada's Indian Residential School System (IRSS) as being "well-intentioned." The Conservative senator argued that, instead of dwelling on the mistreatment and abuse experienced by many of the over 150,000 Indigenous children and youth who attended the more than 130 residential schools across Canada between 1883 and 1997, people should focus on the "good" the system accomplished in terms of assimilating Indigenous Peoples into Canadian society. The senator explained that it was her intent to speak "in memory" of the "kindly" residential school staff whose "remarkable works" and "good deeds" have gone unrecognized because they are too often "overshadowed by negative reports." Though Beyak admitted that "mistakes were made" at Indian Residential Schools (IRS), she used her speech to insist that an emphasis on the system's positives will help "Canada's native people" to thrive "as victors, not victims."[1]

Beyak's speech, made only a year after the Truth and Reconciliation Commission (TRC) of Canada released its *Final Report* in 2015 and showed Canadians the evidence of how residential schooling constituted genocide, sparked an intense public controversy.[2] Beyak's attempt to put a positive spin on the system—that even Stephen Harper, the Conservative prime minister who appointed her to the Senate, called a "sad chapter in Canada's history" during his 2008 apology to Survivors—was not appreciated by many, including her fellow senator and the former chair of the TRC, Murray Sinclair.[3] In response, Sinclair suggested that those trying to downplay the harms of residential schooling were "dim-witted" and posed a serious barrier to meaningful reconciliation.[4] Even the Anglican Church of Canada (ACC), which ran a third of the schools across the country, including the Pelican Lake Indian Residential School near Dryden, Ontario (Treaty 3 Territory) where Beyak lives, made a public statement clarifying that "nothing good" came from the schools. The Church noted that, while a "small minority of survivors" speak of some positive school memories on an individual level, those personal experiences must be understood as occurring in the context of a genocidal school *system* designed to "kill the Indian in the child."[5]

Despite facing wide-spread criticism for her comments, Beyak initially refused to apologize. Instead, she stood behind her "positive" perspective, even attacking criticism of her speech as "fake news and exaggeration."[6] When confronted by reporters, Beyak doubled down on her defence of residential schooling, arguing "there are shining examples from sea to sea of people who owe their lives to the schools." When pressed on how Indigenous Peoples, especially the many former students who were mentally, physically, and sexually abused in the schools, might feel about such statements, Beyak elaborated: "I've suffered with them. . . . I appreciate their suffering more than they'll ever know [but] the best way to heal is to move forward together. Not to blame, not to point fingers, not to live in the past." Asked directly if she had read the TRC's *Final Report* to fully understand the history of the schools and the intergenerational trauma still experienced by many Indigenous Peoples today, Beyak quipped: "I don't need any more education."[7] Beyak was removed from a Senate committee on Indigenous issues in April 2017, but she retained her seat in the Red Chamber until she retired in 2021, and she continually constructed herself as a victim of attacks on "free speech," a common strategy in keeping with what scholars Eve Tuck and K. Wayne Yang refer to as "moves to innocence."[8]

Beyak's speech and subsequent behaviour can be understood as what we call *residential school denialism*. Like other forms of denialism, such as climate and science denialism, residential school denialism is not the outright denial of the system's existence. Denialists rarely say that residential schools never existed, and many, including Beyak, even acknowledge some of the system's harm and abuse. Instead, residential school denial*ism* is a kind of sophistry similar in nature to Holocaust denialism—also known as negationism or historical denialism—where bad faith discourse is used to question or downplay established truths in order to minimize claims of genocide and protect guilty parties. Denialists do the dishonest work of manipulating evidence, developing disingenuous counterarguments, and deliberately planting seeds of doubt.[9] Indeed, many Holocaust "deniers" are actually engaging in denial*ism*. They are deceivers. Dressing up their hate in the garb of pseudo-scholarship, they decontextualize and diminish the Holocaust by questioning its evidence (how reliable are Survivor's testimonies about execution techniques if they survived?); quibbling over the total number of Jews killed (was it 6 million or 3 million or fewer?); and disputing the means and methods of mass death (were gas chambers and Zyklon B really used?).

Building on existing literature on various forms of denialism, we argue that *residential school denialism* can be defined as the rejection, minimization, distortion, or misrepresentation of basic facts about residential schooling to shake public confidence in the truth and undermine reconciliation efforts.[10] It is part of a broader assault on Indigenous Peoples. The end goal is to delegitimize reconciliation and defend the Church, the State, and the colonial status quo in Canada. Only a small handful of people—mostly connected to conservative, Christian nationalist movements and far-right media—are willfully creating and profiting from residential school denialist content. However, such content is alluring to a larger audience fearful of reconciliation and who find comfort in consuming/promoting anti-Indigenous racism as well as other intersecting forms of bigotry and prejudice, that are being boosted by right wing politicians, think tanks, and media, such as anti-immigrant and anti-trans discourse.[11] As scholars from Jean-Paul Sartre and Aileen Moreton-Robinson to Dan Ariely have noted, bigotry of this kind is not always just about hating a scapegoat; as a learned behaviour, it often also provides those who engage in it with a strong sense of community and purpose infused with feelings of power, legitimacy, and superiority.[12]

As Daniel Heath Justice and Sean Carleton outline in their article, "Truth Before Reconciliation," the most common residential school

8 Ways to Identify and Confront Residential School Denialism

1. Genocide: The destruction, in whole or in part, of a nation or an ethnic group. In spite of the United Nation's expansive official definition, denialists strategically narrow the term "genocide" to ethnic cleansing events modelled on the Holocaust. Contrary to historical evidence, denialists contend that genocide is not applicable to Canada. The TRC's final report shows how Canada's treatment of Indigenous Peoples fits the definition of genocide, specifically explaining how the residential school system was a form of "cultural genocide." Some denialists jump on this categorization to suggest that "cultural" genocide is not genocide. That is incorrect. The Canadian Historical Association has recently clarified that genocide is, in fact, the correct term to be using in the Canadian context.

2. School: A place where children are taught a variety of academic subjects. Phys ical assault, sorting of children according t racist assumptions and on the basis of abil and class have long histories in Canadian education. But the particular combination factors distinguish residential schools fron comparative schooling contexts. These factors include: racist assimilationism; cultura shaming and sexual violence combined wi multi-generational collusion of church and state; the explicit aim of isolating children neutralize community resistance to govern ment control. Denialists often make false comparisons between boarding schools an the violent carceral institutions known as "residential schools." Canadian policy mean that for more than 100 years and multiple generations, Indigenous children were removed from their families and cultures t institutions where many were abused, malnourished, trafficked to local white familie and inflicted with substandard education focused on manual labour and servitude—while government also systemically dispos sessed Indigenous lands and resources.

3. "But they learned new skills": Given little meaningful academic or effective vocationa instruction, "new skills" taught in residential institutions included religious indoctrination enforced by corporal punishment and myriad forms of abuse, cultural and bodily shame, alienation from family, disconnection from subsistence economies and substandard orientation for wage labour. Church and state officials often justify this "education" in humanitarian—even sacred—terms. But all of these "skills" directly supported the destruction of Indigenous ways of life and the ostensible training of children and youth for lower-class "productive" service positions. Indigenous children were not put on vocational or profession al paths towards economic or social competition in Canada's capitalist settler society.

Figure 0.1. Eight ways to identify and confront residential school denialism. Daniel Heath Justi and Sean Carleton, "Truth Before Reconciliation," *The Conversation*, 5 August 2021, https: theconversation.com/truth-before-reconciliation-8-ways-to-identify-and-confront-resider tial-school-denialism-164692.

"They had good intentions": No matter how many bodies are found, how many peo-
e testify to the lifelong traumas of extensive abuse at the hands of church officials and
achers, denialists evoke the "good intentions" of some school officials as justification for
eir maintenance of a genocidal school system for over a century.

"You're ignoring all the good things": ything at all that made life bearable under a minant violent context of staff-inflicted cru- ies, deprivations and separations from friends, nily and home is cited by denialists as a "good" residential schooling to absolve churches of pability. Denialists insist on focusing on a nority of individualized, positive recollections m the schools as part of a strategy to discredit se who draw attention to the overall, systemic nocidal effects of the IRS system. Even the glican Church of Canada, which ran approxi- tely 30 per cent of residential schools across country, has clarified that "there was nothing od" about a school system that sought to "kill Indian in the child."

Balance: An equal weighting of different ments. Denialists often engage in a form of s known as "false balance" to wrongly sug- st that the "good" and the "bad" of residential hooling were equal parts of the "whole story." e insistence on focusing on "positives" to pro- le "balance" fundamentally misrepresents the holarly consensus, supported by overwhelm- survivor testimony and backed by historical earch, that the overall effects of the system genocidal.

7. "It was of the times": The idea that we can't judge the past by the values of today. This notion wrongly suggests that no one judged the IRS system harshly during its operation. In fact, Indigenous parents, students and community leaders, church employees and even the Department of Indian Affairs' own medical expert critiqued the system "in their own times." However, powerful church and state officials chose to downplay and discredit dissent and resistance for over a century to protect the IRS system so that it could continue to support settler colonialism and Canadian nation-building—as a way of protecting their assets and defend against litigation.

8. Civility: What some settlers demand from Indigenous people when their denialism is publicly called out, challenged and discredited. Indigenous anger, sadness and refusal are labelled as uncivil and excluded from so-called mainstream dialogue. By contrast, our public institutions accommodate public settler anger and outrage used to defend denialists.

helping to define residential school denialism and bring public attention to its many harms, stice and Carleton created this glossary as the start of an inventory of some common contortions ed by denialists to try to undermine the overwhelming documentary and testimonial evidence widespread, multigenerational, systemic, and ongoing violence of the IRS system.

denialist talking points and rhetorical tricks are well known (Figure 0.1).[13] They include, for example,

1. narrowing the definition of genocide to deny its applicability to Canada;
2. defending the architects of the residential school system, especially Conservative prime minister John A. Macdonald;
3. emphasizing the skills that Indigenous students were supposedly taught;
4. dwelling on the stated good intentions of employees, especially Christian missionaries;
5. cherry-picking any positive student recollections to offer "false balance";
6. arguing that accounts of student abuse are overblown and Survivor testimony is untrustworthy;
7. rejecting evidence of deaths or trying to justify them as being natural or inevitable.
8. obsessing about the ongoing Kamloops investigation into potential unmarked burials, and aggressively demanding exhumation (e.g. "where are the bodies?"), while ignoring confirmed deaths and unmarked burials across the country;
9. misrepresenting media errors about potential unmarked burials to push conspiracy theories about governments and First Nations colluding to guilt Canadians into caring about reconciliation through deliberate lies and deception;
10. denying that the prominent pundits and politicians challenging residential school truths are denialists and instead insisting that they are the real "truth seekers."

All of these arguments and rhetorical tricks—most of them used by Beyak in her 2017 speech—have been rigorously debunked by peer-reviewed studies as well as by the TRC's *Final Report*, but denialists continue to defend and deploy them in their efforts to attack and undermine truth and reconciliation.

Residential school denialism thus deserves more critical analysis in today's era of truth and reconciliation, a time of reckoning with Canada's colonial past to build stronger relations between Indigenous Peoples and Canadians.[14] Before his passing in 2024, Murray Sinclair suggested a useful approach, which we amplify and build on in this collection. After jesting that denialists are just "dim-whited," Sinclair argued that it was, in fact, "not enough for us to simply yell at [denialists] and knock them down." Instead, we must try to understand their reasoning and "show that they are wrong." He elaborated, "I've always been convinced that while we may not deal with all of the [denialists], we can at least take away their tools." By challenging the comments of high-profile people like Beyak and teaching Canadians the truth about residential schooling, Sinclair was hopeful that denialists "will have a diminishing population of people who will believe them."[15] Sinclair, in short, called for a strategy of engagement to disprove and discredit denialism.

Taking away the "tools" of residential school denialism requires a better understanding of them and how and why some people employ and defend them. As a settler historian of schooling and colonialism (Sean Carleton) and an Indigenous Studies scholar and the son of Murray Sinclair (Niigaan Sinclair), we have assembled *Truth Before Reconciliation* to advance such an understanding.

In this Introduction, we historicize residential school denialism and contextualize it in terms of recent literature. We also theorize denialism. Specifically, we engage with Albert Memmi's psychological portrait of the "colonizer who accepts" to highlight the role that denialism plays in justifying ongoing settler capitalism.[16] In this context, we suggest that denialism is neither new nor surprising. Instead, we argue that residential school denialism and attacks on truth and reconciliation, can be understood as a common strategy in which colonizers use discourse to legitimize and defend their material power, privilege, and profit. Building on Murray Sinclair's suggested approach, this book shows how critical analysis of the discursive strategies or "tools" that denialists use—rather than engaging, debating, and thereby platforming and legitimizing denialists themselves—can help check the residential school denialism and support truth and reconciliation efforts.

Historicizing Residential School Denialism

Residential school denialism is on the rise today, but it is important to recognize that it is not new. In fact, settlers downplaying or "silencing" the destructive effects of residential schooling for Indigenous Peoples has a long history.[17] Sociologist Eric Taylor Woods has noted that, for

Figure 0.2. Photographs of Thomas Moore Keesick, from Muscowpetung Saulteaux First Nation, published in 1897 for the Department of Indian Affairs annual report for the year 1896. This image is an example of the kind of propaganda that Church and State officials used to promote the Indian Residential School System as a benevolent, humanitarian project of uplifting and transforming Indigenous children from so-called "savagery" to civilization. Library and Archives Canada/Annual Report of Indian Affairs 1896/OCLC 1771148.

much of the system's 100-year history in Canada, Church and State officials "likened the residential schools to a humanitarian—even sacred—enterprise designed to save Indigenous communities from extinction in the face of an ostensibly higher form of civilization."[18] Even when confronted with evidence of horrific conditions in many of the schools documented in the annual reports of the Department of Indian Affairs (DIA), officials clung to a "humanitarian" discourse and discredited the system's detractors, especially Indigenous leaders and parents who consistently raised concerns about the schools (see Figure 0.3). Officials also disregarded non-Indigenous critics. In 1907, as the system was expanding across the country, Peter Henderson Bryce, a medical official working for the DIA, released a report drawing attention to the abnormally high rate of student death and disease in many residential schools that he argued was exacerbated by the system's indifference and underfunding which led to overcrowding, poor nutrition, and a lack of proper sanitation (see Figures 0.4 and 0.5).[19] The DIA ignored Bryce's report.[20] Bryce tried to blow the whistle on residential

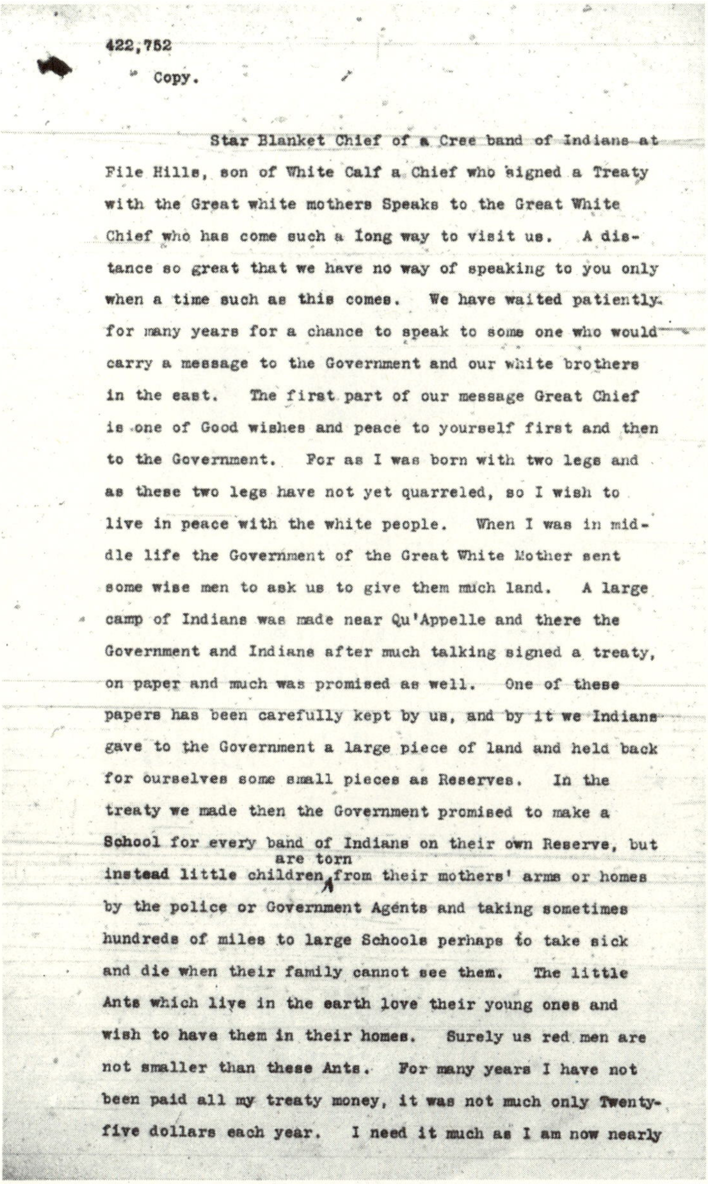

422,752

Copy.

Star Blanket Chief of a Cree band of Indians at File Hills, son of White Calf a Chief who signed a Treaty with the Great white mothers Speaks to the Great White Chief who has come such a long way to visit us. A distance so great that we have no way of speaking to you only when a time such as this comes. We have waited patiently for many years for a chance to speak to some one who would carry a message to the Government and our white brothers in the east. The first part of our message Great Chief is one of Good wishes and peace to yourself first and then to the Government. For as I was born with two legs and as these two legs have not yet quarreled, so I wish to live in peace with the white people. When I was in middle life the Government of the Great White Mother sent some wise men to ask us to give them mich land. A large camp of Indians was made near Qu'Appelle and there the Government and Indians after much talking signed a treaty, on paper and much was promised as well. One of these papers has been carefully kept by us, and by it we Indians gave to the Government a large piece of land and held back for ourselves some small pieces as Reserves. In the treaty we made then the Government promised to make a School for every band of Indians on their own Reserve, but instead little children are torn from their mothers' arms or homes by the police or Government Agents and taking sometimes hundreds of miles to large Schools perhaps to take sick and die when their family cannot see them. The little Ants which live in the earth love their young ones and wish to have them in their homes. Surely us red men are not smaller than these Ants. For many years I have not been paid all my treaty money, it was not much only Twenty-five dollars each year. I need it much as I am now nearly

Figure 0.3. Chief Star Blanket's letter. In 1912, a Cree Chief, Star Blanket expressed his frustration at the government using the treaty right to education, understood as a promise of educational resources to teach children in community, as a pretense to take Indigenous children away to distant residential schools where they often got sick and died far from their families. Library and Archives Canada, RG10, School Files, Volume 4068, File 422, 752.

Figure 0.4. Peter Henderson Bryce (1853–1932), physician, public health official, and author of *The Story of a National Crime: An Appeal for Justice to the Indians of Canada* (1922). Lancefields of Ottawa, 1989, https://en.wikipedia.org/wiki/Peter_Bryce#/media/File:Peter_H._Bryce.jpg.

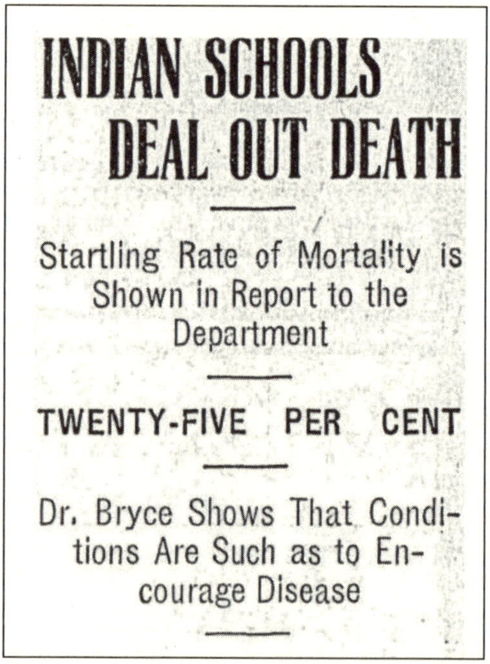

INDIAN SCHOOLS DEAL OUT DEATH

Startling Rate of Mortality is Shown in Report to the Department

TWENTY-FIVE PER CENT

Dr. Bryce Shows That Conditions Are Such as to Encourage Disease

Figure 0.5. *Daily Colonist* headline, c.1907. Bryce's report on residential schools received a lot of press from across the country. This is evidenced by an article from the 16 November 1907 edition of the *Daily Colonist*, a newspaper in Victoria, British Columbia. The article draws attention to high rates of student death and disease that Bryce attributed to systemic problems with the Indian Residential School System.

Figure 0.6. St. Mary's Indian Residential School, Mission, British Columbia, c. 1880s. First opened in 1861, and run mostly by the Missionary Oblates of Mary Immaculate (O.M.I), St. Mary's was the last residential school to close in British Columbia in 1984. More than 2,000 students attended the school, many of them from the Stó:lō Nation. Royal BC Museum, BC Archives, D-08840.

Figure 0.7. The foundation of the Boys' Dormitory, which is still visible on the grounds of the old St. Mary's Indian Residential School, now the Fraser Valley Heritage Park, in British Columbia. The National Centre for Truth and Reconciliation lists the deaths of fifteen students at St. Mary's. The Stó:lō Nation believes that number is higher and is currently undertaking additional research about the institution, including searching its grounds as well as the grounds of other former residential schools in the Fraser Valley for potential unmarked burials. Photo by Sean Carleton.

schooling in its initial phase, but DIA officials chose to selectively focus on the "positive" results the system was having—or, more correctly, that they hoped it would have—in disrupting Indigenous lifeways and supporting continued settler colonialism and Canadian nation-building.[21] It was not until the 1940s, argues Woods, that "the gap between the benign representation of the residential schools and their malign reality had become so wide that it was no longer possible to ignore."[22] Even still, many Church and State officials continued to promote a positive representation of residential schooling. Despite the system's obvious failings, even according to the DIA's own experts, residential schools operated in many parts of Canada for another fifty years. The last school closed in 1997.[23]

It was not until former students began publishing accounts of their abuse at the schools and started organizing for redress that the dominant humanitarian narrative about residential schooling started to shift significantly. Some students admittedly recounted positive experiences, but, by the 1970s and 1980s, more former students were speaking out about the cruelty, abuse, and poor conditions they endured in schools across the country.[24] As more students spoke publicly about their negative experiences and the damage done by the system, they inspired others to break their silence, eventually sparking a movement led by thousands of former students seeking an apology and compensation. With many officials still denying any wrongdoing—and some right-wing pundits vehemently defending the Church and the system's legacy in the 1980s and 1990s (see Figure 0.8)—86,000 students forced the issue by launching one of the largest class-action lawsuits in Canadian history, which the Government of Canada chose to settle out of court by agreeing to the Indian Residential Schools Settlement Agreement (IRSSA, 2006/2007).[25] As a result of the settlement, the federal government officially apologized to former students in 2008 and established the Independent Assessment Process (IAP) to deal with individual claims and an independent commission, which became the TRC, to research and raise national awareness about residential schooling. As part of its research, the TRC consulted thousands of Church and State records and gathered testimony from more than 6,000 witnesses, including school employees and former students. The goal of the commission was to present evidence that would "reveal to Canadians the complex truth about the history and the ongoing legacy" of residential schooling.[26]

Figure 0.8. The O.M.I. Cemetery, which is adjacent to the former St. Mary's Indian Residential School, containing burials connected to the institution as well as other Oblates, including the disgraced Bishop Emeritus of Prince George, Hubert O'Connor. In 1996, O'Connor was charged for rape and indecently assaulting Indigenous girls while he was principal of the St. Joseph's Indian Residential School in Williams Lake, British Columbia. He fathered at least one child, which was put up for adoption. While O'Connor was found guilty, making him one of the first Canadian Catholic bishops to be convicted of sex crimes, the charges against him were appealed and eventually stayed in favour of a community-led restorative justice initiative. Years later, on 4 June 2022, an elderly man, Richard Albert Manuel, drove his truck through a memorial march near the former St. Mary's school while yelling racist slurs. Found guilty of dangerous operation of a motor vehicle, Manuel was sentenced to a nine-month conditional sentence (house arrest) and a twelve-month driving prohibition, but he was not sent to jail. Photo by Sean Carleton.

The TRC released its *Final Report* in 2015. The conclusions shocked many Canadians but confirmed what generations of Indigenous Peoples had been saying: "For over a century, the central goals of Canada's Aboriginal policy were to eliminate Aboriginal governments; ignore Aboriginal rights; terminate the Treaties; and, through a process of assimilation, cause Aboriginal peoples to cease to exist as distinct legal, social, cultural, religious, and racial entities in Canada. The establishment and operation of residential schools were a central element of

Figure 0.9. The 26 January 1998 issue of *Alberta Report*—a conservative weekly newsmagazine based in Edmonton, Alberta—included a number of articles challenging "Canada's Mythical Holocaust." Foreshadowing the approach of more recent denialist publications, the issue's cover cherry-picks a photograph of smiling Indigenous children and suggests that the "horrors" of the Indian Residential School System are "rooted more in fiction than fact." Image courtesy of the Provincial Archives of Alberta, PR2005.0335.33.294.

Figure 0.10. Murray Sinclair, Mazina Ghiizik-iban, at the Truth and Reconciliation Commission of Canada's Closing Ceremony, 2015. Photo by Fred Catroll.

this policy, which can best be described as 'cultural genocide.'"[27] The commission made clear, however, that "shaming and pointing out wrongdoing" was not the TRC's mandate, regardless of how some might feel after learning the truth about residential schooling. Instead, the "focus on truth determination was intended to lay the foundation for the important question of reconciliation."[28] According to the report, reconciliation "requires an understanding that the most harmful impacts of residential schools have been the loss of pride and self-respect of Aboriginal people, and the lack of respect that non-Aboriginal people have been raised to have for their Aboriginal neighbours." The commissioners thus emphasized, "Reconciliation is not an Aboriginal problem; it is a Canadian one."[29] Many Canadians have embraced the challenge put forward by the TRC and are, in differing ways, engaged in reckoning with Canada's colonial past to build new relationships of mutual respect with Indigenous Peoples to aid reconciliation.[30] We must not lose sight of the important work being done across the country.

There are others, however, who are choosing a different path: they are downplaying, disputing, and discrediting the commission's findings specifically and residential school truths generally to reject reconciliation and defend the colonial status quo. To be sure, confronting the

Figure 0.11. In 2017, a new monument entitled łkamnin'tik (The Children) was unveiled on the former grounds of the St. Eugene Indian Residential School near Cranbrook, British Columbia. According to the sculptor, Cameron Douglas, the commemoration honours all the students who attended the school, one of the first residential schools in the country and one of the longest-running institutions (1890–1970). Photo by Sean Carleton.

legacies of genocide and committing to what Stó:lō writer Lee Maracle calls "continued growth and transformation" is not easy, but it is the task that Indigenous and non-Indigenous peoples living in what is currently Canada are being challenged to undertake in the era of truth and reconciliation.[31]

Theorizing Residential School Denialism

Scholarship in the fields of genocide studies, Indigenous studies, and setter colonial studies sheds light on how different countries around the world, including Canada, can deal with the legacies of genocide and address the phenomenon of denialism. Political scientist Adam Jones argues that the manipulation of memory and history often occurs in the aftermath of genocides. In looking at Germany's grappling with the Holocaust, he shows how a "wilful amnesia" and "politicized forgetting" emerged in the immediate post-war period that served to distance the country and its citizens from its recent Nazi past. In reflecting on the psychology of denialism, Jones argues that "individual and collective narcissism play a pivotal role in buttressing denial; in many contexts a denialist stance heads off cognitive dissonance between one's preferred view of self and country, and the grimmer reality." He also points out that "there is also usually an element of material self-interest."[32] Similarly, in *If Auschwitz Is Nothing: Against Denialism*, philosopher Donatella Di Cesare contends that the rise of the internet and social media have contributed to an intensification of denialist discourse in recent decades.[33] Di Cesare points out that denialists, as "attack-dogs of thought" and "assassins of memory," not only seek to expose what they derisively call the "Holocaust Myth," but they also actively depict Jewish people today as liars and scammers complicit in the "Holocaust Industry" to justify further antisemitism and hostility toward Jewish people.[34] Drawing on the Holocaust denialism playbook and repurposing its language, residential school denialists oppose the "genocide myth," brand Survivors and Indigenous Peoples as liars, and decry the so-called "Reconciliation Industry."

Indeed, Canadian genocide scholars such as Andrew Woolford and David B. MacDonald show how the same tactics of denialism, or negationism, are used in Canada against Indigenous Peoples. They argue that Canada's treatment of Indigenous Peoples, particularly in regards to the Indian Residential School System, constitutes genocide, and point out that some Canadians refuse to acknowledge this reality to avoid cognitive dissonance and feeling guilty or responsible for redress.[35] This includes some historians—mostly retired—who have aligned themselves with denialists in recent years to seemingly protest the "woke ideology" infecting the historical profession and universities more broadly. The Canadian Historical Association and its active members have rejected such an assertion and confirmed that the consensus of the field, based on rigorous peer-reviewed research, is that Canada's treatment of Indigenous Peoples constitutes genocide, a fact agreed upon unanimously by the House of Commons in 2022.[36] Overall, then, denialism is at work in Canada and can be understood as part of a conscious or unconscious strategy of selectively remembering the past to protect one's power and privilege in the present and, most importantly, to perpetuate it into the future. In 2022, genocide studies scholar Gregory Stanton argued that Canada, indeed, is stuck in the tenth and final stage of genocide: denial.[37]

Insights from genocide studies overlap with lessons from Indigenous studies and settler colonial studies on the role of denialism. Cree scholars Gina Starblanket and Dallas Hunt contend that Canadians are in denial about the past and present of settler capitalism. They argue that Canadians seek refuge in myths of benevolence that justify colonial policy toward Indigenous Peoples as being well-intentioned, even necessary.[38] Indeed, Maracle argues that "Canadians have a myth [of innocence] about themselves, and it seems this myth is inviolable."[39] She argues that to be Canadian "is to be sunk in deep denial."[40] Mississauga Nishnaabeg writer Leanne Betasamosake Simpson explains that a "large number of Canadians will do everything they can [...including perpetuating colonial mythology] to preserve the social, cultural, and economic systems of the country, even though this system is predicated on violence and dispossession of Indigenous lands and bodies."[41] Similarly, settler scholars such as Eva Mackey, Emma Battell Lowman, and Adam J. Barker argue that Canadians must embrace the transformative possibilities of reconciliation by "unsettling" the myths of Canada as the "Peaceable Kingdom" and challenging "fantasies of entitlement" that some settlers use to legitimize their "right" to lands and resources.[42] In particular, settler researcher Paulette Regan contends that understanding the history and ongoing legacies of residential schooling offers Canadians an "opening" into the work of reconciliation that can facilitate dialogue and help build reciprocal relationships with Indigenous Peoples.[43] Framed in this way, reconciliation and reckoning with residential school history is not a threat but a challenge *and* an opportunity for growth. Nevertheless, Maracle notes that many Canadians "tend towards defensiveness" and engage in denialism as a defensive strategy to protect their power and privilege.[44]

To further theorize the role of denialism in colonial societies, we turn to the works of anticolonial and post-colonial writers. In particular, Albert Memmi's *The Colonizer and the Colonized*, which consists of psychological portraits of "the colonizer" and "the colonized" based on the author's personal experiences in North Africa, is insightful because it looks at the role of denialism in legitimizing colonialism as commonsensical. While scholars such as Métis writer Emma LaRocque have related Memmi's "Portrait of the Colonized" to Indigenous struggles in Canada, we focus on Memmi's "Portrait of the Colonizer" and its applicability to settler Canadians.[45] Memmi argues that colonizers are daily confronted with the illegitimacy of their status. Whether colonizers are immigrants or are born in the colonies, they are always, even if only subconsciously, plagued by the question: what entitles me to live here? In the back of their mind, they understand that their home is not really *their* home. It is their home *on* Native land; it is not *their* native land. Indeed, colonizers are implicitly cognizant that coercion, theft, and bloody violence only recently cleared—and in some cases still clears—the way for them to travel to and take root in a new land. Moreover, fears about revenge and retribution by the colonized, often fuelled by news of anticolonial "protests," "riots," and "rebellions" from around the colony and across the globe, stoke a kind of ever-present anxiety.[46] In an attempt to resolve these unsettled feelings, colonizers devise and deploy different discursive strategies to protect their position of material privilege and to prove to themselves and to others the righteousness of their existence.

In addition to enacting specific laws and creating institutions such as reserves, ghettos, prisons, and schools to contain and control the colonized physically, Memmi contends that colonizers invent and invest themselves in mythology and racist stereotypes that they propagate through various channels, including art and entertainment and even the writing of history. As Memmi's contemporary Frantz Fanon once remarked, "the colonist makes history, and he knows it."[47] Accordingly, colonizers make films and paintings and they write books, plays, and poems that bolster the supposed superiority of the colonizer while simultaneously degrading and dehumanizing the colonized.[48] In advancing an interconnected understanding of the material and discursive elements of colonialism, Edward Said, building on the work of Fanon, explains that the main battle of colonization "is over land, of course; but when it came to who owned the land, who had the right to settle and work on it, who kept it going, who won it back, and who now plans its future—these issues were reflected, contested, and even for a time decided in narrative."[49] Colonizers, in short, produce new knowledge and disseminate it to rationalize the oppressive colonial relationship that underpins their material prosperity as natural, inevitable, and, most importantly, unchangeable, something Tuck and Yang call "settler futurity."[50]

Although Memmi argues that all colonizers benefit from the colonial situation, he differentiates between the behaviour of two main groups: "the colonizer who refuses" and "the colonizer who accepts." The colonizer who refuses comes to the realization that colonialism is unjust and vows to challenge the oppression of the colonized and fight for their freedom. This is no easy task because the liberation of the colonized requires colonizers to challenge and question the legitimacy of the colonial project and thus their own existence. The colonizer's freedom is facilitated by the unfreedom of the colonized. Ending this unequal relationship works against the colonizer's own self-interest, and advocating for such a radical rupture can result in being ostracized by both the colonized—who see colonizers, even well-intentioned ones, as oppressors—and by other colonizers, who see those "who refuse" as traitors and turncoats.[51] As a result of these contradictions, Memmi contends that most colonizers simply resign themselves to embrace colonialism and its benefits, becoming colonizers "who accept." "Justice" and "equality" are threatening concepts to colonizers "who accept" because their prosperity is predicated on prejudice and rooted in the ongoing oppression of the colonized.

As a result, denialism is an especially powerful tool employed by colonizers "who accept." Memmi argues that "to possess victory completely [the colonizer] needs to absolve himself of it and the conditions under which it is attained. This explains his strenuous insistence, strange for a victor, on apparently futile matters. He endeavors to falsify history, he rewrites laws, he would extinguish memories—anything to succeed *in transforming his usurpation into legitimacy*."[52] Moreover, Memmi suggests that colonizers' "disquiet and resulting thirst for justification" requires them to extol the virtues of their righteousness "to the skies and to drive the usurped below the ground at the same time."[53] This type of behaviour reassures colonizers "who accept" that "colonization is eternal," and it encourages them to look toward their "future without worries of any kind."[54]

Properly historicized and theorized, we contend that residential school denialism can be understood as a strategy for protecting the status quo in colonial settings such as Canada. Rather than "unsettle" the history of Canada and confront the ongoing legacies of colonization, including things like residential schools, some people are employing the tools of Memmi's "the colonizer who accepts": they deploy a denialist discourse that justifies their existence through a combination of degrading Indigenous Peoples and clinging to selective and self-congratulatory accounts of the past that they think absolves them of wrongdoing and justifies their lack of support for reconciliation. In this way, we argue that residential school denialism is being used as a tool to downplay the injustices of the past and present to safeguard colonial power and privilege in the unsettling time of truth and reconciliation.

Truth Before Reconciliation

Building on the insights above, this book intervenes and responds to the rise in residential school denialism in Canada. It is important, as scholars of Holocaust denialism have warned, that those engaging in denialism are not viewed as acting in good faith. We must reject the tendency, as Di Cesare explains, "to take individual episodes in isolation, reading them as distasteful incidents which are largely due to ignorance, misinformation and forgetting." This, she explains, "implicitly tells us that the deniers deny because they do not know, and that, if they knew, they would not deny."[55] That is not the case. Instead, to properly confront residential school denialism we need to connect the analysis of its substance to its strategy. We need to see it as a pattern of behaviour and recognize that it is actively being encouraged and supported by a small but coordinated network of pundits and politicians committed to fomenting anti-Indigenous racism and undermining truth and reconciliation for their own benefit.

Since the release of the TRC's *Final Report*, and growing in intensity after the Tk'emlúps te Secwépemc announcement in 2021 about the location of potential unmarked graves at the Kamloops Indian Residential School, residential school denialism has grown in popularity, especially, though not exclusively, on the political right. There have been a number of prominent controversies. We have seen teachers disciplined or fired for inappropriate comments related to residential schooling.[56] Politicians, from Liberals like Jean Chrétien and Conservatives like Erin O'Toole and Pierre Poilievre to the People's Party of Canada leader Maxime Bernier, have legitimized denialist talking points and normalized anti-Indigenous racism.[57] On the far right, think tanks such as the Frontier Centre and media outlets such as *Rebel News*, *True North*, *Juno News*, *Western Standard*, and even the *National Post* have promoted or amplified residential school denialism, and some have gone on to

Figure 0.12. Screenshot of Dallas Brodie (@Dallas_Brodie), "Every child, DOES matter. And so does the TRUTH!" X, 2 October 2025, https://x.com/Dallas_Brodie/status/1973910823375630424. Vancouver–Quilchena MLA Dallas Brodie was expelled from the BC Conservative caucus in May 2025 after mocking residential school Survivors. She has since created her own party, One BC, that regularly promotes anti-Indigenous racism. In October 2025, she posed with a "Zero Bodies" sign in front of an Every Child Matters billboard in Penticton, British Columbia, and posted it on social media. The TRC confirmed 3,200 deaths linked to Indian Residential Schools (including fifty- at the Kamloops Indian Residential School), and ongoing work by Indigenous communities, police, and government agencies is confirming additional deaths. For example, in 2024, an investigation into Ontario residential schools supported by Ontario's Office of the Chief Coroner confirmed 220 additional deaths. In consulting a variety of public and protected archival records, the investigation confirmed the death rate at some Ontario schools was more than double that reported by the TRC. As more research is done, additional deaths of children linked to Indian Residential Schools are being confirmed across Canada. Stunts like Brodie's serve to distract from this grim reality. Elections BC has approved a recall petition against Brodie.

monetize their misinformation in the form of independently published books and documentaries. This content spreads further on social media, and AI is often used for the purposes of "astroturfing," or the deceptive practice of training bots to engage and comment on specific content (often responding to key words such as "reconciliation" or "residential schools") to make it appear that denialism is widely accepted. This is all part of the strategy of "flooding the zone," borrowed from the American far right's playbook, to overwhelm, exhaust, and saturate public discourse with "alternative" information to the point where confusion replaces accountability and doubt supplants well-established evidence.[58] In this way, even firmly documented truths become framed as "controversial," while Indigenous people are recast as untrustworthy liars or manipulative actors of the so-called "Reconciliation Industry." This is all part of what Carleton has identified as the Anti-Indigenous Industry's "war on reconciliation."[59]

The marked increase in residential school denialism is contributing to a surge of anti-Indigenous racism, hatred, and backlash in Canada. For example, in 2021, someone removed items at a memorial outside the Mohawk Institute in Ontario. In 2022, a man drove his truck through a march of Survivors near Mission, British Columbia, while yelling racist slurs, and the monument at the St. Paul's Indian Residential School in North Vancouver, British Columbia, was vandalized. In 2024, a serial killer in Winnipeg, Manitoba, who was posting residential school denialism in the form of the "Mass Grave Hoax" conspiracy theory online at the time he was targeting Indigenous women, was sentenced to four life sentences. In 2025, an Every Child Matters message on the Treaty 8 Tribal Association building in Fort St. John, British Columbia, was defaced with a swastika, and far-right politicians and speakers engaged in political theatre to target public displays (Figure 0.12) and BC universities with unauthorized events questioning residential school truths. In 2026, after two previous acts of vandalism, an Every Child Matters message on a bridge near Port Alberni, British Columbia, was altered with a racist slur and also defaced with a swastika. As Niigaan Sinclair has pointed out hateful anti-Indigenous rhetoric such as residential school denialism sets the stage for acts of hate against Indigenous Peoples.[60]

In this context, *Truth Before Reconciliation* invites readers to learn how to identify and confront residential school denialism as a way of standing up for Survivors, defending the truth, and protecting the promise of reconciliation. The book brings together a diverse group of experts—from Survivors and academics to politicians and educators—to share knowledge in various ways, ranging from academic research to interviews. In different but overlapping ways, the following chapters illustrate that the way forward must be guided by truth-telling, solidarity and collaboration, and an unwavering commitment to confront the rise of misinformation and anti-Indigenous racism as a precondition for reconciliation.

To begin, Chapters 1 and 2 offer personal reflections about the effects of denialism by Phyllis Webstad and Mary Jane Logan McCallum. Webstad is a Survivor of St. Joseph's Indian Residential School in Williams Lake, British Columbia, and she is also the founder of Orange Shirt Day. McCallum is an Indigenous historian who has written about the Indian Residential School System and has faced denialism in public while sharing her academic research. Taken together, these chapters show the personal and professional dimensions of denialism as an attack on truth and truth-tellers.

The subsequent chapters map the problem of residential school denialism and reflect on possible solutions. Chapters 3, 4, 5, and 6 examine the ways in which denialists often deliberately twist and misrepresent Indian Residential School facts to undermine public confidence in truth and reconciliation in Canada. In Chapter 3, Raymond Frogner, the National Centre for Truth and Reconciliation's Head of Archives/Senior Director of Research, discusses the role that archives can play in truth and reconciliation work, and professor Andrew Martindale outlines the contribution of archeology and new technologies such as ground-penetrating radar (GPR) to residential school searches in Chapter 4. Chapter 5, by scholars Sean Carleton, Alan Lester, Adele Perry, and Omeasoo Wahpasiw, exposes residential school denialism's transnational network beyond Canada, while Chapter 6, by education scholars Lindsay Gibson and James Miles, looks at how denialism can be challenged in Canadian schools.

Chapter 7, by researchers Reid Gerbrandt and Sean Carleton, debunks the "mass grave hoax" conspiracy theory and shows how denialists cherry-pick media errors to shake public confidence in the work of Indigenous Nations. Chapters 8, 9, and 10 focus on the question of genocide and the politics of combatting denialism. In Chapter 8, genocide studies scholar Andrew Woolford outlines how residential school denialists use common techniques of genocide denial or "neutralization." In Chapters 9 and 10, writer Michelle Good and Member of Parliament Leah Gazan, respectively, make political arguments for criminalizing residential school denialism. Chapter 11 brings together public history experts Krista McCracken, Jackson Pind, Skylee-Storm Hogan-Stacy, and Erin Millions to discuss the role of public history and commemoration in challenging denialism.

The final chapters address why combatting residential school denialism matters for Survivors, Indigenous communities, and everyone living in Canada. Survivor Neegaunibinessikwe and Indigenous scholars Crystal Gail Fraser and Kisha Supernant highlight the importance of taking care of those most affected by the harms of the residential school system in Chapter 12. In Chapter 13, Kimberly Murray, the former Independent Special Interlocutor for Missing Children and Unmarked Burial Sites associated with Indian Residential Schools, reflects on the need to fight denialism and stand up for the truth. In the Conclusion, we, as the editors of the collection, reflect on the importance of education as the key to reconciliation and building a better future. Overall, this book proves that confronting denialism and standing up for the truth is an important part of our collective responsibility to put truth before reconciliation.[61]

The TRC was clear that reconciliation is not an Indigenous burden but a Canadian responsibility—and an opportunity to build stronger relations with Indigenous Peoples. It is thus crucial for all Canadians to learn how to challenge residential school denialism, denouncing and discrediting it at every turn. This is a concrete way to support reconciliation, as explained by Kimberly Murray in the 2024 *Final Report* of the Office of the Independent Special Interlocutor.[62] Standing up for the truth is, as Murray stresses, an important way of honouring Survivors and extending compassion and solidarity to Indigenous Peoples as they carry on with searches for potential unmarked graves at former residential school sites across Canada and investigations into the complex truth about the residential school experience. This is hard but necessary work that will help support reconciliation and efforts to build a more honourable future in the lands today called Canada.

Figure 0.13. Orange shirt memorial on the site of the former St Michael's Indian Residential School in 'Yalis, Alert Bay, British Columbia. In 2015, the community demolished the old school, but the truth about the harm it created is kept alive through various acts of commemoration such as this installation. Photo by Sean Carleton.

Notes

1 For a full account of the controversy, including the content of Beyak's speech, see Sean Carleton, "'I don't need any more education.'" As a synthesis of our work to date, this Introduction utilizes previously published work, including from Carleton "'I don't need any more education'"; Sinclair and Carleton, "Residential School Denialism is on the Rise"; and Carleton, "Confronting the Far-right's War on Reconciliation," *Canadian Dimension*, 16 January 2026, https://canadiandimension.com/articles/view/confront-the-far-rights-war-on-reconciliation.

2 The Truth and Reconciliation Commission of Canada, *Honouring the Truth, Reconciling for the Future*.

3 Government of Canada, "House of Commons Debates, 39th Parliament, 2nd Session," *Edited Hansard* 142, no. 110, 11 June 2008, www2.parl.gc.ca/HousePublications/Publication.aspx?DocId=3568890&Language=E&Mode=1&Parl=39&Ses=2.

4 "Senator Murray Sinclair Responds to Lynn Beyak's Defence of Residential Schools," *CBC News*, 29 March 2017, https://www.cbc.ca/news/politics/murray-sinclair-lynn-beyak-residential-schools-1.4045465; Brett Forester, "Residential School Deniers, White Supremacists Biggest Barrier to Reconciliation says Murray Sinclair," *APTN News*, 12 January 2021, https://www.aptnnews.ca/national-news/residential-school-deniers-white-supremacists-biggest-barrier-to-reconciliation-says-murray-sinclair/.

5 The Anglican Church of Canada, "There Was Nothing Good: An Open Letter to Canadian Senator Lynn Beyak," 10 March 2017, https://www.anglican.ca/news/nothing-good-open-letter-canadian-senator-lynn-beyak/30018179/.

6 John Paul Tasker, "Senator Beyak Stands By Residential School Remarks, Cites 'Fake News,'" *CBC News*, 16 March 2017, https://www.cbc.ca/news/politics/lynn-beyak-stands-by-fake-news-1.4028126?cmp=rss.

7 John Paul Tasker, "Senator Lynn Beyak Says She Has 'Suffered' With Residential School Survivors," *CBC News*, 27 March 2017, https://www.cbc.ca/news/politics/senator-lynn-beyak-suffered-residential-schools-1.4042627.

8 Tuck and Yang, "Decolonization Is Not a Metaphor," 3.

9 French historian Henry Rousso is often credited with coining the term "négationnisme," which is frequently translated into English as "negationism" or "denialism," to describe the deliberate denial of the Holocaust, particularly the existence of gas chambers at Nazi extermination camps such as Auschwitz. See Henry Rousso, *The Vichy Syndrome: History and Memory in France since 1944* (Harvard University Press, 1991).

Since the 1980s and 1990s, the term denialism has been expanded and adopted to be used in interdisciplinary scholarship. Mark Hoofnagle and his brother Chris Jay Hoofnagle, an American physiologist and lawyer respectively, are frequently credited with broadening "denialism" to the field of science, along with Pascal Diethelm and Martin McKee. Diethelm and McKee define denialism as "the employment of rhetorical arguments to give the appearance of legitimate debate where there is none, an approach that has the ultimate goal of rejecting a proposition on which a scientific consensus exists." In responding to denialists, they argue, "it is necessary to shift the debate from the subject under consideration, instead exposing to public scrutiny the tactics they employ and identifying them publicly for what they are." Pascal Diethelm and Martin McKee, "Denialism: What Is It and How Should Scientists Respond?," *European Journal of Public Health* 29 (January 2009): 2–4.

For more on Holocaust denialism see, for example, Deborah Lipstadt, *Denying the Holocaust: The Growing Assault on Truth and Memory* (Free Press, 1993); Richard J. Evans, *Lying About Hitler: History, Holocaust, and the David Irving Trail* (Basic Books, 2001). For more on scholarly responses to science denialism see, for example, Philip Schmid and Cornelia Betsch, "Effective Strategies for Rebutting Science Denialism in Public Discussions," *Nature Human Behaviour* 3 (2019): 931–9. For a communications studies perspective, see Alexander Godulla, Daniel Seibert, and Tim Klute, "What is Denialism? An Examination and Classification of Definitional Approaches and Relevant Actions," *Journalism and Media* 5, no.1 (2024): 135–147.

10 Building on the work of Survivors and Murray Sinclair, the first peer-reviewed study to examine residential school denialism was Carleton's 2021 article in *Settler Colonial Studies*, "'I don't need any more education.'" Since then, a number of works have contributed to the scholarly analysis of residential school denialism. See, for example, Lisa Howell and Nicholas Ng-A-Fook, "A Case of Senator Lynn Beyak and Anti-Indigenous Systemic Racism in Canada"; Edana Beauvis and Mark Williamson, "The Prevalence and Correlates of Residential School Denialism"; Sean P. Hier, "Moral Panics, Conservative Contrarianism, and the Polarizing Debate about Missing Children, Unmarked Burials, and Residential School Denialism in Canada"; James Miles and Lindsay Gibson, "Telling Truth in History Classrooms: Pedagogical Responses to Denialism and Pseudohistory."

11 Michelle Cyca, "The Dangerous Allure of Residential School Denialism," *The Walrus*, 4 May 2023, https://thewalrus.ca/residential-school-denialism/.

12 See, for example, Jean-Paul Sartre, *The Anti-Semite and the Jew* (Schocken Books, 1948); Aileen Moreton-Robinson, *The White Possessive: Property, Power, and Indigenous Sovereignty* (University of Minnesota Press, 2015); and Dan Ariely, *Misbelief: What Makes Rational People Believe Irrational Things* (HarperCollins, 2023).

13 Justice and Carleton, "Truth Before Reconciliation."

14 "Reconciliation" is an admittedly contested concept. See, for example, Asch, Borrows, and Tully, *Resurgence and Reconciliation*.

15 "Senator Murray Sinclair Responds to Lynn Beyak's Defence."

16 See Memmi, *The Colonizer and the Colonized*, 45–76.

17 Sean Carleton, *Lessons in Legitimacy*. For more on history and power see, for example, Michel-Rolph Trouillot, *Silencing the Past: Power and the Production of History* (Beacon Press, 1995).

18 Woods, "On the Making of a National Tragedy," 29.

19 See P.H. Bryce, *Report on the Indian Schools of Manitoba and the North West Territories* (Government Printing Bureau, 1907).

20 Bryce later published his report independently. See P.H. Bryce, *The Story of a National Crime: Being an Appeal for Justice to the Indians of Canada* (James Hope and Sons, 1922).

21 For more on Bryce's efforts, see Milloy, *A National Crime*, 90–91.

22 Woods, "On the Making of a National Tragedy," 35.

23 For more on the history of residential schooling see, for example, Miller, *Shingwauk's Vision*; Milloy, *A National Crime*; Schissel and Wotherspoon, *The Legacy of School for Aboriginal People*; Mosby, "Administering Colonial Science"; McCallum, "'I Would Like the Girls at Home'"; and Fraser, *By Strength, We Are Still Here*.

24 Woods, "On the Making of a National Tragedy," 40–41. For early accounts that were positive see, for example, Ahenakew, "Little Pine: An Indian Day School" and Moine, *My Life in a Residential School*. For more critical accounts see, for example, Johnston, *Indian School Days*; Fontaine, *Broken Circle*; and Sellars, *They Called Me Number One*.

25 *Alberta Report*'s 26 January 1998 edition focused on "Canada's Mythical Holocaust." Included in the issue are a series of apologist articles defending Christianity and the work of missionaries in the schools. See, for example, Patrick Donnelly, "Scapegoating the Indian Residential Schools: The Noble Legacy of Hundreds of

Christian Missionaries is Sacrificed to Political Correctness," *Alberta Report* 25, no. 6 (26 January 1998): 6–11. See Figure 0.9.

26 *Honouring the Truth*, 23. On how Canada has addressed ongoing issues related to residential schooling, including the Truth and Reconciliation Commission, see Niezen, *Truth and Indignation*; Capitaine and Vanthuyne, *Power Through Testimony*; and MacDonald, *The Sleeping Giant Awakens*.

27 *Honouring the Truth*, v.

28 *Honouring the Truth*, vi.

29 *Honouring the Truth*, vi.

30 See, for example, McNally and Martin, "First Nations, Inuit, and Métis Health," 117–22; and Gaudry and Lorenz, "Indigenization as Inclusion, Reconciliation, and Decolonization," 218–27.

31 Maracle, *My Conversations with Canadians*, 78.

32 Jones, *Genocide: A Comprehensive Introduction*, 352.

33 Di Cesare, *If Auschwitz Is Nothing*, 20.

34 Di Cesare, 30. Di Cesare notes that Pierre Vidal-Naquet borrows and popularizes the phrase "assassins of memory" from Yerushalmi, *Assassins of Memory*, 146.

35 Scholars such as Andrew Woolford have published numerous studies situating Canada's treatment of Indigenous peoples in the field of genocide studies. See, for example, Woolford, "Ontological Destruction," 81–97 and Woolford, *This Benevolent Experiment*. See also MacDonald, *The Sleeping Giant Awakens*, 146–7.

36 For a sampling of these debates, see "Media Coverage/Reaction to the Canadian Historical Association's Canada Day Statement Recognizing the Genocide of Indigenous Peoples in Canada," 17 September 2021, https://cha-shc.ca/media-coverage-reaction-to-the-canadian-historical-associations-canada-day-statement-recognizing-the-genocide-of-indigenous-peoples-in-canada/. See also Sean Carleton and Andrew Woolford, "Ignore Debaters and Denialists, Canada's Treatment of Indigenous Peoples Fits the Definition of Genocide."

37 See Genocide Watch's "Country Report: Canada," February 2022, https://www.genocidewatch.com/country-pages/canada.

38 Starblanket and Hunt, *Storying Violence*, 67–9.

39 Maracle, *My Conversations with Canadians*, 10.

40 Maracle, 27.

41 Simpson, *As We Have Always Been*, 101.

42 Mackey, *Unsettled Expectations*, 9. See also Furniss, *The Burden of History*; Regan, *Unsettling the Settler Within*; and Lowman and Barker, *Settler: Identity and Colonialism*, 44–7.

43 Regan, *Unsettling the Settler Within*, 6–11.

44 Maracle, *My Conversations with Canadians*, 58.

45 See LaRocque, *When the Other is Me*, 3–4.

46 On settler fear and anxiety, see Maracle, *My Conversations with Canadians*, 14; Mackey, *Unsettled Expectations*, 35–36; Rifkin, "Settler States of Feeling"; and Carleton, "Settler Anxiety and State Support for Missionary Schooling."

47 Fanon, *The Wretched of the Earth*, 15.

48 For more on the cultural production of colonialism, see LaRocque, *When the Other is Me*; Said, *Orientalism*; Berkhofer Jr., *The White Man's Indian*; and Francis, *The Imaginary Indian*.

49 Said, *Culture and Imperialism*, xii–xiii.

50 Tuck and Yang, "Decolonization Is Not a Metaphor," 1.

51 Memmi, *The Colonizer and the Colonized*, 37.

52 Memmi, 52, emphasis is added.

53 Memmi, 53.

54 Memmi, 78.

55 Di Cesare, *If Auschwitz Is Nothing*, 57.

56 Liam Britten, "Homework Assignment to List 'Positive' Stories about Residential Schools Under Investigation," *CBC News*, 25 November 2020, https://www.cbc.ca/news/canada/british-columbia/residential-school-homework-assignment-1.5816491.

57 See, for example, Kristy Kirkup, "Jean Chrétien Criticized by Indigenous Leaders, Advocates for Comments on Residential Schools," *Globe and Mail*, 25 October 2021, https://www.theglobeandmail.com/politics/article-jean-chretien-criticized-by-indigenous-leaders-advocates-for-comments/; Peter Zimonjic and Catherine Cullen, "Erin O'Toole Walks Back Claim that Residential Schools were Designed to 'Provide Education,'" *CBC News*, 16 December 2020, https://www.cbc.ca/news/politics/erin-otoole-residential-schools-comments-1.5844307; The Canadian Press, "Indigenous Peoples Grapple with Claims Downplaying the History of Residential Schools," *CTV News*, 4 October 2025, https://www.ctvnews.ca/canada/article/indigenous-peoples-grapple-with-claims-downplaying-the-history-of-residential-schools/.

58 Sean Carleton, "'Flooding the Zone' with Residential School Denialism," *Canadian Dimension*, 23 October 2025, https://canadiandimension.com/articles/view/flooding-the-zone-with-residential-school-denialism.

59 Carleton, "Confronting the Far-right's War on Reconciliation."

60 Niigaan Sinclair, *Wînipêk*, 164–166.

61 Sinclair and Carleton, "Residential School Denialism Is on the Rise."

62 Office of the Independent Special Interlocutor, *Executive Summary: Final Report on the Missing and Disappeared Indigenous Children and Unmarked Burials in Canada*, 2024, https://osi-bis.ca/wp-content/uploads/2024/11/3.OSI-Executive-Summary.pdf.

CHAPTER 1

WHY TRUTH-TELLING MATTERS:

A Survivor's Perspective

an Interview with Phyllis Webstad

SEAN CARLETON AND NIIGAAN SINCLAIR (EDITORS): Thank you for making time to talk about residential school denialism and why, from a Survivor's perspective, it needs to be confronted. It's such an honour to speak with you.

People will be familiar with your story: you are a Northern Secwépemc (Shuswap) from the Stswecem'c Xgat'tem First Nation (Canoe Creek Indian Band); a third-generation Survivor of the St. Joseph's Mission Indian Residential School in Williams Lake, British Columbia; a founding member of Orange Shirt Day–Every Child Matters and the Orange Shirt Society, the owner of your orange shirt story; and a prominent advocate for truth and reconciliation. You are also the author of many successful books, including most recently *Decolonization and Me: Conversations about Healing a Nation and Ourselves*.[1] In the book, you devote a whole chapter to addressing the dangers and harms of denialism from your perspective as a Survivor. To begin, can you share more about how you understand denialism and how you've experienced it personally?

PHYLLIS WEBSTAD: Thank you for including me in this important collection. I've seen a lot of negative denialism, especially online, but no one has ever told me to my face that they don't believe us as Survivors. I've invited that dialogue, but it's never happened, and I speak all across

Canada. If there are denialists in the audience, they don't identify themselves or try to challenge me in person.

I've never gone one-on-one, in person, with somebody saying, "Show me the bodies" or "How come you haven't dug any up yet?" I have mostly seen and experienced that hatred and racism online, on social media. It's never said directly to my face.

The closest I came was one September when I was doing media for one of my children's books in Toronto. I went to a radio interview, and I'm on Toronto time, three hours ahead of British Columbia time, so I'm still waking up. I'm talking about my children's book and Orange Shirt Day and suddenly, the host hit me with all of these questions about denialism and asking me what I think and how to respond. I had to really think on my feet because I was not expecting that. It was live on the radio, too. I walked away from that experience realizing I need to be better prepared. I need to have a set of notes with me in case I'm ever confronted with this again.

EDITORS: What did the host say?

PHYLLIS: They kept asking about or referring to denialists who have websites: Have I seen the websites, and what do I think of them and their arguments? I had never really thought about it that much or paid too much attention. I'm busy doing my work. I still haven't visited any of those websites. What I kept saying was that we, as Survivors, are not liars. There are people alive today who have brothers, sisters, aunts, and uncles who never came home. And they're not lying about their experience.

EDITORS: In *Decolonization and Me*, you talk about some of your social media examples—people saying that residential school deaths are a "hoax" and other hurtful things. These kinds of comments are, unfortunately, quite common as we explain in the Introduction and that subsequent chapters will deal with in greater detail.

It's interesting that you say most of the denialism you've experienced is impersonal—emails, social media, undermining, questioning, and challenging—but never in direct, personal way. We think that also tells us something about the nature of this, which is that denialists and those allured by what they say are not interested in spending time getting to know Indigenous people, Survivors, and learning or investing in the relationship building that's necessary for truth and reconciliation. They are just pot-shotting from the side, making rude, racist, and dehumanizing comments on the internet. They're angry and frustrated that they feel like they're losing power in society. Like other conspiracy theorists, they're not engaging personally. Nevertheless, the damage that can be done with those websites, articles, and social media posts that promote denialism is far-reaching.

As part of your work with the Orange Shirt Society, you've had the opportunity to travel and speak with Survivors, communities, and non-Indigenous people across the country. What have you learned about denialism in talking with other people, Indigenous and non-Indigenous? Why do you think it's so harmful?

PHYLLIS: My motivation for writing *Decolonization and Me*, with Kristy McLeod, was to explore it for myself. My education is in accounting, so I think of things in measurements. The whole residential school story is, say, the length of a ruler. What people understand—about me, about residential schooling generally—is only three or four inches of the ruler, and the rest they don't know. That is where we need to invite people to learn and fill in the gaps in their knowledge. I hope those reading this book will feel invited to learn more about the truth of Survivors and residential schooling. That was my hope with *Decolonization and Me*, and this book, too, is to start filling in the rest that is not understood. But we can't make people care. There'll always be denialists, I think. But the ones who are willing to learn are the ones who we can work with and, I hope, they will change their attitudes and behaviour and hold people around them accountable as well. There will always be the ones who will bury their heads in the sand and there's nothing we can do about that—but the vast majority of Canadians want to listen, learn, and build a better future. I truly believe that.

What I've learned from other Indigenous people, from the stories they tell me as I travel around, is that they want a safe place where they can tell their truths and be heard and believed.

I answer questions with stories a lot of the time. One of the stories is about my eldest aunt, my mom's older sister. She went to St. Joseph's Indian Residential School in British Columbia for nine years, 1953 to 1961. She had a couple of friends who went missing, and she never knew what happened to them. She gave her testimony to the group that was collecting the testimonies of people who knew anything about the missing children and unmarked burials.

My aunt lives on the reserve, she has a phone, cable television, and APTN (Aboriginal Peoples Television Network), but doesn't do computers. She called my cousin, her daughter, crying and upset. My cousin Sarah is my assistant who works and travels with me. My aunt called Sarah, upset and emotional, saying, "Those white people don't believe us. They don't believe me." She had seen the National Chief on APTN addressing the media regarding denialism. She didn't understand why they didn't believe what was being told, what the Survivors were saying about the missing children and unmarked burials. That was hard for her to know that her story wasn't believed by non-Indigenous people. To go through something like that, not knowing what happened to her friends, only to not be believed, it's hard.

I've had many stories told to me by those who have family who didn't come home. It would never occur to me to think they were lying, or to demand to see bodies. Why would anybody lie about something like that? We have enough to deal with in our daily lives because of the genocide, intergenerational effects, and history. That we also have this handful of denialists hurling these hurtful opinions in the media and on social media, it's discouraging, which is perhaps why they do it.

But it's not our responsibility, as Survivors, as Indigenous people, to take on challenging this denialism. I understand that and my brain understands that, but to be thought of as a liar is hard. Nobody wants to be told that they're a liar. That's what is happening with these denialists who boldly declare on the internet: "Where's the bones? Where's the kids? Why aren't you digging them up? I am not going to believe until you do those things." What I say and what comes to mind when I hear and see those kinds of comments is there's a lot more going on in the background than what you understand. These denialists are people who have not lived through what we have and experienced what we have. It didn't happen to them. You have to own it to know it; they don't own it and therefore don't know it. It's as simple as that.

For me and my family, everyone came home. All fourteen of us. But that isn't the case for many families across this country. I put myself in their shoes. If I had an aunt or uncle who didn't come home and faced the decision to talk about that as a family, there is so much to be considered. To get us together financially, emotionally, mentally, and physically, because residential schools have harmed our family so severely, a simple family meeting about a loved one would be almost impossible. So, for those families that need to gather to discuss this as a family and community, those discussions haven't even started yet. There is a process that needs to be followed. It has only been five years since this came out in a big way. We're all still learning. We have always known about deaths and missing loved ones, but dealing with it so openly is new for us.

My aunt worked on the stories of the Kamloops Indian Residential School (KIRS) for years, but the day the Nation made their announcement, in May 2021, even though she knew the stories of the deaths of children first-hand, she came into my office and was just shaking. Finally, the world believes us, she said. To have these denialists try to roll things back, it's hard. We have enough to deal with.

There's a lot of pain in having family members missing and not knowing what happened to them, like with my aunt and her two friends. She still doesn't know, and I don't know if she'll ever know what happened to them. But she thinks about them. She talks about it on occasion and tells us who they were and where she knew they were from. She gave her testimony, and I hope that testimony gets to those families about my aunt's last remembrances of her friends whom she never saw again. There's a lot of stories that have been told to me. I would never think, as they're telling me their truths, that they're not being truthful.

I'll tell you another story. After the Tk'emlúps te Secwépemc's announcement—I live about three and a half hours north of Kamloops—I needed to go check on my mom, who lives in Kamloops. I also needed to check on my son, who's a Survivor, and my grandchildren. When I was done—I was there for about a week—and I was checking out of my room, there was a Native man. First, I noticed his belly and it kind of startled me because he was in the room next to me and standing in the doorway with his cup of coffee. We both said, "Good morning." When I checked out, I usually have everything around my neck and arms, carrying suitcases and dragging things because I want to make one trip, right? As I was going down the walkway on the third floor outside, the balcony, I thought, no, I have to turn around, go back, and say hello. There's something going on there. I turn around with all my stuff and I go back to where my door is and I drop everything and tell him, "Good morning" again and ask where he was from. He said, "Good morning," and the next thing he said was, "I am so ashamed of myself." If I ever find this man, I want to talk to him again. I didn't get his name. He had long braids and said, "I am so ashamed of myself." I opened my mouth to say something, but before I could say anything, he continued and said that he hadn't had a drink of alcohol for thirteen years, but last night he drank because he couldn't stand it anymore—this was a week after the announcement. I don't remember if he mentioned whether he was a Survivor or not, but what he said was, "Those bastards, I think they lied to me. They said my brothers ran away. But I think they are..." He made a gesture that they were in the ground, dead. He said when he was done seeing his grandchildren in Merritt, British Columbia, and they were okay, he was going back to his home in Saskatchewan to do what he can to find out what happened to his brothers and where they are. I want to find him. I don't know who he was. I wouldn't even recognize him. It wouldn't occur to me to walk away thinking that he is full of it or laugh at him and say, "You don't have any bones. You don't have any bodies. You're a liar."

It's just unfathomable how anyone with any ounce of empathy or humanity can be saying Survivors are lying. Why not put your energy into learning Survivor truths and helping us find those who are missing, helping us do research and achieve justice and healing? That would be a more productive way to spend money and energy than to say we're lying on the internet.

EDITORS: When we've been talking to people, they've really been emphasizing how painful this conversation is and how much courage it took for Survivors to begin to share their truth in the first place. There was such a culture of silence around residential schooling, even in the 1980s and 1990s. With the power relationships of speaking out against the Church and leaders in many communities, it was just easier to stay silent. But as a result of a lot of hard work, that culture has shifted, and more Survivors feel comfortable sharing their truth today. To then not be believed or, worse, as you say, to be challenged continuously: "I don't believe you." "No deaths happened." "Abuse is exaggerated." It's a form of intimidation. It's painful. It keeps people silent—"This is why I didn't want to talk about this in the first place." "This is why I didn't want to share this." These are things we are hearing from Survivors.

We think the denialists know what they're doing. Your point of why not put your energy into empathy, compassion, and listening—well, quite simply, because that empathy and compassion would lead to change. It would lead to changes in the way Canada operates. We think that's why denialism is so harmful, as you've explained. There is harm being done and that is why they're doing it—to cause harm and protect the Colonial status quo.

We like your analogy of the ruler—a lot of people who are susceptible or allured by denialism only know part of the ruler. They don't know the whole story. That is why we're optimistic that the work that you're doing can help bridge that gap, tell the whole story, and inform people about what's going on so they can be part of the solution.

One of the things that we keep saying is that it's not just knowledge about residential schooling that's needed to push back against denialism—that's one part, the foundational piece. But another part is knowing how to identify denialism and to be able to effectively challenge it, often in interpersonal situations and relationships. We wonder if you have any thoughts about what non-Indigenous Canadians can do to challenge denialism and support Survivors? What are the kinds of things that you would like to see non-Indigenous people do to step up and take responsibility to confront residential school denialism?

PHYLLIS: Well, the first thing that non-Indigenous people can do is to believe Survivors, listen to us and learn our truths, and have empathy for our experiences. What's the saying by Maya Angelou? "When you know better you do better." As a person learns more about what they don't know on that ruler, a lot of it is the history of this country, how it was formed, Indigenous Peoples, and the ongoing impacts of colonialism. It was apocalyptic, one thing after another that affected us and put us where we are today. Residential schooling was one of those events, but there have been others. Learning about those things is very important. Know your history. That's what I do when I present. I hope I can fill in those gaps of understanding so that non-Indigenous people can think, know, and do differently and better.

There are Survivors I know who are willing to challenge denialists face-to-face. I'm one of them. I sometimes visualize what that would be like. "Bring it on! Go tell me what you think, and I'll tell you what I know." I don't think it would be very productive, but I know that there are Survivors, myself included, who are willing to be in a room with these people. All we can do is tell our truths.

EDITORS: It's now been ten years since the TRC released its *Final Report* and 94 Calls to Action. In many ways, there has been a lot of progress made in terms of increasing awareness around the history of Indian Residential Schools and their ongoing effects. On the other hand, residential school denialism is certainly on the rise as a kind of backlash to this progress and as an attack on truth and reconciliation. Why do you, as a Survivor, think we need to continue to put truth before reconciliation? Why do you think defending Survivors and their truths is so essential for the work moving forward?

PHYLLIS: The genocide in Canada against Indigenous Peoples is not complete. It's ongoing. Denialism is the last step in genocide, a last gasp for control over Indigenous Peoples by undermining our experience.

In 2008, when the TRC started, they said the number of children alive, or Survivors, was around 80,000. In 2023, I was at Survivors Gathering put on by the National Centre for Truth and Reconciliation and they said that number was around 40,000 and rapidly declining. Survivors won't live forever. I can confidently say that those in elementary school right now, in their lifetime, will see a day in the news when the last Survivor has died. When there are no more. That will be in the next fifty or so years. It's very important that those Survivors who are alive, who are willing and able, need to tell their truths and, if they can, have it written down, even if for nothing more than their own family history. I know the IRSSS (Indian Residential School Survivors Society) is running a program where they are matching writers with Survivors to get their stories written down. Truth comes before reconciliation, and the truth is not yet fully told.

When I talk to organizations and they are so proud of their reconciliation action plan, I ask them, respectfully: Can you please put truth in the reconciliation action plan? Even in Ottawa—I need to find out what government agency it is—they have on this big wall in concrete, "Reconciliation." We went by too fast, and I saw it and said, "Somebody didn't put 'truth' before reconciliation."

So, why do I think, as a Survivor, that we need to press on to learn more about residential schooling and the Survivor experience? Because one day we are not going to be here. If we keep talking about it and keep documenting, then maybe those who deny and downplay will come to their senses and believe us. I think that denialists do not have Indigenous people in their lives. At the very least, our truth will be documented for future generations.

EDITORS: You mentioned that the Indian Residential School System (IRSS) is just one part of the larger genocide. A lot of denialists will, as you say, cherry-pick an example and say, "See, this person is saying the system was positive. We were saving Indigenous people from these dysfunctional families." That is a symptom of ignorance about Indigenous history. Where is the understanding of the intergenerational aspect of residential schooling, the Indian Act, land loss, and all of these elements that are contributing to that situation? They are manipulating that story.

As you say, Survivors won't be around forever and the time to establish the truth, to understand the full story, the whole ruler, is now. Denialism is trying to distract us from learning that truth. We need to find ways to challenge that. But the best way is to focus on the truth. The other pieces—the healing, the justice, the reconciliation—will come. But only if we put that truth piece first. We have a lot of work to do.

PHYLLIS: And that truth is so personal. It's not an abstract thing; it's a daily lived experience for us as Survivors. I want people to remember that as they read the rest of the book. It's difficult and ongoing. I think a lot of non-Indigenous people generally don't have a clue about what it means to have lived experience with the Indian Residential School System. But denialists in particular think it's just a game. Debating our humanity, dehumanizing us on the internet, it's just fun for them. It's just another form of racism. As you say, the damage of residential schools and colonialism isn't just the abuse; it's sterilization and the disruption of family and community. That just doesn't get fixed overnight. You don't just flip the switch. That's the genocide.

EDITORS: Genocide studies scholar Andrew Woolford has written a chapter for this collection (Chapter 8) on the techniques of genocide denialism, and we've learned a lot from him. As he explains, genocide is the destruction of a people's group life, in whole or in part, and that was certainly the clear objective of residential schooling to support settler colonialism and Canadian nation-building. That story that you've just shared, that disruption, is what Canada was hoping for. It meant that Indigenous Peoples couldn't resist the development, colonization, and the shift to a settler capitalist economy.

We think there's a lot of truth still to be told. The full truth may never be known, but we have a responsibility, while Survivors are still with us, to learn, listen, and support research and knowledge as much as possible so that we gain a few inches of the ruler of knowledge in our lifetime. That knowledge will deal with a lot of the denialism and the people who don't know. We might not deal with all the denialists, but for the vast majority of people, when they are presented with as much information as we know, it will become harder and harder to justify, consume, or promote denialism. That gives us a lot of hope.

Part of our solution, and it's just one piece, is to really focus on education. Murray Sinclair used to say that education got us into this mess and education is what will get us out. As educators, we see this on a daily basis with our university students. You also see this, thinking about that generation of K–12 students who are learning about this in a different way, and Indigenous Peoples generally. Some of the curriculum changes that are happening are transforming this country and creating a pathway to reconciliation. Simply put, we believe that education, broadly understood, will win the day. It won't be easy, but it will be this multigenerational shift that contributes to reconciliation and helps build a better future.

We have talked a lot about the difficulty, harm, and pain that denialism creates. But what gives you hope for the future?

PHYLLIS: There are a number of things that give me hope. I believe that the future is bright because of what I've witnessed.

I love graduation time and seeing all the graduates—grade twelve, masters, doctors. My cousin received her master's recently in linguistics. She's a language teacher. Every time I think about that I say, "Watch out, world!" We're getting educated, we're getting to learn your colonial system and how to fight back. An example of that is Chief Cadmus Delorme—well, he's not Chief anymore. But part of his story is he got educated and learned. He had an understanding of both worlds. That is what we need. I just love seeing it. I'm fifty-eight, and these thirty-year-olds are just amazing with what they're teaching and learning, and the changes they're going to be able to make with their education. Not only that, but their self-worth and confidence is growing too.

My grandchildren are the first in five generations to be raised by their mother and their father. Granny, Mom, I, and my son didn't have that—we went to residential school. The healing is happening in my family and it's happening in other families where they don't have the craziness, the dysfunction—a healing journey we had to be on to live in this world. They don't come with all of that baggage, so they are free. As the late Murray Sinclair said, "to be who they were meant to be." I'm really witnessing that now. They're not afraid to stand up for what they believe in, and they're going to be the change makers.

I think about my life and my healing journey—I didn't know what I believed. I didn't have the self-confidence to even say what I thought. That's what residential schooling took from me. It's taken a lot of therapy and healing to know that I belong on this Earth just as much as anybody else. To walk on this Earth and to breathe this air, I'm not better than or less than anybody else because I didn't grow up with a mom and a dad. Those who grow up with a mom and a dad who can guide them, or whoever is there for them, are doing a great job, because of what I witness every May and June with all these graduates. They don't have to worry about what we've had to worry about in the past. That gives me a lot of hope. In fact, the gradating class of June 2026 will be the first to have had K–12 exposure to Orange Shirt Day–Every Child Matters and residential school teachings, and they'll be going out into the world with empathy and more of an understanding of what happened to us than, say, people my age. The older generation didn't even know residential schools existed, let alone the impacts and legacy. This is changing in a big way.

Orange Shirt Day was created to honour Survivors and their families and to remember those who never made it home. One of the ways we do that is by keeping the conversation going—keep it out there in the forefront, and keep challenging the denialists. This is our truth, and Survivors are not liars.

EDITORS: Thank you for sharing your knowledge with us. We really appreciate your hope and optimism. It's a good reminder to start off this book not to let the negativity of denialism—whether it's experienced online or in-person, as the next chapter will discuss—distract us from all the good work being done. We need to keep up the momentum behind truth and reconciliation. As Jesse Wente argues in his essay in *The Brightness of Being*, "hope may be our final refuge. So we must take it, and from there, we fight."[2]

We appreciate everything that you do to speak up for Survivors and defend the truth about residential schooling.

Notes

1 See Webstad, Parker, and Nicol, *Phyllis's Orange Shirt*; Webstad and Kewageshig Emily; *With Our Orange Hearts*; and Webstad and McLeod, *Decolonization and Me*.

2 Jesse Wente in Sara Sinclair and Stephanie Sinclair, *A Brightness of Being: Truths, Wisdom, and Love from Celebrated Indigenous Voices* (Penguin, 2025), 68.

CHAPTER 2

ORANGE SHIRT DAY HANGOVER:

Municipalities, Indigenous Historians, and the Long History of Denialism

by Mary Jane Logan McCallum

It is 1 October 2022, and I wake up exhausted and tense, my jaw clenched and my lungs like raisins, still feeling the gut punch that took my breath away the day before. My mind races with regrets.[1]

The day before, I had spoken at public events in Elgin County, southwestern Ontario. These events marked National Day for Truth and Reconciliation, or Orange Shirt Day, now the culmination of the annual Truth and Reconciliation Week.[2] I was on a study leave and living in London, Ontario, while undertaking research with my relatives at Munsee Delaware Nation. My plan that day was to share my recent research on Indian Residential School student labour at Mount Elgin Industrial School at these events, as they were organized by and for Canadians who live in the area of the school.[3] Instead, I ended up being confronted and contradicted by an angry white man as organizers and attendees looked on. Unlike Survivor Phyllis Webstad, who in the previous chapter remarked about not having ever been confronted in-person, this experience brought me face-to-face with residential school denialism. Clashes like this take a toll on Indigenous historians like me for whom none of this is theoretical or detached, a toll that is especially steep at events where Canadians have a responsibility to learn history and adequately support the experts they call on to share it. The experience taught me a lot about the importance of Indigenous

Figure 2.1. My messy kitchen table the morning after Orange Shirt Day. Photo by Mary Jane Logan McCallum.

histories and the dynamics of residential school denialism, and this chapter reflects on the lessons learned.

Mount Elgin Industrial School, like the municipality of Elgin County across the river from it, was named for British colonial administrator and Governor General of the British province of Canada Lord Elgin (James Bruce, 1811–1863). The communities in the area continue to find comfort in this imperial heritage, a comfort that is reflected by the twinned activities of renaming places and erasing foundational and continuing Indigenous history.[4] Founded in 1846, the Mount Elgin Industrial School was to play an important role in this imperial work, and the connected imposition of a new relationship to land and among people. This new relationship was a hierarchical one that was based on the extraction of land and labour to support colonial agricultural entrepreneurship that would create intergenerational wealth from the land for settlers.

Learning about the school alongside relatives and the archival records of the Department of Indian Affairs (DIA) and the United

Church of Canada (UCC) has profoundly shaped my own world view. My great-grandfather, Alonzo, who attended Mount Elgin in the early twentieth century after his mother was hospitalized, did not speak negatively about the school. Neither did his father, who attended the nearby Indian Residential School, the Mohawk Institute, in Brantford, Ontario, in the 1870s. Alonzo's daughter, Norma, would only speak openly about her mid-twentieth-century experience of Mount Elgin under certain conditions. I have also read reels of microfilmed and paper letters that spell out appeals to improve miserable conditions and confident replies that Indians deserved no better and instead needed to learn to devalue themselves, their labour, and their academic gifts and potential.

Indigenous historians' community-based and public education work of researching and analyzing the past and presenting it in ways that make sense in the present has always been tricky. For too long, and even now, a decade after the release of the Truth and Reconciliation Commission (TRC) of Canada's *Final Report*, most Canadians have little to no knowledge of Indigenous history, even if, after the release of the report, some Canadians did realize how little they had learned about Indigenous—and Canadian—history. For many citizens, the National Day for Truth and Reconciliation (NDTR), a Canadian observance that was first established in 2013 as Orange Shirt Day, became especially meaningful in the years following the announcement that 215 suspected "anomalies" were located on the grounds of the former Kamloops Indian Residential School in May 2021. Similar findings have since been made at the sites of other residential schools.[5] Others however, often more vocal, still insist on the "history" they think they know, a history that hangs on thinly veiled stereotypes and shallow misconceptions drawn from general culture and spoken loudly in an effort to drown out carefully researched histories and the voices of Indian Residential School Survivors.[6]

As historians, we can offer various points of entry into the topic of Indian Residential Schools: I focus on health and labour; others, on sport and extracurricular activities, gender, militarism, land and land loss, commemoration, school staffing, architecture, religion and missionization, art and literature, biography, specific schools and regions, and so on.[7] On Orange Shirt Day, however, our work can become generalized and contorted by and for audiences who expect certain types of information delivered in a certain way and to a certain end. There is often an appetite in these places for personal stories of individual pain and suffering.[8] Theorized best by scholar Audra Simpson, our arguments about real anger, real frustration, and real need to identify and reject colonialism in all its forms can be pre-emptively framed in an affective performance of sorrow, contrition, and moving on.[9] We must also contend with unsubstantiated arguments on practically any subject of Indigenous history that gains media attention.[10] In this context, Indigenous historians can struggle to be heard.

When reconciliation events are held in places where Indigenous people are extremely under-represented, they can be especially fraught. For more than twenty years now, I have lived in Winnipeg, amid a much larger Indigenous population than in most cities. But I grew up in the heart of Simcoe County, near Barrie, Ontario, in what was then a predominantly white settler population. In places like Winnipeg, Indigenous people and Indigenous community laws and structures are part of everyday life and part of the bigger conversations about how things should work.[11] For Indigenous historians, this means that at the very least, there is a lot more support to draw on.

Indian Residential Schools have local histories of their own. So far, Canadians have attended almost exclusively to the national history of Indian Residential Schools that the Truth and Reconciliation Commission documented, and that has driven public education efforts over the past decade. This comes at the cost of deeper and more localized understandings of Indian Residential Schools, allowing Canadians today to distance themselves from the schools' day-to-day operations and legacies. Indian Residential Schools operated within and were enmeshed with local geographies and economies; they employed local citizens, and they fed low-skilled farm and domestic labour directly into the homes and communities that surrounded them.[12]

For the most part, citizens of these communities saw First Nations as a federal responsibility, a view that functioned as both mechanism and justification for racial segregation. While Canada's Constitution does indeed give jurisdiction over "Indians" to the federal government, it does not deny provinces, municipalities, or individuals the ability to pursue meaningful relationships with Indigenous people and communities. And it certainly never restricted municipalities from directly reaping the benefits of land dispossession. David Parent's examination of municipal tax rolls to understand Métis land dispossession in Manitoba reveals just how deeply implicated non-federal governing bodies are in Indigenous histories.[13] Local histories of Indian Residential Schools can help citizens make sense of the past and the present, especially those from communities that were established on the borders of reserves they have come to know very little about.[14] Until more of these closer connections can be developed, events organized to mark Orange Shirt Day require significant care and attention, alongside Indigenous history training and education programming, all sewn into municipal governing structures.

On 30 September 2022, after a long chain of email forwards made their way to my mailbox about a week earlier, I spoke at two Orange Shirt Day events in Southern Ontario. There are many things I do not know about the efforts that went into organizing the events, but I imagine it was difficult. The task of organizing the events appeared to have fallen exclusively to women (that is a whole different paper)[15] as part of their work for local municipal government. For employees of settler-dominated institutions, hosting Indigenous speakers can be awkward. This is especially so in places with little Indigenous representation, and given the histories and ongoing tensions of dispossession, racism, and marginalization that lie between municipalities and the Indigenous communities meant to come together in truth and reconciliation.[16] From the email chains that I became a part of, I could gather that the chiefs of all three neighbouring First Nations had declined the invitation to raise the Orange Shirt Day flag and say a few words. The chief of Munsee Delaware Nation was aware of my work on Mount Elgin Industrial School, which is why I was forwarded the email. I accepted because it was an opportunity to be of service to First Nations government and the larger community and share my work among an audience local to Mount Elgin; over the course of the week, I also lectured at Huron University, McMaster University, and Delaware Central Public School.

The first public event that I spoke at was held outdoors under sunny skies at the Sons of Scotland Park and Community Centre in Dutton, Ontario. From the start, it was clear that the sound system was broken. The microphone was working, but the speakers were making a constant loud, grating noise. "It worked on Canada Day," the master of ceremonies said. As far as I could tell, no one made even a motion to fix it, giving me the impression that the municipality did not view the speakers, and what they were saying, as very important. This impression was confirmed by the perfunctory speeches offered by the municipal and Church delegates at the event. It is a special day. Reconciliation is important. But the overwhelming sense that these speakers conveyed was that Indian Residential School history unfolded long ago and far away (in Kamloops, British Columbia, among other distant places).

Before I spoke, I asked to have the system turned off during my talk, as I had my own personal microphone and amp (a COVID-19 purchase for in-class lectures while I was wearing a mask). I made the request lightly and politely—I was, after all, visiting—but it was met with a sneer. I had to wonder if the sound system had been rigged not to work and if I was ruining some juvenile prank. I doubt that was the case, but it is how I felt.

I was anxious to speak about the history of forced child labour that I had uncovered in *Nii Ndahlohke: Boys' and Girls' Work at Mount Elgin Industrial School, 1890–1915*, a history that had unfolded a mere twenty-four kilometres to the east of the Sons of Scotland Park. Mount Elgin Industrial School was operated by the Methodist and United Church of Canada and the federal government at Deshkan Ziibiing, Chippewas of the Thames First Nation, over a period of nearly 100 years. *Nii Ndahlohke* (or "I work" in Lunaape) originated as a project of the Munsee Delaware Language and History Group, which meets informally to learn Lunaape language and Munsee history. With a grant from Heritage Canada, we designed a resource for use in teaching Canadian history in grades seven to nine in the Thames Valley District School Board and other Ontario boards of education.[17] The book includes images, maps, and archival documents, as well as review and discussion sections, and a glossary. Munsee Lunaape language experts provide careful translations of terms and phrases, to help teach about girls' and boys' work in the barns, fields, kitchens, and laundries at Mount Elgin. Munsee artists also provided their interpretations of the book's content in their own artforms. I brought copies of the book to give away to people attending the Orange Shirt Day event.

About thirty to forty students in grades four and five sat on the ground at the front of the audience, and another thirty to forty adults sat on chairs or stood at the back. To me, it seemed like a good turnout. As I was explaining the essential function of child labour at the Mount Elgin Industrial School and the farm connected to it, I could see in my periphery a person walking toward me. I thought it could be an Indian Residential School Survivor, so I respectfully provided space and offered my mic for them to speak. He would not look at me, however, and acted as if I were not even there.

In front of dozens of children and adults, he rebuked my research and made a presentation of his own about the "good intentions" of Mount Elgin's staff and Indians' lack of farming skills. He was later identified to me as "Mr. Ryerson." He was not wearing an orange shirt, nor was he a scheduled speaker, and his interruption showed disrespect and contempt for me and for the research that I presented.

I did not have the words at the time, but Mr. Ryerson's interruption was a form of residential school denialism.[18] It is possible that Mr. Ryerson went to the event with the sole purpose of confrontation and disruption. When he had finished and walked away, I pushed my emotions down as far as they would go and carried on because, well . . . no one had stopped him, and no one stopped me. In fact, no one said or did anything. At the end of the event, a United Church minister asked if he could take a photo of *the two of us*, as he wanted to write a newspaper article on the "debate." Mr. Ryerson refused. The Conservative Member of Parliament for the riding told me that she "got it," because she is a "Mama Bear." Another woman told me blandly that I handled myself well.

Egerton Ryerson, Indian Residential Schools (Including Mount Elgin), and Two Toronto Universities

I do not know Mr. Ryerson, nor his relation, if any, to Egerton Ryerson, but his comments need to be understood in the context of family, community, and national histories of colonialism and education. About six months prior, Ryerson University had announced that it had changed its name to Toronto Metropolitan University (TMU). That change might have seemed swift but it was a long time coming if we consider the longer history since the 1990s of acknowledging the violence of the Indian Residential School system, the massive public investigation led by the Survivors and the Truth and Reconciliation Commission, and the use of the TRC and its recommendations by Canadian university faculty and students and administrators to propel change. A statue of Egerton Ryerson located next to TMU's Kerr Hall had become a site for protesting historical injustice connected to Indian Residential Schools

Figure 2.2. Sit-in at the X statue on Gould Street at X Campus (Ryerson University). Image courtesy of A Great Capture.

and raising support for the TRC's Calls to Action on campus, including a submission to the university president on Canada Day, 2018, that pressed for the statue's removal. Initially, the university added a plaque to provide further context on Ryerson, but this did not satisfy students. The statue was repeatedly defaced, and students and faculty unofficially renamed the school X University. In 2020, University President Mohamed Lachemi appointed a fourteen-member committee, called the Standing Strong (Mash Koh Wee Kah Pooh Win) Task Force, to study Egerton Ryerson and the reasons for the "controversy" on campus. Standing Strong's fifty-seven-page report, based on historical research and community engagement, was released in August 2021.[19] While the report summarized research into the life and legacy of Egerton Ryerson, it also documented his endorsement of a boarding and industrial schooling for Indigenous children in the 1830s and 1840s, and his vision for public education that allowed for both racial segregation and the exclusion of Black students from the public system. The report also provided "principles to guide commemoration . . . of Egerton Ryerson within the context of the University's values" and made twenty-two recommendations including #4: to rename the institution.[20]

Toronto Metropolitan University was not the only institution with Egerton Ryerson honorifics at the time. In 2019, University of Toronto Board of Regents asked then-president William Robins to produce a report that would advise the university on the use of Egerton Ryerson's name in honorifics, including a residence called Ryerson House. That thirty-four-page report, authored by a group of five scholars called the Victoria University Research Panel, was released in March 2021,[21] and provided a summary of Ryerson's achievements as an educator and public official. It also described his work at Victoria University (now part of the University of Toronto), his attitudes toward Indigenous Peoples, and the impact of decisions Ryerson made and influenced, as well as the effect of reports he wrote on Indigenous Peoples and communities.[22]

The University of Toronto's report found that, while it was clear Ryerson was aware of the vision Indigenous Peoples had for their own future, "he, his church, and his government sought to convert and 'civilize' the Anishinaabeg, steal and settle their land, and take their children away from them in both spirit and body." In a document that would later become, as the panel's report states, "one of the seeds for the genocidal residential school system," Ryerson recommended that the government turn "indigenous students into a racialized servant class."[23]

While most writing on Ryerson's legacy focuses on his role in building a universal public education system in Ontario, both the Standing Strong and Victoria University reports addressed what Ryerson said and did to keep Black and Indigenous students out of that system, and his views on the ways Indigenous Peoples should be educated. Those views are spelled out in Ryerson's 1847 "Report on Industrial Schools," submitted to the Assistant Superintendent General of Indian Affairs George Vardon, who had sought Ryerson's opinion on the matter. Ryerson stated, "I understand the end proposed to be the making of the pupils industrious farmers, and that learning is provided for and pursued only so far as it will contribute to that end."[24] His report dutifully proposed a model that would ensure students spent most of their time being "civilized" through the influence of industry and religion. The Victoria University Research Panel report found that "within ten years of their opening, the residential schools precipitated by Ryerson's report . . . were plagued with problems [including] . . . excessive manual labour[,] outbreaks of infectious diseases, and high rates of children running away from the schools."[25] One of those schools was Mount

Elgin Industrial School, the very school my relatives had attended and the one that I was talking about that day in Dutton, Ontario, when Mr. Ryerson confronted me and defended the Indian Residential School System.

Ryersons, Munsees, and the *Longue Durée* of Denialism

At jarring moments like the one I experienced on Orange Shirt Day in 2022, it feels like well-considered Indigenous histories cannot compete with groundless appreciation of and advocacy for the reputations and endeavours of supporters of Indian Residential Schools. Where does knee-jerk denialism with its thin, one-dimensional, carefully chosen story of white conquest, settlement, and entrepreneurship get its strength? Denialism thrives because of its place in a social order in which Indigenous people, land, and history are extinct at worst, or irrelevant at best. *Longue Durée* is a term used by some historians to describe an approach to history that sees current crises as part of enduring structural patterns. In the case of residential school denialism, *Longue Durée* challenges us to consider the founding and systemic patterns of white supremacy, economic exploitation, and Indigenous erasure inherent to settler colonialism in North America if we are to understand the history and phenomenon itself—as outlined by Carleton and Sinclair in the Introduction.

According to Ryerson family historians Phyllis A. Ryerse and Thomas A. Ryerson, Egerton Ryerson's ancestor Marten Reijersz[26] immigrated as a ten-year-old boy alongside his brother Adriaen to Lenapehoking (Lenape homeland) in 1646, possibly on the same ship as Dutch leader Pieter Stuyvesant and other old Knickerbocker families.[27] In 1663, Marten married New Amsterdam-born Annetje Joris Rapalje, whose parents (Joris Jansen Rapalje and Catalina Jeronimus Trico) were on the *Endracht* with other Walloon families in 1624.[28] They arrived intending to build a colony on Lenapehoking for the Dutch West India Company. Annetje's sister Sarah, born 1625, is the famed "first-born Christian daughter" of the colony. Land "purchased from the Indians" supported the family's growth and establishment in New York and New Jersey.

The narrative of a peaceful purchase of land by Dutch people in New York and New Jersey was fixed and popularized in the nineteenth and early twentieth centuries in dioramas and pageants, popular turn-of-the-century artistic forms of commemoration, history, and theatre that involved historical re-enactments, heritage tableaux, and song. The 1924 *Dutch Pageant* celebrating the tercentenary of the arrival of the first permanent settlers in "New Netherland," is a particularly generous site of such history making.[29] *Dutch Pageant* was presented at the newly built "Town Hall," a Progressive theatre, auditorium, and club for political education, discussion, and entertainment[30] organized by the Town Hall's "Historical Department," a group of white settler suffragists between the ages of forty and sixty who, according to one observer, "[we]'re interested in the romance of the founding and growth of the city."[31]

The pageant began with a re-enactment of the land purchase—depicted as a neutral and intelligent transaction prompted by Dutch leaders. Indeed, the written record of this agreement is conveniently and sufficiently vague enough for the Knickerbocker families to celebrate it as a peaceful land purchase. The purchase scene was followed by scenes of "A School in New Amsterdam" (featuring the first clergyman and schoolmaster), "A Dutch Wedding," and "An Address on Toleration." Proceeds from the *Dutch Pageant* were to be directed to the dedication of two special chairs to "commemorate the first white persons born on the Island of Manhattan."[32] The chairs were also said to be dedicated to "the first two mothers of our city—one to Mme Vinge, mother of little Jean, the other to Mme Rapaeljie, mother of little Sarah."[33]

The land purchase, the hero-worshipping of the first white babies, and the erasure of Indigenous mothers exemplify what historian Jean O'Brien calls "firsting and lasting." She identifies an important pattern in the telling of American history:

> Non-Indians narrate their own present against what they constructed as the backdrop of a past symbolized by Indian peoples and their cultures. . . . In the process of asserting their modernity, local writers . . . claimed to be the first people who established cultures and institutions worthy of notice, thereby invalidating Indian ways of life. Indians serve the larger story line of establishing the primacy of the new . . . social order. They are then effectively "replaced" by the rightful owners of the land, followed by a narrative of Indian

> extinction, whereby local historians occasionally tell stories about people they identify as the last Indian who lived in places they claimed as their own.[34]

These commemorative forms both assert and solidify community-driven lore of Dutch non-violent possession and settlement.

Like statues and pageants, museum dioramas are another popular form of historical commemoration. In the well-known 1939 *Old New York* diorama in the Theodore Roosevelt Memorial Hall at the American Museum of Natural History, Pieter Stuyvesant, the colonial governor of the colony of New Netherland, is depicted alongside Lenape during a 1660 encounter. Though the background shows a clear and seemingly regular presence of Lenape men and women alongside Dutch men, they are noticeably separate: Dutch on the right, Lenape on the left. The scene is set amidst Dutch settlement infrastructure with a windmill and a fleet of Dutch ships anchored just offshore. Stuyvesant and the figure of Munsee leader Oratamin are about to meet (with Lenape coming to Dutch), but distance remains between them. Each has a hand outstretched to indicate the peaceful nature of the meeting. Oratamin carries tobacco leaves and a second Lenape man carries a wampum, while Stuyvesant, demanding tribute, holds nothing in return (but his guard carries a gun).[35] It is revealing that the 1939 diorama focuses on diplomacy and downplays the many years of violent conflict between the Dutch colony and the Munsees.[36]

Indigenous studies scholar Aileen Moreton-Robinson argues that European control of Indigenous territories was rationalized and affirmed through logics she calls "the white possessive." These logics are "operationalized within discourses to circulate sets of meanings about ownership of the nation, as part of commonsense knowledge, decision-making, and socially produced conventions."[37] The ubiquity of the *Manhattan Purchase* pageant and story, told over and over and over again across diverse American audiences, essentially disavows not only this particular treaty but all treaties. Treaties that are reconceived as simply sale agreements were in fact understood by First Nations to establish relationships that were to foster trust and mutual prosperity. Whatever kind of peaceful relations that may have existed at some point had given way to violence and white possession that displaced Munsees and their relatives and allies by the time they were re-enacted

Figure 2.3. The *Old New York* Diorama, 1939. Image courtesy of American Museum of Natural History.

in the nineteenth century. Free from the responsibilities of relationality and secure on lands depopulated of Indigenous people, white settlers overwrote First Nations voices and more recent violence in sanitized expressions of a peaceful transfer of power.

The Ryersons and Munsee Lenape families (Westbrook, Turkey, Dolson, Logan, and others) ultimately became neighbours again in southwestern Ontario around the 1780s. In exchange for military alliance with the British Crown, Munsees were promised land along the Thames River in what is now Ontario, where they lived with the consent of the Chippewas, whose relations with Lenape—their grandfathers—are understood in kinship terms.[38] In the 1790s, Lord Simcoe confirmed Munsee title to twelve miles square (7,680 acres) along the Thames when he toured the area.[39]

Egerton Ryerson's father, Joseph, and uncle Samuel also received land grants for their military roles in the Revolution when they left Munsee homelands in New Jersey around 1783, first receiving a Crown land grant in Maliseet, Mi'kmaq, and Passamaquoddy territory in Majorville, Saint John, New Brunswick, then petitioning again in 1797 and receiving a free grant of land in Upper Canada about 100 kilometres east of what was referred to in maps and correspondence as Delaware Villages and Delaware Castle.[40] Here, there were three settlements of Munsee families along the north and south sides of the Thames River. These families raised extensive cornfields around the "flats," where spring flooding of the Thames made the ground very fertile. On the surface, it might appear that the Ryersons and the Munsees followed similar pathways to resettlement. But the extraordinarily polarized experiences that followed demonstrate their very different experiences of the underlying racial and colonial trajectory of land possession and dispossession that laid the foundation for Indian Residential Schools in subsequent years.

Joseph Ryerson (1761–1854) resettled in Norfolk County with his brother Samuel. Simcoe granted Joseph 2,500 acres between Vittoria and Port Ryerse, and a deed to what became Ryerson's Island adjoining Long Point. In contrast, the land promised to Munsees along the Thames River was never formally recognized as belonging to the Munsee People. In the absence of formal title, Munsee lands were dispossessed in various ways until they reached their current size of one square mile (640 acres), falling within Chippewa territory—approximately a 92-percent reduction of the land that was originally promised by Simcoe.[41] At the same time, it was the need for white settlement that drove treaty making in the territory, treaties that excluded Munsees, who have time and time again over the subsequent 250 years reminded the Crown and Canada of the promises that had been made to them.

Early efforts to set things straight included handwritten petitions to the Governor General, the Department of Indian Affairs, and the Department of the Interior, sometimes through the Indian agent and at least once through the local Member of Parliament. Munsees also informed the Bagot and Pennefather Commissions of their history on the Thames. Later, Munsee delegates made in-person visits to Parliament in Ottawa and London. All of these appeals recounted Munsee diplomatic relations with the Crown and the associated loss of life, belongings, and land that they had suffered, as well as the promises made in exchange, promises of clothing, provisions, implements for husbandry, and the replacement of their lands in Canada. Petitions stated that even when clothing and presents stopped arriving, Munsees continued to serve the Crown in the wars of 1812, 1834, and 1838. They wrote of being "excluded from any share of the Queen's bounty," and the Crown's need to restore the relationship with the Munsee.[42] These reminders sometimes referenced strings of white wampum, a tomahawk, and the silver chain as signs of the "covenant made between the Crown and Munsees."[43]

In the context of intransigence over Munsee claims, the experience and success of the Ryerson family, and other families like it, are thrown into sharp relief. Egerton Ryerson, who has, until recently, been presented as a champion of public education (and as a model Methodist), was also part of a society so deeply invested in colonial violence, racial segregation, and land appropriation that it was impossible (and still is for many Canadians) to even contemplate the profits and advantages Ryerson accrued through these processes at the cost of First Nations People. Like so many others, Ryerson and his descendants benefited from a profoundly unjust society. Egerton Ryerson had the means and intelligence to challenge this unjust society, but opted instead to use his abundant social, political, spiritual, and real capital to work within it, bolstering an ideology that always put (and paid) white settlers first.

Conclusion

The work of Indigenous historians bears great significance for Canadian history and history education. A good number of us spent dozens of years in the Canadian public education system, the highest levels of which are accessed through treaty rights negotiated and held onto by those who came before us and maintained by our bands and Nations. Many of us were trained and tested by other university-based historians and historians in our communities, in pursuit of careers invested in peer-reviewed research creation, teaching, governance, and service. Even with this considerable experience, our histories are accused of being deceptive ("cherry-picking" evidence) and petty (intending only to "erase history"). We work in an absurd social, and often professional, context that does not see Indigenous history as mattering, or First Peoples as fully human. We are experts in a subject for which many Canadians cannot or will not distinguish uninformed opinion from expert analysis grounded in evidence. We live in a country where the bar for history is so low and anti-Indigenous that elected municipal, provincial, and federal officials and Church ministers cannot tell the difference between evidence-based expert analysis and uninformed and often reactionary views, or simply do not demand better, even on days devoted to learning a more truthful national history and endeavouring to reconcile Indigenous and non-Indigenous relations.[44]

Orange Shirt Day, and its purpose to educate Canadians about the history of Indian Residential Schools, is one of a range of platforms for denialists to silence and shout over Indigenous history, historians, and expert analysis grounded in evidence.[45] Applying the concept of *Longue Durée* to National Day of Truth and Reconciliation, we can begin to understand the work that denialism has done at every level, from the imperial and national scale to the local. We can also see that denialism is not just arguing alternative interpretations of history. Denialism seeks to perform power by publicly silencing and blocking out Indigenous history in a way that demonstrates who is in control. We see that in the way that Mr. Ryerson pushed his way in and took over on Orange Shirt Day. We see that, too, in the uncomplicated histories of colonial land purchase, Indigenous "disappearance," white Loyalist settlement in Upper Canada, and the hagiographic history of Egerton Ryerson.[46]

As we now know, denialism requires an audience to perform power and does not hold up against critical historical thinking. We can use this knowledge to predict behaviour and take measures to prevent or discourage denialists and denialist events so that speakers are not put into the position that I was, forced into silence by settler distortions and falsehoods.[47] If it is every Canadian's responsibility to become educated about Indigenous history, from policies such as the Indian Residential School System to deeper local histories about the people, places, and events that have impacted the spaces where we live our day to day lives, it is also every Canadian's responsibility to learn about the history of denialism and determine how best to confront it.

Notes

1 A previous version of this essay was published on ShekonNeechie.ca. Xwat anushiik to Jill McConkey, who read earlier, uglier versions of this paper and helped me make it better and then doing it again for this chapter. Thank you also to Anne Lindsay for helping me think through and express an intellectual resistance to denialism, and Mark Meuwese and Kathryn Boschmann for review, comment, and support on New Amsterdam history.

2 Orange Shirt Day, first observed in 2013, is more formally known as National Day for Truth and Reconciliation since 2021, and the name comes from a story told by

Indian Residential School Survivor Phyllis Jack Webstad about having her orange shirt—a gift from her grandmother—taken from her by staff on the first day at St. Joseph's Mission Indian Residential School in British Columbia, never to be returned. The shirt, as she discussed in the previous chapter, is a symbol of the denial of Indigenous children's identity and history within the Indian Residential School system. National Truth and Reconciliation Week falls on the last week of September and culminates on the 30th. Since 2020, the National Centre for Truth and Reconciliation has organized events and programming for students from kindergarten to grade twelve to learn about the history of Indigenous Peoples on this week. September 30 became a statutory holiday for federal employees and workers in federal workplaces in 2021. By 2023, it was a statutory holiday for provincial government employees in Nova Scotia and New Brunswick and all workers in British Columbia, Manitoba, Northwest Territories, Prince Edward Island, and Yukon. Notably, the 30th of September is not a statutory holiday in the province of Ontario.

3 Mount Elgin Residential School has been called various names over the years, including Mount Elgin Industrial School, Mount Elgin Industrial Institution, Mount Elgin Industrial Institute, The Muncey Institute, and Mount Elgin Industrial Farm.

4 Aroha Harris, "The Future of History Is Māori," *Te Pouhere Korero* 10 (2023): 5–18.

5 Hundreds of Indigenous communities are now leading search and recovery efforts. At the time and since, at many schools and school memorials, people leave children's toys and shoes to remember the children and to protest Canada's failure to prioritize the identification of missing children and unmarked burials at Indian Residential Schools. The 2024 *Final Report* of the Office of the Special Interlocutor for Missing Children and Unmarked Graves and Burial Sites associated with Indian Residential Schools studies this work and builds a case for a robust Indigenous-led Reparations Framework that involves four elements: activating and enforcing international obligations; implementing Indigenous laws and decolonizing the Canadian legal framework; finding truth, rematriating lands, and repatriating the children; and supporting Indigenous-led healing and countering settler amnesty. Office of the Independent Special Interlocutor for Missing Children and Unmarked Graves and Burial Sites associated with Indian Residential Schools, *Executive Summary: Final Report on the Missing and Disappeared Indigenous Children and Unmarked Burials in Canada* (2024), https://osi-bis.ca/wp-content/uploads/2024/11/3.OSI-Executive-Summary.pdf.

6 For example, in his response to a history faculty survey on the University of Winnipeg's Indigenous course requirement, Dr. Ryan Eyford noted that his students often cite that Native people "used all of the buffalo." Mary Jane Logan McCallum, "History Faculty and History Indigenous Course Requirement Courses," paper delivered at the 2017 Ethnohistory conference in Winnipeg, Manitoba. Also see Mark Cronlund Anderson and Carmen L. Robertson, *Seeing Red: A History of Natives in Canadian Newspapers* (University of Manitoba Press, 2011) and the 2022 story of kids making feathered "headdresses" of orange construction paper at a British Columbia preschool in preparation for National Day for Truth and Reconciliation: https://www.cbc.ca/news/canada/british-columbia/headdress-activity-coquitlam-bc-1.6603631.

7 Crystal Fraser, *By Strength, We Are Still Here*; Richard W. Hill Sr., Alison Norman, Thomas Peace, and Jennifer Petit eds., *Behind the Bricks*; Alexandra Giancarlo, Janice Forsyth, and Braden Te Hiwi, with Kelly Bull, Chris Chromarty, and

David Wesley, *Beyond the Rink*; Survivors of the Assiniboia Indian Residential School, *Did You See Us?*; Cathleen Cahill, *Federal Fathers and Mothers: The United States Indian Service, 1869–1933* (University of North Carolina Press, 2011); David Garneau, "Imaginary Spaces of Conciliation and Reconciliation: Art, Curation, and Healing," in *Arts of Engagement: Taking Aesthetic Action in and beyond the Truth and Reconciliation Commission of Canada*, ed. Keavy Martin and Dylan Robinson (Wilfrid Laurier University Press, 2016).

8 Audra Simpson, "Reconciliation and Its Discontents: Settler Governance in an Age of Sorrow," 15 March 2016, University of Saskatchewan, YouTube, https://www.youtube.com/watch?v=vGl9HkzQsGg.

9 Simpson, "Reconciliation and Its Discontents."

10 In an "Open Letter" on the "Genocide Myth," several Canadians who never studied any Indigenous history at all opined confidently and ignorantly on the history of Indian Residential Schools. See Paul Burrows, "Genocide, Genocide-Denial, Nationalism, and the Canadian Historical Profession," Black Cat Red River, 10 August 2021, https://blackcatredriver.ca/index.php/2021/08/10/genocide-and-denial-in-canadian-history/; Council of the Canadian Historical Association, "The History of Violence Against Indigenous Peoples Fully Warrants the Use of the Word 'Genocide,' Canada Day Statement," 30 June 2021, https://cha-shc.ca/advocacy/the-history-of-violence-against-indigenous-peoples-fully-warrants-the-use-of-the-word-genocide-2021-06-30.htm; and Brenda Macdougall, Mary Jane McCallum, Kim Anderson, et al., "Open Letter to the Council of the Canadian Historical Association and the Canadian Public," Shekon Neechie.ca, 13 August 2021, https://shekonneechie.ca/2021/08/13/open-letter-to-the-council-of-the-canadian-historical-association-and-the-canadian-public/

11 See, for example, Sinclair, *Wînipêk*.

12 Mary Jane Logan McCallum, *Nii Ndahlohke*. See also: Nii Ndahlohke website at www.niindahlohke.ca.

13 David Parent, "Governing Metis Indigeneity: The Settler-Colonial Dispossession and Regulation of the Metis in Mid-Twentieth Century Manitoba," PhD diss., University of Alberta, 2021. For work on provincial governments and Indigenous history, see, for Manitoba, Aimée Craft and Jill Blakley, eds., *In Our Backyard: Keeyask and the Legacy of Hydroelectric Development* (University of Manitoba Press, 2022); and, for Ontario, see Brittany Luby, *Dammed: The Politics of Loss and Survival in Anishinaabe Territory* (University of Manitoba Press, 2020); and Helen Olsen Agger, *Dadibaajim: Returning Home Through Narrative* (University of Manitoba Press, 2021).

14 One example of this is Survivors of the Assiniboia Indian Residential School, *Did You See Us?* This book shows what change is possible from more localized attention. Assiniboia Indian Residential School barely registered on people's radar before the book, but because of this work, and deliberate engagement with it, it is clear that many more know about it. A new city park and memorial have been built as a site for public engagement and education. Other examples include Crystal Gail Fraser, *By Strength, We Are Still Here*; Richard W. Hill, Sr., Alison Norman, Thomas Peace, and Jennifer Pettit eds., *Behind the Bricks*; and Sean Carleton, *Lessons in Legitimacy*.

15 Rose Hackman, *Emotional Labor: The Invisible Work Shaping Our Lives and How to Claim Our Power* (Flatiron, 2023). See also Candace Brunette-Debassige, *Tricky Grounds: Indigenous Women's Experiences in Canadian University Administration* (University of Regina Press, 2024).

16 This tension exists everywhere in a colonial nation state, but notable examples are the unresolved land claims at Oka, Quebec, and Caledonia, Ontario. Laurence Brisson Dubreuil, "Oka Backtracks on Land Protection," *Toronto Star*, 24 January 2022, https://www.thestar.com/news/canada/2022/01/24/oka-backtracks-on-land-protection.html; and the 1492 Land Back movement, which seeks to draw attention to land development on disputed territory without First Nations consent (Yellowhead Institute, "Yellowhead Statement at 1492 Land Back Lane," 8 September 2020, https://yellowheadinstitute.org/2020/09/08/statement/). More recently the Cowichan decision, the Saugeen First Nation at Sauble Beach, and, on a different scale, Bloodvein First Nation banning non-community hunters all successfully assert Indigenous Title in areas long claimed to be simply non-Indigenous land. Canadian Press, "Cowichan Tribes Win Rights and Title along Fraser River in B.C.'s Lower Mainland," *CBC News*, 9 August 2025, https://www.cbc.ca/news/canada/british-columbia/first-nation-vancouver-island-1.7605235; Andrew Lupton, "Saugeen First Nation Looks to the Future after Supreme Court Denies Appeal in Dispute over Ontario Beach," *CBC News*, 28 August 2025, https://www.cbc.ca/news/canada/london/sauble-beach-saugeen-first-nation-land-dispute-supreme-court-appeal-decision-1.7618999; and Lauren Scott, "Bloodvein First Nation Will Bar Non-Indigenous Hunters from Land amid Overhunting Issues," *CBC News*, 24 August 2925, https://www.cbc.ca/news/canada/manitoba/bloodvein-first-nation-moose-hunting-1.7616562.

17 *Nii Ndahlohke*—also available as an audiobook—is the first modern accessible, published, analytical history book to include Munsee language. It was short-listed for an Indigenous Literature Award from the 2023–2024 First Nations Communities READ Awards in the Adult/Young Adult category (a prize that celebrates Indigenous literature and increases awareness about First Nation, Métis, and Inuit writing, illustration, and publishing). The Thames Valley (Ontario) District School Board developed a Teachers' Resource to accompany the book and distributed the book to over 130 elementary schools. Subsequently, my cousin Julie Tucker and I developed an award-winning art exhibition based on the book. The exhibition, entitled "Nii Ndahlohke / I work," won a Community Impact Award from the Association of Tribal Archives, Libraries and Museums (2024) and Exhibition of the Year Award (2024) from Galeries Ontario/Ontario Galleries.

18 Justice and Carleton, "Truth Before Reconciliation." This article identifies some of the arguments used by denialists to undermine grounded research on the residential schools, some of which were made by this man at the Orange Shirt Day event.

19 Mash Koh Wee Kah Pooh Win, and Standing Strong Task Force, *Standing Strong Task Force Report and Recommendations: Acknowledging the Past, Learning from the Present, Looking to the Future*, 18 August 2021, https://www.torontomu.ca/content/dam/next-chapter/Report/SSTF-report-and-recommendations-Aug_24_FINAL.pdf. The members of the Task Force were: co-Chairs Joanne Dallaire and Catherine Ellis, Frank Walwyn, Tracey King, Gerald McMaster, Heather Rollwagen, Tay Rubman, Amorell Saunders N'Daw, T'hohahoken Michae Doxtater, Riley Kucheran, Dennis Mock, Cecile Farnum, Julia Spagnuolo, and Natasha Henry.

20 Mash Koh Wee Kah Pooh Win and Standing Strong Task Force, *Standing Strong Task Force Report*, 17.

21 Victoria University Research Panel on the Legacy of Egerton Ryerson, report, 25 March 2021, https://vicu.utoronto.ca/assets/PDFs/Ryerson-Research-Panel-Report.pdf. The members of the Research Panel were: Pamela Klassen, Heidi Bohaker, Bonnie Jane Maracle, Margaret Sault, and Roxanne Korpan.

22 Victoria University Research Panel on the Legacy of Egerton Ryerson, report, 1.

23 Victoria University Research Panel, report, 1, 2.

24 Egerton Ryerson, "Report on Industrial Schools, 26 May 1847," in *Statistics Representing Indian Schools* (Government Printing Bureau, 1898), as cited in Appendix 2 of Victoria University Research Panel on the Legacy of Egerton Ryerson, report, 30.

25 Victoria University Research Panel on the Legacy of Egerton Ryerson, report, 18.

26 He was also known as Reijersen after immigration, also Reyerzoon, Reyertz, Ryerse, and Reijersz.

27 Phyllis A. Ryerse and Thomas A. Ryerson, *The Ryerse-Ryerson Family 1574–1994: The Early Generations in the Netherlands and America and the History of the Brothers Samuel Ryerse–Joseph Ryerson and Their Descendants, Early Pioneers of Norfolk County, Ontario, Canada* (Phyllis A. Ryerse and Thomas A. Ryerson, 1994), 6, viii. "Knickerbocker" refers to Dutch settlers who came to the "New World," especially those who came to New York in the 1600s. The term was first coined by author Washington Irving in the early nineteenth century; Irving wrote the book of local history satire *A History of New York: From the Beginning of the World to the End of the Dutch Dynasty* (1809) under the pseudonym Diedrich Knickerbocker.

28 The Walloon families who moved to North America in 1624 were Calvinist refugees from the Habsburg-controlled southern Netherlands (now Belgium and northern France).

29 "Dutch Pageant at the Town Hall, 1924: Purchase and Disappearance at the Tercentenary of the Settlement of New Amsterdam," an unpublished paper by Mary Jane Logan McCallum delivered at the 2024 Munsee Language and History Symposium, Institute for Advanced Study, Princeton University Library, New Jersey, YouTube video, accessed 1 September 2025, https://www.youtube.com/watch?v=eP7JVTV7dhE .

30 While the object of the pageant was entertainment, it was also hoped that the pageant would "stimulate interest in the Town Hall of today, which bears the same relation to the life of the modern city as did the first, the Stadt Huis, as it then was called, to the life of the early Dutch settlers." Initially, a tavern was built in 1642 by Governor Kieft, which later became the City Hall of New Amsterdam. *New York Times*, 11 May 1924.

31 Entry for Tuesday 12 February 1924 of the Diary of (League of Nations activist) Annie Hughes-Griffiths. Available at Casgliad y Werin Cymru People's Collection Wales Website, accessed 8 April 2026, https://www.peoplescollection.wales/items/1886876.

32 "Dutch Pageant to Show Old New York Days: Descendants of Original Settlers Are to Appear at Town Hall Thursday–Features of Novel Show," *New York Times*, 11 May 1924, 9.

33 Judith Stuyvesant, "Social Activities of the Week," *New York Evening Post*, 17 May 1924, 2.

34 Jean O'Brien, *Firsting and Lasting*, xxiv.

35 In 2018, Menominee and Stockbridge Munsee People offered Indigenous perspectives on the Munsees in the diorama, and the diorama has since been re-interpreted with "call-outs" of the original diorama labels and images on its glass display for what it says about colonialism and cultural representation. On one panel, Wasalaangweew (Bright Star, Molly Miller), Clan Mother of the Turtle Clan and

Elder from Stockbridge-Munsee, states, "The early years of colonization caused much intergenerational trauma and the hiding of our culture. We now celebrate over 40 years of cultural reawakening and the 13th year of Lenape-Munsee language revitalization. Our knowledge of our history, culture, and language is most important to our survival as a people." American Museum of Natural History, "Teaching the Old New York Diorama," 2019, accessed 1 September 2025, https://www.amnh.org/content/download/261483/4450517/file/teaching-the-old-new-york-diorama-3-5.pdf.

36 From 1640 to 1645, a cycle of violence between Munsees and settlers broke out known as "Kieft's War," which included two massacres of Munsees in 1643, at Pavonia and Corlears Hook. See Mark Meuwese, "Mass Murder on Manhattan" in the National Archives of the New Netherlands Website Blog Series "400 Years of Dutch-American Stories," no date, accessed 8 April 2026, https://www.nationaalarchief.nl/en/research/400-years-of-dutch-american-stories/mass-murder-on-manhattan. From 1645 to 1664, sporadic outbreaks of violence continued between Dutch and Indigenous people including a resistance in 1655 known as The Peach War (or Peach Tree War), and the Esopus War in 1659-60 and 1663-1664.

37 Moreton-Robinson, *The White Possessive*, xii.

38 Haldimand guaranteed the land; wampum strings were given to restore/reconfirm this relationship, according to several people, including Chief Thomas Fisher, 8 November 1886, in a statement before A. Dingman, Inspector of Indian Agencies, and Thomas Gordon, Indian agent, relative to the land dispute between the Chippewa and Muncey bands on the Caradoc Reserve. Library and Archives Canada (LAC) RG 10 B-3-a, vol. 2189, file 38112-1.

39 LAC RG 10 B-3-a, vol. 2189, file 38122-1, reel T-16652. Minutes of a Council held at the Garrison, 25 January 1828.

40 For example, see Sir Frederick Haldimand, "Sketch of Part of Ontario Showing Delaware Village," 1784, Unpublished Papers and Correspondence, 1758–1784, British Library, UK, ADD MSS no. 21829, folio 73; Patrick McNiff, "Field Notes on 'the Country from Detroit towards River La Tranche (Now Thames),'" 1793, MNR, Peterborough, *Surveyors Field Book*, vol. 1, 274–78; Major E.B. Littlehales, "Extract from Journal from Niagara to Detroit," 1793, in E.A. Cruickshank, ed., *The Correspondence of Lieut. Governor John Graves Simcoe*, vol. 1 (Ontario Historical Society, 1923), 288–93; and Patrick McNiff, "Extract of a Survey of the River Thames formerly River La Tranche," 1793, Ontario, Ministry of Natural Resources, Crown Land Survey Records, Plan no. SR 7089.

41 Reid, "'Compound Dispossession' in Southern Ontario," 92.

42 "Delaware Indian Address. Presented to the Marquis of Lorne," *Gazette Montreal*, 21 January 1879, 3.

43 No author, no title, *Dover Express*, 17 June 1892, 2. Munsee petitions to resolve the claim to territory are in written record from at least the following: 1826, 1830, 1845, 1852; by Pennefather 1858, 1869; by Bagot 1870; in Ottawa in 1872, 1877, 1878; in London in 1882; and in 1884, 1886, and 1895.

44 See also "Open Letter," *Dorchester Review*, 12 August 2021, signed by fifty-three individuals, only one of whom has undertaken sustained primary research on the topic of residential schools, that argues there are "no grounds" for the claim that Canada's treatment of Indigenous Peoples was genocidal. See also Shekon Neechie Board, "Open Letter to the Council of the Canadian Historical Association and the

Canadian Public," Shekon Neechie: An Indigenous History Site, 13 August, 2021, accessed on 12 April, 2026, https://shekonneechie.ca/2021/08/13/open-letter-to-the-council-of-the-canadian-historical-association-and-the-canadian-public/.

45 Sean Carleton, Alan Lester, Adele Perry, and Omeasoo Wahpasiw, "Exposing Residential School Denialism's Transnational Network," *Active History: History Matters,* 10 December 2024, accessed on 10 April 2026, https://activehistory.ca/blog/2024/12/10/exposing-residential-school-denialisms-transnational-network/.

46 See Victoria University Research Panel on the Legacy of Egerton Ryerson, report, especially the Works Cited and Recommended Readings, 22-23; and Mash Koh Wee Kah Pooh Win and Standing Strong Task Force, *Standing Strong Task Force Report*, especially Appendix D: Life and Legacy of Egerton Ryerson, accessed 12 April, 2026, https://www.torontomu.ca/content/dam/next-chapter/Report/Appendix-D_Life-and-legacy_Aug-26.pdf.

47 A no longer accessible Twitter thread by Eve Tuck dated 19 June 2019 was helpful in thinking about how events and events organizing plays a role in the staging and legitimation of denialist arguments. The thread, about mediating "Q & A" sessions, was accessed 25 March 2026 here, https://threadreaderapp.com/thread/1141501422611128320.html.

CHAPTER 3

WHAT WE CHOOSE TO FORGET:

Residential School Denialism and the National Centre for Truth and Reconciliation Archives

by Raymond Frogner

I wish to begin by recognizing the rights, dignity, and well-being of First Nations, Inuit, and Métis Peoples across Turtle Island.[1] As the Senior Director of Research and Head of Archives and Collections for the National Centre for Truth and Reconciliation (NCTR), I approach this dialogue with deep humility and respect, knowing that the legacy of Indian Residential Schools in these lands we co-inhabit represents a painful and unresolved chapter in our shared history. I recognize the strength and resilience of First Nations, Inuit, and Métis communities, and I hope to contribute to this conversation in a way that honours those who were lost, supports those who continue to grieve, and aligns with ongoing efforts toward justice and reconciliation.

In this chapter, I discuss how residential school denialists have exploited and mischaracterized archival evidence to deny, downplay, or minimize the punishing impact of Indian Residential Schools (IRS). Those engaging in denialism often refuse to acknowledge the preponderance of evidence of traumatic childhood experiences of residential school Survivors, the negligently recorded and disproportionately high rates of death, or the ongoing intergenerational legacy of this trauma. They argue that the intent and legacy of the system was benign or even beneficial and that they are truth seekers attempting to rebalance an inaccurate depiction of a positive social program. They suggest the operation of the schools was well documented, and in calling for what they describe as "balanced" history, they maintain the records have not been completely made available. Many denialists claim this is a question of academic freedom and free speech, and that those who argue for the productive benefit of the schools are in fact the real heroes, taking risks of persecution.[2]

Residential school denialists often defend the forced assimilation, systemic neglect, destruction of families and communities, and the physical and cognitive erasure of Indigenous culture, memory, and identity that is the core function of residential schools. As historian Crystal Gail Fraser (and contributor to Chapter 12) has noted, such statements are "denying survivors' experiences, how they experienced their institutionalization as a child, but also the so-called intent of residential schools."[3]

Denialists also decline to admit that for decades, public archives in colonial jurisdictions have played an embedded role in the settlement process, serving as documentary armouries acquiring and storing archival evidence as ammunition to assert the settler fact. In this chapter, I will offer examples that highlight denialists' misuse and mischaracterization of colonial archival records. I show that the existing archival record of the Indian Residential School System is in fact inconsistent, unreliable, incomplete, and misrepresentative; that records of unmarked and neglected burial sites exist nonetheless; and that the argument that the schools were productive and beneficial is selective propaganda disproven by considerable archival evidence.

When discussing the documentary evidence of residential schools, denialists often overstate the completeness and accuracy of archival records. In highlighting the accuracy of recorded evidence, they also marginalize the remembrance of Survivors, whose voices—remembered in community oral histories, art and ceremony, and Elders' teachings—were not recorded in the juridical record of administrative operations. Recently, the International Council on Archives (ICA) released a statement on the relationship between public archives and Indigenous Peoples, the Tandanya Declaration. It recognizes that settlers in colonial jurisdictions around the world have exploited public archives in defence of the colonial process. It reads in part: "Evidence is not a fact but a matrix of relationships, and like all relationships they are open to trust and mistrust; good faith and manipulation; the dynamic nature of the social provenance of colonial records must be expressed in the collaborative descriptive representation of archival material."[4] The ICA's Tandanya Declaration asserts that Survivors' voices must be heard in the interpretation of residential school records. This is the fundamental challenge of a decolonizing archive: to give cognitive space to the Indigenous remembrance of such colonial experience. With the guidance of Survivors, this is the goal of the NCTR Archives.

Inconsistent Record Keeping

Denialists commonly state that "to some extent abuses occur in all schools,"[5] and Survivors' experiences in Canada's Indian Residential Schools were no worse than any other boarding school system around the world. To make this argument, denialists make a twofold claim on the nature of the residential school records. First, they claim that the administrative and operational records of the residential school system were reliably and consistently created, stored, and made available. Second, they claim that the Truth and Reconciliation Commission (TRC) and the NCTR have acquired the complete record of the residential school experience from this effective record-keeping system; the NCTR has simply not made the records fully available.

Nina Green, a researcher possibly writing under a pseudonym who often downplays the severity of residential schools in online writings, has commented on the reliability of government records:

> The federal government mandated that the names of treaty Indians who had died were to be deleted from the treaty lists, that Band lists were to be maintained, and that the death of every status Indian adult and child was to be registered with provincial vital statistics agencies. There was thus an official government record at both the federal and provincial levels of every status Indian death. . . .
>
> As well as requiring the routine registration of the children's deaths with provincial authorities, the Department of Indian Affairs (DIA) mandated that the local Indian Agent conduct a formal inquiry into the death of every child who died while enrolled at a residential school. . . . Moreover provincial vital statistics offices across Canada long ago handed over thousands of death records to the TRC and NCTR.[6]

This is simply untrue. The historical records of the Indian Residential School System are inconsistent, unreliable, incomplete, and inaccurate. It is striking to note there was no formal, unique, and comprehensive record-keeping system for one of the longest serving and most profoundly impactful federal social programs in the history of the country. Not a single residential school listed in the Indian Residential Schools Settlement Agreement (IRSSA) has a complete set of admission files, quarterly returns, and discharge records—the most valued record sets to prove attendance at a residential school. It is untrue to claim that "provincial vital statistics offices across Canada long ago handed over thousands of death records to the TRC and NCTR."[7] For example, after years of discussion, the NCTR finally struck a data-sharing agreement with Manitoba Vital Statistics in 2022 for access to death certificates of residential school children. As part of the agreement, the NCTR agreed to provide Vital Statistics with "available personal information" about "missing Indigenous children that attended a residential school in Manitoba . . . for the purposes of the Vital Statistics Branch searching and providing Records to the NCTR about the children referenced in the Applications."[8] Manitoba Vital Statistics, like many of the provincial vital statistics agencies, did not keep metadata to identify residential school children in their registrations of deaths.[9] Several provincial coroners agencies have also not produced complete sets of coroners' reports involving deaths of residential school children despite their national organization committing to do so shortly after the release of the *Final Report* of the TRC.[10]

A recent article by Library and Archives Canada archivist Bill Russell, in the journal *Archivaria*, describes the high volume of record destruction, loss of records, and records policy uncertainty in the Indian Affairs Branch (IAB) record keeping from 1932 to 1947.[11] Russell observes that a paucity of record-keeping resources "prompted the Treasury Board's decision in 1932 to provide a directive that permitted departments to undertake regularized destructions."[12] He goes on to say, "There is ample evidence, most visible in the area of [Indian Affairs Branch] I.A.B. field office records practices, that, into the 1940s, there was neglect (e.g., storage that failed to protect documents from the effects of the elements or from vermin) and ignorance of, or indifference to, approved records policies and procedures, with unauthorized elimination the result."[13] The resource strain brought on by the Great

Depression and the Second World War resulted in several hundred thousand I.A.B. records being deliberately destroyed.[14] Many more records were lost or poorly archived, making them all but impossible to locate.

Provincial government record keeping concerning Indigenous Peoples' vital events was also inconsistent. Each province is responsible for its vital statistics process. In British Columbia, for example, provincial vital statistics excluded recording Indigenous vital events for the periods from 1872 to 1877 and from 1899 to 1916. The province began to register Indigenous Peoples' deaths, births, and marriages in 1916. Legislation appointed Indian agents as district registrars for Indigenous communities. But until 1943 registration was not mandatory and was only as reliable as the unique agency's agent. The province applied special "Indian registration" forms from 1916 until 1956. Indian agents unreliably completed these unique, and frequently unavailable, registration forms. Due to delays and other inconsistencies, these registrations were filed separately. In addition, a contemporary researcher must be aware that these complications are compounded by the fact the Indigenous registration forms are stored on separate sets of microfilm for access at the British Columbia Provincial Archives.[15]

Another way to measure the incomplete nature of the records of Indian Residential Schools is through the NCTR Survivor inquiry process. The NCTR prioritizes the requests of Survivors. It has an established process that will create a comprehensive dossier on every file found concerning a Survivor in the Archives holdings of over four million documents and over 7,000 Survivor and relations statements. To date, 800 of the 2,065 individual names/profiles researched for Survivor inquiries from 2015 to 31 March 2025 have resulted in "no records found." That accounts for approximately 39 percent of individual profiles researched to date. Such gaps in the NCTR's holdings have led to accusations that the NCTR Archives is holding back records. Frances Widdowson, someone who contributes to publications and websites promoting denialism, has declared on her web blog: "Shame on the NCTR" for holding back records.[16] To be perfectly clear, the NCTR is transparent and accountable in its access process. A researcher can apply for the complete "pro-active release" of all records related to an individual identified in an application for records access. In addition, a researcher can sign a memorandum of agreement with the NCTR to gain full access to the NCTR's internal database of records. There is no other public archive in the country that supplies such a complete level of public access to its archival records.

Records of Religious Orders—The "Mysterious Mother House" Record-Keeping Systems

Green paints a similarly erroneous picture of efficient record keeping by Christian religious organizations that operated residential schools. She suggests these religious orders reliably documented their activities and stored their records at central records repositories. At these "mother houses," records were supposedly safeguarded and accountably processed and made accessible. The Indian Residential School Records website Green is linked to states:

> The Sisters who taught, nursed and cared for Indian children at residential schools kept records of daily events which were periodically forwarded to the mother houses of their religious orders.
>
> Similar records, called codices, were kept by the Oblates of Mary Immaculate at their missions across Canada, many of which had residential schools.
>
> Most of these chronicles were sent to the TRC years ago in response to its requests for records from religious orders across Canada, but the NCTR has not digitized them for its archives, and they are thus not available to the general public.[17]

This is a misleading account of the inconsistent and unreliable nature of record keeping in religious orders. To be clear, due largely to the research efforts of NCTR staff, the records of religious orders have been located, digitized, and transferred to the NCTR Archives as authentic digital copies.[18] In fact, the NCTR has usually paid for the cost to both research and digitize relevant records. This has nothing to do with the good record-keeping practices of religious orders. The NCTR is not holding back records from the public; quite simply, there are enormous gaps in the documentation of religious orders. To date, the NCTR has consulted over 105 private records repositories to find residential school records of Christian denominations.

Because of their preponderant influence on residential school operations, I will focus on the records of the Catholic order Oblates OMI Lacombe, a regional province of the Missionary Oblates of Mary Immaculate.[19] In the history of the residential school system, Oblate missionaries operated and administered forty-eight residential schools across the North and the West. The records of the Oblates are misleadingly incomplete, inconsistent, and fragmented. The Oblates do not reject the claims of physical and sexual abuse at the schools they operated. In fact, they apologized over thirty years ago with a promise of supplying evidence of school abuse for the purpose of reconciliation. On 24 July 1991, in front of media and an audience of almost 20,000 Indigenous people attending the Lac St. Anne Annual Pilgrimage, the president of the Oblate Superiors of the Canada Region, the Reverend Douglas Crosby, OMI, expressed a formal apology now preserved in the NCTR Archives.[20] Without citing it by name, Father Crosby apologized for the mentality of superiority ingrained in the Doctrine of Discovery, how "deep, unchallenged, and damaging was the naïve cultural, ethnic, linguistic, and religious superiority complex of Christian Europe."[21] He apologized for the cultural erasure and the attempted assimilation. He also wished to publicly acknowledge that there were instances of individual physical and sexual abuse: "We wish to state publicly that we acknowledge that there were inexcusable, intolerable betrayals of trust in one of its most serious forms. We deeply, and very specially, apologize to every victim of such abuse and we seek help in searching for means to bring about healing."[22] Father Crosby closed his four-page apology with a promise to "support an effective process of disclosure vis-à-vis Residential Schools. We offer to collaborate in any way we can so that the full story of the Indian Residential Schools may be written, that . . . an effective healing process might take place."[23]

Over thirty years later, after much negotiation, in 2022 the NCTR finally drafted a Memorandum of Agreement making the NCTR "the principal archives of reference, access, preservation and use, of all Oblates records that document the Oblates operation and/or administration of the 48 residential schools that functioned under the Oblates' authority."[24] This provided the NCTR with full access to the files of the Oblates OMI Lacombe with permission to research, digitize, and transfer relevant materials to the NCTR Archives. Two years later, the two parties struck a second agreement to create personnel files, identifying and digitizing the Oblate records documenting the career of Oblate missionaries who were responsible for the administration and operation of a residential school. The result is a page on the NCTR's website profiling each missionary with links to the records of school(s) where they worked.[25] Our negotiations to gain access to these records were making little progress until 2021 when the discoveries of potential unmarked burials across the country cast a spotlight on the nature of the records. Even then, despite Green's claims, the Oblates were initially reluctant to release the codices.[26]

Locating Oblate records related to residential schools is no simple task. Since our Oblate agreements, the NCTR has reached agreements and established supported research in each of the archival institutions known to house the majority of Oblate school records: the Royal British Columbia Museum (Archives) in Victoria, British Columbia; the Provincial Archives of Alberta, in Edmonton, Alberta; the Centre Patrimoine, in Winnipeg, Manitoba; and Dechatelêts Archives in Longueil, Québec. Predominantly done by NCTR-funded researchers, save the Provincial Archives of Alberta, work continues to review Oblate records, digitize, and transfer copies to the NCTR to create a more complete resource base of records to understand the residential school experience. To claim, as Green does, that "most of these chronicles were sent to the TRC years ago in response to its requests for records from religious orders across Canada" is quite simply wrong. And this is only the Oblates of OMI Lacombe. Significant volumes of records of Catholic nuns' orders remain to be fully collected. In a recent visit to the Archives and Collections of The Grey Nuns in Montréal, the order that worked closest with the Oblates, the order's archivist conceded that they did not produce for the TRC all the records that documented their activities with the residential school system. We mutually agreed to install a researcher at this archive, at the cost of the NCTR, to review all file lists and begin to acquire digitized records to better document the Grey Nuns' relationship to the residential school system.[27] The sisters' order also categorically refused to consider opening personnel files, similar to the Oblates, to make accessible the records of those sisters who operated most of the schools maintained by the Oblates OMI Lacombe.[28]

The Roman Catholic Church (RCC) in Canada lacks a central record-keeping authority, and any claims to easy and full access to comprehensive Catholic records sets are misinformed. There is no central record-keeping "mother house." One of the most in-depth contemporary studies on the question of Catholic records is a master's thesis by Jackson Anderson titled "Records of Manitoba Residential Schools in Oblate Archives."[29] In the thesis, he notes that the most recent "inventory of the Oblate Province of Manitoba's archives [was] completed by Romuald Boucher, O.M.I. in June 1983 [and it] provides some of the only information on what records were accumulated by the province and how these records may have been managed."[30] Not only does Anderson confirm it has been forty-two years since the Oblates performed any significant research on the records they created and held, he also notes darkly that the custodial history of these records remains unclear: "Many records from the Oblate Province of Manitoba's archives were transferred to Deschâtelets in 1984. . . . It is also possible that Boucher or other archivists re-arranged the provincial records in preparation for their transfer to Deschâtelets."[31] This has led to "significant discrepancies" that have not been resolved. In the end, the Catholic record-keeping environment in Canada is "the result of a fluid and inconsistent mix of regulations of the congregation, canon law, and the federal government."[32] Records such as codices, correspondence, and sacramental files can be randomly found, often stored in ad hoc fashion, in local parish offices, regional provincial centres, archdiocese offices, private records centres, or public archival institutions.[33] Rarely are these records in a digital format to facilitate accessibility.

To give one final example of the unreliability of Catholic record keeping, OMI Lacombe invited me to Rome for a five-day visit to the Archivum Generale O.M.I. Romae (AG)—Oblate General Administration Archives. I focused a portion of my brief visit on the records of personnel files to determine a clearer picture of how missionaries operated schools. What I found was that the Archivum Generale O.M.I. Romae (AG) held only skeletal administrative profiles of Oblate missionaries.[34] Oblate case files document fulfillment of the Oblate's *formation*, his vows and responsibilities as a priest.[35] The documentation of the Oblate's case file focuses almost exclusively on records of the priest's completion of religious milestones. It is therefore not very informative of his activities working in residential schools. In a missionary's case file, the lives of children at residential schools are of marginal significance.

I will discuss the records of one priest, Father Garand, to understand what is typically stored in a missionary personnel file in the Archivum Generale O.M.I. Romae (AG). This will also provide insight into the mysteries of Catholic record keeping.

Father Benoit Garand's is the only file I found in the Archivum Generale O.M.I. Romae (AG) that documented in detail a priest's abuse of children. But even here, the record is incomplete. To truly understand Garand's nefarious career, one must *combine* research from his file in the Whitehorse Archdiocese Archives, records of Indian Affairs located at Library and Archives Canada in Ottawa, and the available documentation the NCTR holds from the Royal Canadian Mounted Police (RCMP). Father Garand received his priestly ordination on 17 February 1945 in Richelieu, Québec. Early in his career his religious superiors wrote in their moral assessment that Father Garand had a marked weakness for children: "Assez sensible, doux de caractère, calme, un peu ferme; entreprenant, surtout lorsqu'il s'agit de s'occuper des enfants, pour qui il a un faible marque, bien qu'il paraisse anime des meilleurs intentions."[36] Further attached to the assessment:

> Son point faible, la pierre d'achoppement c'est son penchant pour l'affection des enfants. Il a été averti souvent sur ce point mais ça semble plus fort qui lui, il aime trop caresse les enfants. Le danger c'est qu'il ne semble pas se douter que c'est une faiblesse. Comme il est indiqué plus bas sur le rapport, avec surveillance normale des supérieurs, il pourra faire un excellent religieux, mais si jamais il y une faiblesse, ce sera de ce côté-là. N'ayant personnellement peu d'expériences dans le discernement des vocations religieuses, je ne sais jusqu'à quel point les supérieurs tiennent compte de pareille disposition.[37] (English translation provided in the endnotes)

By 1955, Father Alexis Monnet, OMI, was writing as the Vicariate Apostolic of Whitehorse about Garand's flagrant child abuse.

> Vous trouverez ci-joint une lettre du Frère Garand. Il qualifie maintenant «d'histoire d'enfants» ce qu'il a plusieurs fois admis comme des faits. Il met à sa réadmission des conditions tellement inacceptables qu'on se demande s'il est sincère à moins que ce soit une expression on nouvelle de son manque

> de jugement. A le lire on dirait qu'il ne s'était fait religieux que pour son Supérieur. Si je commente ainsi sa lettre ce n'est pas que je sois tend la main. C'est aussi l'avis du Père Dréan auquel j'ai montré cette lettre la semaine dernière. Ce dernier semble être en faveur d'un retour a Lower Post, mais pas avant Sept.[38]

The letter goes on to suggest that other clerical authorities including Père Dréan support Garand's return to Lower Post. The Oblate solution to Garand's abuse of children was to move him to another school where he continued his crimes against children, not to contact the police, or reach out to communities or families. One year later, Father Coudert wrote a letter that includes a question on how Rome would like to document Garand's problems: "Je viens d'écrire au Très Rev. Père General au sujet du Frère B. Garand et lui envoyer sa Déclaration de libre acceptation de la Dispense de ses Vœux. Je ne me souviens pas où se trouve la filière couvrant son cas; je crois que vous trouverez cela dans le 'filing cabinet' de droite, sous le titre 'Cas Spéciaux-Confidentiel' afin de s'y rapporter si la Maison Générale demande le reste de la filière ou quel qu'autre document s'y rapportant."[39]

As expected, the General Administrative Archives in Rome held final decision on the material kept to document such a volatile case. But the directions were not in the personnel file. Father Coudert OMI expressed uncertainty over where the file is located, but there is clearly a set of files titled "Special Cases—Confidential" to manage these matters. The documentation in the Roman Catholic Diocese of Whitehorse Archives, the local archives of the religious Province, holds a much more complete record.

Included in Father Garand's file is a summary of his career as an Oblate teacher in residential schools from the Vicariate Apostolic of Whitehorse: "Ce frère a toujours été d'une familiarité troublante avec les enfants partout où il a passé, et dès ses débuts en mission; à Dawson, aussi bien qu'ici a notre résidence Vicarial il introduisait constamment des enfants dans sa chambre, malgré les remarques répétées qu'on lui faisait; quand des plaintes plus sérieuses nous parvenaient (sembles a celles du père Fleury) il déniait avoir fait quoi que ce soit de mal, et se retranchait sur le fait que 'chacun a sa conscience' en ces matières."[40]

The summary continues:

> J'avais pense qu'a l'École-pensionnat de Lower Post, ou les enfants sont toujours tenus sous stricte surveillance, il serait plus facile d'arrêter tout abus de sa part, tout en lui permettant d'être en contact journalier avec les enfants, dont il aime certainement la compagnie. A cause de cela, nous ne l'avons jamais mis en charge de la surveillance des enfants, mais, malgré cela, il s'arrangeait toujours pour en recevoir dans sa chambre, en amener avec lui dans les camions, sous toutes sortes de prétextes. Bien des scènes ont eu lieu entre lui et le père Principal a ce sujet; il avançait toujours des excuses pour se justifier, et malgré les ordres stricts qu'on lui donnait il recommençait aussitôt. Malgré touts nos craintes et tous nos soupçons, nous avons toujours essaye des nous persuader que c'était de l'enfantillage et qu'il n'y avait rien de grave, car le frère autrement était dévoue a son travail et paraissait pieux. Les mêmes plaintes, cependant, se remettent comme celles que nous avons entendues précédemment. Savourera-t-il enfin coupable? J'aimerais que vous le fassiez interroger par un père d'expérience de vtre conseil, avec les documents ci-inclus en mains, et de ma part.[41]

The document notes that the damage of concern for Oblate authorities is not the welfare of the children but the public reputation of the Oblate Order: "Je ne sais quelle sera votre décision a son sujet mais je vous avoue que je redoute son retour après le longue expérience que nous avons eue avec lui; il est maintenant trop connu de notre jeunesse, et circulent dans le public et causent un scandale majeur au détriment de la réputation de nos missionnaires et de notre œuvre de conversion parmi les natifs."[42]

Finally, the letter laments the loss of a brother with so many useful technical skills: "Son départ fera un vide immense dans notre Vicariat, car au point de vue de ses aptitudes techniques (chauffeur, ingénieur, Menuisier) il est difficile à remplacer. Nous sommes déjà si à court de frères; mais oserai-je vous demander un bon frère, au moment où je vous offre de reprendre un frère à qui on ne peut se fier? Je crois, cependant, que dans une maison d'éducation ou il n'y a pas d'enfants, ce frère pourrait se reprendre et rendre encore à votre Province de réels services."[43]

Even after having a well-documented history of Garand's child abuse at residential schools, which included moving him to other schools where he continued to sexually abuse children, Oblate authorities still discussed Garand's utility and future career in the Order. The ultimate goal remained "conversion parmi les natifs." Included as a capstone to the life of Father Garand in the NCTR Archives is a piece of documentation not found in the General Administrative Archives in Rome or in the Diocesan Archives in Whitehorse. It is titled "R.C.M.P.—N.I.R.S. Tip (Subject) Report." It is the file of [Name redacted] dated 1995. The remarks section addresses the case of a young boy who "Attended Lower Post R.S. where he was sexually assaulted by Maczynski and Garand. Both men were convicted at separate trials and sentenced to lengthy terms in prison. Garand died in prison on 1995-05-27."[44]

Garand's personnel file in Rome is fifty-three pages, one of the largest I examined. But his formal RCMP record is not included in the file, and the records repository in Whitehorse holds a much more complete file. Although some crimes are acknowledged, the life of the Oblate fulfilling his formation as a member of the Order is the "religious case" documented in the personnel case file, not the "legal case" of an abuser. There is no documentation of children, parents, or community representatives. Civil law is addressed very rarely. Based on this confused and misleading set of records, one must conclude that Indigenous children were confronted with two menacing systems conceived for their spiritual, cultural, and familial demise: the residential school system of the settler community, and the evangelical Catholicism of the Oblate Order.

There is a purposeful strategy to this documentation. It is noted in the advice of the Oblates' legal council. Frank Morissey, professor of canonical law and legal counsel to the Oblate Order, has written record-keeping advice to the Oblate Order: "We are going to have to find some way to protect the documents (and the reputations of all concerned), and, yet, at the same time, observe the applicable civil legislation. We can see as an offshoot of this new situation that dioceses and religious institutes are going to be very careful about what documents they retain in their archives for the future."[45]

Records of Death—Counting Is a Moral Act

The records that produce the evidence of a death are another example of the inconsistency of residential school record keeping. However, denialists often downplay the insufficient record keeping of student deaths. In *Grave Error*, a collection of essays and blogs independently published by True North in collaboration with Dorchester Books, the editors note that "no persuasive evidence has yet been offered by anyone for the existence of unmarked graves, missing children, murder or genocide in residential schools," but a few documentary facts will demonstrate this to be untrue.[46] It was not until 1935 that the Indian Act declared a policy to investigate and report the death of a child at residential school.[47] Nevertheless, "[a]s late as 1942, the principal of a residential school in Saskatchewan was unaware of any responsibility to report a death to provincial vital statistics officials."[48]

Old Sun Indian Residential School, in southern Alberta, was founded in 1890. By 1909 47.4 percent of children who had attended the school had passed away; 20 percent of the children died "at school." For this period in total, the annual death rate at Old Sun was 46.6 per 1,000 students. This is likely higher if we add recent NCTR research. The national average death rate per 1,000 children between five and fourteen years at the time was 4.3 per 1,000. Old Sun's average death rate was almost eleven times higher.

Oftentimes, there are indications of death in the school records that remain undetermined. For example, the admission process for residential schools involved assigning a child an ID number as well as an English or French name. Often these numbers were used instead of a language-based name in reports. Such is the case in Albany Indian Residential School in Ontario. In the quote below, an Indian Affairs official remarks that in the September 1942 quarterly return for Albany, which reported children by number, there are thirty-one fewer numbers than in the previous quarterly return. The official lists the numbers that are not included with the observation that there is no evidence of discharge:

> The Department has just received the September quarter return of the Albany Indian Residential School.... The names of the pupils numbered as follows were shown on the June

quarter return but do not appear on the September return, although no application has been received for their discharge:

No. 105	No. 126	No. 0130	No. 0163
No. 111	No. 127	No. 0139	No. 0166
No. 113	No.128	No.0152	No.0167
No.114	No.133	No.0155	No.0168
No.115	No.134	No.0157	No.0170
No.116	No.136	No.0159	No.0176
No.120	No.078	No.0160	No.0180
No.121	No.0106	No.0161[49]	

NCTR Archives staff have not found a resolution to these missing numbers. They have been identified at the NCTR as records of missing children that require more research. The NCTR's Missing Children Project has identified slightly over 17,600 "indications of loss." These are cases such as Fort Albany above, where the records of loss remain unresolved.

In another chapter in *Grave Error*, Hymie Rubenstein notes, "It is somewhat disappointing that despite six years of investigation and a $72 million budget, the TRC was not able to provide updated and comprehensive figures on the total number and percentage of students attending residential schools beyond its rough 150,000 estimate."[50] Rubenstein has his facts wrong. The NCTR, in collaboration with Carson Leung (Canada Research Chair in Data Mining, Faculty of Computer Science, University of Manitoba) and two computer science graduate students from the University of Manitoba Faculty of Computer Science, has produced a study that calculates through algorithms a reliable number range of students who attended the residential school system over its lifetime: 170,000 to 175,000 students. The NCTR began with a list of almost ten million names taken from all historical documentation in 2015. With this research, the NCTR will move on from the TRC estimate. As Leung explains, "To elaborate, we designed and developed a data science solution, which comprises a rule-based name matching algorithm that combines fuzzy string similarity metrics with a graph traversal technique to cluster related names. The algorithm was implemented by incorporating a fast and comprehensive string-matching library in Python programming language. It also applies depth-first search to construct transitive chains of matches based on pre-defined thresholds chosen through human-in-the-loop process."[51]

Researchers will use this comprehensive list to interrogate the meaning of the residential schools; Survivors and their families and communities can reference this list to understand the destiny of loved ones and perhaps to heal; general media and educators will use the list to better inform the national dialogue on residential school history and legacy. It is difficult to account for the dead when they were not properly counted in the first place. Counting is not just statistical—it is moral. Who gets counted reflects who is valued.

The Tragedy of Burial Sites

Muscowequan Residential School

Another common denialist claim is that there is no evidence of unmarked burials, that the remains of children were appropriately cared for. If there are any unidentified burials, it is because the environment naturally degraded the markers of unattended graves. Or as Rubenstein so callously puts it, "The fact that wood rot[s] is a natural occurrence, not a sign of malign intent [*sic*]."[52] The unmarked burials of the Muscowequan Residential School in Saskatchewan disprove this.

The Muskowekwan Education Centre (MEC) was established in 1889 and was administered by the Oblate Order of the Roman Catholic Church. It was designed to be an industrial school with students working at a trade or in industry to help make the school self-financing.[53] There was a historical pattern of encountering and disregarding students' burials for building development. Referencing Muscowequan Residential School, W.H. Pope, executive assistant to the director of Indian Affairs, reported to the director in 1960, "There is a Roman Catholic residential school run by the Oblate Fathers. This school has been in operation since about 1905. Until about 1930 there was a cemetery at the school where Indians were buried. Then a new cemetery was started about a mile from the school. This summer a new staff house was built at the school, right on the old cemetery grounds. Rumours among the Indians are to the affect [*sic*] that bones were dug up. Some of the Indians have taken great objection to this."[54]

Saskatchewan Member of Parliament Hanzen Robert Argue wrote to Director Jones to inquire on this issue. Argue cites the same information, that "a new staff house was built at the school, right on the old cemetery grounds." But after noting the concern of the Indigenous community, he closes with a troubling observation: "According to an Elder who attended the residence, a priest levelled the remaining graves in 1944."[55]

With almost each round of construction at the school, there seem to have been discoveries of unmarked burials. Amongst the structures thought to have been built on student remains are the kindergarten, nursery, grade one building, and a residence formerly used to house single child care staff. Other structures built during the 1960s and 1970s are thought to be located on the burial ground.[56]

All of these issues came to a head in the construction of a sewage system that began with a planning study in 1991.[57] The project brief notes that in 1935, "Some graves were moved to accommodate one wing of [a school] residence."[58] As planning progressed:

> the Project Team was made aware that a section of the proposed sewage collection system would run through the site of an unmarked graveyard. A site sketch of the unmarked graveyard was provided by a M.E.C. Board member on February 28, 1992. No plans, other than the site sketch, identifying the gravesite could be located in either INAC or Energy Mines and Resources (EMR) files.
>
> Following uncovering of the graves however, EMR did locate a site plan which was provided to the Project Officer. Survey field notes, also provided by EMR, did not indicate how the gravesite boundaries were established.[59]

Local members of the MEC team noted that "graves had been uncovered during previous excavation work in the area. In several instances the remains unearthed were reburied in the same excavation and on another occasion the remains were reburied in a new cemetery."[60] In spite of the directions of local members of the MEC team, digging for the sewers uncovered several sets of remains. On 20 July 1992, workers with NIS Construction Ltd. uncovered three unmarked graves during installation of the gravity main down the roadway between the residences.[61] Then again, the next day, "an additional 15 graves were encountered." Another set of remains was encountered the next day and all excavation was stopped. According to the project brief, "All remains unearthed were placed in plastic bags and stored in a locked building."[62] The band council was consulted. Local Elders met on-site and advised that no further excavation work was to take place in the area behind the student residence building. The MEC board agreed to follow the Elders' advice. As a result of this decision, no buildings located behind the student residence were connected to the new sewage system. The project brief states, "On July 25, 1992 the remains unearthed were ceremoniously re-buried in a cemetery located on the Reserve."[63] Finally, with the advice of the band and Elders, "Honouring the Dead," a brief outline of appropriate process, was drafted.[64]

In 2018, members of the band council of the Muskowekwan First Nation contacted the NCTR with the news that soil erosion was turning up children's remains in fields around the local residential school. The NCTR Archives staff visited the site at the request of band council authorities. Following investigation, the NCTR staff created a short documentary on the fields of unmarked burials.[65] The interviews in the documentary provide the Indigenous voice to institutional reports.[66] Following the NCTR investigation and documentary, Terence Clark, William T.D. Wadsworth, and Kisha Supernant visited the school site with a team and performed ground-penetrating radar research on fields where school Survivors indicated human remains existed. The field searches all returned indications of remains, and the next chapter by Andrew Martindale will explain more about the role of archeology and tools such as ground-penetrating radar in establishing the truth about residential schooling.[67]

The "Good Life"

Denialists also claim that children lived a good life at Indian Residential Schools. The children, they argue, were well educated, well nourished, and treated with the care every child deserves. As Rubenstein notes, "The archival record . . . supplies thousands of photos of residential school life, including a 1962 CBC documentary about the residential school in Kamloops that depicts many apparently healthy, animated, neatly dressed, and well-fed children."[68] But it is well known that schools were perpetually underfunded, and as a result, children were malnourished, lacked adequate shelter and clothing, spent countless hours working school farmlands instead of in classrooms, and never received proper health care. School administrators were frequently advertising the success of their schools to promote greater funding. Staged photographs and film footage were often used as part of propaganda campaigns to gain resources. In the case of the Catholic orders, such as the Oblates of OMI Lacombe and the Grey Nuns, photos also served as recruitment material for staff. But for every photo of happy schoolchildren, the NCTR Archives holds fivefold examples of evidence of trauma. I will cite two examples of the traumatic life of students: Dunbow Residential School and Alberni Indian Residential School.

Dunbow Residential School

The photo below is under a warning on the NCTR website to caution viewers of the image's disturbing content.

This is a photo from 1918 of a gravesite near St. Joseph's or Dunbow Indian Residential School in Alberta. It depicts twenty-seven women and girls attending to a graveyard with crosses and gardening equipment. It is a posed photo: The girls are wearing summer hats; they are facing the camera and have not yet been at work in the gravesite. This is a type of propaganda photo common for its time. In their constant effort to convince the federal government to fund their work in residential

Figure 3.1. Des étudiantes dans le cimetière de Dunbow, 1918. / Cemetery at the Dunbow Indian Residential School, c. 1918. Courtesy of the National Centre for Truth and Reconciliation.

schools, religious orders such as the Catholic Grey Nuns, who operated the Dunbow school, would regularly accompany their quarterly reports and correspondence with images giving proof of the social legitimacy of residential schools. Such photos were commonly circulated in news bulletins to Catholic audiences located predominantly in the province of Québec, from where most of the IRS teachers in western Canada, significantly priests and nuns, were recruited. The school was one of the first three industrial schools set up in western Canada in 1884. A federal order-in-council gave the Catholic Oblate Order responsibility for the Treaty 7 area encompassing the southern region of the province of Alberta. Father Lacombe, a leader in the history of the Oblate Order in Canada, set up the school. The Blackfoot (now Siksika) community was one of the closest reserves and the subject of Lacombe's attention.

Funding from the federal government was directly linked to enrolment numbers. This led Father Lacombe's successors to cast an increasingly wider net for students to attend Dunbow. Over the next decades, Cree, Métis, Sarcee (now Tsuut'ina Nation) and Stoney children were recruited.

In all, the Dunbow Indian Residential School (also known as Dunbow Industrial School) operated for thirty-eight years, with a total of approximately 430 students attending. Health conditions at Dunbow were always poor. Indigenous children lacked resistance to European diseases. The operating agreement included the provision for a medical doctor from Calgary to pay regular visits, but this rarely occurred. Students were almost constantly sick: colds, influenza, and especially tuberculosis (TB). Records indicate that by 1909 virtually every student at Dunbow had TB. Quarters were so tight that healthy children were forced to sleep in the infirmary, exacerbating the spread of disease. At last estimate, seventy-three students died at the school, which closed in 1922. That's one in six. To date, thirty-four children who were interred in this graveyard have been named. This particular cemetery is near the edge of the Highwood River. In 1996, flooding eroded the banks. Caskets and bones spilled into the river; remains were washed away, many found by local Indigenous children. Environmental erosion occurred at several schools across the country, including Kuper Island, Assiniboine, Muskowekwan, and Brandon, to name a few. This is a direct result of the poor, or non-existent, care of these burial sites.

There is no federal gravesite legislation in Canada; there is only a patchwork of provincial laws that apply to unmarked burials, gravesites, and collective remains. The Dunbow site fell into a no man's land in terms of Alberta provincial government jurisdiction: too young to be archaeological; too old to have been recorded as a cemetery in provincial records. No government department was immediately prepared to step forward and assume responsibility for the disposition of these remains.

To research this question, one must consider multiple sources: government and clergy, public and private. In the case of the Dunbow School, the records of the Grey Nuns, located in their Montréal archival centre, the records of the Oblates OMI Lacombe, located in the Provincial Archives in Edmonton, and the federal government sources in Ottawa at Library and Archives Canada are the most important sources of documentary evidence. This must be read in the context of community social memory. In cross-indexing the resources, it is possible to identify the names of who is in the picture by examining the discharge records of the school and the annual reports of who attended. These are the reports that were submitted to the Department of Indian Affairs.

It is also possible to review the original discharge register to confirm what were often inconsistent reports. It is not uncommon to find important information written into the comments of the discharge register. Furthermore, the children were often given European names and numbers for recording in registers, and these must be confirmed. There is evidence of the Indian Affairs headquarters cautioning school officials to stop naming children after Indian Affairs officers such as Hayter Reed.[69] Different registers frequently had different spellings or identifications for the same child. There are examples of children with over fifteen different spellings, languages, and numbers, all identifying the same child.

The school's day journals are also a useful documentary source. In this case, the journals note that the children who learned farming dug the graves and boys learning carpentry made the coffins for their classmates. Another journal indicates that during the influenza outbreak, more than one child was placed in a coffin due to resource restraint. Also from these journals, I determined that the local Indian agent was instructed to give a special pass to permit a family to visit a child at school once a year, more often if the child was sick.

With the photo from the Grey Nuns, the reports from Indian Affairs, and the journals from the Oblates, it is possible to weave together an impression of the IRS experience and get a view of the nature of the contested archives of residential schools in Canada. Together with the testimony of Survivors, we begin to get a glimpse of the Indigenous experience of the period of the "healthy, animated, neatly dressed, and well-fed children" attending Dunbow Residential School.

Researchers and Survivors of Dunbow Residential School began to research the history of the gravesite after years of negotiation with local authorities.[70] In 2001, several Elders gathered to rebury in ceremony dozens of children's remains from the eroded gravesite. The ceremony lasted for almost a week and involved Elders from all the surrounding communities.[71]

Alberni Indian Residential School

The Alberni Indian Residential School (AIRS) in British Columbia is notable as another notoriously dangerous school for Indigenous children. This is in terms of death rate as well as child abuse by teachers. In the first nine years of operation, the death rate at Alberni was 11 percent. In defence of this record, R.P. MacKay of the Presbyterian Church commented that "while the conditions at Alberni are admittedly bad, the records of some other schools are equally unenviable."[72]

The physical and sexual violence committed against children sent to the Alberni Indian Residential School was endemic across the twentieth century. The RCMP Native Indian Residential School Task Force, Project E-NIRS (1995–2003), investigated abuse at fifteen British Columbia schools, including Alberni IRS. Unavailable until 2025, the results of the investigation recorded 103 sexual assault offences and ninety-one physical assault offences.[73]

The abuse began in the 1910s. A series of correspondence in 1918 notes that a male student at the Alberni Indian Boarding School was subjected to a "most brutal beating" at the hands of an employee of the school.[74] The employee was the principal, Authur Currie. Another series of correspondence from 1922 indicates that an employee of the school whips, hits, and chokes the boys.[75] In 1922, Andrew Paull, the corresponding secretary of the Allied Tribes of British Columbia, wrote to W.E. Ditchburn, the chief inspector of Indian agencies in British Columbia, to complain that the principal of the Alberni industrial school "unmercifully whips the boys on their backs, which is objected to as well as Mr. Currie fighting and kicking the boys for the purpose of correction. It is further reported that Mr. Currie gets extremely mad at the slightest provocation, and whips or hits the boys with his fists, or chokes them."[76] The "AIRS Narrative," drafted as part of the IRSSA negotiations, fails to mention Principal Currie in its list of abusers, even though documenting crimes against children was one of the purposes for these narratives. As historian Tyla Betke notes, Principal Currie was transferred to Birtle Indian Residential School in Manitoba in 1927, and by 1930, the principal, who falsely claimed to be an ordained Presbyterian minister, was charged with multiple cases of sexually abusing children. As with the case of Father Garand, the records indicate, "A multitude of actors and institutions were involved in the coverup: the Indian agent and the Department of Indian Affairs, the Presbyterian Church, the court systems, and the public press. Strategies of concealment included blatant bribery, transferring accused principals to other schools, document falsification, forced marriages, and misreporting runaways, along with the IRS system itself, which kept children from their families and support systems."[77]

Currie, however, was not simply a bad apple. Conditions at Alberni failed to improve even after Currie's departure, with sexual abuse being prevalent at the school into the 1950s. Most notably, this decade included the rampant abuse committed by Arthur Plint, one of the most notorious serial sexual abusers in the history of the Indian Residential School System. Things became so bad in the early 1960s that a student uprising forced school authorities to call in the RCMP. Alberni Indian Residential School is one of the only schools in the history of the system to require RCMP forces to quell student resistance. In 1995, Arthur Henry Plint pleaded guilty to eighteen counts of indecent assault against victims at Alberni. In 1997, Plint pleaded guilty to ten more counts of indecent assault, relating to nine victims, and three counts of assault causing bodily harm, relating to three victims, all at the same school. In October 2003, Donald Bruce Haddock pleaded guilty to four counts of indecent assault, which occurred at Alberni between 1948 and 1954.[78] In November 2003, Michael Dennis Flynn and David Henry Forde were charged in connection with the allegations of sexual abuse at the Alberni Indian Residential School.[79]

The IRSSA "Narrative" for Alberni identified five teachers, including the principal, found guilty of sexually abusing children in the school's history.[80] This "Narrative," the legal list used in the settlement agreement, suggests a much lower number of assaults than reported in the "Final Report" of the Native Indian Residential School Task Force report. This restricted report, it bears noting, was made available only in 2025 after investigative reporting forced its release. It is important to recognize this report was not made available when the IRSSA was being negotiated and terms of settlement agreed to on the basis of what was known to have occurred in schools.

As a result of the Plint investigations, the case known as *Blackwater v. Plint* recognized vicarious responsibility of Christian orders in the crimes against children at residential schools.[81] This decision forcefully brought Christian orders to the negotiating table for the crimes committed at residential schools during the IRSSA.

In front of the Nuu-Chah-nulth band office is a totem in honour of Tsaqwasupp, Art Thompson, a lead witness and victim in the trial against Plint. At the close of the trial, Tsaqwasupp was given the opportunity to make a final impact statement.

> You know, as victims, as a victim, you know, I want to erase this notion of being very nostalgic and how I carried my life on; all of the "I wishes" that didn't happen. You know, I wish I wasn't born. I wish I was born white. I wish that I had different parents. I wish there wasn't a guy by the name of Plint . . . that nostalgic notion doesn't carry me through my life, and I've learned that. Those kinds of issues, I've learned to accept the fact that I do have a history, and that history has made me who I am today. I believe this human being, a contributing human being to society, one that has contributed artistically both to the state at large and to my own community at large. I've contributed, I feel, enormously to this society with my artist background. And it hasn't come without consequences, and those consequences are having to relive the notion that I represent all of my assailants. And I understand that in my heart that's a very sickly thing to pack around. So, purge that, let it go. Public at large is a lot better than, you know, the assailants that are named in this suit.[82]

This is the human measure of the residential school system that denialists are trying to discount, disregard, or downplay. Residential schooling erased Tsaqwasupp's Indigenous identity, denied his family, and attempted to dissolve his community. And this is why the voices of First Nations, Inuit, and Métis, and Inuit, and First Nations Survivors must be centred and prioritized in the remembrance of schools. The events at Dunbow and Alberni represent only two examples of the *systemic* abuse of children persistent throughout the history of the residential school program. There was no nostalgic good life.

The Decolonization of Archival Memory

The uncertainty of death at residential schools was matched by the inconsistency of its appointed documentation. Denialists claim to exclusively follow Enlightenment principles of positivist, objective evidence, as Widdowson claimed repeatedly during a presentation at Brock University in 2024.[83] What denialists often fail to acknowledge is that many political, philosophical, and legal perspectives influenced the design and operation of residential schools: the social gospel, Christian evangelism, British colonialism, nascent capitalism, and stages theories of social development. Often competing, this plurality of ideologies came together in the residential school program with the mutual agreement that Indigenous Peoples' best and final destiny was total eradication and assimilation. These competing ideas of social development and nation building compounded any attempt to build a comprehensive and trustworthy record-keeping system for the Indian Residential School System. Ultimately, one of the most thorough and profound social programs in the history of the nation was inconsistently and irregularly coordinated and resourced through random orders-in-council and legislative amendments. Records were lost through under-resourcing, lack of planning, inconsistent record keeping, and simple lack of concern. As I have demonstrated, the result was that the reliability and availability of the record of a student death varied in each residential school across Canada. The indifference and neglect applied to the records of the residential school program are both a product and a profound statement on the value placed on the lives lost. And that is why remembrance is also a moral act.

The liberatory research that the NCTR supports shifts the purpose of research from extraction to empowerment, from documentation to transformation.[84] It highlights how traditional Enlightenment research values have banished Indigenous world views and research methods to the cognitive wilderness. Liberatory research validates the voices and lived experiences of residential school Survivors, whose memories were marginalized for much of the twentieth century. With the guidance of Survivors, the NCTR approaches the histories of residential schools with profound questions of identity and belonging: Who benefits from this research? Who controls it? And, most importantly, who is healed by it?

Notes

1 I offer my position relative to the information I am sharing. This is an acknowledgement of Indigenous research methodologies built on Indigenous epistemologies. I reject the denialist claims for the neutrality of Enlightenment research models. All knowledge is socially mediated, and it is best understood when those who create, store, and share the knowledge under study declare their relationship to the knowledge. Placed in *Nêhiyaw* (Cree) knowledge epistemology, this is *nisitohtamowin,* a Cree word for "understanding," or, more accurately, "self-in-relation." Margaret Kovach, *Indigenous Methodologies: Characteristics, Conversations, and Contexts* (University of Toronto Press, 2021), 26. As the head of archives for the National Centre for Truth and Reconciliation, since 2016 I have had an intimate role in the discovery, acquisition, preservation, and access of evidence concerning the history and legacy of the residential school system in Canada. My mother attended Shaftsbury Mission, an Oblate-administered mission school in northern Alberta. For a fuller background of my personal relationship to these matters, see R.O. Frogner, "The Train from Dunvegan: Implementing the United Nations Declaration on the Rights of Indigenous Peoples (UNDRIP) in Public Archives in Canada," *Archival Science* 22 (2022): 209–38. https://doi.org/10.1007/s10502-021-09373-0.

2 It has even been suggested the reason so many residential school denialists are of retirement age is because they do not risk losing their jobs if they speak out. C.P. Champion and Tom Flanagan, eds., *Grave Error: How the Media Misled Us (and the Truth About Residential Schools)* (True North and Dorchester Books, 2023), 12.

3 Crystal Gail Fraser, associate professor in history and Native Studies at the University of Alberta, quoted in Samantha Schwientek, "Residential School Denialism: What Is It and How to Recognize It," *CBC News*, 17 March 2025, https://www.cbc.ca/news/indigenous/residential-school-denialism-explainer-1.7485959.

4 International Council on Archives Expert Matters Indigenous Group, *Tandanya–Adelaide Declaration* (International Council on Archives, 2019), https://www.ica.org/app/uploads/2024/01/tandaya_adelaide_declaration_eng.pdf.

5 Champion and Flanagan, *Grave Error*, 3.

6 Death Records—Indian Residential School Records, accessed 8 January 2025, https://indianresidentialschoolrecords.com/death-records/.

7 To be clear, the NCTR has received authentic copies of records, not the originals. This crucial archival distinction seems to be lost on Green.

8 Agreement for Data Sharing Between The University of Manitoba on behalf of its National Centre for Truth and Reconciliation and Her Majesty the Queen in Right of the Province of Manitoba as represented by the Minister of the Department of Finance on behalf of the Vital Statistics Branch of Manitoba, 4.

9 The NCTR continues to hold discussions to acquire copies of vital statistics on residential school children from Quebec and Saskatchewan. In the case of Ontario, the provincial vital statistics agency employed a team of researchers who spent approximately two years identifying the deaths of Indigenous residential school students.

10 Most provincial coroners' offices are still in discussion with the NCTR to produce records of investigations into the deaths of children at residential schools.

11 Russell, "Probing a Dark Decade."

12 Russell, 113.

13 Russell, 134–35.

14 Russell, 134–35.

15 As a former archivist at the British Columbia Provincial Archives, I can confirm the countless hours archival staff spent explaining to researchers the arcane randomness and inconsistencies of Indigenous vital events records in British Columbia.

16 Frances Widdowson on X: "Next stop @Umanitoba - on September 25 and 26. I am also looking forward to the #SpectrumStreetEpistemology session on September 25 and the other 'Truth and Reconciliation' events (except the official prayers, which should not be held at a secular institution, @UMSU). https://t.co/3InYMF8A5v" / X.

17 Indian Residential School Records, accessed 1 August 2025, https://indianresidentialschoolrecords.com/staff-chronicles/.

18 Over 95 percent of the records that religious orders made available to the TRC and the NCTR were authentic digital copies.

19 The Oblates OMI Lacombe merged several western and central Canadian Oblate provinces in 2003.

20 NCTR Archives, "An Apology to the First Nations of Canada by the Oblate Conference of Canada," 24 July 1991, https://archives.nctr.ca/BB-0252-003. For an update Oblate statement on residential schools and the Missionary Oblates of Mary Immaculate, see https://omilacombe.ca/indian-residential-schools-missionary-oblates-mary-immaculate-q/

21 NCTR Archives, 1.

22 NCTR Archives, 4.

23 NCTR Archives, 4.

24 Memorandum of Agreement between The Missionary Oblates of Mary Immaculate, OMI Lacombe Canada (Oblates) and The University of Manitoba on behalf of The National Centre for Truth and Reconciliation (NCTR), 2022, 2.

25 NCTR Archives, "Oblate Priests," https://archives.nctr.ca/Oblate-Priests.

26 The term *Codex Historicus* typically refers to historical chronicles or records maintained by religious institutions, such as dioceses or institutions of Catholic orders. Under canon law, Catholic orders are not explicitly required to keep these codices. However, canon law (Canon 486) does require religious orders to keep

a historical archive. Dioceses around the world implement canon law's archival requirements in diverse ways, often influenced by their size, resources, and historical context. In the case of the Oblates OMI Lacombe, the record-keeping efforts seem underfunded, ad hoc, and desultory.

27 Interview with the archival staff of the Grey Nuns Order, Montréal, Québec, 29 April 2025.

28 Interview with the archival staff of the Grey Nuns Order. To give another example, the Sisters of St. Anne was the women's order that taught at Kamloops Residential School from 1890 to 1970. When they produced daily chronicles for the TRC, they redacted the names of all the sisters mentioned on every page of the chronicles. They did not redact the names of children, or even Oblates and other authorities responsible for running the schools. Strangely, they even redacted the salaries the sisters received.

29 Jackson Anderson, "Records of Manitoba Residential Schools in Oblate Archives," MA thesis, University of Manitoba, 2023, http://hdl.handle.net/1993/37842

30 Anderson, 102.

31 Anderson, 102.

32 Anderson, 46.

33 The confused disposition of the Sacramental files is particularly difficult, since these are the Catholic records of birth, baptism, marriage, and death.

34 For my complete report on the records held at the Archivum Generale O.M.I. Romae (AG)—Oblate General Administration Archives, see 2022.09.03—Oblates Rome Archive Final Report.docx.

35 "Formation," Oblates, OMI, Constitutions and Rules of the Congregation of the Missionary Oblates of Mary Immaculate (Rome 2018), 45, https://www.omiworld.org/wp-content/uploads/CCRR-ENG-08-02-2019.pdf. This document offers a detailed list of the information required to be created and kept to document a missionary's "*formation*."

36 "Quite sensitive, gentle in character, calm, a little firm; enterprising, especially when it comes to taking care of children, for whom he has a marked weakness, although he seems to have the best intentions" (trans. author), Frère Convers, Vicariat des Missions de Whitehorse, Garand Benoit, 16 Février 1941.

37 "His weak point, the stumbling block is his penchant for the affection of children. He has often been warned on this point but it seems stronger than him, he loves caressing children too much. The danger is that he does not seem to suspect that it is a weakness. As indicated below in the report, with normal supervision by superiors, he could make an excellent religious, but if ever there is a weakness, it will be on that side. Personally having little experience in the discernment of religious vocations, I do not know to what extent superiors take such a disposition into account" (trans. author), Frère Convers, Vicariat des Missions de Whitehorse, Garand Benoit, 16 Février 1941, Commentaire Sur la Note Rédigée par le Conseil Vicarial.

38 "Attached you will find a letter from Brother Garand. He now calls 'a child's story' what he has repeatedly admitted to be fact. He places such unacceptable conditions on his readmission that one wonders if he is sincere, unless it is a new expression of his lack of judgment. If I comment on his letter this way it is not that I am holding out my hand. This is also the opinion of Father Dréan to whom I showed this letter last week. The latter seems to be in favor of a return to Lower Post, but not before Sept. 1956" (trans. author), "Alexis Monnet, OMI, Vicariate Apostolic of Whitehorse,

Chancery Office, to S.E. Mgr. J.L. Coudert, OMI," 15 Novembre 1956, Roman Catholic Diocese of Whitehorse Archives, 40a-c000014-d0003-001 NCTR.

39 "I have just written to the Very Rev. Father General about Brother B. Garand and send him his Declaration of free acceptance of the Dispensation from his Vows. I don't remember where the filing covering his case is; I believe you will find this in the filing cabinet on the right, under the heading 'Special Cases-Confidential' in order to refer to it if the General House asks for the rest of the filing or any other document relating to it" (trans. author), "Coudert O.M.I. to Pere A. Monnet O.M.I" 1 Novembre 1956, 40a-c000018-d0003-001 NCTR.

40 "This brother has always been disturbingly familiar with children wherever he went, and from his beginnings on the mission; in Dawson, as well as here at our Vicarial residence, he constantly brought children into his room, in spite of the repeated remarks made to him; when more serious complaints reached us (similar to those of Father Fleury) he denies having done anything wrong, and entrenches himself on the fact that 'everyone has his conscience' in these matters"(trans. author), Roman Catholic Diocese of Whitehorse Archives, 1969.

41 "I had thought that at the Lower Post Boarding School, where the children are always kept under strict surveillance, it would be easier to stop any abuse on his part, while allowing him to be in daily contact with the children, whose company he certainly enjoys. Because of this, we never put him in charge of looking after the children, but, despite this, he always managed to receive some in his room, bring some with him in the trucks, under all sorts of pretexts. Many scenes took place between him and the Principal on this subject; he always put forward excuses to justify himself, and despite the strict orders he was given he started again immediately. Despite all our fears and all our suspicions, we always tried to persuade ourselves that it was childishness and that there was nothing serious, because the brother otherwise was devoted to his work and seemed pious. The same complaints, however, recur as those we heard earlier. Will he finally confess guilt? I would like you to have him interviewed by an experienced father of your counsel, with the enclosed documents in hand, and on my behalf" (trans author), Roman Catholic Diocese of Whitehorse Archives, 1969.

42 "I don't know what your decision will be about him, but I confess that I dread his return after the long experience we have had with him; it is now too well known to our youth, and is circulating in the public and causing a major scandal to the detriment of the reputation of our missionaries and of our work of conversion among the natives" (trans. author), Roman Catholic Diocese of Whitehorse Archives, 1969.

43 "His departure will leave a huge void in our Vicariate, because from the point of view of his technical skills (driver, engineer, carpenter) he is difficult to replace. We are already so short of brothers; but dare I ask you for a good brother, at the moment when I offer to take back a brother who cannot be trusted? I believe, however, that in a house of education where there are no children, this brother could pull himself together and still render real service to your Province" (trans. author), Roman Catholic Diocese of Whitehorse Archives, 1969. Note: this letter is a copy. Where it has been distributed is unclear.

44 "NIRS Tip File 1113," 1995-06-08, RCMP-903871, NCTR.

45 Frank Morissey, "Confidentiality, Archives, and Records Management: Canon Law Provisions," Catholic Archivist Group Conference, Pierrefonds, 27 September 2012, 3. Unpublished presentation, copy in possession of author.

46 Champion and Flanagan, *Grave Error*, 13.

47 Truth and Reconciliation Commission (TRC), National Records Archive, LAC, RG10, vol. 6016, _le 1-1-23, part 1, A. F. MacKenzie to Indian Agents, Principals of Indian Residential Schools, 17 April 1935 [SBR-001147-0000],

48 TRC, NRA, LAC, RG10, vol. 6302, _le 650-23, part 2, Inspector, Commanding Prince Albert Sub-Division to the Officer in Charge, RCMP, Regina, Saskatchewan, 10 September 1942 [BVL-000822], cited in *The Final Report of the Truth and Reconciliation Commission of Canada*, vol. 4, *Canada's Residential Schools: Missing Children and Unmarked Burials* (McGill-Queen's Press, 2015), 9.

49 Dr. T.J. Orford, Indian Agent, Moose Factory, to P. Langlois, Principal, Les Missionnaires Oblats de Marie Immaculée, École-pensionnat Indien d'Albany, 19 January 1942, NCTR Archives, c-7922-01438-01467. The destinies of the missing children, identified with numerical identifiers in M. Langois's September 1941 Quarterly Report, remain unknown.

50 Hymie Rubenstein, "Digging for the Truth," in *Grave Error*, 89.

51 Correspondence with Dr. Carson Leung, 19 August 2025. Dr. Leung has drafted an article on the construction of the algorithms and other methods he used to filter names. His article is forthcoming.

52 Rubenstein, "Digging for the Truth," 69.

53 In the over 7,000 Survivors' and relations' recordings stored in the NCTR Archives, manual labour is a common theme. Students recall spending large portions of their day on farmwork because it was often the only way to avoid malnutrition.

54 "W.H. Pope, Executive Assistant to Colonel H.K. Jones, Director of Indian Affairs, 6 October 1960," Strategic Research and Analysis Directorate, Indian and Northern Affairs Canada, file no. MDD-006305-0002.

55 "Hanzen Argue, M.P. to Colonel H.K. Jones, 6 October 1960," Strategic Research and Analysis Directorate, Indian and Northern Affairs Canada, file no. MDD-006305-0002.

56 No author, "Muskowekwan Education Centre Relocation of Buildings, Project Brief," p. 4, INAC—Resolution Sector—IRS Historical Files Collection—Ottawa Muscowequan Box 23, File 28, report (no author listed) to Department of Indian Affairs and Northern Development, 23 March 1993, DocID MDD-006177-0002, 5.

57 The official project title was the "Muskowekwan Education Centre Sewer System—Project No. 62469."

58 "Muskowekwan Education Centre Relocation," 5.

59 "Muskowekwan Education Centre Relocation," 5.

60 "Muskowekwan Education Centre Relocation," 5.

61 "Muskowekwan Education Centre Relocation," 5.

62 "Muskowekwan Education Centre Relocation," 6.

63 "Muskowekwan Education Centre Relocation," 6.

64 "Muskowekwan Education Centre Relocation," 7.

65 NCTR, *Remembering the Forgotten Children—Muskowekwan Residential School*, YouTube, 2 January 2018, https://www.youtube.com/watch?v=hwjpFTob4r0.

66 It should be noted that over half the Survivors of the residential school who gathered to discuss the situation with the NCTR staff refused to go the school to record the documentary for fear of being retraumatized.

67 Terence Clark, William T.D. Wadsworth, and Kisha Supernant, "Technical Report on the GPR Survey Conducted Around the Muskowekwan Residential School, SK.," 21–22 June 2018.

68 Rubenstein, "Digging for the Truth," 92.

69 Beginning as an Indian agent in Battleford in 1881, Reed concluded his career as deputy superintendent general of Indian Affairs (1893 to 1897). His principal role in shaping nineteenth-century Indigenous policy, including residential schools and the pass system, makes this eponymous naming of residential school children particularly ironic.

70 Tammy Rollie, "Horrors of Residential Schools Existed Not Far from Okotoks," *Western Wheel*, 8 June 2021, https://www.westernwheel.ca/local-news/horrors-of-residential-schools-existed-not-far-from-okotoks-3849354.

71 Ed Struzik, "The Dunbow School," *Edmonton Journal*, 5 December 2005, Media Clips.doc, https://barge.ca/dunbow/edjournal.pdf.

72 Quoted in Miller, *Shingwauk's Vision: A History of Native Residential Schools*, 132.

73 Royal Canadian Mounted Police, "Final Report of the Native Indian Residential School Task Force," Project E-NIRS, Prepared by Cpl. M.W. Pacholuk, 2003, 67.

74 Indian Affairs, RG 10, Vol. 6431, file 877-1, part 1, ARS Narrative file 00742.

75 Indian Affairs, RG 10, Vol. 6431, file 877-1, part 2, ARS Narrative file 00750.

76 Item 70a-f003263-d0038-001—[Request of Opinion Pertaining Certain Charges Against Mr. Currie, Principal of Alberni Boarding School] (Draft); Item 70a-f003263-d0039-001—[Charges of Physical Violence on Willie Mitchell Against Mr. Currie, Principal of Alberni School] (Draft); Item 70a-f003263-d0040-001—[Request for Investigation and Report Concerning Charge Made by George Mitchell Against Mr. Currie, Principal of Alberni Indian Boarding School] (Draft).

77 Betke, "'Not a Shred of Evidence.'"

78 Jeff Holubitsky, "Tofield Man Jailed for 1950s Sexual Abuse of Children," *Edmonton Journal*, 24 January 2004.

79 Royal Canadian Mounted Police News Release, E-Division File: 1994E-14664, "Final Set of Charges Laid in Native Indian Residential School Task Force Investigation," 14 November 2003.

80 "Alberni IRS School Narrative," 25 March 2004, NCTR, "School Narratives," https://archives.nctr.ca/NAR-NCTR-018, 8.

81 *Blackwater v. Plint*, 2005 SCC 58 (CanLII), [2005] 3 SCR 3.

82 Art Thompson and Evelyn Thompson-George, *The Defiant 511 of the Alberni Residential School* (Friesen Press, 2025), 118.

83 Frances Widdowson, "'Grave Error' at Kamloops Residential School," Lecture at Brock University, 29 October 2024.

84 For a good example of this approach to research, see Leslie Brown and Susan Strega, eds., *Research as Resistance: Critical, Indigenous, and Anti-oppressive Approaches* (Canadian Scholars' Press, 2005).

CHAPTER 4

UNDERSTANDING THE ROLE OF ARCHAEOLOGY IN RESIDENTIAL SCHOOL SEARCHES

an Interview with Andrew Martindale

SEAN CARLETON AND NIIGAAN SINCLAIR (EDITORS): Thank you for taking time out of your busy schedule in the field to be in dialogue with us about the role of archaeology and different technological tools used in truth and reconciliation work. Residential school denialists often target this particular aspect of residential school research, like they do with archival records. They try to twist the complex nature of ground-penetrating radar and related technologies in the public mind to cast doubt on residential school truths such as deaths. We are honoured to be in conversation with you, a non-Indigenous scholar and a highly respected archaeologist who works with community on searches for potential unmarked burials. To start, can you introduce yourself and explain how you've come to truth and reconciliation work?

ANDREW MARTINDALE: I'm a professor in the Department of Anthropology at the University of British Columbia (UBC). I'm an archaeologist with expertise primarily in working with Indigenous communities in tracing Holocene history through explorations of material culture, typically in settlement patterns, and in Oral Traditions in the Indigenous oral record. I began working with geophysics in 2006 when I joined UBC. I reached out to our local Indigenous hosts, xʷməθkʷəy̓əm (Musqueam), and they proposed the development of a field school that I would instruct and would be hosted at Musqueam. We were asked if there was a way that one could locate unmarked graves without excavation. I said, yes, there are some geophysical tools that archaeologists use, including ground-penetrating radar (GPR), which have been shown to have value in this. The community, the Elders, and then the Advisory Committee at Musqueam, who were supporting our work, recommended we do this. So that summer we were actually able to find quite an antiquated array of ground-penetrating radar at UBC in the Department of Earth, Ocean, and Atmospheric Sciences. There was a very generous faculty member who brought it all out and set it up, and we did a basic line through ancestors in one of the Musqueam cemeteries with positive results.

It was on that basis, then, that a team from Musqueam and UBC co-applied to an educational fund through the university to get our own equipment so that we could expand our field school to include a geophysical component. Then for the next three years we taught students this method while mapping out the Musqueam cemeteries, looking for and locating unmarked graves. As with many historic cemeteries, there had been a degree of loss of knowledge of where ancestors were. Monuments that were made of wood eroded. Caretakers, at times, had moved monuments and markers around. With GPR we were able to relocate the patterns of ancestor burials, so our success was considerable.

One of the Elders, the famous Delbert Guerin, of the well-known *Guerin* decision in Canadian law, told me that there are two graves in the cemetery that are different, and to tell him if I found them.[1] When I went back in the fall, I told him that there are two graves in the cemetery perpendicular to everybody else. He said, yes, they were outsiders who had asked to be buried in the cemetery and the community agreed but not in the alignment that their people are buried in. It was a little internal test on whether this technology was working.

From that point on, we helped other communities. We had a master's graduate thesis by Steven Daniel that was based on this work.[2] Around 2011, I was approached by Eldon Yellowhorn and Alex Maass from the Truth and Reconciliation Commission (TRC).[3] They asked if I might be interested in supporting the work on residential schools. Honestly, for several years, I said no. I just didn't have the capacity. But then, in 2013, Alex proposed that the community of Penelakut were interested in support for their work at the Kuper Island Indian Industrial School, an Indian Residential School (IRS) in British Columbia. At that point, my calendar was clearer, and I recognized the need. So, I said yes, knowing that it would be a lifetime commitment, and here we are more than ten years later.

We began the work in 2014. This was a time long before there was any support. It was before the TRC had released its *Final Report*. We were working as volunteers with the support of the Supne'luxutth Sulxwe'en (Elders Committee). It was difficult work for a lot of reasons. There had been very little health and wellness support for the Survivors; the committee were all Survivors. They knew of stories and had witnessed events but when they were confronted with a tool that could actually provide some specific spatial information on the modern landscape, that became, for some, quite overwhelming and difficult. We proceeded slowly. We found some results early on that were pretty clearly associated with a residential school burial ground.[4] Then, we pivoted and started working in their main cemetery, partly because it needed doing. Eric Simons is focused on this work as part of his PhD at UBC. Our most recent count shows that there are almost 400 unmarked graves in their cemetery, which is not uncommon for historical cemeteries of some antiquity. We also know that there are some known and marked burials in the cemetery of children who went to and died at the residential school. This step helped us refine our craft and gave us some confidence since the ancestors in the cemetery are in the right place. It's an appropriate spiritual setting for them.

We also supported the community when they were building new developments and constructions in the environment of the school. They wanted to know if there was anything of concern in the areas around the former IRS site there. We continue to do a lot of scanning of the ground to help the community identify any potential areas of concern.

We had just presented at a symposium at the Canadian Archaeological Association conference in early May of 2021 on GPR in IRS landscapes when, two weeks later, the Kamloops results were announced. Our symposium had invited people who were doing this work across the country—academics working in partnership with Nations, exploring residential school landscapes, and using different methods including geophysics—to try to investigate the land to identify the locations of unmarked graves. I had encountered a few documents—geotechnical reports—that, in my mind, were inadequate for the task. Their data collection parameters were not appropriate for what they were looking for. In fact, in some cases, they said there was nothing there when I could see results that were significant in their reports. I felt there was a need for a degree of expertise and scholarship in this space. That's really where my work has been focused on since. I have been working in partnership with Musqueam, supporting Penelakut and, by extension, other Nations. The task has been to develop results but also to refine best practices around these technologies. We've been focusing on radar, but we're also using a range of other methods including magnetometry, underwater methods, and remote sensing tools like LiDAR (Light Detection and Ranging) from drones. In 2022, I was invited to be on the National Advisory Committee on Residential Schools Missing Children and Unmarked Burials (NAC), which was a great honour. I participated in those conversations for two years, again largely to speak to technical issues around remote sensing and geophysics.

EDITORS: Can you explain more about what ground-penetrating radar is, how it works, and how it differs from LiDAR? We think it's important to understand the technology being used to search for potential unmarked burials because denialists often try to exploit the public's lack of specific knowledge to cast GPR as unreliable, suggesting that all that is being located is just tree roots and rocks, not graves.

ANDREW: Well, there are two basic categories of technology that we use—three if you count underwater, but let's not talk about that right now since it's an emergent one that we're just on the cusp of. Remote sensing typically includes LiDAR but can include photographs and other kinds of investigations of the surface of the ground from a distance via satellites, airplanes, drones, or hand-held devices. They typically observe surface patterns. Occasionally, we will find subsurface patterns through remote sensing by proxy such as, for example, crop marks or thermal signatures. But the main technology we use is what's called LiDAR.[5] It's a relatively modern method but is used in document scanning, automated doors, and self-driving vehicles. It sends out an infrared signal in great quantity: Modern LiDAR sensors from drones emit 100,000 to two million data points every second. LiDAR sensors send out this stream of signals and then track the telemetry of their reflection off objects they encounter, generating a model of surfaces from all these points—known as a point cloud.

It's a technological innovation that has revolutionized many field sciences in the last five years. I use that word intentionally because it has enabled us to create a huge amount of data from landscapes with precision and accuracy relatively quickly. The point cloud of data represents the physical space of every reflection point, hundreds of millions of them. That point cloud can then be reviewed and evaluated depending on your purpose.[6] Foresters, for example, want to know what's in the tree cover; so, they model the canopy, and they can use this kind of technology to evaluate timber stock. We edit out the trees, essentially, and what we're left with is a ground surface model that gives us a surface shape of what the ground looks like under the vegetation.[7] You can't see through things, but because vegetation is not perfectly opaque, some signal passes through and the result is a model of the ground surface.

We know from other researchers and our work in cemeteries like Penelakut that graves typically will have a surface contour, especially in formal cemeteries.[8] Those shapes are positive indicators of graves. In more clandestine spaces it is less clear how useful it will be. All of these technologies have roles in other forms of heritage and archaeology so their value is not restricted to residential schools.

LiDAR also gives us a really good base map upon which we can layer other pieces of data. It identifies trees, buildings, paths, roads, potential gravesites, fencelines, gateposts, et cetera. We can add in other search method results, whether it's a Survivor's information, an archival map, an air photo, or another technology like geophysics. In the case of Kuper, we're working in reserve lands and, typically, reserve lands are not serviced well by the federal government. There's not a good history of maps, there's no government-supported Geographic Information System (GIS), and there's no municipal database. The community is left to create these, and our ability to make our own base map can be useful beyond heritage issues.

The second class of methods we use are geophysical. These are tools that will look into materials, so can discern patterns under the ground. They are specifically designed to do that. We are working with two methods—one is through radar and the second is through magnetic fields.[9] We do both, but the one that has received the most attention is radar, partly because it's shown to be valuable for this kind of work. Geophysicists and archaeologists have used it to map out both natural and anthropogenic subsurface features including graves, in cemeteries, for decades.[10] It exists as a technology for industrial applications, for finding service lines and other buried infrastructure, and for evaluating material within other materials, such as steel within concrete.

Magnets are a different thing, but you can imagine it's an iteration of metal detection. Anything that has a magnetic signature or responds to a magnetic field can generate a result. Radar is a little bit different. It sends out an electromagnetic (EM) signal into the ground using a transmitting antenna. Then, it captures reflections of these signals in a receiving antenna. The electromagnetic signal is of a certain wavelength and strength that will travel a certain distance into the ground and capture reflections of things of a certain size. That can be quite varied. People use these to map out the terrain beneath glaciers, for example, so they go through metres of ice. You have to have a very big array and use really low wavelengths. If you want to find something close to the surface, you use a higher wavelength that won't travel as deep but provides higher resolution. That's the basic exchange. The deeper you go, the more resolution you lose. We typically use about 400 to 500 megahertz. That goes down about one to two metres, and you can see something approximately the size of a basketball. That is suitable resolution and depth for most archaeological and industrial applications. This is the format that most people looking for service lines will use, and it has application in unmarked graves. The return signal reflection is based on qualities of the subsurface. It's those qualities that we're trying to identify and interpret.

The reflected signal responds to changes between materials that influence the EM signal differently through a physical property known as dielectric permittivity that influences the speed of the signal. The relative difference between materials influences the reflection, which is stronger when the difference is high. One of the main influences on GPR is the dielectric difference between air and water, which is large. Disturbed soil, such as in a grave shaft or a service trench, tends to absorb higher concentrations of moisture from the surrounding undisturbed sediment through capillary action. Undisturbed sediments have different water and air concentrations relative to disturbed sediments. As the signal crosses the boundary between the two, some of it is reflected back to the receiving antenna, allowing GPR to capture the patterns of their margins. The signal is also reflected back by very high permittivity materials such as metals or large rocks. Shape of the boundary also influences the reflection, and small, reflective curved surfaces—such as metal pipes in cross-section—provide a characteristic point target hyperbolic pattern.[11] Flat metal plates produce a different result—known as a ringing pattern. Voids also create distinctive patterns. Importantly, when different refractive boundaries are close to each other, they not only reflect back to the antenna but off of each other, creating a characteristic suite of reflected patterns. Recent work from Japan, for example, suggests that GPR can distinguish between graves with or without coffins based on patterns in the reflected polarity of the signal.[12] Voids of different shapes produce characteristic patterns as well. The point here is that the geophysics of GPR are well known and the reflective effects of refraction on different kinds of subsurface patterns are well modelled and documented. You can even simulate results in software based on the geophysical principles. Our work in unmarked graves simply uses this well-established scholarship.

There are two issues that are important to note here. Geophysicists studying near surface geology typically are looking for broad planar patterns in sediments. Reflections from small objects and small planar surfaces add noise to this effort. As a result, geological geophysicists tend to filter out the resulting patterns through a process called migration. Migration filters clarify large horizontal patterns made of small objects but tend to erase the very evidence of anthropogenic patterns that archaeologists are interested in. I have heard from well-established geophysicists who think you cannot find patterns the size of graves in GPR because they essentially filter them out as part of their best-practice workflow. The second issue is that GPR is not actually identifying graves, per se. Rather, it is creating a composite pattern of reflective surfaces that together characterize a grave. Geophysicists sometimes argue that GPR cannot find graves, which is sort of true in the strictest sense.

EDITORS: This fact is what denialists try to emphasize out of context, especially to their audience of non-experts, to discount the technology and by extension all searches for unmarked burials at former residential schools that use it.

ANDREW: However, what they ignore is that GPR can, in fact, find the surfaces and contents that make up a grave. Thus, the results of GPR are interpreted as a grave from constituent arrangement of patterns of the reflected signal.

The key question that we get is, "You can map out all sorts of subsurface things; how do you know it's a grave?" That's the question that most of us who do this work focus on. I've written some papers and I've got some website guidance on how to do this. There are about twenty-three possible traits and five basic characteristics of graves that are visible in GRP results. You'll see them in a few other places. I actually had an email exchange with a retired geophysicist from the Geological Survey of Canada (GSC) who didn't believe I could do what I was doing because what we look for in the anthropogenic landscape rarely occurs in the natural landscape. If you're mapping natural geography, you do not see vertical discontinuities. They rarely occur in nature, but when you're working with human-made subsurface patterns, whether architecture, burials, et cetera, small vertical discontinuities are a common feature. Indeed, the reflections between vertical and other discontinuities create some of the most distinctive evidence of anthropogenic patterns in GPR—patterns that my colleague from the GSC had never really seen.

My point is that you can be a geophysicist and still not be particularly well attuned to this kind of application of GPR. There are a few people around the world—archaeologists typically, or geophysicists who become archaeological—who know this kind of work and publish it. But it is not a well-known subject. With a lot of these technologies, if a signal is clear, you don't need to know why; you just need to know you found a buried pipe. You and I could get together and push this device around, and if we found a pipe, you would, with no experience, be able to say there's a pipe because it's pretty obvious. It stands out as a dramatic linear feature in vertical and horizontal profiles against a background where there isn't much else. You can do an interpretation quite quickly.

Recently, I presented interim results from work at the Kuper landscape with the Penelakut Tribe. We noted that we have found almost 400 unmarked graves in GPR results at the Penelakut Cemetery, about a third each of possible, probable, and likely graves, using research and a logical matrix we had published in 2023. I've since received an email from a UBC alumni of geology who has launched a formal complaint of academic integrity against me with my employer, UBC. He is arguing that it is impossible for GPR to locate graves in cemeteries, thus I must be presenting fabricated evidence. Now, this person has not seen my results or the data but has concluded that I am a fraud based simply on the idea that the patterns I have identified using radar cannot be burials because, he assumes, GPR cannot detect burials. Leaving aside the details of why these might be burials (which I discuss below), we can ask: What else would they be? If we find a lot of patterned differences in the subsurface within a formal cemetery in rectangular shapes that form rows, most of which align with existing visible rows of graves—then what are they most likely to be? You almost don't need any geophysical understanding to see that the most likely answer is that they are graves.

The challenge then is: Why is it a grave? What are the qualities of the GPR signal that allow us to move from simply noting a pattern of difference to interpreting its nature? What are the interactions between the EM wave and the various subsurface patterns that are generating that interpretation? These issues are especially important when the signal interpretation is ambiguous, such as we might find in unmarked or clandestine graves.[13] So that's where we need to start unpacking the signal. I apologize for getting so far into the weeds, but it's important that people understand the difference between different applications of geophysics.

EDITORS: This is why we wanted to have this conversation, and we're learning a lot as well. This detailed, expert knowledge is so necessary to push back on denialist claims that the technology is sloppy, unreliable, and unprofessional.

ANDREW: There are different kinds of graves. In a historic cemetery, a grave often has a standard shape and size.[14] It will have relatively straight walls, it will have a certain depth, and it will be of a certain size in order to accommodate a human body. Typically, in historic graves, people are laid out in an extended position, so they're not flexed, as happens in some traditions. This produces a rectangular shape of about one by two metres. Because of the water effect discussed above, the grave shaft itself is usually the strongest signal from the grave: the four vertical discontinuities plus two horizontal discontinuities defining its shape. These are pretty visible boundaries in GPR, especially if you consider that when people build cemeteries, they don't just build them anywhere. They find places where the geological background is made of relatively small sediments of even particle size—not too much clay, not a lot of big boulders, not a lot of tree roots, not a lot of bedrock. Any of those things would make it hard to build a cemetery, especially if you're using hand tools, which is how most of these historic cemeteries began. These contexts are, it turns out, just the kinds of places where the GPR signal is not particularly reflective.

When we find things that are reflective, against a background that's not very noisy or reflective, it becomes relatively straightforward to identify where graves are. In historic cemeteries, GPR is a very reliable tool, partly because there's not much else in cemeteries other than graves. When the background isn't particularly reflective, the grave itself has this association of characteristics that mediate the reflection of the wave signal back to the receiving antenna. It's then able to appear in our results, which are visualizations of this reflection, so that we can identify those traits and say there is the edge of a vertical discontinuity, here's a second edge of it, it's a metre apart. If they are that close together, they often create a shape above and between the two vertical patterns caused by reflections between them. If the discontinuities are two metres apart, you can see each of them, but the shape above does not occur, since the discontinuities are too far apart to generate it.

This is why GPR can detect service trenches—there is no burial, though the service line or pipe is usually reflective. However, you can see the trench in GPR because water migrates into it because of the breaking apart of the compaction of the soil, and then the consequent absorption of water into its porous nature through capillary action. It doesn't work, by the way, in deserts because there's no water to absorb. It also doesn't work in really waterlogged environments because everything is wet to the same degree. But in temperate environments, when you've got a mix of clays, sands, and loams in places where there's seasonal water, excavations such as service trenches or grave shafts produce a result in GPR.

The challenge comes when we change some of those parameters or when we move away from any of those qualities. What if we move outside of a context that's conducive for putting in a historic cemetery like a forested landscape? You wouldn't put a cemetery in there, but maybe there's a clandestine burial. What happens if the burial shape is not vertical and rectangular but basin-shaped? What happens if it's smaller than what we expect, such as the size of a child or an infant? Are the signal patterns still going to produce positive results? It becomes more challenging, partly because of their smaller size, the change of shape, and the background signals, but they still produce a result. We have identified graves as small as infants in cemeteries. We have also seen graves that are more basin-shaped. We have identified ancestors within burial mounds—very unconventional forms of burial treatment by Western standards—and they're still visible. In all cases, GPR produces a pattern of the elements of the subsurface because of the differential reflections from boundaries between materials of different dielectric permittivity. The interpretive task is to identify and describe these and then ask which are associated into larger features such as a grave. We are in the midst of assembling enough data to evaluate correlations with statistics, which is an important next step.

In short, there are applications for this technology, even as we move outside of the most straightforward context, which is the historic cemetery. That's really where the contemporary scholarship is working. That's why most of the results that you'll hear about, including our own from Penelakut, begin with a cemetery. Then, we can move into cemeteries that are not recognized as such, including less formal spaces and ultimately clandestine spaces. That is what we did at Penelakut. We have a formal cemetery with 381 unmarked graves visible in radar. We have an informal cemetery—it was formal at one point, but it was not recorded as such—with staff from the original school back in the late nineteenth century. We found five staff members with twenty-six signals in three to four rows behind them. The last row is a little bit unclear, so three to four rows. We have what look like twenty-six potential graves in that place. Then, we have one clandestine grave where we were taken to a place where a murdered child was buried. We had a positive signal in GPR there as well.

Before GPR was applied to residential schools, it was a standard tool for mapping out cemeteries by archaeologists and other people working in cemetery management. It is the go-to technology, and it has gotten even better now with new innovations. Our approach includes the application of the data collection parameters. What should the settings be? How do you collect your data? What are the protocols of data collection? How do you filter your result to get a visualization where your interpretation is most clear? Then, what are you interpreting? What are the descriptions of the patterns in your visualized results that you can then associate with a particular geophysical pattern? The constellation of that points to a grave. This is where scholarship is at today.

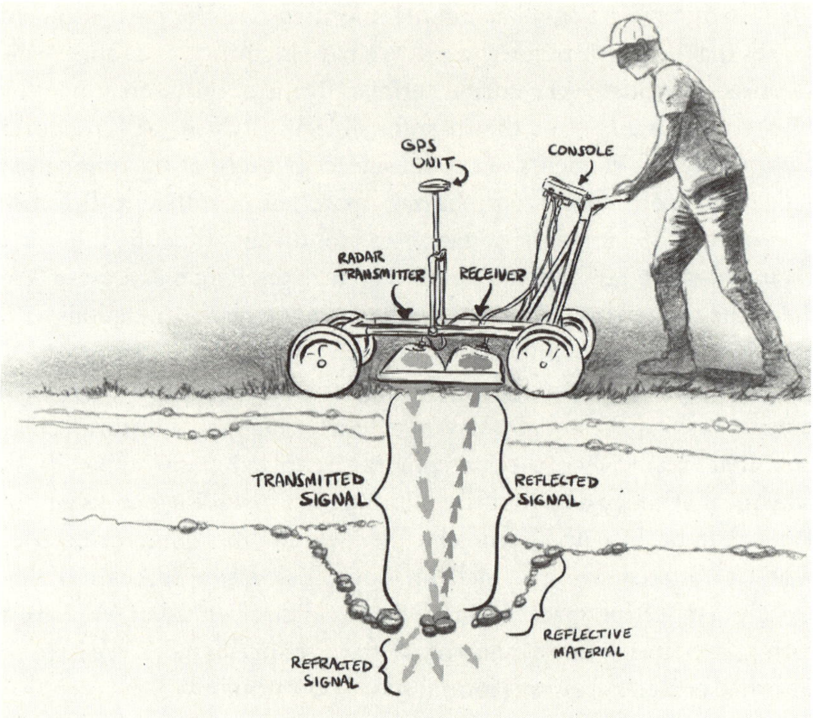

Figure 4.1. Ground-penetrating radar. Illustration by Eric Simons.

EDITORS: Thanks for this detailed and nuanced discussion of the important technology and its practical application regarding residential school deaths. There's this popular perception that you get this machine, roll it over the ground, and it shows you skeletons. With all of the nuance you've outlined, it sounds like what you're really doing is collecting another kind of incomplete evidence—similar to what Raymond Frogner was talking about in terms of the archival records in the previous chapter. Similar to archival research, then, you're looking for patterns and you're analyzing, interpreting, based on a range of data. It's very similar to what historians do, actually. The truth isn't just sitting there in an archive—you have to wade through different materials, map things out, see patterns, and interpret. We think one of the elements about your work with Penelakut—and this is certainly the case with other teams that we're working with—is that GPR and other technology is complementary. Archives on their own can show

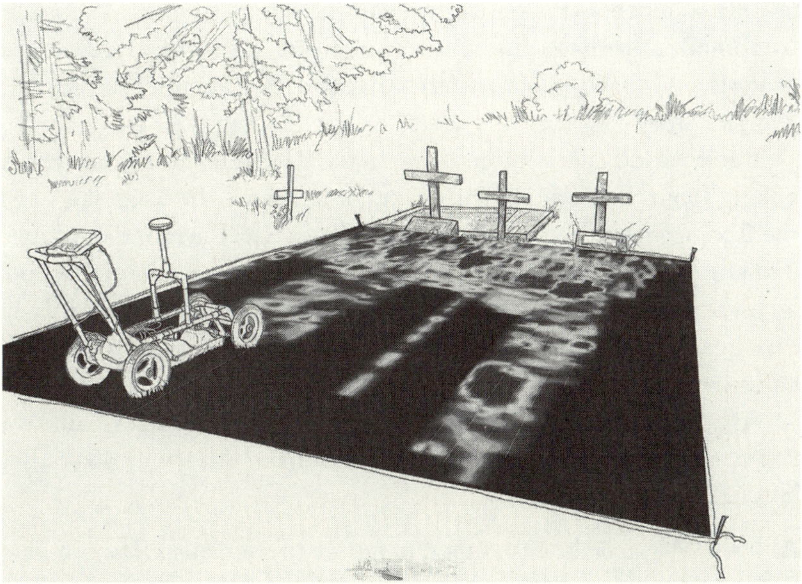

Figures 4.2 and 4.3. How ground-penetrating radar can help identify marked and potential unmarked graves in the field. Illustrations by Eric Simons.

us only so much; GPR on its own can show only so much. It's in the combination of these different technologies, forms of evidence and analysis, and drawing out patterns that then you begin to see the full, complex story.

But what denialists often want to do is exploit the nuance you're talking about to cast doubt and shake confidence in the technology and the findings regarding residential schools, just as Raymond described denialists do regarding the incomplete nature of residential school archival records. It's part of a strategy: engaging disingenuously in dialogue, in bad faith, to shift the conversation and create a counter-narrative.

As an expert using this technology in the field, can you explain how you've experienced residential school denialism? Also, why do you see it as being so harmful?

ANDREW: To be honest, I tend to ignore the denialists. I know what their purpose is, and it's not to engage in a scholarly debate. I don't mind disagreement, critique, or opposition, to be clear. But the wilful gainsaying of conclusions based on a rejection of observable truths is not really debate; that's just ideological. That's really why I haven't paid a whole lot of attention to denialists. I know they're there and they've increasingly taken an interest in my work, which is a new step for me.

My encounters with them have mostly been indirect. The Penelakut Elders Committee has not made any public announcements until recently. They did that intentionally. They also acknowledged that other communities who had released results were confronted by these denialists, and they wanted to get to a position where they felt more comfortable with the preliminary results before going public. They chose to announce the results this year (2025) partly because we now have a robust archival report, which came from Ashley Whitworth, the lead researcher of the archives. Then, we could combine that with my own ground search results to give them—not so much the wider audience, but the peers, families, and communities of Penelakut Survivors—an understanding of what we've done and some assurance that we are proceeding with this work. I haven't encountered too many denialists.

I'm familiar with some of their arguments, though. Typically, they are founded on the notion that residential school violence and trauma are somehow in question. If that's your starting point, then the conversation is largely over because we already know the answer to that. It was demonstrated in the Truth and Reconciliation Commission's *Final Report* and the alternative claims process. We've got tens of thousands of Indigenous people who have individually described their trauma, including the death of children at these places. This is supplemented now with archival work and ground searches, and they confirm the same thing. Our knowledge of the number of children who died at these schools is only rising as more work is completed and new records consulted.

I know that at Kuper, we had a number of 121 that came to us from the National Centre for Truth and Reconciliation's Memorial Register. Some of those were redundancies, and some were erroneous. After Ashley Whitworth's archival compilation and analysis, we now have a number of 171 deaths connected to the school. These numbers and this history are clear. If you want to say that they are somehow in dispute, logically you must be arguing that all of those thousands of Indigenous people are lying, that Church and State records are wrong. On what basis would you make that case? There isn't really a basis. The fact that you would suggest that an entire group of people are lying based on, for example, their race or ethnicity, well, there's a word for that, isn't there? That's a form of racism. The starting point of a denialist's logic is that we don't yet have enough information to determine the nature of this history, and that is obviously false. If you're going to advocate for that premise, you're clearly not thinking or debating in good faith. You're debating based on a premise that is unconscionable and erroneous. So why bother having that debate?

They're engaged in ad hominem attacks now. I'm on their radar, but I was ignored before. Some of my colleagues have been subjected to violence and threats. The argument that denialists often start with is not to say that our evidence or logic is wrong but that people who find the data are dishonest and incompetent. If you can say that person is an unreliable source, then everything that they have concluded becomes suspicious. But ad hominem attacks are typically not the kind of rhetorical avenues that we allow people to use in scholarly publications and academic work. If you're reviewing somebody's paper, you don't argue that they shouldn't be published because you don't like them. That would be nonsense. You are required to evaluate only the evidence they present. This line of rhetorical effort is spurious. I would also observe that in the modern era of social media and fraught ideological differences in political debates, this approach seems to be gaining traction. However, ignoring evidence and insulting people is not a robust form of scholarship.

Another avenue of denialism is a misunderstanding of the concept of ambiguity. In a scientific frame, it's part and parcel of doing research. For example, I am sure many denialists have gone in for medical tests, perhaps even for some very serious things like cancer. There's an uncertainty around that diagnosis, whether it's an X-ray, an MRI, or a blood test. Is it really cancer? We might have to do more tests. It doesn't mean the test is nonsense just because there's ambiguity. It means that sometimes these phenomena manifest themselves differently in different people, in ways that are less clear than others.

It is standard scientific method to evaluate two basic forms of uncertainty. This is not the same meaning as in the vernacular language of a mistake. Rather, it is about coming to terms with uncertainty. First, all measuring devices have a limit of precision beyond which we cannot see difference, typically half the smallest unit of resolution. A ruler with one-millimetre gradations can measure only +/- 0.5 mm. That is its measurement error. It does not mean that rulers don't work, only that there is a limit to their precision. The GPR arrays are complex instruments, but they also are fundamentally measuring devices: They measure time, polarity, and signal intensity. Each of these has a measurement error. This means that there are limits to what a GPR device can observe. However, as I noted above, adult-size graves in cemeteries are well within that measurement error. Children's graves are as well, while infant graves are getting closer to the limit but still possible to discern. Conditions influence this, so small graves near the surface can be identified with higher frequencies arrays, for example. However, the idea that GPR cannot measure the parameters of a grave is simply wrong.

The second facet of uncertainty is accuracy: how close the measurement is to reality. You can have precision without accuracy, in which you collect precise reproducible data that do not correlate with reality. For example, a precision clock set to the wrong time would be precise but inaccurate. Accuracy can also exist without precision, such as measuring time with a sundial; you know the time but only in general terms. Ideally, our measurement data are both precise and accurate, but there are always limits of uncertainty to both. The key issue is whether these limits are within the parameters of what is being identified. The analysis of GPR results from burials is clearly within these limits. We know this from the accumulated evidence of GPR results from known burials over many decades of work around the world.

The third avenue of denialist logic is a different form of the scientific concept of uncertainty: equifinality, where different processes can produce similar results. Denialists often argue that results from GPR analyses are not burials but rather some other feature that looks like a burial such as a service trench or rodent burrow. The range of variation between graves means that they will all have some similarities, generating a pattern in which most graves have a set of recognizable traits that correlate with graves and are not present or are less common in other subsurface features. Outliers will exist that are graves and have less clear signals, and we do find geological or other features that can at times have some of the traits of graves. This gives us a scale of uncertainly in which signals that have all the traits are likely to be graves, but fewer of those are probable or possible graves. The existence of outliers in a sample does not mean that the central trends are spurious. Quite the opposite: Patterns of central tendency are easily defined and quantified even in complex results. There are numerous academic publications, including those I have contributed to, that explore the traits specific to graves, especially those in historic cemeteries.[15] As I discussed above, our logic is strongest when we ask not if something is a burial but rather if the geophysical results conform to the physical parameters of the geology in traits and arrangements that correlate to burials. This is the detailed work that geophysical interpretation is based on. All GPR work does this within the population of areas where a team works. We are slowly comparing notes across different landscapes to arrive at a more complete understanding of the patterns in geologically varied locales.

The denialist strategy is to focus on the examples at the margins of uncertainty and to ignore the majority of the results that are clear. This is a form of rhetoric known as anecdotal evidence or cherry-picking. One example of something does not always reflect a trend if it is an outlier to a clear pattern of central tendency. Weather is an example that is familiar to many. I have very occasionally been caught in a sun shower—rained on when the sun is overhead. I know that this is an outlier of a correlation between cloud cover and rainfall; it generally rains when it's cloudy. Even though this has happened to me, I do not take an umbrella or raincoat with me on a sunny day—sun showers are an outlier to a well-understood association between rain and clouds. In GPR we do have some examples of ambiguous signals, but the vast majority—the statistically significant majority—are clear about the association of a constellation of specific traits and graves. Ignoring the pattern of these data is a wilful act of ignorance.

If denialists are going to argue that our evaluation of uncertainty in interpretation is evidence that the fundamental logic of the interpretative matrix is flawed, then they should similarly reject opinion polling, weather forecasts, medical diagnoses, the use of GPR in locating service trenches, et cetera. The truth is that they only ever have concerns about the evidence from graves from Indian Residential Schools; they are unconcerned about graves in historical non-Indigenous cemeteries or the application of GPR to service trenches, which is based on similar logic. Their selective opposition tells you all you need to know about the vacuousness and double standard of their views. They are picking a target to reject not because of the evidence but because it does not align with their preconceived beliefs.

EDITORS: We want to end our conversation on some hope. It's been ten years since the TRC released its *Final Report* and 94 Calls to Action. Given the rise of denialism, specifically in the last five years, and some of the backlash that we are seeing, what gives you hope for the future? What inspires you to keep doing the work that you're doing to help put truth before reconciliation and challenge denialism?

ANDREW: I suppose what gives me hope for the future is this larger recognition that this is a significant part of our history in Canada—this coming to terms by non-Indigenous Canadians about this part of our past and the landscapes that remain. That's important because the issue isn't just missing children, as important as that is; it's about colonialism, disenfranchisement, racism, and double standards. That's the larger challenge that non-Indigenous Canada needs to face. Residential schools, I think, give us a point of conversation that is important, but it is not the only point of conversation. The country seems to have arrived at the conclusion that it is Indigenous voices that need to lead this discussion, which I admire and I approve of. Nobody else has stepped in to say, "This is how we find the missing children." It's all being led by communities. Although I will relay this to you, the former Chief of Penelakut Joan Brown said, "Why do we have to do this work? We didn't build this place. Why are we the ones who have to carry the weight of finding all of these children?" There's no answer for that, except that there is nobody else. But that gives us hope, because in the process of following the guidance of the Elders and/or Indigenous communities in locating missing children from these schools, we will learn more about pathways toward the future that we aspire to—that we might, at one point, have hoped we actually had in Canada as a just society but recognize now we didn't. It gives me some hope that this is a relationship that could serve as a model for other work.

I'm also encouraged by the support we're getting from some politicians, and that it's no longer something that can be ignored. They're recognizing that it's a responsibility that they have. At our event at Penelakut recently, we didn't get any federal representatives, but we did get a lot of provincial representatives—significant voices too. I was pleased that they were humble and thoughtful about the challenges but also grateful for the work that was being led by the community, while pledging support. That's an important step that gives me hope that politicians are not tiptoeing around this, showing up only when opportune, or stepping away when it becomes challenging. At least some of them seem to be dedicated to this work, regardless of the political calculus, and that gives me hope.

I also feel that colleagues, such as yourselves, and communities doing the searching of archives and landscapes and Survivor testimony are making good progress. These are challenging issues and it will take decades to complete the search. I think that the progress we're seeing is a positive step. I have hope for those things.

Mostly, I am inspired by the Supne'luxutth Sulxwe'en. The Elders meet every month, more often usually. These are all Survivors of Kuper. They sit in a boardroom in the front of where that school was and they work together to advance the work of locating the children who went missing. They're telling their stories, helping the families who lost their children to know about them, and advancing their own well-being and that of their community and other communities. They are walking and inviting others to join them on a healing journey. I find that extremely inspirational. It's a model for being a good human in a way that I rarely see in the world. Certainly, we don't see it on the denialists' side very often, if at all. These community members are people who are willing—despite the many burdens they carry—to do good work, do the right thing for others, and show the respect and kindness and the care that we all deserve.

Notes

1 John Boileau, "Guerin Case," *The Canadian Encyclopedia, 4 January 2021,* https://thecanadianencyclopedia.ca/en/article/guerin-case.

2 Stephen Daniel, "Ground Penetrating Radar Applied: A Model for Quantifying Interpretation of Human Burials in Historical Contexts," MA thesis, University of British Columbia, 2015.

3 Alexandra Maass, "Finding the Missing: Residential School Cemeteries for Indigenous Children in Canada. A National Strategy for Identification, Recording, Preservation, and Commemoration," PhD thesis, Faculty of Humanities, Archaeology, University of Southampton, 2018.

4 Jillian Harris, Alexandra Maass, and Andrew Martindale, "Practicing Reconciliation."

5 Lovre Panđa, Ante Šiljeg, Fran Domazetović, et al., "Evaluating the Absolute Accuracy of UAV RTK Photogrammetry and LiDAR for 3D Cultural Heritage Documentation: A Comparative Study of DJI Xenmuse P1 and L1 Systems," *Applied Geomatics* (2025): 1–21. DOI:10.1007/s12518-025-00642-6.

6 Daniel Lamhonwah, Erin Seagren, and Robin Pike, "An Overview of LiDAR for Watershed Applications in British Columbia," *Water Science Series*, WSS2025-07, Province of British Columbia, Victoria, 2025.

7 I. Korost and O. Korotia, "Results of LIDAR Surveys of Archaeological Sites within the Historical and Cultural Reserve," *Archaeology and Early History of Ukraine* 54, no. 2 (2025): 180–90.

8 K.A. Corcoran, A.Z. Mundorff, D.A. White, and W.L. Emch, "A Novel Application of Terrestrial LIDAR to Characterize Elevation Change at Human Grave Surfaces in Support of Narrowing down Possible Unmarked Grave Locations," *Forensic Science International* 289 (2018): 320–28. https://doi.org/10.1016/j.forsciint.2018.05.038.

9 Daniel P. Bigman, "The Use of Electromagnetic Induction in Locating Graves and Mapping Cemeteries: An Example from Native North America," *Archaeological Prospection* 19, no. 1 (2012): 31–39. https://doi.org/10.1002/arp.1416.

10 See Victoria Berezowski, Xanthé Mallett, Justin Ellis, and Ian Moffat, "Using Ground Penetrating Radar and Resistivity Methods to Locate Unmarked Graves: A Review," *Remote Sensing* 13, no. 15 (2021): 2880, https://doi.org/10.3390/rs13152880; Christopher Gaffney, Chrys Harris, F. Pope-Carter, James Bonsall, Robert Fry, and Andrew Parkyn, "Still Searching for Graves: An Analytical Strategy for Interpreting Geophysical Data Used in the Search for 'Unmarked' Graves," *Near Surface Geophysics* 13, no. 6 (2015): 557–69, https://doi.org/10.3997/1873-0604.2015029; Dean Goodman and Salvatore Piro, *GPR Remote Sensing in Archaeology* (Springer Berlin Heidelberg, 2013); Carlos Martín Molina, Jamie Keith Pringle, Miguel Saumett, and Gethin Evans, "Geophysical Monitoring of Simulated Graves

with Resistivity, Magnetic Susceptibility, Conductivity and GPR in Colombia, South America," *Forensic Science International* 261 (2016): 106–15, DOI:10.1016/j.forsciint.2016.02.009; Armin Schmidt, Paul Linford, Neil Linford, Andrew David, Chris Gaffney, Apostolos Sarris, and Jörg Fassbinder, "EAC Guidelines for the Use of Geophysics in Archaeology: Questions to Ask and Points to Consider," *EAC Guidelines 2*, https://zenodo.org/records/10671299; Namur, Belgium, Europae Archaeologia Consilium (EAC), Association Internationale sans But Lucratif (AISBL), 2015, 73–74, 135; Immo Trinks, Alois Hinterleitner, Wolfgang Neubauer, et al., "Large-area High-resolution Ground-penetrating Radar Measurements for Archaeological Prospection," *Archaeological Prospection* 25, no. 3 (2018): 171–95, DOI:10.1002/arp.1599; William T.D. Wadsworth, Andrew Martindale, Kisha Supernant, and Colin Grier, "Sensing Houses: New Investigations of Ground Penetrating Radar at Tsimshian Villages Sites on the Northern Northwest Coast," in *Abstracts of the 18th International Conference on Ground Penetrating Radar—GPR 2020 Colorado School of Mines* (Society of Exploration Geophysicists, 2020), https://doi.org/10.1190/gpr2020-012.1; William T.D. Wadsworth, Carl-Georg Bank, Katherine Patton, Dena Doroszenko, "Forgotten Souls of the Dawn Settlement Project: A Geophysical Exploration of Unmarked Graves in Southwestern Ontario," *Historical Archaeology* 54, no. 3 (2020): 624–46, DOI:10.1007/s41636-020-00251-7; Brian Whiting, "Community-led Investigations of Unmarked Graves at Indian Residential Schools in Western Canada—Overview, Status Report and Best Practices," *Archaeological Prospection* 31, no. 4 (2024): 403–18, DOI:10.1002/arp.1914.

11 Keun Wang Lee and Joon Kyu Park, "GPR Exploration of Non-metallic Water Pipes Linked with Network RTK," *Journal of the Korea Academia-Industrial Cooperation Society* 22, no. 2 (2021): 296–301, DOI:10.5762/KAIS.2021.22.2.296.

12 Rene Lee-Yee Kwan and Wallace Wai-Lok Lai, "Archaeological Investigation of Burials Preluded by Ground Penetrating Radar and Geospatial Technologies," *Journal of Archaeological Science* 170 (2024): 106058, https://doi.org/10.1016/j.jas.2024.106058.

13 A. Juerges, J.K Pringle, J.R. Jervis, and P. Masters, "Comparisons of Magnetic and Electrical Resistivity Surveys over Simulated Clandestine Graves in Contrasting Burial Environments," *Near Surface Geophysics* 8, no. 6 (2010): 529–39, https://doi.org/10.3997/1873-0604.2010041.

14 Aidan Armstrong, Kennedy Doro, Katrina Cristino, Agathe Ribéreau-Gayon, Shari L. Forbes, Willian T.D. Wadsworth, et al., "Comparison of GPR Signals over Simulated Clandestine Graves with Domestic Pigs (Sus Scrofa domesticus) and Human Remains," *Journal of Forensic Sciences* 69 (2024): 2054–68, DOI:10.1111/1556-4029.15622.

15 Andrew Martindale, William T.D Wadsworth, Eric Simons, Brian Whiting, Colin Grier, "The Challenges of Signal Interpretation of Burials in Ground-penetrating Radar," *Archaeological Prospection* 31, no. 4 (2024): 337–51, DOI:10.1002/arp.1920.

CHAPTER 5

EXPOSING RESIDENTIAL SCHOOL DENIALISM'S TRANSNATIONAL NETWORK

by Sean Carleton, Alan Lester, Adele Perry, and Omeasoo Wahpasiw

Residential school denialism is on the rise in Canada and meaningful reconciliation is at risk.[1] After the release of the Truth and Reconciliation Commission's (TRC) *Final Report* in 2015, and especially since the Tk'emlúps te Secwépemc Nation's 2021 announcement about the location of potential unmarked graves at the former Kamloops Indian Residential School and the confirmation of additional deaths at other schools across the country, many priests, pundits, and politicians have engaged in residential school denialism.[2]

Denialists, as previous chapters have established, do not usually deny the residential school system's existence or even that it caused harm. Rather, denialists employ a disingenuous discourse that twists, distorts, and misrepresents basic facts about residential schooling to shake public confidence in truth and reconciliation efforts, defend guilty and culpable parties, and protect Canada's colonial status quo.

Denialism tends to spike at predictable times, such as the anniversary of the Kamloops announcement (27 May) and Orange Shirt Day (marked in Canada on 30 September as the National Day for Truth and Reconciliation). Indeed, this has been the case in the past several years, where there have been a number of concerning incidents of denialism—from the usual far-right publications promoting the "positives" of the genocidal Indian Residential School System to the spreading of conspiracy theories and disinformation by politicians and social influencers.[3]

In response, Indigenous writers such as Tanya Talaga and Drew Hayden Taylor, and prominent organizations such as the Union of BC Indian Chiefs, have addressed the community harms of denialism. As public figures and organizations, they stress the need for settler Canadians to confront this dangerous phenomenon if Canada is serious about its commitment to truth and reconciliation.[4]

What gets less attention, however, is residential school denialism's global connections and spread. Residential school denialism may have its origins in Canada, but it is increasingly circulating and being used around the world as part of a wider matrix of imperial apologetics—a transnational network of discourse that aims to defend the legacy of the British Empire in the metropole and former colonies.[5] In this chapter, we contend that this global dimension of residential school denialism demands greater attention. Indeed, residential school denialism must not be thought of as a nation-bound problem but rather one component of a recently reinvigorated transnational political project.

Circuits of Empire

To better understand denialism's transnational nature, it is important first to contextualize this phenomenon as a continuation of the imperial project itself. Denial and disavowal have been part of the fabric of British colonialism since the establishment of the first colony in Ireland. As historian Jane Ohlmeyer notes, "the daily reality of anglicisation was for many people extraordinarily grim, robbing them of their homes, their livelihoods, their dignity and even their lives."[6] From the very beginning, colonization was characterized by "scorched earth" tactics, meaning the destruction of the local population's means of subsistence. Famine and colonization went hand-in-hand. The seventeenth-century wars between Gaelic lords and English usurpers devastated Gaelic society, with atrocities committed on both sides. These colonial wars took the lives of some 20 percent of the Irish population during the 1640s. Oliver Cromwell's reconquest from 1649 caused up to a third more of the inhabitants to die in certain districts. At the same time, propaganda in England and Scotland extolled the virtues of Irish land for purchase. Merchant companies depicted Ireland's "plantation" as a land of milk and honey. British colonists were encouraged to improve the land, as their investment would be met with Gaelic gratitude.[7]

Over twenty million British emigrants fanned out to the settler colonies of North America, Australasia, and southern Africa between the late eighteenth and early nineteenth centuries. In their great migration, they extended the transimperial networks of communication that circulated their own justifications. When antislavery activists objected to the trafficking in British ships of some 3.1 million African captives for enslavement in the Americas, their enslavers mobilized powerful rationales. The human buyers and sellers activated their network, cultivated a West India Interest in Parliament, and lobbied friends in high places including the Royal Family. They extolled the need for African removal from the "savage continent" on the path to civilization, and, ultimately, the injustice of depriving slave owners of their human property.[8] Denial and disavowal is about far more than simple justification. It has always leveraged beneficial material support too. In this case, enslavers successfully resisted emancipation until they had persuaded Parliament to grant them a sum of twenty million pounds (around two billion pounds today), an amount equivalent to 40 percent of government revenue in 1833, in compensation.[9] Ironically, their recompense was called reparations.

In the 1930s, the heirs of the antislavery campaigners, the evangelical and paternalistic colonial philanthropists or humanitarians, condemned the violence of settler colonization in South Africa, Australia, and North America. In response, settler colonial communities mobilized and founded new propaganda networks. Newspapers sprang up in Britain, sponsored by colonial funds and ideals. Again, self-justification continued alongside requests for military, political, and economic support from the British government and people. Together, settler editors around the anglophone world conspired to justify the displacement of "irreclaimable" savages and, failing their complete removal, forced assimilation.[10]

The end of the British Empire inspired an intensive bout of denial and disavowal about its nature and effects. The 1940s and 1950s were a moment of reckoning, according to historian Stuart Ward, as apologists "employed all manner of techniques to insulate the country from overly harsh judgement, not just about the empire's evident moral shortcomings but also the wider culpability of the British people themselves."[11]

At the same time that documentary records of the empire's late colonial wars in Kenya, Malaya, Aden, and Suez were being destroyed or "displaced," British officials attempted to persuade the anticolonial leaders of newly independent colonies to remain open to British and U.S. influence rather than move into the Soviet Cold War orbit. The idea that the empire must be considered as a moral balance between the "bad" things, which anticolonial leaders knew all about, and the long-term "good" brought by railways, schools, hospitals, free trade, and good governance, was cemented in this moment, its purpose to deflect from the denial of self-determination for people of colour.[12]

The current culture war within the West, between right-wing populism and progressivism, is another moment in which imperial denial and disavowal is wielded across globally extensive networks to defend Britain's record of violent colonization and its continuation by local officials in settings such as Canada. Key intellectual participants on the right, such as Nigel Biggar, operate across a transnational Christian Nationalist sphere with ideological connections in Hungary and funding from the USA. They now insist that to question the empire's legitimacy is to weaken the democratic West from within, at a time when it needs all its strength against autocratic regimes in Russia and China. The irony, of course, is that nothing suits these regimes better than the right-wing, authoritarian populist resurgence in the West. It is no coincidence that Russia's electoral interference has been geared toward the success of culture war–oriented, nationalist, and populist right-wing parties. With its authoritarian, "antiwoke" politics and refusal to admit colonialism's racist and exploitative traits in the face of contemporary anti-racist movements like Black Lives Matter, the populist right fuels divisions within the West and undermines democracies. The West's rivals do not have to lift a finger.[13]

Culture War Connections

The old circuits of Empire, then, are being repurposed in the bitterly contested debates about history today. Current discussions are prefigured and scaffolded by previous ones, some long-standing and others more recent. These include the heated 1980s and 1990s conversations known as the "history wars." This framing nodded to the wider, ongoing "culture wars," a largely conservative backlash to the prevalence of gendered, racial, and religious voices and newly influential knowledge creation and legitimacy.[14]

The history wars played out differently in different contexts around the world, but there are important connections.[15] In Australia, debates pivoted on questions of colonial violence, Indigenous loss, and settler agency and complicity. In 1999, historian Ann Curthoys explained that a generation of national leaders were raised on histories where "the conflict between settlers and indigenous people in the past was elided, suppressed, forgotten, or viewed as so long ago that we in the present have no connection with those people or those events."[16] A growing awareness of Indigenous histories, including of child removal and incarceration, held real power to destabilize national narratives. The response was a fevered campaign against what became known as "Black Armband" history.[17]

Canada had its version of these history wars, but they had little to say about colonialism, dispossession, or Indigenous Peoples. The hot-button issues were different, and the chronologies stretched into the 2000s. In 1992, Michael Bliss linked historians' interest in diverse histories and identities to an imperilled Canadian nation. His analysis included a brief nod to "the aboriginal or native people of Canada" and a "Manitoba representative" who brought down a recent attempt at constitutional reform. In this brief note, Bliss left Anishinninew Manitoba Member of the Legislative Assembly Elijah Harper entirely unnamed.[18] Six years later, historian Jack Granatstein's polemic book *Who Killed Canadian History?* gave even less space to these histories. In a chapter on "Multicultural Mania," Granatstein included "that the Indians were victims of white genocide" as one item on a long list of interpretative sins. The book also included a footnote mention of the federal government's 1998 apology for the Indian Residential School system, made as the book went to press.[19] The revised edition of *Who Killed Canadian History?* was published in 2007, a year after the Indian Residential Schools Settlement Agreement, which called for the creation of the Truth and Reconciliation Commission. This version of Granatstein's book did not include a footnote to Indian Residential Schools.[20]

The history wars that occurred in Canada in the 1990s and 2000s left historians mainly cold, and continue to do so.[21] The most visible combatants have not been major voices in residential school denialism, though one—the late James Rodger (J.R.) Miller—is a signatory to the

2021 open letter about the Canadian historical profession and what it called the "Genocide Myth."[22] But Canada's versions of the history wars did produce a surprisingly durable discursive language and argumentative posture. The combatants voiced outrage and claimed they were bravely telling truths in the face of powerful threats to the nation and the historical profession. These modes of dissemination were repurposed in the 2010s, especially immediately after the release of the TRC's *Final Report* in 2015, to defend Canada's honour and reputation. Canada's history warriors had a new target: the stories Indigenous people told about residential schools, and those who believed them. While the history wars that occurred in Canada in the 1990s and 2000s were of little interest outside Canada's borders, today's imperial apologists find homegrown residential school denialism a useful part of their transnational struggle to redeem the Empire, protect its spoils, and weaponize imperial heritage as a political tool.[23] Building on debates from the past, residential school denialism has become a key part of the recent surge in imperial apologetics across the former British Empire.

The Truth About Empire

Exposing residential school denialism's transnational network is one contribution of a chapter we (Carleton, Perry, Wahpasiw) have written about the manipulation of Canadian and Indigenous histories by imperial apologists for a new collection, *The Truth About Empire: Real Histories of the British Empire*, which is edited by our fellow co-author (Lester).[24] As a team comprised of Indigenous (Wahpasiw), non-Indigenous/Canadian (Carleton and Perry), and British (Lester) historians, we worked together to challenge the misuse of Indigenous and Canadian history. *The Truth About Empire* brings together the expertise of historians from different parts of the former Empire to confront the tactics of denial and disavowal used by apologists generally and, as an example, specifically Nigel Biggar's bestselling book, *Colonialism: A Moral Reckoning*.[25]

As Lester explains in *The Truth About Empire*'s introduction, "the culture war is about politics rather than historical understanding."[26] Moreover, he explains, "For its most avid participants, interpretations of the past are simply a weapon to be wielded in a struggle between progressive and reactionary philosophies and instincts."[27] In gathering subject experts "intent on telling the truth based on the evidence we have analyzed and debated over many years," *The Truth About Empire* marshals a defence not of the imperial past but of the expertise of imperial historians.[28]

Yet, the power of the collection, at least in our eyes, is that we do not simply assert our expertise as the truth because we say so. Instead, we *do* the work of historians. We reveal how Biggar's argumentation (like imperial apologetics generally) is flawed. Biggar depends on fanciful interpretations about the colonial past to guide public perceptions. We base our analyses on careful examinations of records generated at the time and preserved in oral history, written records kept in archives, and published accounts that draw out nuance, complexity, and historical understanding. This may hold less appeal to a popular audience than the easy comforts offered by right-wing writers and pundits. Individual and collective apologists profit from producing books, articles, and podcasts that soothe the conflicted consciences of many during another period of imperial reckoning. Our nuanced work certainly generates less clickbait revenue for the "war on woke," but it is important to stick up for the truth about empire nonetheless.[29]

Residential School Denialism's Transnational Network

Biggar's recent efforts are a good example of how apologists outside of Canada *use* residential school denialism as part of their efforts to justify British imperialism on the whole. As Lester makes clear, cherry-picking, or the selective use of evidence to misrepresent the complex truth, is a key tactic of apologists. It is easy to see how writers like Biggar—in ways similar to those examined by Frogner in Chapter 3—cherry-pick the history and historiography of residential schooling for the purposes of justification.[30]

In *Colonialism*, Biggar turns settler colonialism, as described and explored by Canadian and Indigenous scholars, into a beneficent movement. Biggar draws on dubious and often discredited sources, such as the work of right-wing strategist Thomas Flanagan and the pseudohistory magazine *The Dorchester Review*. With these questionable sources as the foundation for his work, Biggar makes a number of problematic arguments. For example, he suggests that Métis resistance leader Louis Riel recognized a logical rationale for colonization. A recurring tactic of Biggar's and other apologists is to discount and discredit Indigenous experience and epistemologies. Moreover, he selectively engages with

Canada's colonial history, leaving out important aspects that do not fit his narrative. The long history of the Hudson's Bay Company, for instance, receives no mention in *Colonialism*. Finally, Biggar defends Indian Residential Schools as "humanitarian" institutions.[31]

In regards to residential schooling specifically, Biggar draws on right-wing sources to discredit the Truth and Reconciliation Commission's *Final Report*. The TRC found the Indian Residential School system was genocidal. In response, Biggar relies upon and cherry-picks from one book, J.R. Miller's *Shingwauk's Vision*, to stress the so-called positive aspects of the system. Given Biggar's strenuous reliance on Miller's work, it is instructive to pause to examine *Shingwauk's Vision* as a source more carefully.

Miller published *Shingwauk's Vision: A History of Native Residential Schools* in 1996 at a time when many Canadians were just beginning to learn about the system. Miller was born in 1943, and hired in 1979 as a professor of history at the University of Saskatchewan. His career focused on "Native-Newcomer Relations" and often explained Indigenous perspectives to a non-Indigenous audience. In *Shingwauk's Vision*, one of the first peer-reviewed works on the residential school system, Miller sought to weigh responsibility for Indian Residential Schools out amongst Indigenous leaders and their "vision" and those of Church representatives and government agencies. A mere three years later, John S. Milloy, then professor of Native Studies at Trent University, published *A National Crime: The Canadian Government and the Residential School System*. These two books, ostensibly telling the same history, reveal divergent theses. Both books arrived several years after the revelations of sexual abuse at Indian Residential Schools were shared publicly for the first time by then–Manitoba Regional Assembly of First Nations Chief Phil Fontaine.[32] The year 1996 also saw the conclusion and publication of the *Final Report* of the Royal Commission on Aboriginal Peoples, an effort Milloy lent his expertise to as a researcher and historian.

Although it was not readily apparent at the time, *Shingwauk's Vision*, now a work heavily relied upon by residential school denialists, laid out its mission in more than title.[33] In his book, Miller first outlines his lukewarm assessment of the residential school's genocidal intent, which he later expanded.[34] He dismisses his acknowledgement of "European cultural aggression" with the innocence of the system, which "gradually bec[a]me the vehicle of the newcomers' attempts to refashion and culturally eliminate the first inhabitants' way of life and identity."[35] These euphemisms—"cultural aggression," "gradually," "refashion," and "culturally eliminate"—have given residential school denialists a vocabulary to downplay and minimize the harms and crimes of the system. In contrast, Milloy's book clearly argues that "the system, was, even as a concept, abusive."[36] Indigenous Peoples knew this, as did many "newcomers." The evidence of this is not hard to find, much of it cited within both Miller's and Milloy's books, such as the 1907 report to the Department of Indian Affairs by medical official Dr. Peter Henderson Bryce, which laid out many of the systemic problems with residential schooling in its initial phase. Frustrated that his report was mostly ignored, Bryce self-published his findings along with damning correspondence with department officials to reveal governmental indifference to student suffering. Bryce called the residential school system "a national crime." Biggar, in his evaluation of the system, chooses not to engage with Milloy's work, or Bryce's report, but instead relies exclusively on his own particular take on Miller's more sympathetic interpretation. This allows him to deny and disavow the full truth about residential schooling, especially as told by Survivors themselves.

Canadian historians will, of course, see through Biggar's flimsy argumentation for what it is: disingenuous source engagement that minimizes what scholars agree—despite a handful of detractors—was a genocidal school system.[37] Even Miller's work, which denies the genocidal *intent* of the system and stresses certain positive aspects, acknowledges the residential school system's overall destructive consequences for Indigenous Peoples. Quite simply, *Shingwauk's Vision* does not support Biggar's assertion that residential schools were "humanitarian" institutions. The issue is that Biggar's UK audience is not likely to pick up on the misrepresentation of the history and historiography in Canada, and his ideas are spreading as legitimate knowledge rather than a repackaging of dubious and discredited denialism that must be refuted.

Biggar has doubled down on denialism in even more recent writing.[38] Worse, he has moved from a simple misrepresentation of scholarly work to an open embrace of far-right, conspiratorial publications on residential schooling. In a 2024 op-ed for the UK (United Kingdom) weekly magazine *The Spectator*, Biggar weighed into the discourse on Empire again and invoked the positives of residential schooling as the crescendo of his argument. For his evidence, he references the book *Grave Error: How the Media Misled Us (and the Truth about Residential Schools)*. Biggar does not inform his readers that, in Canada, *Grave Error* has been discredited by experts as right-wing propaganda.[39] Among many falsehoods, the book promotes the debunked "mass grave hoax" conspiracy theory addressed more fully in Chapter 7.[40] *Grave Error* is not a peer-reviewed book; the majority of authors are not scholars; there are no residential school historians included; and there is not a single First Nations author included. Nevertheless, Biggar draws on the book's clumsy argumentation to cast doubt on deaths in residential schools and thereby minimize their hurt and harm. Specifically, he employs a discursive sleight of hand used in the book: insisting that not one "murdered" child has been proven, strategically changing the narrative/moving the goalposts to deliberate killings and murder rather than the TRC-documented neglect, abuse, disease, and death in the institutions.[41]

Self-published works such as *Grave Error* find an audience happy to consume denialism as legitimate and comforting discourse. Given Biggar's receptivity and amplification of residential school denialism, some people on the far right in Canada have tried to give him a larger platform. Biggar has been interviewed for far-right publications and podcasts and he has given a series of invited talks to spread his message further.[42]

In 2025, Biggar offered his most detailed engagement with residential school denialism to date, this time to a mainstream Canadian audience. In an op-ed for the right-leaning newspaper *National Post* subsequently republished as a chapter in the sequel to *Grave Error*, *Dead Wrong: How Canada Got the Residential School Story So Wrong*, Biggar distills many of the core denialist talking points to argue that "residential schools were no 'atrocity.' Just look at the evidence."[43] In classic cherry-picking fashion, drawing on all of the tactics established in the book so far, Biggar twists evidence and nuance in favour of defending the Indian Residential School System. In doing so, he follows the denialist playbook carefully: He cites Miller to suggest that Indigenous leaders asked for the system; he contends students were not forced to attend the schools; he downplays the number of deaths in the schools and minimizes their causes; he defends John A. Macdonald against accusations of racism; he promotes *Grave Error* and argues that the system was not genocide or an "atrocity"; and he suggests that the people who most need a reckoning are not the Church and State officials who oversaw and maintained the system for over 100 years but rather those who are guilting Canadians into caring about truth and reconciliation today by pushing "the 'atrocity' fabrication."

Biggar's regurgitation of the same old denialist charges—already debunked in this and other chapters—demonstrates that the spread of misinformation and disinformation about residential schooling is no longer a provincial, local matter; it is a global one. The problem, however, is bigger than Biggar. His work is but one example of the dangers of residential school denialism's transnational network. Culture warriors looking for new ways to defend the British Empire, such as those associated with the UK group that Biggar co-founded, History Reclaimed, eagerly consume and promote residential school denialism created in Canada. They repurpose denialism and use it to stress the Empire's beneficent and humanitarian nature. Ultimately, they are at "war," a war to resist an imperial reckoning and refuse calls for reparations and reconciliation.[44]

It is important to note, as we reveal residential school denialism's broader transnational connections, that there is also connective tissue that links this denialism to other issues and approaches that intersect with the global far-right, including anti-feminist and anti-trans advocacy. The vociferous dismissal of *Reclaiming Power and Place*, the 2019 final report of the National Inquiry into Missing and Murdered Indigenous Women and Girls, and Elon Musk's recent mocking of Canada's gendered genocide on social media are two examples.[45] In terms of anti-trans rhetoric, historian Jarvis Brownlie explained in 2024 that the "open assault on trans people's human rights has begun much later in Canada, but it is here now."[46] Frances Widdowson, for example, clearly hangs her hat on two "issues": delegitimizing Indigenous Peoples and what she calls an "objection to 'progressive' gender dogmas."[47] She shares this particular ground with a global community that includes Biggar, who places himself among the "gender-critical."[48] The "gender critical" oeuvre both centres gender and exceeds it, tethering a defence of supposedly biological sex to a set of anxieties that cluster around civilization, authority, and race. In 2025, Widdowson's public presentations ping-ponged between attacking recent research on residential schools and undermining the view that there are more than two legitimate ways of living with gender. Likewise, Biggar's responses to recent scholarship on British imperial history gathers steam from his disapproval of feminist, trans, and queer readings of gender. Biggar's 2026 attack on teaching at one UK university leads with an anonymized email reportedly from a student "in mild despair." The unnamed student encountered critiques of "Eurocentric and cisgendered" knowledge, openness to a "queer and trans lens," and frequent use of the word "decolonisation." "We are doomed," they declared.[49] The way that anti-trans and anti-gender rhetoric circulates alongside denialism's transnational network brings us back to a long-standing contention in feminist scholarship, namely the need to see gender, sexuality, and intimacy as constitutive of empire. Unrestrained bodies are a direct threat to Empire's operation and legacy. These interconnections deserve greater study.

Truth and Justice Before Reconciliation

As this chapter demonstrates, residential school denialism is no longer restricted to Canada. It circulates as part of a transnational network used globally to shape international opinion in opposition to access to knowledge and social justice. It is also linked to a range of other issues, including about gender and particularly trans and queer lives. Putting truth before reconciliation, as the TRC stressed, is thus no longer a domestic issue but rather an international one as well with connections to other issues. This means that new transnational tools and strategies—as the recent *Final Report* by Kimberly Murray, the Special Interlocutor for Missing Children and Unmarked Graves and Burial Sites associated with Residential Schools recently made clear—are desperately needed to combat the rise of residential school denialism.[50] Indeed, Murray makes clear (as she reiterates in Chapter 13) that governments, Churches, institutions, and Canadians have legal, moral, and ethical obligations to confront denialism as part of the implementation of an Indigenous-led Reparations Framework for Truth, Accountability, Justice, and Reconciliation. The truth will set us free, and that includes everyone. We must have truth—at home and abroad—before reconciliation.

Notes

1 See Sinclair and Carleton, "Residential School Denialism Is on the Rise"; Forester, "Residential School Deniers, White Supremacists Biggest Barrier to Reconciliation Says Murray Sinclair." An earlier version of this chapter appeared as Sean Carleton, Alan Lester, Adele Perry, and Omeasoo Wahpasiw, "Exposing Residential School Denialism's Transnational Network," *Active History*, 10 December 2024, https://activehistory.ca/blog/2024/12/10/exposing-residential-school-denialisms-transnational-network/.

2 Justice and Carleton, "Truth Before Reconciliation"; Ashley Joannou, "At Least 55 Children Died or Disappeared at Residential School Near Williams Lake, B.C.: Report," *Global News*, 12 October 2024, https://globalnews.ca/news/10809465/williams-lake-residential-school-remains/; Brett Forester, "Coroner's Probe Finds 220 Additional Deaths at Ontario Residential Schools," *CBC News*, 2 December 2024, https://www.cbc.ca/news/indigenous/coroner-ontario-residential-schools-investigation-1.7396884.

3 See, for example, Cheryl Chan, "BC Election: Conservative Candidate Under Fire Again, This Time over Residential Schools," *Vancouver Sun*, 11 October 2024, https://vancouversun.com/news/local-news/bc-election-conservative-candidate-under-fire-again-this-time-over-residential-schools.

4 Tanya Talaga, "Canada Must Stand Against Residential School Denialism," *Globe and Mail*, 10 October 2024, https://www.theglobeandmail.com/opinion/article-canada-must-stand-against-residential-school-denialism/; Drew Hayden Taylor, "Opinion: Residential-School Denialists Are Adding Insult to Injury," *TVO Today*, 9 October 2024, https://www.tvo.org/article/opinion-residential-school-denialists-are-adding-insult-to-injury.

5 Sathnam Sanghera, "Imperial Nostalgia Has Become So Extreme," *The Guardian*, 8 June 2024, https://www.theguardian.com/books/article/2024/jun/08/imperial-nostalgia-has-become-so-extreme-sathnam-sanghera-on-the-conflict-surrounding-colonial-history.

6 Ohlmeyer, *Making Empire*, 35–36.

7 Montano, *The Roots of English Colonialism in Ireland.*

8 Hall, *Lucky Valley.*

9 Draper, *The Price of Emancipation.*

10 Lester, "British Settler Discourse and the Circuits of Empire."

11 Ward, "No End of a Reckoning," 253.

12 Linstrum, "Escape From Empire."

13 Lester, *Deny and Disavow.*

14 See Tony Taylor and Robert Guyver, eds., *History Wars and the Classroom: Global Perspectives* (Information Age Publishing, 2012).

15 On these connections see, for example, Michel-Rolph Trouillot, *Silencing the Past: Power and the Production of History* (Beacon Press, 1995); David B. MacDonald, "Canada's History Wars: Indigenous Genocide and Public Memory in the United States, Australia, and Canada," *Journal of Genocide Research* 71, no. 4 (2015): 411–31.

16 Curthoys, "Expulsion, Exodus and Exile," 14–15.

17 Curthoys, 17.

18 Michael Bliss, "Privatizing the Mind: The Sundering of Canadian History, the Sundering of Canada," *Journal of Canadian Studies/Review d'Attitudes Canadiennes* 26, no. 4 (Winter 1991): 16.

19 Jack L. Granatstein, *Who Killed Canadian History?* (HarperCollins, 1998), 94.

20 Jack L. Granatstein, *Who Killed Canadian History?* rev. ed. (Phyllis Bruce Books, 2007).

21 See, for instance, Ruth Sandwell, "'We Were Allowed to Disagree, Because We Couldn't Agree on Anything': Seventeen Voices in the Canadian Debates over History Education," in *History Wars and the Classroom: Global Perspectives*, ed. Tony Taylor and Robert Guyver (Information Age Publishing, 2012); Tom Peace, "No One Killed Canadian History: It Is Time to Move On," *Active History*, 2 January 2024, https://activehistory.ca/blog/2024/01/02/no-one-killed-canadian-history-it-is-time-to-move-on/.

22 Open Letter, "Historians Rally vs. 'Genocide' Myth," *Dorchester Review* (12 August 2021): https://www.dorchesterreview.ca/blogs/news/historians-rally-vs-genocide-myth?.

23 Charlotte Lydia Riley, "Battleground in the Culture Wars," *New Lines Magazine*, 5 July 2024, https://newlinesmag.com/essays/britains-imperial-past-has-become-a-battleground-in-the-culture-wars/.

24 Lester, ed., *The Truth About Empire*.

25 Nigel Biggar, *Colonialism: A Moral Reckoning* (William Collins, 2023).

26 Lester, *The Truth About Empire*, 11.

27 Lester, 11.

28 Lester, 15.

29 On the profitability of promoting residential school denialism, see Barbara Kay, "Success of Residential School Book Shows Writers Don't Need Big Publishers," *National Post*, 28 January 2024, https://nationalpost.com/opinion/barbara-kay-success-of-residential-schools-book-shows-writers-dont-need-big-publishers.

30 Lester, "The British Empire in the Culture War."

31 Perry, Carleton, and Wahpasiw, "The Misuse of Indigenous and Canadian History."

32 See "Phil Fontaine's 1990 Account of Physical and Sexual Abuse at Residential School," *CBC* (Archives), 29 October 1990, https://www.cbc.ca/player/play/video/1.3332787.

33 James Pew, "The Frances Widdowson Interview and the CBC Documentary on 'Residential School Denialism,'" *Woke Watch Canada Newsletter*, 20 February 2023, https://wokewatchcanada.substack.com/p/the-frances-widdowson-interview-and.

34 See J.R. Miller, "Genocide, Macdonald and Canadian History," *National Post*, 8 January 2021, https://nationalpost.com/opinion/j-r-miller-genocide-macdonald-and-canadian-history.

35 Miller, *Shingwauk's Vision*, 10.

36 Milloy, *A National Crime*, 57.

37 See Miller, *Shingwauk's Vision*. On the matter of genocide see, for example, Woolford, *This Benevolent Experiment*; Carleton and Woolford, "Ignore Debaters and Denialists, Canada's Treatment of Indigenous Peoples Fits the Definition of Genocide."

38 Nigel Biggar, "History Lessened: Who Gets to Decide How We See the Past?" *The Spectator*, 12 June 2024, https://nigelbiggar.uk/2024/06/13/history-lessened-who-gets-to-decide-how-we-see-the-past/.

39 Richard Butler, "This Is a Worrying Book," *British Columbia Review*, 2 July 2024, https://thebcreview.ca/2024/07/02/2216-butler-champion-flanagan/.

40 Sean Carleton and Reid Gerbrandt, "We Fact-Checked Residential School Denialists and Debunked Their 'Mass Grave Hoax' Theory," *The Conversation*, 17 October 2023, https://theconversation.com/we-fact-checked-residential-school-denialists-and-debunked-their-mass-grave-hoax-theory-213435.

41 C.P. Champion and Tom Flanagan, eds., *Grave Error: How the Media Misled Us (and the Truth About Residential Schools)* (True North and Dorchester Books, 2023), 10. For more of this kind of rhetorical strategy, see Alan Lester, "The Right Wing Culture War and the Refusal to Listen," *Blog*, 19 November 2024, https://alanlester.co.uk/blog/the-right-wing-culture-war-and-the-refusal-to-listen/.

42 See, for example, Peter Shawn Taylor, "Reckoning with Canada's Colonial Past: In Conversation with Nigel Biggar," *C2C*, 6 April 2023, https://c2cjournal.ca/2023/04/reckoning-with-canadas-colonial-past-in-conversation-with-nigel-biggar/; "Was Colonialism All Bad? Nigel Biggar's Surprising Insights," *Nuanced with Aaron Pete*, 2024, YouTube, https://www.youtube.com/watch?v=lTwYWAa5gqI; Macdonald-Laurier Institute, "An Honest Conversation About Colonialism: Nigel Biggar," 2025, YouTube, https://www.youtube.com/watch?v=ERIIpS3sD7o.

43 Nigel Biggar, "Residential Schools Were No 'Atrocity': Just Look at the Evidence," *National Post*, 2 April 2025, https://nationalpost.com/opinion/nigel-biggar-residential-schools-were-no-atrocity-just-look-at-the-evidence. The article was republished in C.P. Champion and Tom Flanagan, eds., *Dead Wrong: How Canada Got the Residential School Story So Wrong* (True North and Dorchester Books, 2025), 164–171.

44 See, for example, "'Astonishing Bit of Fake News' Exposed in Canada," *Sky News Australia*, 1 February 2022, YouTube, https://www.youtube.com/watch?v=egbXE18omy0; "Indigenous Residential Schools—Frances Widdowson," *History Reclaimed*, 23 May 2023, YouTube, https://www.youtube.com/watch?v=pR_YTiwlN5I; Matt Walsh, "The Newest and Most Shameless Hoax to Demonize Christians," 21 August 2023, YouTube, https://www.youtube.com/watch?v=yZ5qHwxDM50.

45 See *Reclaiming Power and Place: The Final Report of the National Inquiry into Missing and Murdered Indigenous Women and Girls* (2019), https://www.mmiwg-ffada.ca/final-report/; "What is MMIWG2SLGBTQQIA+: Canadian Acronym Sparkes Online Frenzy," *Newsweek*, 9 April 2026, https://www.newsweek.com/mmiwg2slgbtqqia-meaning-canada-explained-11806539.

46 Jarvis Brownlie, "Organized Transphobia and the University," *At the Forks*, 3, no. 1 (2024): 3, https://ojs.lib.umanitoba.ca/index.php/forks/article/view/950.

47 Frances Widdowson, "The Campus Trans Diktat: No Debate, No Dissent – And No Jokes," *Quillette*, 6 September 2022, https://quillette.com/2022/09/06/for-campus-pronoun-puritans-the-rules-are-no-debate-no-dissent-and-no-jokes/.

48 Nigel Biggar, "Dissent Is Not Hatred: We Must Resist the Idea that Disagreement with Modish Believes Is Reducible to Ill-feeling," *The Critic*, 17 April 2024, https://thecritic.co.uk/dissent-is-not-hatred/. On "gender critical" thinking, see Judith Butler, *Who's Afraid of Gender? Canadian Edition* (Knopf Canada, 2024) esp. Chapter 5.

49 Nigel Biggar, "The University of Sussex Must Stop Force-feeding Students Bad History," *The Spectator,* 20 February 2026, https://www.spectator.com.au/2026/02/the-university-of-sussex-must-stop-force-feeding-students-bad-history/. See Lester's response, "Smearing Sussex (and Me): Responding to Nigel Biggar's Latest Attack in *The Spectator,*" 27 February 2026, https://alanlester.co.uk/blog/smearing-sussex-and-me-responding-to-nigel-biggars-latest-attack-in-the-spectator/.

50 Kimberly Murray, *Upholding Sacred Obligations: Reparations for Missing and Disappeared Indigenous Children and Unmarked Burials in Canada*, 2024, 2 vols., https://osi-bis.ca/osi-resources/reports/.

CHAPTER 6

CONFRONTING RESIDENTIAL SCHOOL DENIALISM IN CANADIAN CLASSROOMS

by Lindsay Gibson and James Miles

As demonstrated in this book and in several recent publications, residential school denialism is growing at an alarming rate.[1] While residential school denialism has its origins in Canada, it is, as the previous chapter made clear, increasingly being taken up by a transnational network of imperial apologists who defend the legacy of the British Empire.[2] Historical denialism has become a transnational phenomenon as the result of increased culture wars, globalization, mass migration, and the rise of global media. It can also be seen as a backlash to the "age of apology,"[3] where states, public institutions, and other organizations have engaged in processes of truth telling, acknowledgement, memorialization, and the provision of material and/or symbolic reparations to the victims of injustice.[4] These public responses to historical injustices have caused grievances and resentment among those who fear a loss of privileges and/or others gaining advantages, which is a strong motivator for historical denialism.[5]

Given the surge of residential school denialism in public discourse, it is not surprising that it has also made its way into schools. In recent years there have been several news stories about school assignments and tests that ask students to respond to questions focused on the positive aspects of residential schools, a talking point frequently used by residential school denialists.[6] For example, Bambi Bertholet contacted the superintendent of the Hanover School Division in Steinbach,

Manitoba, after a friend's daughter was given a take-home assignment that asked them to "make a list of what you think are two positive and two negative effects of residential schools."[7] Similarly, a Mi'kmaw student from the L'sitkuk First Nation in Nova Scotia was enrolled in a grade ten English correspondence course and was asked to read an article, write a personal response, and create a chart based on the article that listed the "benefits" and disadvantages of being placed in a residential school.[8]

Residential school denialism has important consequences for teaching and learning about the history of Indian Residential Schools (IRS) and Canadian history more generally, and it poses a significant barrier to truth and reconciliation processes in Canada.[9] The *Final Report* of the Truth and Reconciliation Commission of Canada (TRC) identified education as "the key to reconciliation" and called for changes in order to "remedy the gaps in historical knowledge that perpetuate ignorance and racism."[10] Additionally, the TRC's Calls to Action addressed federal, provincial, and territorial governments to make K–12 curriculum and learning resources about the history and legacy of residential schools and Indigenous Peoples in Canadian history, and to share "information and best practices on teaching curriculum related to residential schools and Aboriginal history."[11] If left unaddressed, residential school denialism has the potential to distort students' understanding of the history of residential schools and Canadian history more broadly and undermine truth and reconciliation efforts. The challenge for teachers and students is to understand what residential school denialism is so they can identify it and know how to respond to it when they encounter it.

In this chapter we, as non-Indigenous educators committed to truth and reconciliation, add to current definitions of residential school denialism by describing the techniques and strategies that residential school denialists commonly use and providing illustrative examples. We then describe five *pedagogical* strategies for addressing residential school denialism in schools—detect, debunk, disregard, debate, and deconstruct—and discuss their strengths and limitations.

What Is Residential School Denialism?

As noted in the Introduction by Sean Carleton and Niigaan Sinclair, defining residential school denialism is complicated because the line between historical denialism and legitimate historical revisionism is somewhat blurry. Historical denialism, which is also referred to as historical negationism, is the falsification, trivialization, or distortion of the historical record for ideological and political purposes.[12] Historical revisionism, on the other hand, is the reinterpretation of orthodox or accepted scholarly historical narratives based on new facts, evidence, questions, methodological frameworks, or analysis.[13] Closely related to denialism is pseudohistory, which gives the appearance of scholarly expertise, including primary sources, footnotes, citations, and bibliographies, but has an explicit political agenda and purposefully intends to deceive readers by appearing scholarly and rational.[14] Both denialism and pseudohistory attempt to deceive people for ideological and political reasons by falsifying, trivializing, or distorting history, but pseudohistory attempts to give the appearance of scholarly expertise, whereas denialism usually does not.

Berber Bevernage describes three broad types of denialism that are helpful for understanding residential school denialism: literal denial, interpretive denial, and implicatory denial.[15] Literal denial is the most obvious type and challenges the facticity of events. For example, claiming that Indigenous children received a good education at residential schools is an example of literal denial. Interpretive denial does not involve denial of the facts but aims to revise established interpretations by changing words, introducing new words, and using euphemisms. Refusing to acknowledge that residential schools constituted a genocide or referring to residential schools as boarding schools are examples of interpretive denial that downplay the significance and scope of the harms experienced by Indigenous children. Implicatory denial focuses on the denial of present-day ethical implications and responsibilities to respond to a historical wrong. Implicatory denial does not challenge the facticity or interpretation of events or actions, but denies responsibility for responding to the implications of the event or action in the present or future. For example, implicatory denialism might involve acknowledging that students experienced harms and abuses in residential schools but that contemporary Canadians have no responsibility to redress or respond because the harms were perpetrated by governments and people from a long time ago. They might also argue that what happened in the past has no relationship to the present, and Survivors just need to move on.

As established by Daniel Heath Justice and Sean Carleton, residential school denialism does not involve "the outright denial of the Indian Residential School system's existence, but rather the rejection or misrepresentation of basic facts about residential schooling to undermine truth and reconciliation efforts."[16] Instead, Justice and Carleton argue that denialists use an array of rhetorical strategies, arguments, and fallacies, including the misrepresentation of basic facts, to obscure the truth about Canada's IRS system, undermine truth and reconciliation efforts, protect the status quo, and defend guilty and culpable parties.[17] If we use Bevernage's typology of the three types of denialism, Justice and Carleton's definition suggests that residential school denialism features more interpretive and implicatory denialism than literal denialism.

We provide two examples to illustrate residential school denialism and pseudohistory. On 30 January 2025, the *Canadian Encyclopedia* published two editorials commissioned to provide "sharply different views" about the ongoing debate about Sir John A. Macdonald and his government's approach to Indigenous Peoples in Canada.[18] The two editorials—"John A. Macdonald Was No Friend to Indigenous Peoples" by Niigaan Sinclair and Sean Carleton, and "A Few Facts Every Canadian Should Know about Sir John A Macdonald" by Greg Piasetzki—provide completely contradictory conclusions about the intents and consequences of Macdonald's Indigenous policies, his purposes for creating residential schools, and the degree to which the residential school system can be considered a genocide.

Sinclair and Carleton's central argument is that "the historical record is clear: Macdonald may have had Indigenous friends, but he was no friend to Indigenous peoples." They maintain that Macdonald saw Indigenous Peoples "who insisted on their sovereignty and nationhood" as a barrier to "Canada's development as a settler capitalist society" and enacted policies that attempted to "erase and eliminate autonomous Indigenous nations." This included making Indigenous people wards of the Canadian state, seizing and settling Indigenous lands for resource extraction, and enacting "genocidal polices" such as the Indian Residential School system, "starving resistant First Nations on the Prairies into political submission," and banning Indigenous cultures and ceremonies like the Potlatch and Sundance in 1884.

In the second editorial, Greg Piasetzki, an intellectual property lawyer who is not an expert in Canadian history or the history of residential schools, argues, "An objective assessment of Macdonald's record shows that, far from engaging in genocide, his policies likely saved more Indigenous lives than those of any other prime minister." Piasetzki acknowledges that "more recently" Macdonald's "reputation has come under attack" because of his "alleged mishandling of Indigenous issues" including "residential schools, claims of cultural genocide and even, occasionally, actual genocide." However, he contends "that a closer review of the historical record," particularly Department of Indian Affairs records, "shows that such claims do not stand up to scrutiny." Piasetzki's editorial includes several examples of historical denialism including mythologizing Macdonald as a nation builder, downplaying the impact his genocidal policies had on Indigenous Peoples, and deploying rhetorical tactics such as whataboutism, cherry-picking, and half-truths in order to, according to Sinclair and Carleton, "distract from the historical consensus on Macdonald's controversial legacy."[19] Despite including clear examples of residential school denialism, Piasetzki's editorial remains publicly available on the *Canadian Encyclopedia* website, which is particularly worrying, given that many people believe the website is a trusted and vetted source of information.

Piasetzki also wrote a chapter in the book *Grave Error: How the Media Misled Us (and the Truth about Residential Schools)*, which aims to "analyze and critique the false narrative of unmarked graves, missing children, forced attendance and genocidal conditions at residential schools."[20] This independently published book, edited by known residential school denialists Christian Paul (C.P.) Champion and Tom Flanagan, is an example of pseudohistory: It gives the appearance of being scholarly because it makes an "appeal for rationality and truth" and claims to offer "a powerful, research- and facts-based indictment of the moral panic over residential schools."[21] However, *Grave Error* includes many falsehoods and conspiracy theories (including the debunked "mass grave hoax"), it is not peer-reviewed, the majority of authors are not academic historians, none of the authors are experts on the history of residential schools, and not a single First Nations author is included.[22] A recent scholarly review of *Grave Error* titled "This Is a Worrying Book" concluded that it "adds nothing to an understanding of truth and stands directly in the way of widespread reconciliation."[23]

Common Techniques Used by Residential School Denialists

In 2021, Justice and Carleton created an inventory of eight "common contortions used by denialists to try to undermine the overwhelming documentary and testimonial evidence of widespread, multigenerational, systemic and ongoing violence of the IRS system."[24] This inventory, included in the Introduction (see Figure 0.1), provides an excellent starting point for identifying common examples of residential school denialism; however, it does not categorize and label the examples in terms of the techniques commonly used by residential school denialists.

According to psychologist Albert Bandura's theory of moral disengagement, people adopt moral standards to serve as guides for conduct; they do things that bring them a sense of self-worth and refrain from doing things that violate their moral standards and trigger self-condemnation.[25] However, Bandura identified eight "psychosocial mechanisms" that people use to selectively disengage moral self-sanction from inhumane conduct, which enables them to do immoral and inhumane things free from self-censure.[26] The mechanisms described by Bandura are particularly helpful for identifying the techniques that residential school denialists commonly employ. In this section we draw from the work of Bandura, Justice, Carleton, and historians who have focused on historical denialism and pseudohistory[27] to describe the techniques that residential school denialists commonly use.

- *Assuming worthy ends justify harmful means.* People morally justify violent and harmful means if they serve an end they believe is honourable.[28] For example, residential school denialists regularly justify the harms that Indigenous students experienced in schools by claiming that the skills students learned at residential schools prepared them for vocational or professional jobs and that they would not have learned them otherwise.[29]
- *Making comparisons that make harmful practices seem less destructive.* Denialists regularly contrast harmful actions or events with those that are more harmful to make the actions or events seem less unjust and reprehensible. In his editorial for the *Canadian Encyclopedia*, Greg Piasetzki described how an American government representative sent to study the Canadian Indian Residential School system in 1915 "praised the Canadian policy for its success in preserving Indigenous culture—unlike the American approach,

which was intended to "'obliterate his racial identity.'"[30] He also praised Macdonald's governments for signing treaties and creating the Royal Canadian Mounted Police, which guaranteed that "there were no deaths in Indian Wars in Canada," unlike in the United States where "60,000 Indigenous people and 40,000 settlers and soldiers died."

- *Using euphemisms and sanitized language to conceal harm.* Denialists use sanitized language (for example, they refer to residential schools as boarding schools) to make them seem less harmful. As another example, denialists regularly argue that the Indian Residential School system in Canada was not a genocide or argue that it was a "cultural genocide" to imply that it is not a real genocide. Denialists also use agentless passive voice to give the appearance that harmful acts were the work of nameless forces rather than people who worked at residential schools. For example, in 2020 Erin O'Toole, the leader of the federal Conservative Party, used passive voice when he falsely stated that residential schools were designed to provide education for Indigenous children, but "became a horrible program that really harmed people."[31]
- *Displacing responsibility for residential schools.* This mechanism focuses on how responsibility for harmful practices and actions are reduced when people believe they are not personally responsible for their actions because they were following orders from authorities.[32] It is similar to implicatory denial described by Bevernage, which focuses on denying responsibility for responding to a historical event in the present or future. Residential school denialists often try to absolve the people responsible for the harms that occurred at residential schools by focusing on the good intentions of the people who worked there, or by displacing responsibility by arguing that the people who committed the harms were merely following orders. Duncan Campbell Scott, the deputy superintendent of the Department of Indian Affairs, is regularly blamed for enforcing and expanding the system of residential schools in order to "get rid of the Indian problem." However, focusing solely on his actions displaces responsibility from other people who perpetrated the harms.
- *Diffusing responsibility for residential schools.* This mechanism focuses on how responsibility for inhumane behaviour is diffused

or dispersed by subdividing tasks into parts that seem harmless in isolation, or through collective decision-making where no one can be held personally responsible for making decisions that caused harm. Residential school denialists regularly claim that Sir John A. Macdonald and other politicians should not be held responsible for the harms committed at residential schools by a "few bad apples." They also claim that few people at the time knew about the conditions and harms that were occurring in residential schools, despite persuasive evidence that shows that many people knew what was happening.[33]

- *Ignoring, minimizing, distorting, or disputing harms.* Denialists regularly use various methods to disregard, minimize, distort, or dispute the harmful effects of residential schools for Indigenous Peoples. These include focusing on the benefits of residential schools, including, according to Justice and Carleton, "a minority of individualized, positive recollections from the schools as part of a strategy to discredit those who draw attention to the overall, systemic genocidal effects of the IRS system."[34] In his editorial, Piasetzki minimized the mortality rate of Indigenous students who attended residential schools, and distorted the number of students who actually attended residential schools.[35] Denialists also use the false balance fallacy, also known as "bothsidesism," to suggest that the good and bad aspects of residential schools are more equally balanced than historians have suggested. The demand to focus on the positives of residential schools also misrepresents Survivor testimony, historical research, and the scholarly consensus that residential schools had predominantly negative consequences for Indigenous Peoples.[36]
- *Dehumanizing residential school students and Survivors.* Dehumanizing people makes it easier to mistreat them without experiencing self-condemnation, whereas perceiving them as humans activates empathetic responses. One residential school denialist justified the dehumanizing practices that students experienced upon arriving at residential schools at the end of the summer as being completely normal and necessary. This includes assigning students a number rather than using their name, removing their clothes from home and giving them a uniform, forcing them to be vigorously scrubbed clean and sanitized in showers, and cutting their hair off.

- *Blaming the victim.* Another method residential school denialists use is to blame Indigenous Peoples for bringing the harm on themselves through their behaviour and actions. For example, denialists often erroneously claim that Indigenous students and parents did not resist attending residential schools, which implies that they either consented to attending the schools or they did not have a problem with it. Crystal Gail Fraser outlined various ways Indigenous Peoples, including parents and students, fought against and resisted residential schools.[37]
- *Arguing for presentism.* Denialists often claim that residential schools were commonly accepted and supported by people at the time, and argue that it is problematic to judge the actions of people in the past using contemporary values. There are several problems with this argument. First, when we deem actions or beliefs from the past to be commonplace, it is difficult to blame anyone for those actions, and past injustices can easily be justified. Teaching students that we can judge past actions only by standards that existed at the time normalizes unacceptable beliefs and attitudes. It also reinforces the mistaken notion that everyone in the past thought the same way and suggests that those who opposed unjust actions behaved inappropriately.[38] Assuming that everyone at the time supported residential schools ignores the fact that Indigenous parents, students, Church employees, and even the Department of Indian Affairs's own medical expert opposed residential schools.[39] Second, the idea that we cannot judge the past by today's values is a fundamental misunderstanding about what history is and how it works. The present inevitably shapes the topics and questions historians choose to investigate, the evidence they analyze, and the interpretations they write. No matter how detached historians try to be, it is impossible to make historical judgments that are not influenced by the present.[40]
- *Suppressing evidence.* Cherry-picking, or what is known as suppressing evidence or the fallacy of incomplete evidence, is a technique denialists use to highlight evidence that confirms their position, while ignoring or suppressing contradictory evidence. This technique can also involve using out-of-context quotes to support an argument, or using quotes to support their position that actually say

the opposite of what is being claimed. For example, in Piasetzki's editorial, he describes how after the collapse of the bison population in 1880, Sir John A. Macdonald's government initiated one of the largest famine relief operations in Canadian history, which fed an estimated 10,000 to 20,000 Indigenous people. Piasetzki claims that even historian James Daschuk, who was "one of his [Macdonald's] harshest critics," in his book *Clearing the Plains: Disease, Politics of Starvation, and the Loss of Aboriginal Life* "conceded that the famine relief program saved thousands of lives and avoided a 'region wide mortality.'" However, in the book Daschuk was extremely critical of how Macdonald's government handled the famine after being elected in 1878. Daschuk describes how the famine took on a "sinister character," including the refusal of emergency rations "until the Indians were on the verge of starvation, to reduce the expense."[41] Given Daschuk's criticism of Macdonald's role in exacerbating the famine, it is deceitful to suggest that he praised Macdonald's actions for avoiding widespread mortality in the region.

- *Deflecting with whataboutism.* Deflection is an argumentation technique used by a person or group in response to an accusation or difficult question.[42] Whataboutism is a fallacy closely related to the ad hominem fallacy where a person responds to an accusation by attacking the person making it, except in the case of whataboutism they may not attack the person, but make another accusation that does not defend whoever or whatever is being accused.[43] In Piasetzki's editorial, he argued that "Macdonald was close friends with two prominent Indigenous persons of his time," Oronhyatekha (Burning Cloud) and Kahkewāquonāby. Piasetzki argues that Oronhyatekha and Kahkewāquonāby would not have been friends with Macdonald and supported his political campaigns if he "harboured the ill will towards Indigenous people in Canada that his critics suggest." This is whataboutism because stating that Macdonald had Indigenous friends does not prove that his policies were not genocidal in intent.

Five Possible Pedagogical Responses

In this section, we describe five pedagogical approaches for responding to residential school denialism. For simplicity's sake we have named these approaches the 5Ds: detect, debunk, disregard, debate, and deconstruct.[44] Teachers can teach students to *detect* residential school denialism by identifying techniques that denialists commonly used to undermine the truth about residential schools. Teachers can teach students to *debunk* historical facts, arguments, and interpretations that promote mistruths, mislead, or distort history for political or ideological purposes. Teachers can *disregard* denialist historical interpretations by ignoring them and accepting the interpretations produced by experts and confirmed by peer review and disciplinary consensus. Teachers can teach students to *debate* competing interpretations and evaluate the validity and credibility of the historical arguments presented. Lastly, teachers can teach students to *deconstruct* denialist interpretations by analyzing author intentions, purposes, and motives, decoding the rhetorical strategies utilized, and evaluating the evidence provided and the trustworthiness and truthfulness of the interpretation.

Detect

The first step in addressing residential school denialism in classrooms is detecting it. Of the 5Ds, detecting residential school denialism might be the most important pedagogical approach because the other 4Ds (debunk, disregard, debate, and deconstruct) depend on teachers and students being able to identify residential school denialism. For example, debunking a denialist fact or argument requires students and teachers to first identify the fact or argument as a possible example of residential school denialism that requires further investigation or analysis using the other approaches.

In the introduction to this chapter, we discussed two examples of school assignments that asked students to respond to questions focused on the positive aspects of residential schools, which is a common talking point used by residential school denialists. However, it is unclear whether the teachers who asked students to complete the assignments were aware that they included a common example of residential school denialism.

Both examples highlight the importance of teachers scrutinizing learning resources before using them in the classroom. However, it cannot be assumed that teachers (or students) know how to detect examples of residential school denialism. Thus, one of the most important pedagogical responses to residential school denialism is to teach students how to detect it in various sources. To do this, teachers and students need to understand what residential school denialism is, and the techniques and strategies that denialists commonly use. For example, teachers could introduce students to definitions of historical denialism and pseudohistory, provide different historical examples, and discuss the similarities and differences between the different historical examples. They could also teach students about the techniques residential schools denialists regularly employ and provide examples to illustrate them. Next, teachers could provide students with examples of residential school denialism and see if they can identify the techniques used.

The detect approach is an essential first step for addressing residential school denialism in classrooms, but it is not the end point. If denialism is detected, the next step is for students and teachers to consider which of the other 5D approaches are effective for confronting it. As we discuss below, the pedagogical approach taken after detecting residential school denialism needs to consider the students, the school and community, and the nature and extent of the denialism they have identified. There are some instances where teachers might disregard and ignore denialist interpretations to avoid introducing them to students and providing a platform for these harmful views. However, there are also instances where it is beneficial for students to deconstruct denialist residential school interpretations to determine what the author's purposes and political and ideological motivations are, whether the interpretation can be considered an example of denialism, and how it should be responded to. For example, students could deconstruct Piasetzki's editorial and decide whether it should continue to be available on the *Canadian Encyclopedia* website. The four approaches can be used on their own or in combination with each other. Each approach also has potential limitations.

Debunk

One possible response to denialist interpretations is to teach students how to debunk misinformation and assess the accuracy of the facts and evidence provided in an interpretation. An important goal of debunking is for students to identify misinformation, misleading statements, and inaccuracies through close reading, analysis, and fact checking. A debunking approach requires students to know how to check facts, find reliable sources of historical evidence, and embody dispositions that will help them debunk misinformation. This might include dispositions such as being critically minded and willing to evaluate information and evidence to detect bias and identify and interrogate claims that might be inaccurate, being attentive to detail, and being committed to ensuring that claims meet basic standards of truth and accuracy.

A debunking approach is an effective strategy for confronting literal denialism such as blatant lies and factual inaccuracies. In Piasetzki's *Canadian Encyclopedia* editorial, there are several factual errors that students could debunk. For example, he claims that the mortality rates of Indigenous children at residential schools were "unexceptional" and "lower but not by much" compared to non-Indigenous school-aged children. Volume 4 of the TRC's *Final Report, Canada's Residential Schools: Missing Children and Unmarked Burials,* shows this claim is false. The report unequivocally states that "Aboriginal children in residential schools died at a far higher rate than school aged children in the general population."[45] The TRC *Final Report* also includes statistical analysis that shows the death rate was 4.9 times higher for Indigenous children in residential schools than for non-Indigenous school-aged children as late as from 1941 to 1945.[46]

Although debunking is effective for dealing with literal denial, it is less effective for responding to interpretive and implicatory denialism. Denialist publications like the *Grave Error* book and articles published on the Indian Residential Schools Research Group website[47] claim to be scholarly, dispassionate, and based on rigorous research, accurate facts, and reliable evidence. However, the problem is not that the facts and evidence they present are always inaccurate but that they are presented in misleading ways that promote positive interpretations of residential schools and downplay, dismiss, or ignore evidence that highlight widespread abuse and genocide. Examples of interpretive denialism include focusing on stories of Indigenous students who had positive experiences at residential schools or showing school photos of smiling Indigenous children as proof that residential schools were not harmful places. Misleading uses of evidence such as these examples, also discussed by Raymond Frogner in Chapter 3, cannot be addressed by simply debunking or fact checking. Some students did have positive experiences at residential schools, but this does not mean that these experiences can be generalized to all students, or that these experiences lessen the overall harms that occurred. One of the main problems with the debunking approach is that it fails to consider how facts are assembled into larger narratives. History educator Peter Lee illustrated this problem by writing a highly problematic interpretation of Adolf Hitler's rise to power using only factual statements. His interpretation showed how "singular factual statements in an account might be true but the meaning of the account may still be highly contestable."[48] Likewise, a denialist could write a deeply flawed interpretation about the positive benefits of residential schools for Indigenous children that contains factual statements that cannot be discredited by debunking alone.

Disregard

Another pedagogical approach is to disregard denialist and pseudohistorical interpretations to avoid giving them attention or legitimacy, and focusing instead on credible interpretations accepted by the scholarly community and the process of peer review. This might include interpretations published in peer-reviewed journals or academic presses written by professional historians with expertise on the topic. On 1 July 2021 (Canada Day), the governing Council of the Canadian Historical Association (CHA), with input from Indigenous and settler experts on the history of violence and dispossession Indigenous Peoples experienced in what is today Canada, released a statement that recognized "that this history fully warrants our use of the word genocide."[49] While there is widespread consensus among historians that the violence and dispossession Indigenous Peoples experienced in what is now Canada constitutes a genocide, this is not to suggest that there is unanimity among historians. In fact, several historians signed an open letter to the Council of the CHA and the Canadian public calling on the CHA to retract its statement because they claim that there is not scholarly consensus that Canada's treatment of Indigenous Peoples was genocidal.[50] Experts have also harshly critiqued and dismissed the *Grave Error* book as an example of historical denialism and pseudohistory.

A disregard approach begins from the assumption that reactionary right-wing forces are using denialism and pseudohistory to make hateful and bad-faith arguments to support their political and ideological positions. Scholars have suggested that these right-wing arguments are untrustworthy, unacademic, unsupported by historiography, and generally apologetic of colonial violence, and they advocate for the removal of denialist perspectives from public discourse.[51] In September 2024

Leah Gazan, the New Democratic Party Member of Parliament for Winnipeg Centre, introduced a private member's bill in the House of Commons to add residential school denialism to the Criminal Code in the same way that Holocaust denialism is criminalized in multiple countries including Canada, as will be discussed in Chapter 10.[52]

Disregarding offers clear benefits for confronting residential school denialism in the classroom. First, it refuses to give denialism a platform or a sense of legitimacy and acceptability. In a disregard approach, teachers would focus on trustworthy historical interpretations that have been accepted by the scholarly community. The Truth and Reconciliation Commission report was based on years of in-depth research by professional historians and archivists and includes the testimony of over 6,750 residential school Survivors. Thus, the TRC report represents a trustworthy and comprehensive account of residential schools freely available to teachers and students. To justify disregarding denialist interpretations, teachers could explain that the TRC report is authoritative, comprehensive, and trustworthy. Teachers would also inform students that Piasetzki's editorial should be rejected and ignored because it is an example of residential school denialism written by a non-historian who lacks the expertise to speak about this topic.

While the disregard approach has clear benefits, it does not fully resolve the problem that teachers and students are facing, and has the potential to create new problems. Residential school denialism cannot be easily ignored and disregarded because denialist publications are regularly shared by right-wing media, politicians, and denialists on social media and other online platforms. For example, Piasetzki's editorial has been given significant legitimacy by being published on the *Canadian Encyclopedia* website, which is a trustworthy resource commonly used by teachers and students. Furthermore, *Grave Error* and its sequel *Dead Wrong* are currently bestsellers on Amazon, and public libraries across Canada have purchased these and other denialist publications.[53] Thus, disregarding residential school denialism might be impossible given the widespread availability of denialist publications.

Furthermore, scholarly critiques of residential school denialism have also been weaponized by right-wing commentators to demonstrate the untrustworthiness of academics and politicians opposed to denialism. Right-wing critics have argued that referring to their interpretations as denialism is a form of censorship that restricts their free speech.[54]

Disregarding residential school denialism also has the potential to further increase polarization and lead students or teachers who agree with denialist arguments to feel like they are the victims of censorship, or that their perspectives are being unfairly dismissed as morally and socially unacceptable. In Germany and other countries, criminalizing Holocaust denial has also been somewhat counterproductive because it has produced free speech martyrs and led to further dissemination of falsehoods.[55] If people see residential school denialism as subversive truths that the government or experts are trying to suppress, it is possible that it will continue to circulate and expand. Given the increasing popularity of denialism online, disregarding denialism seems inadequate for fully addressing this problem in schools.

Debate

A third approach is to invite students to debate both denialist interpretations and trustworthy interpretations by evaluating the strengths and limitations of both. For example, teachers could provide students with the two *Canadian Encyclopedia* editorials and ask them to debate which one is more valid by offering reasons and evidence to support their conclusion. An appealing aspect of this approach is that it could lay bare the problematic arguments, faulty reasoning, and weak evidence used to support denialist arguments, while also helping students develop their ability to assess the validity and trustworthiness of historical interpretations.

One glaring problem with the debate approach is that it places denialist and legitimate historical interpretations on equal footing and suggests both are worthy of investigation and discussion. It also exposes students to ideas and interpretations that are hateful, misinformed, and unsupported by scholarly consensus, and introduces the possibility that students could defend and support denialist interpretations. Sam Wineburg described a case where middle school teachers in California asked students to debate whether the Holocaust was real and gave students two interpretations, one that argued it was real and the other from an antisemitic, Holocaust-denying website that argued it was fake. The result was that some students were convinced by the denialist interpretations and made arguments that the Holocaust was fake and a propaganda tool of "world Jewry."[56] This example clearly highlights one of the main problems with the debate approach.

Inviting students to debate residential school denialism is dangerous territory. We are not suggesting that teachers should never use debates to teach about conflicting historical interpretations. However, teachers should consider whether the topic being investigated is an open debate between legitimate viewpoints, or whether it is a settled issue that is not controversial because a consensus opinion has formed or evidence suggests that contrary views should not be considered legitimate.[57]

Deconstruct

The deconstruct pedagogical approach invites students to critically interrogate, analyze, and deconstruct denialist and pseudohistorical interpretations to evaluate their trustworthiness and truthfulness. A deconstruct approach takes a skeptical stance towards denialist interpretations and focuses on understanding what the interpretation is saying, and what values, purposes, ulterior motives, and techniques are being utilized to persuade the intended audience. Deconstructing is more complex and comprehensive than debunking or fact checking because it asks students to consider the larger ideological and political contexts that underpin denialist interpretations and understand the intended meaning, purposes, and uses of the historical interpretation.

To deconstruct historical interpretations, students need to develop the background knowledge, skills, dispositions, and vocabulary to understand why pseudohistories and denialist interpretations are written and what political, ideological, and social motivations influence their creation. While deconstructing denialism involves aspects of debunking such as evaluating the facts presented, it also focuses on who the authors are, what their political and ideological commitments and motivations might be, and how trustworthy they are in terms of offering good-faith historical interpretations. For example, understanding Piasetzki's background and possible motivations for writing the *Canadian Encyclopedia* editorial is important for analyzing his interpretation. He is an intellectual property lawyer and not a trained historian or expert in the history of residential schools in Canada. He has written several articles in right-wing publications decrying cancel culture and wokeness, and has regularly defended controversial historical figures including Macdonald, Henry Dundas, and Egerton Ryerson. This information suggests that Piasetzki has a clear agenda and lacks credibility as an expert on the historical topics he writes about.

A deconstruct approach might also involve students investigating and analyzing the denialist techniques they identified. For example, if an interpretation makes a presentism argument that everyone thought a certain way in the past, students might look for evidence that disproves this argument, such as evidence that shows that Macdonald was criticized in his day for his harmful policies towards Indigenous Peoples.

The goal of deconstruction is not to analyze interpretations and break them down into separate parts, but to evaluate whether an interpretation is trustworthy and its author is attempting to be truthful. A trustworthy interpretation considers available evidence, addresses counter-arguments, and is accurate and transparent in the facts it employs, the evidence it analyzes, and the interpretations it makes. Truthfulness focuses on whether the author operates in good faith, attempts to tell the truth about an issue or topic in a sincere and accurate way, and tries to be ethically commendable.

While deconstruction has the potential to effectively combat residential school denialism, it also has several limitations. Deconstructing historical interpretations requires considerable time, knowledge, and skill to do it well. Teachers might not have the time or resources required to adequately teach students how to do this. This is not to suggest that students are incapable of deconstructing interpretations, only that this approach might be difficult for some students and will require significant teacher scaffolding and instruction. Given this reality, we recognize that disregarding residential school denialism might be a better approach in situations where teaching students to deconstruct denialist interpretations is not feasible. Furthermore, like the debate approach, deconstruction invites students to spend significant time with denialist interpretations that include offensive information, arguments, and perspectives.

Conclusion

The growing prevalence and popularity of residential school denialism on social media and in other right-wing media in recent years is alarming. Helping students confront denialist interpretations has become an essential task for Canadian history and social studies teachers. We argue that this problem cannot be ignored and goes far beyond academic disagreements among historians. Residential school denialism is an important public and political conversation that reflects the increasingly polarized and contested views of Canada's past and the responsibility that Canadians have for responding to it in the present. We described five approaches educators can utilize to address this problem: detect, debunk, disregard, debate, and deconstruct. These five approaches for confronting residential school denialism are interrelated and overlapping, and, as we have discussed, can be used in combination with each other. We also recognize that there are probably additional approaches we have not considered that may also be effective for responding to this problem. This chapter reveals the myriad challenges teachers and students are facing during this time of post-truth and political polarization. While the TRC report was intended to offer a comprehensive and truthful account of what happened in residential schools, it has also sparked a proliferation of interpretations about residential schools rooted in half-truths, pseudohistories, conspiracies, and denialism. Confronting untrustworthy and denialist historical interpretations has become one of the most significant challenges facing teachers and students today.

Notes

1 Michelle Cyca, "The Dangerous Allure of Residential School Denialism," *The Walrus*, 8 January 2024, https://thewalrus.ca/residential-school-denialism/; Sinclair and Carleton, "Residential School Denialism Is on the Rise"; Jillian Kestler-D'Amours, "'Denying Our Truth': The Fight Against Residential School Denialism in Canada," *Al Jazeera*, 7 February 2025, https://www.aljazeera.com/news/longform/2025/2/7/denying-our-truth-fighting-residential-school-denialism-in-canada; Beauvais and Williamson, "The Prevalence and Correlates of Residential School Denialism in Canada."

2 Sean Carleton, Alan Lester, Adele Perry, and Omeasoo Wahpasiw, "Exposing Residential School Denialism's Transnational Network," *Active History*, 10 December 2024, https://activehistory.ca/blog/2024/12/10/exposing-residential-school-denialisms-transnational-network/; Sathnam Sanghera, "'Imperial Nostalgia Has Become So Extreme': Sathnam Sanghera on the Conflict Surrounding Colonial History," *The Guardian*, 8 June 2024, https://www.theguardian.com/books/article/2024/jun/08/imperial-nostalgia-has-become-so-extreme-sathnam-sanghera-on-the-conflict-surrounding-colonial-history.

3 Mark Gibney, *The Age of Apology: Facing up to the Past* (University of Pennsylvania Press, 2008).

4 Bevernage, "Denial in the Age of Apology."

5 Bevernage, 50.

6 Justice and Carleton, "Truth Before Reconciliation."

7 Ian Froese, "Manitoba School Division Apologizes after Students Asked to List 'Positive' Qualities of Residential Schools," *CBC News*, 24 May 2024, https://www.cbc.ca/news/canada/manitoba/hanover-school-division-list-positives-residential-schools-classroom-1.7214155.

8 Frances Willick, "Grade 10 Distance Course Asks about Benefits of Residential Schools, Calls First Nations Alcoholism 'Common,'" *CBC News*, 18 June 2021, https://www.cbc.ca/news/canada/nova-scotia/n-s-correspondence-course-residential-schools-stereotypes-1.6069747.

9 Forester, "Residential School Deniers, White Supremacists Biggest Barrier to Reconciliation Says Murray Sinclair"; Murray Sinclair, "Will Truth Bring Reconciliation? Justice Murray Sinclair Says Not Without Education," *Unreserved*, CBC Radio, 4 December 2015, http://www.cbc.ca/radio/unreserved/taking-the-first-steps-on-the-road-to-reconciliation-1.3347611/will-truth-bring-reconciliation-justice-murray-sinclair-says-not-without-education-1.3348070.

10 *Honouring the Truth*, 234.

11 Truth and Reconciliation Commission of Canada (TRC), *Truth and Reconciliation Commission of Canada: Calls to Action* (Truth and Reconciliation Commission of Canada, 2015), 7, http://nctr.ca/assets/reports/Calls_to_Action_English2.pdf.

12 Wikipedia, "Historical Negationism," 26 July 2025, https://en.wikipedia.org/w/index.php?title=Historical_negationism&oldid=1302640900.

13 Banner, *The Ever-Changing Past.*

14 Gudonis and Jones, "Who Controls the Past?"

15 Bevernage, "Denial in the Age of Apology."

16 Justice and Carleton, "Truth Before Reconciliation."

17 Carleton et al., "Exposing Residential School Denialism's Transnational."

18 Niigaan Sinclair and Sean Carleton, "John A. Macdonald Was No Friend to Indigenous Peoples," *Canadian Encyclopedia* (Historica Canada), 30 January 2025, updated 5 December 2025, https://www.thecanadianencyclopedia.ca/en/article/john-a-macdonald-was-no-friend-to-indigenous-peoples; Greg Piasetzki, "A Few Facts Every Canadian Should Know about Sir John A Macdonald," *Canadian Encyclopedia* (Historica Canada), 30 January 2025, updated 5 December 2025, https://www.thecanadianencyclopedia.ca/en/article/a-few-facts-every-canadian-should-know-about-sir-john-a-macdonald.

19 Carleton and Sinclair, "John A. Macdonald Was No Friend."

20 Tom Flanagan. "No Evidence of 'Mass Graves' or 'Genocide' in Residential Schools," Fraser Institute, 12 February 2024, https://www.fraserinstitute.org/commentary/no-evidence-of-mass-graves-or-genocide-in-residential-schools.

21 Champion and Flanagan, *Grave Error*, 14.

22 Carleton et al., "Exposing Residential School Denialism's Transnational"; Carleton and Gerbrandt, "We Fact-Checked Residential School Denialists and Debunked Their 'Mass Grave Hoax' Theory."

23 Richard Butler, "This Is a Worrying Book: *Grave Error: How the Media Misled Us (and the Truth)* by C.P. Champion and Tom Flanagan (Eds.)," Book Reviews, *British Columbia Review*, 2 July 2024, https://thebcreview.ca/2024/07/02/2216-butler-champion-flanagan/.

24 Justice and Carleton, "Truth Before Reconciliation."

25 Bandura, "Moral Disengagement."

26 Bandura, "Mechanisms of Moral Disengagement."

27 Evans, *Lying about Hitler*; Gudonis and Jones, eds., *History in a Post-Truth World.*

28 Bandura, "Moral Disengagement."

29 Justice and Carleton, "Truth Before Reconciliation."

30 Piasetzki, "A Few Facts."

31 Brett Forester and Jamie Pashagumskum, "O'Toole Walks Back 'Reprehensible' Comments on Residential Schools," *APTN News*, 16 December 2020, https://www.aptnnews.ca/national-news/otoole-reax-residential-schools-ryerson/.

32 Bandura, "Moral Disengagement."

33 Kathleen McKenzie and Sean Carleton, "Hiding in Plain Sight: Newspaper Coverage of Dr. Peter Bryce's 1907 Report on Residential Schools," *Active History*, 29 September 2021, https://activehistory.ca/blog/2021/09/29/hiding-in-plain-sight-newspaper-coverage-of-dr-peter-bryces-1907-report-on-residential-schools/.

34 Justice and Carleton, "Truth Before Reconciliation."

35 Piasetzki, "A Few Facts."

36 Justice and Carleton, "Truth Before Reconciliation."

37 Crystal Gail Fraser, "Resistance and Residential Schools," in *Canadian Encyclopedia* (Historica Canada), 6 May 2020, https://thecanadianencyclopedia.ca/en/article/resistance-and-residential-schools.

38 Miles and Gibson, "Rethinking Presentism in History Education"; Martell Stevens, *Teaching History for Justice.*

39 Justice and Carleton, "Truth Before Reconciliation."

40 Armitage, "In Defense of Presentism."

41 Daschuk, *Clearing the Plains*, 134.

42 Benjamin Curtis, "Whataboutism: What It Is and Why It's Such a Popular Tactic in Arguments," *The Conversation*, 20 May 2022, http://theconversation.com/whataboutism-what-it-is-and-why-its-such-a-popular-tactic-in-arguments-182911.

43 Curtis, "Whataboutism."

44 We expand on our approach in the article, Miles and Gibson, "Truth Telling in History Classrooms."

45 Truth and Reconciliation Commission of Canada (TRC), *The Final Report of the Truth and Reconciliation Commission of Canada,* vol. 4, *Canada's Residential Schools: Missing Children and Unmarked Burials* (2015), 1, https://publications.gc.ca/collections/collection_2015/trc/IR4-9-4-2015-eng.pdf.

46 TRC, *Canada's Residential Schools,* 18.

47 "Articles," Indian Residential Schools Research Group, accessed 21 August 2025, https://irsrg.ca/articles/.

48 Lee, "Putting Principles into Practice," 59.

49 "The History of Violence Against Indigenous Peoples Fully Warrants the Use of the Word 'Genocide,'" Canadian Historical Society, 1 July 2021, https://cha-shc.ca/advocacy/the-history-of-violence-against-indigenous-peoples-fully-warrants-the-use-of-the-word-genocide/.

50 "Historians Rally vs. 'Genocide' Myth," *Dorchester Review*, 12 August 2021, https://www.dorchesterreview.ca/blogs/news/historians-rally-vs-genocide-myth.

51 Perry, Carleton, and Wahpasiw, "The Misuse of Indigenous and Canadian History."

52 Olivia Stefanovich, "Bill before Parliament Would Outlaw Residential School Denialism," *CBC News*, 26 September 2024, https://www.cbc.ca/news/politics/ndp-mp-private-members-bill-residential-school-denialism-1.7334916.

53 As of August 2025, there is a wait-list to access the fourteen copies available in Toronto Public Libraries.

54 Joanna Baron, "Criminalizing Residential School 'Denialism' Is Both Unnecessary and Unconstitutional," *The Hub*, accessed 21 August 2025, https://thehub.ca/2023/07/06/joanna-baron-criminalizing-residential-school-denialism-is-both-unnecessary-and-unconstitutional/.

55 Bazyler, *Holocaust, Genocide, and the Law*, 200.

56 Wineburg, *Why Learn History*.

57 Zimmerman and Robertson, *The Case for Contention*; Hess, *Controversy in the Classroom*.

CHAPTER 7

DEBUNKING THE "MASS GRAVE HOAX" CONSPIRACY THEORY

by Reid Gerbrandt and Sean Carleton

In the years since Tk'emlúps te Secwépemc's 2021 announcement about the location of 215 potential unmarked graves at the former Kamloops Indian Residential School (KIRS), a number of priests, pundits, and politicians have downplayed and questioned the validity of the findings.[1] Some have declared the news of potential unmarked graves at many former residential school sites across Canada to be a deliberate deception and a "huge lie."[2] Others insist that mainstream media, the federal government, and First Nations have conspired to create a "hoax" by misrepresenting the news of potential unmarked burials sites as a "mass grave" to shock and guilt Canadians into caring about Indigenous Peoples and reconciliation.[3] Erroneous accounts of mass graves, which one pundit claims were reported "almost universally," are said to be directly responsible for church burnings in the summer of 2021 and for sending Canadians into "paroxysms of shame, guilt and rage."[4] Despite Church and State archival records already confirming the deaths of more than 3,200 Indigenous children at residential schools,[5] many people—in Canada and internationally—are accepting and promoting the narrative of the "mass grave hoax," with some even suggesting that the whole thing is a "fake news story."[6]

Given the growing popularity of the mass grave hoax narrative, especially on the far right in Canada and globally, and recent calls for Canadians to take responsibility for countering such harmful misinformation,[7] we—as non-Indigenous academic researchers—decided to investigate the claims of a media conspiracy and fact-check them against the evidence of what was actually reported in Canada. What did Canadian journalists report in the immediate aftermath of the Kamloops announcement? To answer this question, we conducted a study that analyzed 386 news articles across five Canadian mainstream media outlets released between 27 May and 15 October 2021. This chapter outlines our research, results, and recommendations.

Overall, our major finding is that a foundational claim of the "mass grave hoax" narrative—that all mainstream media reported the findings as "mass graves"—is not supported by the evidence. The mass grave hoax is more myth than truth. Myths, however, are not pure fiction; they often contain a kernel of truth that is exaggerated or misrepresented for specific purposes, as the previous chapter outlined.[8] This selective representation of evidence is commonly referred to by experts as cherry-picking, and it is easy to see how the narrative of the mass grave hoax utilizes this strategy.[9] We thus conclude that the narrative of the mass grave hoax hinges on a misrepresentation of how Canadian journalists actually reported on the identification of potential unmarked graves at former residential school sites during the spring, summer, and fall of 2021. Those spreading the hoax narrative are engaging—intentionally or unintentionally—in a strategy of cherry-picking, of suppressing or distorting evidence to confirm a preconceived position (i.e., the existence of a mass grave hoax). Based on our findings, we recommend that the mass grave hoax narrative be understood as an expression of residential school denialism. Denialist discourse, in this case taking the form of the mass grave hoax narrative, attempts to minimize or distort basic facts about residential schooling and its legacy to shake public confidence in truth and reconciliation and protect the colonial status quo against a reckoning related to Canada's genocidal treatment of Indigenous Peoples.[10] Indigenous communities have identified this discourse as "dangerous" and a key barrier to meaningful reconciliation.[11]

Methodology

To determine the media narrative in Canada, we selected mainstream media outlets for analysis: CBC, *National Post*, *Globe and Mail*, *Toronto Star*, and the Canadian Press. We examined articles published between 27 May and 15 October 2021. We chose these dates to correspond to the news cycle between the 27 May announcement by Tk'emlúps te Secwépemc and 15 October, which is two weeks after the first National Day for Truth and Reconciliation on 30 September 2021. While news outlets continue to cover the ongoing searches at many former residential school sites across Canada, focusing on the media narrative from the spring, summer, and fall of 2021 is necessary to investigate the foundation of the mass grave hoax narrative, which is the extent of mass grave media errors during that initial news cycle.

We searched for relevant news articles posted on the selected media outlets' websites, as well as the online ProQuest database portal through the University of Manitoba library. To identify articles relevant to the study, we used a word search that included key phrases such as "mass graves," "unmarked graves," "residential schools," "Kamloops residential school," and "Cowessess residential school." The next step was to analyze media and historical discourse in the articles.

Methods of historical discourse analysis are important to this study because the results can challenge the false reality that some people or groups try to create in order to maintain a desired status quo.[12] In the case of potential unmarked graves at former residential schools, some people argue that media, government, and First Nations are purposefully misreporting the issue for political or ideological reasons. Our analysis of the articles disproves this notion, demonstrating—with evidence—how the language used by some journalists was mostly correct in the majority of articles. In terms of the minority of articles that contained inaccuracies, our analysis suggests that these can be understood as limited factual errors, which while unfortunate are a normal part of the journalism industry and not, as is suggested by some, a deliberate cover-up designed to destroy Canada and justify an attack on Christianity.[13]

It is important to first acknowledge the journalistic process and explain how and why media errors occur. According to journalism scholar Dan Berkowitz, even when news stories on events such as disasters break, a "good journalist" must cover the story quickly but correctly, knowing how to identify and present the proper information.[14] Even though journalism, unlike other professions, does not have a "predetermined" approach, a good journalist will know the proper processes for handling such cases and taking care not to introduce error.[15] That said, factual errors by journalists and media outlets are not uncommon, especially in the rush to report on a developing story outside of a reporter's area of expertise. As CBC Editor-in-Chief Brodie Fenlon acknowledges, "Though we try hard, we make mistakes and on occasion, fail to live up to our high standards."[16]

The danger is that media errors, while a normal part of the journalistic process, can easily be cherry-picked by those looking to create conspiracy theories to understand—or distort—major events. Media scholars have used the immediate aftermath of the 2012 mass shooting at Sandy Hook Elementary School in the United States as an example of how media mistakes can fuel misinformation and disinformation and be pounced upon for political ends. In the Sandy Hook case, insufficient information from public officials along with the initial haste to report on the developing story led to factual errors in some of the initial media accounts of the shooting.[17] As more details surfaced, these errors were quickly corrected. When conspiracy theorists tried to spin the errors as proof of a government plot to introduce stricter gun laws and regulations, journalists quickly came to the media's defence: "It wasn't a conspiracy at Sandy Hook Elementary; it was honest human error. Law enforcement sources told journalists things that turned out to be inaccurate. . . . The mistakes were corrected."[18] While ideally avoided, errors need to be understood as part of the journalism industry, as should the efforts made by journalists to correct inaccuracies over time to get the story right and properly inform the public.

In terms of investigating the claims of a mass grave hoax relating to residential schools in Canada, our analysis involved two stages. The first was to determine which articles were relevant to the study. Not all articles had potential unmarked graves as the central issue of the story. In addition, we removed articles that only mentioned potential unmarked graves in passing, and even if they were about certain issues concerning Indigenous Peoples. To be considered relevant, the articles had to focus on the discovery of possible unmarked graves or the reckoning that was taking place across Canada during that period, and they had to mention potential unmarked graves consistently. Adjacent topics included the toppling of statues of prominent figures connected to residential schooling; discussions of Canada Day 2021; church burnings and vandalism taking place across Canada; and the first National Day for Truth and Reconciliation.

The second part of the analysis was to determine how the articles reported on the location of potential graves at residential school sites. Our

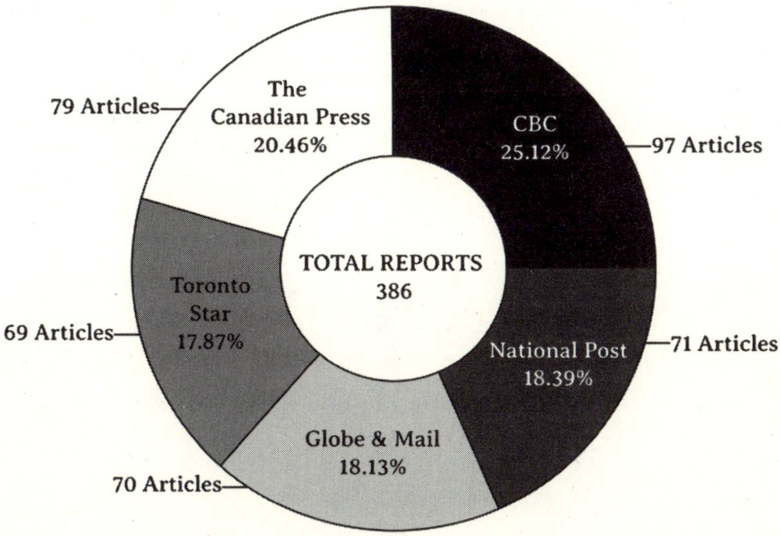

Figure 7.1. Article distribution by Canadian media outlets—CBC, the *National Post*, *Globe and Mail*, the *Toronto Star*, and the Canadian Press—from 27 May 2021 to 15 October 2021. Graph by Anoja Muthucumaru-Barham.

questions included: Did journalists refer to the findings as "mass graves" where "bodies were discovered" or "unmarked graves" with "potential remains"? How did journalists describe ground-penetrating radar (GPR) and its purposes? Were articles accurate when reporting on the announcements made by Tk'emlúps te Secwépemc or by the Cowessess First Nation in May and June 2021? We initially grouped the articles as "accurate articles" and "articles containing inaccuracies," followed by a further examination of the articles containing inaccuracies to better determine what errors journalists made and the extent of the mistakes.

In total, 386 relevant articles were published between 27 May and 15 October 2021. Figure 7.1 shows the breakdown between media outlets. One important note about the sample is that the Canadian Press, unlike other media outlets, has no business-to-consumer mandate. The Canadian Press distributes articles and press releases to Canadian media outlets, including the other four outlets in this study. Outlets that subscribe to the Canadian Press are granted licence rights to their content. This gives the Canadian Press a distinct advantage, as their stories can reach a wide range of Canadians, regardless of which media outlet people normally get their news from. Given the potential

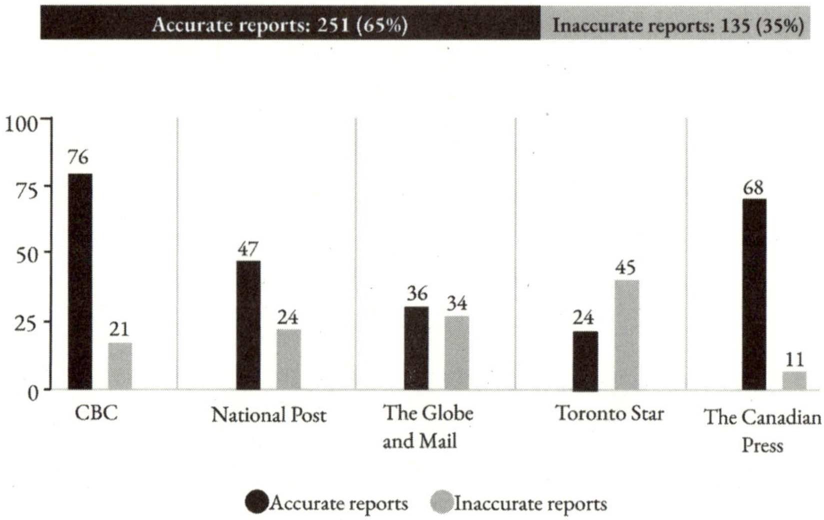

Figure 7.2. Accurate vs. inaccurate articles on potential unmarked graves by Canadian news sources, 27 May 2021–15 October 2021. Graph by Anoja Muthucumaru-Barham.

for these stories to be seen by and influence readers across the different outlets, we chose to include the Canadian Press in the study.

Results

Overall, the major finding of our research is that the foundation of the mass grave hoax narrative in Canada is not supported by the evidence. Of the 386 articles examined, the majority reported correctly on news related to the location of potential unmarked graves in Canada between 27 May and 15 October 2021. It is true that some articles contained some level of inaccuracy. Figure 7.2 shows the breakdown of inaccuracies in the articles:

- CBC: twenty-one (21.6 percent of all CBC articles; 5.4 percent of all articles studied)
- *National Post*: twenty-four (33.8 percent of all *Post* articles; 6.2 percent of all articles studied);
- *Globe and Mail*: thirty-four (48.6 percent of all *Globe* articles; 8.8 percent of all articles studied);
- *Toronto Star*: forty-five (65.7 percent of all *Star* articles; 11.6 percent of all articles studied);

- Canadian Press: eleven (13.9 percent of all Canadian Press articles; 2.8 percent of all articles studied).

It is important to examine the mistakes some journalists made for two reasons. First, revealing that journalists made some errors in their reports, but not to the extent claimed by those insisting there is a mass grave hoax, debunks conspiratorial talking points. Second, such an analysis can assist journalists in reporting on this ongoing news story in ways that avoid contributing to public confusion and fuelling residential school denialism.

The Mass Grave Hoax

Writers advancing the mass grave hoax narrative argue that mainstream media "almost universally" reported the news of First Nations locating potential unmarked graves as the discovery of mass graves.[19] The findings from this research, however, disprove this claim. Of the 135 articles that contained inaccuracies, only twenty-five referred to the discoveries as mass graves. When compared to the 386 total articles, this number represents just 6.5 percent. Put another way, 93.5 percent of articles—the vast majority—did not report on the discoveries as being mass graves. Moreover, we found that only three articles included the words *mass grave* in the title.[20] These numbers do not add up to a universal error, nor do they constitute evidence of a cover-up or conspiracy to mislead the public, even if there was some confusion.

We also found that, of the twenty-five articles that describe the findings as mass graves, thirteen consisted of journalists quoting other people who called these discoveries mass graves, not the authors themselves. This represents 52 percent of the articles that included the words *mass graves*. This was not the case for the *National Post*, as the one article that used *mass grave* was by the reporter. In *Globe and Mail*, four of its six articles used quotes that referred to potential unmarked graves as mass graves. Of the twenty-five articles, three used the phrase *mass graves* outside the context of the Kamloops announcement. One mentioned that Indigenous leaders asked Ottawa to create laws that prohibited the destruction of, or interfering with, mass graves, which still could be located in Canada at the sites of former residential schools.[21] Another article suggested that every former school site needs to be searched for mass graves.[22]

The *Toronto Star*, CBC, and the Canadian Press also released articles that quoted people using the words *mass graves*. In one *Toronto Star* article, the author used a quote from Mississauga Mayor Bonnie Crombie referring to the findings as mass graves.[23] Similarly, of the eight CBC articles that used the words *mass graves*, seven used quotes from interviewees. In the one Canadian Press article that referred to the Kamloops findings as mass graves, the author had quoted someone but followed up by describing the Marieval findings as "what are believed to be 751 unmarked graves."[24]

While some of these authors did correctly refer to the discoveries as potential unmarked graves, they still included errors, such as the words *mass graves*, that could cause confusion. The Canadian public might not understand the difference between an "unmarked grave" and a "mass grave," so when both show up in the same article without context and clarification, it is understandable if some people have further questions. However, to conclude that mainstream media in Canada "almost universally" referred to these discoveries as mass graves is simply incorrect.[25] Further, additional analysis shows that initial mistakes made by journalists were mostly corrected in future reports and by academics and Indigenous communities.

Additional Inaccuracies

We identified three common errors in our analysis that overlap with the articles that included the words *mass graves* (Figure 7.3). In total, we found additional inaccuracies in 120 (31.1 percent) of the total articles studied. In the analysis of only the articles that included this group of errors, including those using the words *mass graves*, this represents 88.9 percent of the 135 articles (Table 7.1). This shows that these errors were more common than the "mass grave" error that people have used to create the narrative of the mass grave hoax.

Of the media outlets that had additional inaccuracies:

- CBC had fifteen articles
- *National Post* had twenty-three articles
- *Globe and Mail* had thirty articles
- *Toronto Star* had forty-one articles
- Canadian Press had eleven articles

It is important to note that the total error percentages presented below by outlet include articles that contained the "mass grave" error.

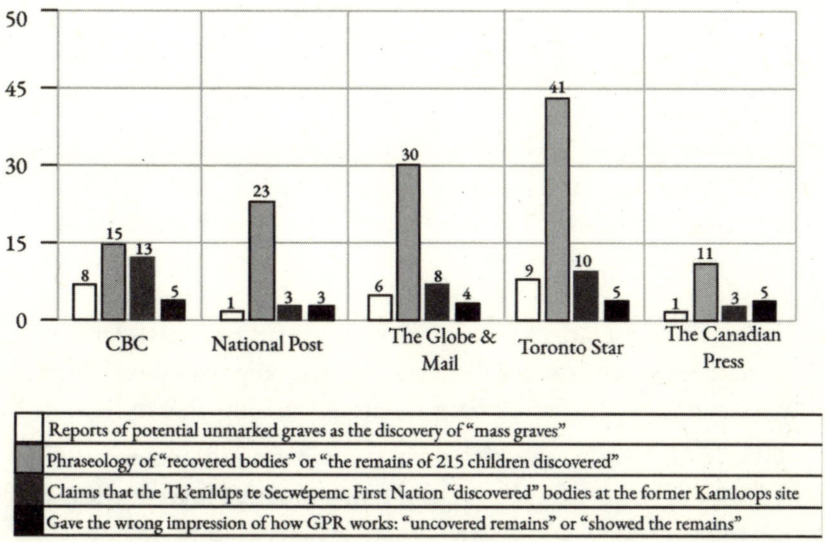

Figure 7.3. Inaccuracies in articles on First Nations locating potential unmarked graves, by news source, between 27 May 2021 and 15 October 2021. Graph by Anoja Muthucumaru-Barham.

Table 7.1. Totals and averages of inaccuracies in articles on First Nations locating potential unmarked graves, by news source, between 27 May 2021 and 15 October 2021. Table by Anoja Muthucumaru-Barham.

Inaccuracies	**Total**	**Total of all articles studied (%)**
Reports of potential unmarked graves as the discovery of "mass graves"	25	6.5%
Phraseology of "recovered bodies" or "the remains of 215 children discovered"	120	31.1%
Claims that Tk'emlúps te Secwépemc "discovered" bodies at the former Kamloops site	37	9.6%
Gave the wrong impression of how GPR works: "uncovered remains" or "showed the remains"	22	5.7%

Error 1: Student Remains at Residential School Sites

The first common error was reports suggesting that Indigenous Nations had recovered bodies from the former residential school sites, with a particular error in phraseology being that the "remains of 215 children were discovered" from the Kamloops site.[26] This error was found in all 120 (31.1 percent) articles that contained errors other than the words *mass graves*. This is incorrect; none of the sites were exhumed in 2021, so all of the anomalies detected at that point had not been confirmed to be remains. Instead, they are potential unmarked burials, and First Nations are in the process of determining next steps based on community consultation. This error was present in the following outlets:

- CBC: found in fifteen articles that contained additional errors (71.4 percent of the total CBC articles that contained inaccuracies; 15.5 percent of total CBC articles; and 3.9 percent of all articles studied)[27]
- *National Post*: found in all twenty-three articles that contained additional errors (95.8 percent of *Post* errors; 32.4 percent of the total *Post* articles; and 6.2 percent of all articles studied)[28]
- *Globe and Mail*: found in all thirty articles that contained additional errors (88.2 percent of *Globe* errors; 42.85 percent of total *Globe* articles; and 7.8 percent of all articles studied)[29]
- *Toronto Star*: found in forty-one articles containing additional errors (91.1 percent of all *Star* errors; 59.4 percent of total *Star* articles; and 10.6 percent of all articles studied)[30]
- Canadian Press: found in all eleven articles[31]

Error 2: Tk'emlúps te Secwépemc Uncovers 215 Bodies

The second common error was that Tk'emlúps te Secwépemc, and specifically Kukpi7 (Chief) Rosanne Casimir, announced that they had discovered 215 bodies at the former Kamloops site. For example, one article in *The Globe and Mail* stated: "Kukpi7 (Chief) Rosanne Casimir said last week that preliminary findings of a search with ground-penetrating radar discovered the remains of 215 children at the site of the Kamloops Indian Residential School."[32] This same phraseology was found in thirty-seven articles (9.6 percent of all articles and 27.4 percent of the articles that contain inaccuracies). This is an error because the

Nation announced that preliminary findings of a GPR survey detected what they believed to be the remains of an estimated 215 children, confirming prior community knowledge. It is true that the initial press release stated that, "with the help of a ground penetrating radar specialist, the stark truth of the preliminary findings came to light—the confirmation of the remains of 215 children who were students at the Kamloops Indian Residential School."[33] However, this same report also stated that the search was "still developing,"[34] and early media reports did indicate that a few days after the 27 May announcement, the First Nation "clarified their statement to say the survey had identified what is believed to be unmarked burial sites."[35]

- CBC: found in thirteen articles (61.9 percent of CBC errors; 13.4 percent of CBC articles; and 3.4 percent of total articles)[36]
- *National Post*: found in three articles (14.3 percent of *Post* errors; 4.2 percent of total *Post* articles; and 0.8 percent of all articles studied)[37]
- *Globe and Mail*: found in eight articles (23.5 percent of *Globe* errors; 11.4 percent of total *Globe* articles; and 2.1 percent of all articles studied)[38]
- *Toronto Star*: found in ten articles (22.2 percent of *Star* errors; 14.5 percent of total *Star* articles; and 2.6 percent of all articles studied)[39]
- Canadian Press: found in three articles (27.3 percent of Canadian Press errors, 3.8 percent of all Canadian Press articles, and 0.8 percent of all articles studied)[40]

Error 3: Ground-penetrating Radar Uncovers Remains

The third error we identified is that ground-penetrating radar "uncovered remains" or "showed the remains" underneath the earth.[41] This error was found in twenty-two articles, 5.7 percent of all articles, and represents 16.3 percent of the articles that contain inaccuracies. These articles gave the wrong impression of how GPR works. Ground-penetrating radar, as Andrew Martindale explained in great detail in Chapter 4, is a technology that detects anomalies and soil disturbances, or "turned soil," as some experts describe it, but does not provide an image of organic matter.[42] One of the lead experts who uses this technology to help Indigenous communities with their searches, Kisha Supernant, explained that First Nations need to be careful about relying solely on

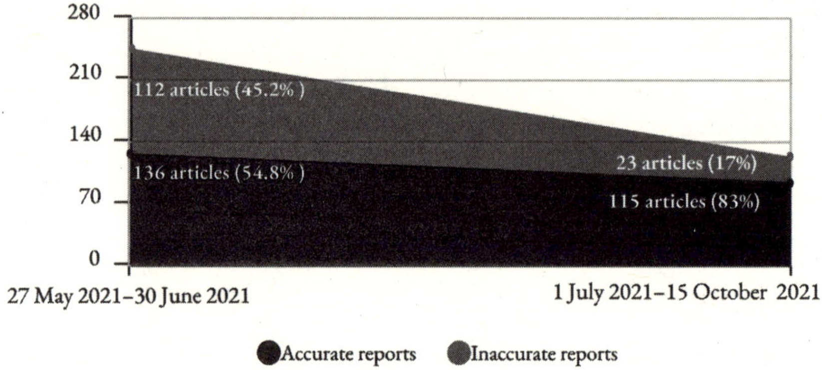

Figure 7.4. Changes in accurate vs. inaccurate reporting of potential unmarked graves in articles on First Nations locating potential unmarked graves between May 27, 2021 and 15 October 2021. Graph by Anoja Muthucumaru-Barham.

GPR results: "At best, ground-penetrating radar can find anomalies in the ground that look grave shaped, based on interpretations of results from scans. In some cases, such as in unmarked sections of historic cemeteries, these are likely to be graves. In other cases it is less clear. In all cases, further investigation is warranted."[43]

To break down the data:

- CBC: five articles (23.8 percent of CBC errors; 5.15 percent of CBC articles; and 1.3 percent of total articles)[44]
- *National Post*: three articles (12.5 percent of *Post* errors, 4.2 percent of total *Post* articles, and 0.8 percent of all articles studied)[45]
- *Globe and Mail*: four articles (11.8 percent of *Globe* errors, 5.7 percent of total *Globe* articles, and 1 percent of all articles studied)[46]
- *Toronto Star*: five articles (11.1 percent of *Star* errors, 7.2 percent of total *Star* articles, and 1.3 percent of all articles studied).[47]
- Canadian Press: five articles (45.45 percent of Canadian Press errors, 6.3 percent of all Canadian Press articles, and 1.3 percent of all articles studied)[48]

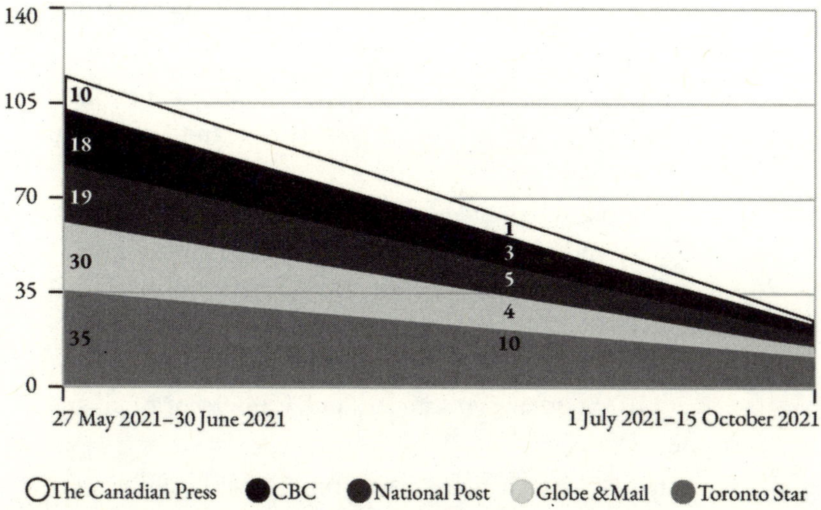

Figure 7.5. Changes in inaccurate reporting in articles on First Nations locating potential unmarked graves by news sources between 27 May 2021 and 15 October 2021. Graph by Anoja Muthucumaru-Barham.

Mistakes over Time

It is important to note that many of the errors across the five outlets were clustered around a small range of dates and then became more sporadic over time. One hundred and twelve of the 135 articles across the five media outlets that contained inaccuracies were published between 27 May and 30 June 2021. This represents 83 percent of total media errors and 29 percent of all articles that were used for this study. The remaining twenty-three articles that included inaccuracies were released between 1 July and 15 October 2021. This represents 17 percent of all errors and 5.95 percent of all articles that were studied.

As Figures 7.4 and 7.5 show:

- *Toronto Star* posted thirty-five articles between 27 May and 30 June that contained inaccuracies (77.8 percent of *Star* errors; 50.7 percent of total *Star* articles; and 9.1 percent of all articles studied)
  - o Ten articles were released after 1 July (22.2 percent of all errors; 14.5 percent of total articles; and 2.6 percent of articles studied)
- *Globe and Mail* posted thirty articles that contained inaccuracies between 27 May and 30 June (88.2 percent of *Globe* errors; 42.85

percent of the total *Globe* articles; and 7.8 percent of all articles studied)

  - Four articles were released after 1 July (11.8 percent of the *Globe* errors; 5.7 percent of the total *Globe* articles; and 1 percent of all articles studied)

- *National Post* posted nineteen articles containing inaccuracies between 27 May and 30 June (representing 79.2 percent of *Post* errors; 26.8 percent of total *Post* articles; and 4.9 percent of all articles studied)
  - Five were released after 1 July (20.8 percent of *Post* errors; 7 percent of the total *Post* articles; and 1.3 percent of all articles studied)
- CBC posted eighteen articles containing inaccuracies between 27 May and 30 June (85.7 percent of CBC errors; 18.55 percent of the total CBC articles; and 4.7 percent of all articles studied)
  - Only three inaccurate articles were released after 1 July (14.3 percent of CBC errors; 3.1 percent of the total CBC articles; and 0.8 percent of all articles studied)
- Canadian Press posted ten articles containing inaccuracies between 27 May and 30 June (90.9 percent of Canadian Press errors; 12.65 percent of all Canadian Press articles; and 2.6 percent of all articles studied)
  - Only one inaccurate article was released between 1 July and 15 October (representing 9.1 percent of Canadian Press errors; 1.3 percent of all Canadian Press articles; and 0.3 percent of all articles studied)

One final set of statistics concerns how many articles that included the words *mass graves* were found between 27 May and 30 June 2021. Of the twenty-five articles that included the words *mass graves*, nineteen (76 percent of "mass graves" articles) were published during that initial time period. However, this number represents only 17 percent of the 112 articles containing inaccuracies released between 27 May and 30 June. This is important because some pundits cite the mass grave error as being almost universal in the immediate weeks after the Kamloops announcement. Though one writer confirmed that, "in the following weeks, while the term 'mass graves' generally gave way to 'unmarked graves,'" their article gives the impression that this was the main error made immediately following the announcement.[49] This claim is not supported by the evidence.

The statistics examined in this section are also important because they show that a change occurred around the end of June 2021 that resulted in fewer articles with inaccuracies overall, confirming the idea that journalists correct inaccuracies over time as part of their professional practice and as more information becomes available.

Media Accuracy

Despite the inaccuracies discussed in the previous section, it is important to underscore the finding that 251 articles, or 65 percent, were accurate in their reporting on the news of potential unmarked graves at former residential school sites. This challenges the notion that there was a universal mass grave hoax pushed by mainstream media, the federal government, and First Nations to mislead the public. The breakdown for the extent that each outlet had accurate reportage is:

- CBC: seventy-six (78.35 percent of CBC articles; 30.3 percent of all accurate articles; and 19.7 percent of all articles studied)
- Canadian Press: sixty-eight (86.1 percent of all Canadian Press articles; 27.1 percent of all accurate articles; and 17.6 percent of all articles studied)
- *National Post*: forty-seven (66.2 percent of *Post* articles; 18.7 percent of all accurate articles; and 12.2 percent of all articles studied)
- *Globe and Mail*: thirty-six (51.4 percent of all *Globe* articles; 14.3 percent of all accurate articles; and 9.3 percent of all articles studied)
- *Toronto Star*: twenty-four (34.3 percent of all *Star* articles; 9.6 percent of all accurate articles; and 6.2 percent of all articles studied)

While the percentages vary, four out of five media outlets posted more accurate articles than articles containing inaccuracies. It is true that the *Toronto Star* posted more articles containing inaccuracies (65.2 percent) than accurate articles. However, one media outlet does not represent all media, and the preceding analysis shows how even the errors made by the *Star* do not confirm the existence of a mass grave hoax.

There are several ways to examine accurate reporting, and the results are a testament to the hard work that many journalists put into their reports about potential unmarked graves at former residential schools. One way to examine accurate reporting is to look back at the cluster of articles containing inaccuracies that were posted between 27 May and 30 June. Along with the 112 articles containing inaccuracies that were published during that time frame, 136 accurate ones were also published. Taken together, this represents 248 articles. While 45.2 percent contained inaccuracies of some kind, 54.8 percent were accurate, meaning that a majority of journalists were giving correct reports on the news of potential unmarked graves in the initial period. To put this in context, the remaining 138 of 386 articles were posted between 1 July and 15 October. One hundred and fifteen (83.3 percent) of these articles were accurate, while just twenty-three (16.7 percent) were inaccurate. This demonstrates that reporting on this story improved over time. We can also re-examine the articles containing the words *mass grave* posted between 27 May and 30 June. Along with representing 17 percent of articles containing inaccuracies released during this period, the twenty articles that made the mass grave error represent only 7.7 percent of the 248 articles released during this period.

Concerning the mass grave error and the three other common inaccuracies, these 251 articles did their job in avoiding such inaccuracies during a confusing time when even one of the editors of this book erred in the immediate period while trying to understand the extent of the announcement. For example, with the mass grave label, four of the five media outlets contained articles that clarified this mistake, such as making the correction themselves, or quoting Indigenous leaders confirming that what was discovered were possible or potential unmarked graves and not mass graves.[50]

In the case of the GPR inaccuracies, all five outlets posted articles that properly explained what GPR is and how the technology was used to detect anomalies, and confirmed that it does not provide pictures of actual remains.[51] What is particularly significant about the article by Tyler Dawson, which appears in the *National Post*, is that it quotes GPR experts who give more confidence that the anomalies located could likely be confirmed as graves. Experts who have used this technology to locate burials for other projects know when anomaly patterns are the shape of a grave, and they found similar patterns when investigating the former Kamloops site. This can be coupled with the article from the *Globe and Mail* that quotes Sarah Beaulieu, who stated that we need to identify findings as "probable unmarked graves." However, she notes that she is confident that the anomalies are graves because of the similar patterns she saw in other unmarked grave searches. Journalists Jana G. Pruden and Mike Hager note Beaulieu's explanation: "She pointed out the indicators that led her to conclude that disruptions picked up in the radar were, in fact, the graves of children—their placement, size, depth and other features."[52]

In the case of inaccuracies about discovering or digging up bodies at former residential school sites, all five media outlets included articles that correctly used the Tk'emlúps te Secwépemc's clarified statements of "potential unmarked graves of 215 children" instead of "confirmed remains of 215 children." These media statements include "as many as 215 children could be buried on the site,"[53] "215 children whose remains are believed to be buried at the former Kamloops Residential School,"[54] "the discovery of up to 215 unmarked graves of children who died while attending the Kamloops Indian Residential School,"[55] "as many as 215 children were buried in unmarked graves,"[56] and "the Tk'emlúps te Secwépemc First Nation announced last week that ground-penetrating radar had located what are believed to be the unmarked graves of 215 children."[57]

It is also worth noting that some journalists who wrote articles that initially contained inaccuracies corrected their reporting when writing subsequent articles on the same subject. One example comes from the Canadian Press, which posted an article on 31 May where the author stated that GPR searches "uncovered the remains of 215 children on the site of the former Kamloops Indian Residential School."[58] The author made a similar error on 1 June when they noted "215 children whose remains were recently discovered on the grounds of a former residential school in Kamloops, B.C."[59] However, by 22 June the same author published an article where they stated that "what are believed to be the remains of 215 children" were identified at the Kamloops site.[60] Moreover, they authored or co-authored two more articles that also had accurate reporting.[61] This type of correction shows that some journalists revised their reporting over time as they and the public became more knowledgeable about the work Indigenous Nations are undertaking. This challenges the claims that no media outlets have attempted to correct inaccuracies they made in earlier reports. As the weeks and months passed, the gap between accurate articles and articles containing inaccuracies grew, with a higher percentage of accurate articles being published after 1 July 2021.

Analysis

In light of the evidence presented above, we argue that the narrative of the mass grave hoax is not simply reasonable skepticism or contrarianism but rather should be understood as residential school denialism. According to Daniel Heath Justice and Sean Carleton, residential school denialism cherry-picks evidence and distorts basic facts and the overall legacy of the Indian Residential School (IRS) system in order to alleviate settler guilt and block important truth and reconciliation efforts.[62] Denialists believe, or at least they purport to believe, that they are asking reasonable questions and conducting rigorous reporting in order to provide the public with the real "truth" about residential schooling. Yet, in regards to news of possible unmarked graves at former residential school sites, what their version of "truth" amounts to is five identifiable denialist talking points that are challenged below.

Denialist Talking Point 1: Mass Grave Errors

The first talking point is that most, if not all, media reports about Kamloops stated that a "mass grave of children's bodies was discovered at the site."[63] Some pundits admit that this reporting did not last, but they contend that the use of the words *mass graves* was how mainstream media "almost universally reported on the issue."[64] In the case of *The Canadian Mass Grave Hoax* documentary on YouTube, the film presents a theory that the media purposefully misquoted the discovery in order to create a hysteria over mass graves. Yet, this chapter shows that only 6.5 percent of articles studied included the words *mass grave*, and many of those instances were quotes from other people and not the words chosen by journalists or Indigenous Peoples. Moreover, some instances were about the need to check for possible "mass graves," which may still be located. Of the articles released between 27 May and 15 October 2021, 93.5 percent did not contain the words *mass grave*. The mass grave hoax narrative thus rests on a misrepresentation of the evidence collected.

Denialist Talking Point 2: Remains Found

The second talking point is the assertion that all mainstream media reported that the potential unmarked graves definitively contain the remains of children. Some pundits focus on this inaccuracy in particular, stating that media consistently misquoted Indigenous Nations concerning the confirmation of likely or probable burials, not actual remains or bodies of children.[65] *The Canadian Mass Grave Hoax* documentary also erroneously states that all media believed the bodies of 751 children were found in unmarked graves at the former Marieval site in June 2021. Again, our research reveals that while 35 percent of the total articles studied contained some inaccuracies, including mistakenly reporting that "remains had been discovered," these can be understood as part of the journalistic process of reporting on breaking news and not evidence of a conspiracy or cover-up. As new details were made available, and the public became more knowledgeable about the story, journalists quickly corrected most inaccuracies in their reporting to help Canadians better understand the story of potential unmarked graves at former residential school sites.

Denialist Talking Point 3: Indigenous Cover-Up

Denialists target journalists, but they also criticize Indigenous Nations who, they argue, are purposefully spreading misinformation in their announcements to gain sympathy and money. Some denialists contend that Indigenous Nations did not correct the mass grave narrative or the fact that bodies were not discovered at Indian Residential School sites on purpose to create a false rage to justify attacks on churches and Christianity.[66] Drea Humphrey of *Rebel News* also suggests that Tk'emlúps te Secwépemc was attempting a cover-up at the Kamloops site. In Humphrey's view, if there were remains at the site, the Royal Canadian Mounted Police would be conducting an investigation on the grounds, and there was no police presence.[67] Humphrey and her team believed Kukpi7 (Chief) Rosanne Casimir was creating a cover-up when they (discreetly) caught her on camera stating that no excavation on the site has begun and they are not sure when it will begin. Our research shows that only twenty-five articles, or 6.5 percent, included the words *mass grave* and just thirteen quoted people, Indigenous and non-Indigenous, used those words. As others have pointed out, this does not prove the existence of a widespread conspiracy between media, government, and First Nations to create a cover-up.[68]

Denialist Talking Point 4: Misrepresenting GPR

The fourth talking point revolves around denialists discrediting GPR technology. *The Canadian Mass Grave Hoax*, for example, focused on the fact that Indigenous Nations and media were using this technology only to locate possible unmarked graves. Also, because GPR detects anomalies, it does not prove that there are bodies underground, nor does it show how these individuals died. The *Rebel News* documentary *Kamloops: The Buried Truth* argues that the rib bone found at the Kamloops site is not human because the coroner said 95 percent of discovered bones people report are usually animal bones. The filmmakers emphasize this point by showing pictures of animal and human bones that look identical to one another, claiming this is proof that no children are buried on the grounds. Humphrey does not acknowledge the other methods that Indigenous Nations are using to locate and search potential burial sites already discussed in this book (i.e., Chapter 3 and 4). This chapter shows that some articles contained inaccurate or confusing understandings of the GPR technology and what it is capable of uncovering, but it also revealed how many journalists reported on the many nuances of the technology and how it was being used by search teams as one tool among many.

Denialist Talking Point 5: Truth Seekers

Denialists often present themselves as the only "true" reporters who are attempting to challenge the mass grave hoax. They position themselves as truth seekers in opposition to "advocacy journalism start-ups" and cast themselves instead as proponents of "traditional journalism," thus making them more believable.[69] This "advocacy journalism" consists of relying on testimony from Survivors or Indigenous Knowledge Keepers, which, as reported in Terry Glavin's article "The Year of the Graves," leads to a "careless conflation of horrific, verifiable crimes with second- and third-hand accounts of childhood horror stories."[70] This is the kind of undermining of Survivors as unreliable witnesses to their own experience that Phyllis Webstad discussed in Chapter 1. This chapter shows how many of those promoting the mass grave hoax narrative are not truth seekers but rather truth distorters; they are cherry-picking and misrepresenting evidence to bolster backlash claims as a way of attacking and undermining Survivor testimony and shaking public trust in the truth and reconciliation process.

Conclusion

This chapter shows that the foundation of the mass grave hoax narrative—that all mainstream media made errors in reporting on the findings as mass graves—is not supported by the evidence. This research is important for two reasons. First, it gives credit to Indigenous Nations and to the journalists who have reported on potential unmarked graves at former residential school sites and helped Canadians understand this important story. While some mistakes were made, and reportage errors need to be addressed as the story continues to develop, that is all they were: errors. Errors that journalists make but correct in subsequent reporting, as we showed was largely the case concerning news of potential unmarked graves in Canada, is part of the journalism industry. Understood in context, the evidence presented debunks the claims of a media-led conspiracy to create a fake news story about residential schools to attack Christianity and destroy Canada.

Second, this research shows how detailed analysis can be an effective tool in confronting the growing threat of residential school denialism and other kinds of misinformation and disinformation, as many Indigenous communities have called for. Instead of ridicule and outrage—which can give denialists a larger platform—what is needed is deep and reasoned analysis of their discourse to show why they are wrong. This is the strategy of disempowering and discrediting residential school denialism advocated by Truth and Reconciliation Commission chair Murray Sinclair and called for by the editors in the Introduction.[71] We recommend that more research of this kind be undertaken to help Canadians learn how to identify and confront residential school denialism and support meaningful reconciliation.

Notes

1 An earlier version of this chapter appeared as Reid Gerbrandt and Sean Carleton, *Debunking the 'Mass Grave Hoax': A Report on Media Coverage and Residential School Denialism in Canada* (Centre for Human Rights Research, 2023), https://chrr.info/resource/debunking-debunking-the-mass-grave-hoaxa-report-on-media-coverage-andresidential-school-denialism-in-canada/. We thank the Centre for Human Rights Research at the University of Manitoba for funding this research. We acknowledge also Adele Perry and Andrew Woolford for providing helpful comments on an earlier draft. We thank Pauline Tennent, Ha B. (Cassie) Dong, and Kyla Neufeld for their support and help with design.

2 Anya Zoledziowski, "Video Shows Catholic Priest Calling News of Residential School Graves 'Huge Lie,'" *Vice*, 11 August 2021, https://www.vice.com/en/article/epn88m/ video-shows-catholic-priest-calling-news-of-residential-school-graves-huge-lie.

3 Lauren Southern, *The Canadian Mass Grave Hoax*, 2021, YouTube, https://www.youtube.com/watch?v=Go6Fpp03Voc.

4 Terry Glavin, "The Year of the Graves. How the World's Media Got it Wrong on Residential School Graves," *National Post*, 27 May 2022, https://nationalpost.com/opinion/the-year-of- the-graves-how-the-worlds-media-got-it-wrong- on-residential-school-graves; Southern, *Canadian Mass Grave Hoax*.

5 *Honouring the Truth*.

6 Southern, *Canadian Mass Grave Hoax*; Dana Kennedy, "'Biggest Fake News Story in Canada': Kamloops Mass Grave Debunked by Academics," *New York Post*, 27 May 2022, https://nypost.com/2022/05/27/kamloops- mass-grave-debunked-biggest-fake-news-in- canada/; Drea Humphrey, *Kamloops: The Buried Truth*, *Rebel News*, 31 August 2022, https://www.rebelnews.com/kamloops_the_buried_truth_documentary; Sky News Australia, "'Astonishing Bit of Fake News' Exposed in Canada," 1 February 2022, YouTube, https://www.youtube.com/ watch?v=egbXE18omy0; Matt Walsh, "The Newest and Most Shameless Hoax to Demonize Christians," 21 August 2023, https://www.youtube.com/watch?v=yZ5qHwxDM50.

7 Office of the Independent Special Interlocutor for Missing Children and Unmarked Graves and Burial Sites associated with Indian Residential Schools (Office of the Special Interlocutor), *Interim Report, Sacred Responsibility: Searching for the Missing Children and Unmarked Burials*, 2023, https://osi-bis.ca/wp-content/uploads/2023/06/OSI_InterimReport_June-2023_WEB.pdf.

8 Francis, *National Dreams*; Starblanket and Hunt, *Storying Violence*.

9 Alan Lester, "The British Empire in the Culture War: Nigel Biggar's *Colonialism: A Moral Reckoning*," *Journal of Imperial and Commonwealth History* 51, no. 4 (2023): 763–95.

10 Justice and Carleton, "Truth Before Reconciliation."

11 Office of the Special Interlocutor, *Interim Report*.

12 Martin Reisigl and Ruth Wodak, "The Discourse-Historical Analysis of the Rhetoric of Racism and Antisemitism," in *Discourse and Discrimination: Rhetorics of Racism and Antisemitism* (Routledge, 2021); Marianne Jørgensen and Louise Phillips, *Discourse Analysis as Theory and Method* (SAGE Publications, 2002).

13 Southern, *Canadian Mass Grave Hoax*; Walsh, "Newest and Most Shameless Hoax."

14 Dan Berkowitz, "Telling What-a-Story News Through Myth and Ritual: The Middle East as Wild West," in *Media Anthropology*, ed. Eric Rothenbuhler and Mihai Coman (Sage, 2005), 211.

15 Berkowitz, "Telling What-a-Story," 211.

16 Brodie Fenlon, "I Run CBC News. Elon Musk's Twitter Changes Had to Be Called Out," *National Post*, 20 April 2023, https://nationalpost.com/opinion/i-run-cbc-news-elon-musks-twitter-changes-had-to-be-called-out.

17 Dan Berkowitz and Zhengjia Michelle Liu, "Media Errors and the 'Nutty Professor': Riding the Journalistic Boundaries of the Sandy Hook Shootings," *Journalism* 17, no. 2 (2016): 155–72.

18 Carl Hiaasen, "Keep Nutty Professor Around as Case Study," *Tampa Bay Times*, 21 January 2013, http://www.tampabay.com/opinion/columns/keep-nutty-professor-around-as-case-study/1271614.

19 Glavin, "Year of the Graves."

20 Stephanie Levitz, "Under Fire over Indigenous Children's Mass Grave, Trudeau Defends His Government's Work on Reconciliation," *Toronto Star*, 31 May 2021, https://www.thestar.com/politics/federal/2021/05/31/trudeau-cant-just-say-he-is-sorry-about-the-discovery-of-a-mass-grave-of-indigenous-children-jagmeet-

singh-says.html; Nadine Yousif, "Survivors Helping Survivors: Residential School Hotlines Flooded with Calls after Kamloops Mass Grave Discovery," *Toronto Star*, 31 May 2021, https://www.thestar.com/news/canada/2021/05/31/survivors-helping-survivors-residential-school-hotlines-flooded-with-calls-after-kamloops-mass-grave-discovery.html; Amira Elghawaby, "Discovery of Kamloops Mass Grave Compels our Collective Action," *Toronto Star*, 1 June 2021, https://www.thestar.com/opinion/contributors/2021/06/01/discovery-of-kamloops-mass-grave-compels-our-collective-action.html.

21 Kristy Kirkup and Mike Hager, "Murray Sinclair Says More Remains Will Be Found at Residential School Sites," *Globe and Mail*, 1 June 2021, https://www.theglobeandmail.com/politics/article-murray-sinclair-says-more-remains-will-be-found-at-residential-school/.

22 Patrick White, Kristy Kirkup, and Mike Hager, "Ottawa Pledges Funds to Locate Unmarked Indigenous Graves at Residential Schools," *Globe and Mail*, 2 June 2021, https://www.theglobeandmail.com/canada/article-ottawa-pledges-27-million-for-uncovering-unmarked- indigenous-graves/.

23 Jenna Moon, "Mississauga Paster Apologizes After Asking Canadians to See 'the Good That Was Done' in Residential Schools," *Toronto Star*, 24 June 2021, https://www.thestar.com/news/gta/2021/06/24/mississauga-pastor- apologizes-after-asking-canadians-see-the-good-that-was-done-in-residential-schools.html.

24 James McCarten, Canadian Press, "Canada's Tragic Residential-School Reckoning Could be Grim Harbinger for U.S.," *Toronto Star*, 27 June 2021, https://www.thestar.com/politics/2021/06/27/canadas-tragic-residential-school-reckoning-could-be-grim-harbinger-for-us.html.

25 Glavin, "Year of the Graves."

26 Tony Davis, "P.E.I. First Nation to Honour Residential School Victims from Kamloops, B.C.," *CBC News*, 30 May 2021, https://www.cbc.ca/news/canada/prince-edward-island/pei-shoes-first-nation-residental-school-victims-may-2021-1.6046224.

27 Courtney Dickson, "Residential School Survivors Society Calls for Action Following Discovery of Children's Remains," *CBC News*, 28 May 2021, https://www.cbc.ca/news/canada/ british-columbia/indian-residential-school-survivors-society-calls-for-action-1.6045448.

28 Tasha Kheiriddin, "The Push to #cancelCanadaDay Misunderstands That Our Flawed Nation Is Still Worth Celebrating," *National Post*, 8 June 2021, https://nationalpost.com/opinion/tasha-kheiriddin-the-push-to-cancelcanadaday-misunderstands-that-our-flawed-nation-is-still-worth-celebrating.

29 Andrea Woo and Jeffrey Jones, "Discovery of Remains of 215 Children at Former Kamloops Residential School Prompts Calls from Indigenous Leaders to Investigate All Sites," *Globe and Mail*, 30 May 30, 2021, https://www.theglobeandmail.com/canada/article-calls-for- action-follows-discovery-of-childrens-remains- at-kamloops/.

30 Douglas Quan, "Prayers Mixed with Calls from Justice in Kamloops: Mourners Honour Lives of 215 Children Whose Remains Were Found at Residential School Site," *Toronto Star*, 31 May 2021, https://www.thestar.com/news/canada/2021/05/31/no-words-just-cries-in-kamloops-calls-for-healing-calm-and-accountability-for-215-children-lost.html; Stephanie Levitz, "Amid Calls for Urgent Action in Response to Deaths in Residential Schools, Ottawa Says There's No Speedy Solution," *Toronto Star*, 1 June 2021, https://www.thestar.com/politics/federal/2021/06/01/amid-calls-for-urgent-action-in-response-to-deaths-in-residential-schools-ottawa-says-theres-no-speedy-solution.html.

31 Maan Alhmidi, Canadian Press, "Discovery of Indigenous Children's Bodies Reminder of Canada's Genocide: Experts," *Toronto Star*, 1 June 2021, https://www.thestar.com/politics/2021/06/01/discovery-of-indigenous-childrens-remains-evidence-of-canadas-genocide-experts.html.

32 Kristy Kirkup and Mike Hager, "RCMP Investigating Former Kamloops Residential School Site, Sinclair Tells MPs," *Globe and Mail*, 3 June 2021, https://www.theglobeandmail.com/politics/article-rcmp-investigating-former-kamloops-residential-school-site-sinclair/.

33 Tk'emlúps te Secwépemc, "Remains of Children of Kamloops Residential School Discovered," 27 May 2021, press release, https://tkemlups.ca/wp-content/uploads/05-May-27-2021-TteS-MEDIA-RELEASE.pdf.

34 Tk'emlúps, "Remains of Children."

35 CBC, "Central B.C. First Nations Hold Ceremony Honouring Residential School Victims, Survivors," *CBC News*, 20 June 2021, https://www. cbc.ca/news/canada/british-columbia/central-b-c-first-nations-hold-ceremony-honouring-residential-school-victims-survivors-1.6072828.

36 CBC, "Flags on Federal Buildings Lowered in Memory of Kamloops Residential School Victims," *CBC News*, 30 May 2021, https://www.cbc.ca/news/politics/flags-lowered-residential-school-victims-1.6046152.

37 Ryan Tumilty, "Trudeau Jets to Tofino, B.C. for Vacation on First Truth and Reconciliation Day," *National Post*, 30 September 2021, https://nationalpost.com/news/politics/trudeau-jets-to-tofino-b-c-on-first-truth-and-reconciliation-day.

38 Walsh, "The Newest and Most Shameless Hoax."

39 Alex McKeen, "He's Found Graves Before. As First Nations Push to Find Children's Remains Across Canada, He and Others Are Ready to Go Back to Work," *Toronto Star*, 16 June 2021, https://www.thestar.com/news/canada/2021/06/16/hes-found-graves-before-as-first-nations-push-to-find-childrens-remains-across-canada-he-and-others-are-ready-to-go-back-to-work.html.

40 Brenna Owen, "'Reconciliation Demands Honesty and Transparency,' says Chief of B.C. First Nation,"The Canadian Press, 30 September 2021, https://www.thestar.com/politics/2021/09/30/reconciliation-demands-honesty-and-transparency-says-chief-of-bc-first-nation.html.

41 Brian Platt, "Trudeau Calls on Catholic Church to 'Step up' on Residential Schools and Release More Records," *National Post*, 3 June 2021, https://nationalpost.com/news/canada/canadian-press-newsalert-trudeau-calls-on-catholic-church-to-take-responsibility.

42 Mark Gollom, "How Radar Technology Is Used to Discover Unmarked Graves at Former Residential Schools," *CBC News*, 14 June 2021, https://www.cbc.ca/news/canada/ground-radar-technology-residential-school-remains-1.6049776.

43 Kisha Supernant, "'Every Child Matters': One Year After the Unmarked Graves of 215 Indigenous Children Were Found in Kamloops," *The Conversation*, 26 May 2022, https://theconversation.com/every-child-matters-one-year-after-the-unmarked-graves-of-215-indigenous-children-were-found-in-kamloops-183778.

44 Gareth Hampshire, "Former Site of Shubenacadie Residential School Scanned for Human Remains," *CBC News*, 31 May 2021, https:// www.cbc.ca/news/canada/nova-scotia/shubenacadie-residential-school-kamloops- radar-remains-1.6047347.

45 Ryan Tumilty, "After PM's Vacation, Trudeau Minister Says Important Part of Reconciliation Is 'Listening,'" *National Post*, 2 October 2021, https://nationalpost.

com/news/politics/after-pms-vacation-trudeau-minister-says-important- part-of-reconciliation-is-listening.

46 Kristy Kirkup, "Federation of Sovereign Indigenous Nations to Receive Funding for Research of Burial Sites," *Globe and Mail*, 22 June 2021, https://www.theglobeandmail.com/politics/article-federation-of-sovereign-indigenous-nations-to-receive-funding-for/.

47 Alex McKeen, "RCMP Say They're Playing Supportive Role Only After Remains of 215 Children Discovered at Kamloops Site," *Toronto Star*, 3 June 2021, https://www.thestar.com/news/canada/rcmp-say-they-re-playing-supportive-role-only-after-remains-of-215-children-discovered-at/article_bd50d658-6dd0-548c-a29b-8509a6d69997.htm.

48 Daniela Germano, "'Delicate, Sensitive Process': Expert Talks on Searching for Burial Sites with Radar," *Toronto Star*, 1 June 2021, https://www.thestar.com/news/canada/2021/06/01/delicate-sensitive-process-expert-talks-on-searching-for-burial-sites-with-radar.html.

49 Glavin, "Year of the Graves."

50 Bryan Eneas, "Sask. First Nation Announces Discovery of 751 Unmarked Graves Near Former Residential School," *CBC News*, 24 June 2021, https://www.cbc.ca/news/canada/saskatchewan/cowessess-marieval-indian-residential-school-news-1.6078375; Tom Blackwell, "Residential School Remains Could Reveal How 215 Children Lived—and Died, Experts Say," *National Post*, 2 June 2021, https://nationalpost.com/news/canada/forensic-probe-of-residential-school-graves-could-reveal-much-about-tragic-lives-experts-say; Jana G. Pruden, "'There's Still So Much Work Yet to Be Done,' Chief of Tk'emlúps te Secwépemc Says," *Globe and Mail*, 5 June 2021, https://www.theglobeandmail.com/canada/article-chief-of-tkemlups-te-secwepemc-says-theres-still-so-much-work-yet-to/; Brendan Kennedy and Alex Boyd, "'We Will Not Stop Until We Find All of Our Children': Discovery of 751 Unmarked Graves Only the Beginning, Say Saskatchewan Indigenous Leaders," *Toronto Star*, 24 June 2021, https://www.thestar.com/news/canada/we-will-not-stop-until-we-find-all-of-our-children-discovery-of-751-unmarked/article_c1178e88-38f9-520a-85ee-9193a22d90f1.html.

51 Gollom, "How Radar Technology Is Used"; Tyler Dawson, "How Ground-Penetrating Radar Is Used to Uncover Unmarked Graves," *National Post*, 31 May 2021, https://nationalpost.com/news/canada/how-ground-penetrating-radar-is-used-to-uncover-unmarked-graves; Jana G. Pruden, "How the Ground-Penetrating Technology Used to Locate Unmarked Graves Is Both Amazing and Complex," *Globe and Mail*, 3 June 2021, https://www.theglobeandmail.com/canada/article-the-technology-used-to-search-for-lost-graves-is-amazing-and-murky/; Kennedy and Boyd, "'We Will Not Stop'"; Mike Raptis, Canadian Press, "More than 160 Unmarked Graves Found at B.C. Residential School Site: First Nation," *National Post*, 13 July 2021, https://nationalpost.com/pmn/news-pmn/canada-news-pmn/more-than-160-unmarked-graves-found-at-b-c-residential-school-site-first-nation.

52 Jana G. Pruden and Mike Hager, "Anthropologist Explains How She Concluded 200 Children Were Buried at the Kamloops Residential School," *Globe and Mail*, 15 July 2021, https://www.theglobeandmail.com/canada/article-kamloops-residential-school-unmarked-graves-discovery-update/.

53 John Paul Tasker, "Catholics Need to 'Ask Their Church to Do Better' in the Wake of Kamloops Discovery, Minister Says," *CBC News*, 2 June 2021, https://www.cbc.ca/news/politics/un-calls-canada-prompt-exhaustive-investigations-1.6049912.

54 Frances Bula, "Victoria Cancels Canada Day Celebrations as Mayor Says They Would Be Damaging to Reconciliation Efforts," *Globe and Mail*, 10 June 2021, https://www.theglobeandmail.com/canada/british-columbia/article-victoria-cancels-canada-day-celebrations-as-mayor-says-they-would-be/.

55 Tristin Hopper, "The Graves Were Never a Secret; Why So Many Remain Unmarked," *National Post*, 2 June 2021, https://nationalpost.com/news/canada/the-graves-were-never-a-secret-why-so-many-residential-school-cemeteries-remain-unmarked.

56 Levitz, "Amid Calls for Urgent Action."

57 Teresa Wright, Canadian Press, "Canada's Justice Minister Mulls Legal Protection of Residential School Burial Sites," *Toronto Star*, 2 June 2021, https://www.thestar.com/politics/2021/06/02/indigenous-services-minister-wants-pope-to-apologize-for-canadas-residential-schools.html.

58 Julia Peterson, Canadian Press, "Indigenous Leader, Saskatchewan Want Federal Action on Residential School Deaths," *Toronto Star*, 31 May 2021, https://www.thestar.com/politics/2021/05/31/indigenous-leader-saskatchewan-want-federal- action-on-residential-school-deaths.html.

59 Julia Peterson, Canadian Press, "Saskatchewan First Nation Honours Children Who Disappeared from Residential School," *Toronto Star*, 1 June 2021, https://www.thestar.com/news/canada/2021/06/01/saskatchewan-first-nation-honours-children-who-disappeared-from-residential-school.html.

60 Julia Peterson, Canadian Press, "Federal Government Gives Money for Residential School Site Research in Saskatchewan," *Toronto Star*, 22 June 2021, politics/2021/06/22/federal-government-gives-money-for-residential-school-site-research-in-saskatchewan.html.

61 Julia Peterson, Canadian Press, "Ground-Penetrating Radar Search for Graves Begins in Delmas, Sask," *Toronto Star*, 17 July 2021, https://www.thestar.com/politics/2021/07/17/ground-penetrating-radar-search-for-graves-begins-in-delmas-saskatchewan.html; Julia Peterson and Kelly Malone, Canadian Press, "First Nation Says 751 Unmarked Graves Found at Saskatchewan Residential School Site," *Toronto Star*, 24 June 2021, https://www.thestar.com/politics/2021/06/24/first-nation-says-751-unmarked-graves-found-at-saskatchewan- residential-school-site.html.

62 Justice and Carleton, "Truth Before Reconciliation"; Michelle Cyca, "The Dangerous Allure of Residential School Denialism," *The Walrus*, 4 May 2023, https://thewalrus.ca/residential-school- denialism/.

63 Glavin, "Year of the Graves"; Southern, *Canadian Mass Grave Hoax*.

64 Glavin, "Year of the Graves."

65 Glavin, "Year of the Graves."

66 Southern, *Canadian Mass Grave Hoax*.

67 Humphrey, *Kamloops*.

68 Meaghan Walker-Williams, "Residential Schools Tragedy Lost in the 'Mass Grave' False Narrative," *National Post*, 14 September 2023, https://nationalpost.com/opinion/meaghan-walker-williams-residential-schools-tragedy-lost-in-the-mass-grave-false-narrative.

69 Glavin, "Year of the Graves."

70 Glavin, "Year of the Graves."

71 CBC, "Senator Murray Sinclair Responds to Lynn Beyak's Defence of Residential Schools," *CBC News*, 29 March 2017, https://www.cbc.ca/news/politics/murray-sinclair-lynn-beyak-residential-schools-1.4045465.

CHAPTER 8

IDENTIFYING THE TECHNIQUES OF SETTLER COLONIAL GENOCIDE DENIALISM

by Andrew Woolford

Wherever there exists a claim of genocide, one will find those who distort or minimize the events and processes addressed under the claim. Even with respect to the most researched and established case of genocide, the Holocaust, denialists continue to challenge, misrepresent, and misdirect the historical record, as explained in the Introduction and previous chapters.[1] In this chapter, I, as a settler professor of sociology and criminology and a genocide scholar, identify six "techniques of neutralization" commonly used by denialists to refute the charge of settler colonial genocide, particularly as it relates to the case of Canada's Indian Residential School (IRS) system.

Denialism is made possible by the nature of genocide and its *phenomenological complexity*—its scale and scope cross multiple regions, time periods, and even, in some cases, political regimes. This is why genocide scholars generally agree that genocide is a process and not an event.[2] Another factor that creates space for denialism is the *definitional complexity* of genocide. In its most basic formulation, genocide is the intentional destruction of a group in whole or in part. But questions inevitably arise, such as: What constitutes intent? What types of groups are protected? What forms of destruction are included? And how large a part of a group must be impacted for it to be genocide? Genocide is thus an "essentially contested" notion in that we agree that such a phenomenon exists, but we have very different ideas about what it entails.[3] This is so even though there is a legal definition of *genocide*, the Convention on the Prevention and Punishment of the Crime of Genocide (the United Nations Genocide Convention [UNGC], adopted in 1948), which is the basis for all international and domestic definitions of genocide (as explained in greater detail in the next chapter). Legal and scholarly debates continue in relation to all elements of the genocide concept. These debates include whether physical destruction is a necessary component of genocide; whether mass bombing campaigns and other acts of war should be considered genocidal; whether groups based on other criteria, such as politics or sexual identity, should be included as targets of genocide; and whether group destruction resulting from instrumental or other goals, rather than a specific intent to eliminate a despised group, should be considered genocide.[4] Debates such as these allow for critical discussion of the genocide concept, its potentials and limitations, but also create room for doubt and denialism based on contested criteria. Denialists deliberately seek to exploit this discursive space to neutralize genocide claims and normalize minimization as a technique.

Motivations for and Techniques of Denialism

What do denialists hope to achieve by countering narratives of genocide? Denialists often perceive the question to be one of genocide or innocence. With respect to residential school genocide denialists, their reasoning often plays out as either Canada is guilty of the genocide charge, or it engaged in acts of benevolence that misfired or succeeded only in part. However, in more serious legal discussions of Canada's Indian Residential School System (IRSS), this is not the choice faced. There is no doubt that Canada quite often forcibly removed children from their families and subjected them to harmful and violent conditions within residential schools. The fact that Canada settled the class action lawsuits launched by Survivors through the Indian Residential School Settlement Agreement in 2006/2007, and the government apologized to Survivors in the House of Commons in 2008, is testament to this. Even if one insists on an overly narrow and rigid definition of genocide that excludes its application to Canada, an approach I have elsewhere critiqued,[5] crimes against humanity—which includes harms against civilian populations ranging from murder to rape and torture to persecution—would still stand. As one of the primary atrocity crimes under international humanitarian law, crimes against humanity are considered an equally severe charge to genocide.[6]

In the end, the payoff for denialism is its capacity to neutralize bad feeling and re-establish a sense of innocence helpful in protecting the settler colonial status quo.[7] Put differently, denialism allows one to purify their identity, removing any association of being Canadian with genocide, violence, dispossession, and other historical wrongs.[8] Identity is protected, given certainty, and made less susceptible to devaluation. Such identity protection, of course, has real consequences, as denialists seek to preserve their power and privilege, especially in terms of claims to resources and land.[9]

In the next section, I examine a sample of written statements made by those promoting or engaging in residential school denialism. These statements arose in response to key moments, such as the release of the *Final Report* of the Truth and Reconciliation Commission of Canada, the National Inquiry for Missing and Murdered Indigenous Women and Girls, the revelation of potential unmarked graves located at the former Kamloops Indian Residential School (KIRS) and other sites, and the Canadian Historical Association's Canada Day Declaration.

Techniques of Neutralization in Residential School Genocide Denialism

In 1957, Gresham Sykes and David Matza identified five techniques of neutralization based on a study of young offenders and the strategies they used to rationalize their misbehaviour. The authors noted that criminology had sought to identify how potential offenders learned the techniques of crime commission but had ignored the skills required to engage in guilt avoidance.[10] Since their study, their techniques have been used widely within criminology and also extended into fields such as genocide studies. For example, Stanley Cohen uses the techniques of neutralization to critique state justificatory discourses deployed when accused of human rights violations.[11] Below, I apply all five techniques of neutralization to the case of residential school genocide denialism. These techniques are not mutually exclusive and quite often overlap or blend into one another. Nonetheless, they are a useful rubric for assessing the work done through denialist discourses, including how they operate to dampen the blow of genocide accusation. They often do so through contrasting residential schools to other genocides, most prominently the Holocaust and Rwanda, or by professing a desire to preserve the purity of the genocide concept.

The five techniques of neutralization identified by Sykes and Matza and explained below—denial of responsibility, denial of injury, denial of the victim, condemnation of the condemners, and appeal to higher loyalties—when applied to settler colonial genocide denialism tend to traffic primarily in the phenomenological complexity of the genocide concept. To capture how definitional complexity is specifically deployed to deny genocide claims, I add "denialism through definitionalism" as a sixth technique of neutralization.

Denial of Responsibility

The first technique of neutralization is the denial of responsibility whereby a perpetrator professes that they did not have agency when committing the acts, and, if damage occurred, it was due to other forces. This mode of denialism arose most prominently in response to the discovery of potential unmarked graves at residential schools such as Kamloops and Merieval in 2021. In addition to being upset at how some journalists initially reported these discoveries as "mass graves,"[12] detractors were at pains to blame sources other than Canada and the Churches for any deaths that did occur. Christian Paul (C.P.) Champion's claim that "most of the children likely died of disease (meaning they were not murdered)"[13] is echoed by others engaging in denialist writing, such as Brian Giesbrecht and Peter Holle, who argue: "It is far more likely that the deaths simply reflected the sad reality of life back then."[14] Such claims rest on a false notion that disease is solely a natural phenomenon, unrelated to the social conditions that enable its spread and severity.[15] But they also effectively displace responsibility, directing it toward a non-human agent.

If the social conditions that made disease more deadly are acknowledged, the argument shifts to noting that the social conditions themselves were the product of a lack of education among the Indigenous population, as in this passage from Mark DeWolf: "Little or no education at all must certainly be considered a major cause of poverty, its related social ills, and all kinds of negative intergenerational effects, but this glaring fact rarely gets a mention in articles dealing with First Nations poverty, unemployment, and related social problems."[16]

Blame is transferred to Indigenous children and communities for resisting education, rather than resting on the education itself.

With respect to the question of genocide, these denials of responsibility reject that Canada possessed an intent to destroy Indigenous Peoples. These authors focus on the importance of specific intent in the UNGC. And, in doing so, they ignore how genocide perpetration can include cultural techniques of destruction. James Rodger (J.R.) Miller, for example, argues that "the government's aim was assimilation, not extermination" and further adds: "If Canada had wanted to destroy First Nations, it would not have devoted so much effort to trying to turn them into Euro-Canadians."[17] In this manner, Miller bypasses the originator of the genocide concept—Raphaël Lemkin's discussion of assimilation as a potential tool of genocide—as well as subsequent scholarship on cultural techniques of destruction.[18] This is also true for Champion, who states that accusations of genocide operate "as if the children had been deliberately killed or death were the norm rather than the very sad exception."[19] Some even go so far as to reinforce the disingenuous claims of benevolent intent espoused by government figures. Nina Green, for example, denies government intent by cherry-picking a single statement, and one that reveals the goal to assimilate Indigenous Peoples to menial positions, isolated on reserves: "In fact, the Canadian government made clear at the time that the purpose of educating status Indian children in residential schools was 'to develop the great natural intelligence of the race and to fit the Indian for civilized life in his own environment.'"[20] The quoted statement in this passage comes from a Department of Indian Affairs report from 1910. Not all superintendents working in the residential school era were as willing to acknowledge the "natural intelligence" of Indigenous children, but even with this seeming compliment, one cannot ignore the language of evolutionary racist science within the quotation, or the important work done by the word *civilized* in conveying meaning. The notion of the "Indian problem" very much frames this statement and signals the underlying intent to forcibly transform Indigenous Peoples. Such statements neutralize any sense of responsibility, since they purport that intentions were benign.

Denial of Injury

The objective of the denial of injury is to demonstrate that the damage done was lesser than claimed or even that no real damage was done. In many cases, detractors will admit that residential schools could be bad places but then pivot to explain why they were not as bad as perceived, or their impact is smaller than stated. In making this argument, a few key points are regularly voiced: one, that reserve communities were themselves harsh places where Indigenous children experienced hardship; two, that most Indigenous young people were not sent to residential schools; three, that there is no official record or physical evidence of Indigenous children being killed in residential schools; and four, that Indigenous populations have increased rather than decreased.

On the first point, Bruce Dowbiggin asserts that "the sobering death rates of Rez [*sic*] children were in line with the terrible mortality rates for children from all causes in the years the schools were employed from 1870–2000."[21] Rather than using this claim to reinforce the overall deprivations caused by settler colonialism, Dowbiggin deploys it to suggest that residential schools were not as bad as they are commonly presented. The indignity of one situation seemingly justifies the indignity of another.

The second point neutralizes the injury through a focus on the number of children who did not attend residential schools. DeWolf writes, "As government records clearly show, the great majority of First Nations children were never enrolled in a residential school."[22] Similarly, Green attests, "In fact in almost any year throughout the entire period during which the residential schools were in operation, fewer than one-third of status Indian children were actually enrolled at a residential school."[23] By removing Indian Residential Schools from a broader system of assimilative education that also included public and day schools as well as other missionary and seminary institutions, the authors are able to advance a calculus that minimizes the injury to Indigenous communities. They leave out of the equation the relational and community-level impacts of having children forcibly removed and then returned, bringing with them varying levels of trauma that subsequently circulated through these communities over generations.

The third denial of injury technique is to defer to certain types of evidence, usually documents from the colonial archive, to claim a lack of assimilative violence. DeWolf leans in this direction with the following minimizing passage: "Cultural repression, abuse of all kinds, forcible incarceration, and even preventable deaths did happen, and a system that should have done far more to prevent such things can rightly be condemned. But the facts show that they happened much less frequently than is commonly believed, and arguably had much less effect on First Nations communities than has been confidently stated."[24] The facts here apparently do not include the ample testimony from residential school Survivors as recounted to the Truth and Reconciliation Commission of Canada. Likewise, Tom Flanagan and Brian Giesbrecht argue, "There is no documentary evidence to support these stories. There is no record, for example, of a single student being murdered at a residential school—never mind thousands—in the 113-year history of residential schools."[25] This ignores that residentials school archives are often, as fellow traveller Miller notes in his significant book *Shingwuak's Vision*, "scanty" and "sanitized,"[26] and created by the very parties who would be accused of such crimes.

The fourth denial of injury is a classic denialist manoeuvre and can be found in most postgenocide contexts. Population growth of the targeted group is presented as evidence against genocide. This of course ignores the violence of cultural erasure and restricts genocide to its physical and biological forms. But even when evaluated through the narrowest reading of the genocide concept, it misses the fact that genocides are rarely completed. Champion and Flanagan remark with respect to genocide accusations in the wake of the discovery of suspected unmarked graves: "It is a strange genocide in which the target population has increased rather than decreased."[27] Any discussion of population growth in relation to the crime of genocide needs serious contextualization. Since genocide is also a crime in its intent, to the extent that it targets a group "in whole or in part," one does not need to prove substantial population reduction that lasts long after the event to prove a charge of genocide so long as a significant proportion of a group has been targeted. It is also the case that the shock of genocide can affect matters of population growth in different ways. In some cases, a target group may face severe fertility challenges because group members killed or sterilized were primarily of an age for reproduction. In others, cultural promotion of reproduction may result in periods of population catch-up in response to genocidal pressures. Population growth is a complex topic in relation to genocide and not served by denialist misappropriation.[28]

A selective use of residential school contextualization, sources, and data thus provides an opportunity for denialists to minimize the injury caused by Indian Residential Schools.

Denial of the Victim

The third technique of neutralization, denial of the victim, simply asserts that the victim deserved the harm they received. Most brazen perhaps is Conrad Black's dismissive description of Indigenous Peoples as a "Stone Age civilization that was almost entirely nomadic."[29] Others are only slightly more subtle, as with Hymie Rubenstein's claim that Indigenous people were eager to throw off their culture for one they saw as superior: "Aboriginals willingly abandoned many of their traditional beliefs and practices for Western technology, medicine, foodstuffs, religion, and languages from first contact to the present."[30] Here, cultural adaptation is confused with a willingness to cede culture. Green refers to how, "in 1925, for example, Father James McGuire wrote of parents 'clamouring' for their children's admission to the Kamloops Indian Residential School."[31] Use of this statement naïvely accepts Father McGuire's point of view, ignoring how Church leaders worked to convince the government to increase student numbers so that they could increase their budgets,[32] as well as how Indigenous parents were often desperate to find alternatives for their children because of the aforementioned settler colonial–caused destitution of reserves.[33]

In other instances, victim harm is denied by the suggestion that all children were equally at risk of harm from the misguided practices of that era. The British Home Child program, which operated between 1883 and 1939 and sent poor and sick British children to colonies such as Canada to work as indentured labour, is a common example given of the similar wrongs done to white children.[34] Giesbrecht and Holle express this claim as follows: "Many died alone and forgotten. It is a coincidence that the number of 'Home Children' roughly equaled the total number of children who attended residential schools—150,000."[35] The Home Child program, of course, operated on a very different set of motives, which were also problematic in how they sought to civilize the British poor, but they did not use these children as a vector for the erasure of distinct and persistent cultures. Indeed, the transfer of Home Children was understood to strengthen the empire and further establish British culture by emigrating more settlers to the colonies.[36] Yet, with this comparison, victims are denied by making all removed children into equivalent victims.

Condemnation of the Condemners

The fourth technique of neutralization shifts blame from the accused and places it upon the accusers, charging them with being unfair or hypocritical. The claims of the unfairness of the settler colonial genocide charge are often expressed through deployment of the Holocaust as the prototypical genocide, claiming that it is outrageous to compare residential schools to concentration camps. For these denialists, it is as though the application of the legal or sociological concept of genocide means that two distinct events are somehow the same. Champion follows this approach with his protestation, "They [Indian Residential Schools] weren't ideal and were sometimes horrible, but they were a very far cry from concentration camps."[37] As well, he accuses residential school Survivors of co-opting the term *Survivor* toward their own ends: "But anyone over the age of 40 knows that the term 'survivor' was specifically used for 'Holocaust survivor,' meaning European Jews not exterminated in the Shoah, and that the word has since been co-opted by others for its political emotiveness rather than its accuracy."[38] This disregards the fact that the Survivor terminology gained purchase first among psychoanalysts in the late 1970s and early 1980s, who used it to describe the ongoing trauma of Holocaust Survivors and several other groups, such as women who had lived through domestic or sexual violence.[39] Denialists instead imagine an exclusivist etymology to condemn residential school Survivors for the misuse of the term. Champion also condemns claimants as members of a "multi-billion dollar grievance industry."[40] The emergence of reparations politics, however, grew out of the Holocaust, whereby victims of atrocity crimes followed the model advanced by Holocaust Survivors who sought compensatory justice in instances where other forms of moral reckoning were hard to reach.[41] What changed, historically, was not that it suddenly dawned on victims of atrocity crimes that they could grasp for monetary gains based on their suffering; rather, the Holocaust and post–Second World War shifts in the geopolitical order and the global economy created an opening for Survivors to pursue this form of redress alongside a general shift from victor's to victim's justice.[42]

When those who argue for the existence of settler colonial genocide in Canada are not denounced for co-opting the Holocaust or for possessing greedy motives, they are assailed for "concept creep."[43] This idea draws on a dilution argument that enables genocide gatekeeping to deny some groups the right to claim genocide since they are not held to match a pure prototype. For historian Christopher Dummit, "Concept creep weakens the original term. Expansion entrepreneurs use powerful terms to borrow their potency. Yet by stretching the meaning of genocide to fit an ever-broader array of actions, the term loses severity. It just doesn't mean the same thing anymore."[44] Aside from his longing for a static genocide concept that need not attend to the empirical question of how Indigenous communities persist and what actions threaten their persistence, Dummit's framing allows for representation of so-called expansion entrepreneurs as the real guilty parties because they dilute the notion of genocide.

This condemnation of the condemners enables denialists and minimizers to reverse the victimization claim. No longer are Indigenous Survivors of assimilative education the wronged party. The wronged are the Christian churches and the State, who are diminished by their accusers. With respect to the former, Flanagan and Giesbrecht write, "This anti-Christian sentiment has been largely directed against the Catholic Church and the Catholic religious orders which operated and staffed many residential schools."[45] As such, they reduce criticism of Church participation in genocide to the prejudice of the accusers.

Appeal to Higher Loyalties

In its initial formulation, the fifth technique of neutralization, the appeal to higher loyalties, referenced how young people viewed their felt obligations to friends, a gang, or a specific individual to override social norms. In the context of genocide denialism, the appeal is often to a higher order ideal or value, though it can also speak to group loyalty. Discussion of the Holocaust, for example, can operate both as condemnation of the condemners and an appeal to higher loyalties. It fits the latter technique because the Holocaust is a world historical event and the Holocaust Survivor a sacred figure in global genocide consciousness.[46] Loyalty to these victims, it is argued, must be preserved against those who wish to expand the genocide concept. Irwin Cotler's remarks are a key touchstone for those using this technique. Dowbiggin quotes Cotler as follows: "'If we say everything is a genocide, then nothing is a genocide.'"[47] It would seem, according to this reasoning, that one cannot acknowledge the distinct genocide experiences in both the Holocaust and the IRS system. We are dragged back into the tired uniqueness debate, which holds the Holocaust as, if not the only genocide, at minimum one that should be treated as incomparable to others.[48]

In other appeals to higher loyalties, loyalty is given to a notion or value rather than a specific group or event. For many, the value protected is simply the idea of Canada as a just and inclusive society. DeWolf, for example, minimizes the harms of residential schools by assigning them the noble role of sponsoring inclusion: "The IRS system was a deeply flawed attempt to accomplish two main objectives: to give native children education and training that would help them survive economically and socially in a white man's world, and to eradicate those aspects of native culture that would hold them back from achieving those goals."[49] But the national imaginary appealed to by others is a set of values, institutions, laws, and symbols they feel necessary for a Canadian future.[50] Rather than confront the attempted destruction of Indigenous nations, denialists tend to foreground the potential destruction of Canadian unity. Flanagan and Giesbrecht put the matter this way: "The strong belief within the indigenous community that Canada has acted murderously towards them in the past and is continuing to commit genocide against them and their culture in the present will poison relations for years to come, and make it very unlikely that indigenous young people will have happy and successful lives."[51] For Miller, it is reconciliation that is at stake with the claim of genocide: "Canadians of good will can hope that, once charges of 'genocide' in Canadian policy die down, we will focus on what is important. Continuing controversy over terminology is pointless and distracting. It inhibits necessary action to implement many of the recommendations of the Truth and Reconciliation Commission that remain unaddressed five years after it reported."[52] Under this logic, the truth of genocide is the barrier to reconciliation and thus reconciliation the higher loyalty.

Denialism Through Definitionalism

In his model of the ten stages of genocide, Gregory Stanton, under the final stage of denial, includes Israel Charny's notion of "definitionalism," whereby actors wade into the intricacies of the genocide definition to sow doubt about the term's applicability to a specific case, past or present.[53] Definitionalism can be added as a technique of neutralization because of its specific prominence in genocide denialism strategies. Too often, disingenuous contrarians espouse half-baked and under-researched notions of genocide to muddy the waters regarding a Survivor group's claims, and in doing so, they distract attention from the harms themselves so that they might focus instead on matters of law.

A common definitionalist tactic is the claim that cultural genocide has no legal status. This is not an entirely unfounded argument; powerful members of the General Assembly of the United Nations worked very hard to ensure that Lemkin's recognition of cultural techniques of genocide would be excluded from the UNGC.[54] Rubenstein thus has a basis to argue "they do not add up to cultural genocide, partly because the term itself has no legal definition."[55] But it is not so simple. Techniques of cultural genocide were foundational to the original conceptualization of genocide, and colonized nations were under-represented in the discussions that led to their removal. Even still, Lemkin felt that article 2(e) of the UNGC retained an element of his notion of cultural genocide in its reference to "forcibly transferring the children of the group to another group."[56] This is an undertested element of the UNGC, so it remains to be seen if future judges will follow Lemkin's leanings, or instead reinforce the interpretation made by the International Law Commission that privileges the preparatory discussions at the UN that took place mostly among colonial powers.[57] But even with this interpretation, we have seen how courts are beginning to consider cultural techniques of genocide as evidence of an intent to physically destroy a group.[58] As well, other legal scholars have built compelling cases against Canada that examine the combination of cultural, physical, and biological techniques used against Indigenous Peoples, as well as the intricacies of working under Canadian and international legal frameworks for examining genocide.[59] Statements such as Rubenstein's seek to isolate the cultural genocide argument, and dismiss it based on a frozen notion of genocide law.

Michael Melanson and Green likewise use as an example a case brought to the International Criminal Court (ICC) by a group of Canadian lawyers against the Vatican for crimes against humanity for the deaths of children in their care.[60] The case was rejected, for one, because of the principle of complementary, which makes domestic courts the venue of first resort when they are available and have the capacity to hear a claim. This is a procedural rather than substantive refutation of the case, but this point is ignored so that the case can be used to advance definitionalist distraction. Second, Melanson and Green also note that no single individual was identified to be accused of the crime, which makes the case impossible to determine for a criminal court focused on individual guilt. And they point out that there was no jurisdiction for cases before 2002 when the Rome Statute came into force. This case is relatively marginal to the discussion of genocide in Canada, but Melanson and Green seek to use it in definitionalist terms to rebuff the charge of genocide. It should be noted that the individualizing justice of the ICC is part of the reason that we have seen more cases go to the International Court of Justice, which addresses claims against nation-states rather than trying individual perpetrators.[61] Too often, the complexity of genocide perpetration, and the fact that it coordinates the actions of diverse actors in a pattern of destruction, makes it more difficult to isolate individual perpetrators. Melanson and Green also suggest that the lawyers sought a ruling on "crimes against humanity," knowing the genocide convention would not apply.[62] This is a piece of technical definitionalism that misuses the tactical manoeuvre made by a group of lawyers whose goals were to push for further investigation of the violence of the IRS system to suggest that they did not believe genocide an appropriate charge in the case. Melanson and Green ignore that law is a field of play where strategic moves are often made with other goals in mind. It is crass definitionalism to try to cite such an endeavour to discount genocide in Canada.

Conclusion

We can see in such examples, too, how denialists remain set in seeing the world through the lens of the so-called Indian problem. They neutralize accusations against Canada and the Churches and seek to make the issue one of Indigenous Peoples lacking something or not fitting into the dominant society. For this reason, some have sought to flip the script and refocus on a settler rather than Indian problem.[63] It is settlers who have come to stay, erase, and eliminate, and until we unsettle these relations, there is little hope for breaking the frame of the Indian problem. Techniques of neutralization, as deployed by genocide denialists and minimizers, accept the basic premise of assimilation and ask that we ignore the truth of its violence.

Notes

1 For example, see Deborah E. Lipstadt, *Denial: Holocaust History on Trial* (Ecco Publishing, 2016).

2 Rosenberg, "Genocide Is a Process, Not an Event," article 4.

3 Gallie, "Essentially Contested Concepts," 167–98.; Powell, "What Do Genocides Kill?" 527–47.

4 For summaries of these and other debates, see A. Dirk Moses, *The Problems of Genocide: Permanent Security and the Language of Transgression* (Cambridge University Press, 2021); and A. Dirk Moses, "Conceptual Blockages and Definitional Dilemmas in the 'Racial Century': Genocides of Indigenous Peoples and the Holocaust," *Patterns of Prejudice* 36, no. 4 (2002): 7–36.

5 See, for example, Woolford, "Ontological Destruction," 81–97; Woolford, *This Benevolent Experiment.*

6 Akhavan, "Cultural Genocide," 243–70. William Schabas is quoted within Daniel Schwartz, "Cultural Genocide Label for Residential Schools Has No Legal Implications, Expert Says," *CBC News*, 13 June 2015, https://www.cbc.ca/news/indigenous/cultural-genocide-label-for-residential-schools-has-no-legal-implications-expert-says-1.3110826.

7 Eve Tuck and K. Wayne Yang's concept of settler "moves to innocence" overlaps with the techniques of neutralization discussed in the chapter. They note how settlers distance themselves from harms against Indigenous Peoples, restricting them to a "dark chapter" or something that happened "a long time ago." Or they claim an Indigenous ancestor, which allows them to also claim membership as part of the victimized rather than victimizing group. Tuck and Yang, "Decolonization Is Not a Metaphor."

8 Richard Sennett speaks of the purified identity as arising when the "threat of being overwhelmed by difficult social interactions is dealt with by fixing a self-image in advance, by making oneself a fixed object rather than an open person liable to be touched by a social situation." Sennett, *Uses of Disorder*, 6.

9 Carleton, "'I don't need any more education.'"

10 Sykes and Matza, "Techniques of Neutralization," 664–70.

11 Cohen, *States of Denial*; Kjell Anderson, *Perpetrating Genocide.*

12 Gerbrandt and Carleton, *Debunking the "Mass Grave Hoax."*

13 C.P. Champion, "From Katyn to Kamloops," *Dorchester Review*, 17 June 2021.

14 Brian Giesbrecht and Peter Holle, "The Kamloops Cemetery," Frontier Centre for Public Policy, 6 June 2021, https://fcpp.org/2021/06/06/the-kamloops-cemetery/.

15 Latour, *We Have Never Been Modern.*

16 Mark DeWolf, "Myth Versus Evidence: Your Choice," *Essays on the Frontier*, Frontier Centre for Public Policy, 22 August 2018, https://fcpp.org/2018/08/22/myth-versus-evidence-your-choice/.

17 J.R. Miller, "Genocide, Macdonald and Canadian History," *National Post*, 8 June 2021. This is similar to Prime Minister Benjamin Netanyahu's deflection about genocide in Gaza, claiming that if Israel had wanted to commit genocide, "it would have taken exactly one afternoon." Perpetrators and their apologists often ignore that genocide is a crime that targets a group "in whole or in part." See *Times of Israel* Staff, "Netanyahu: 'If We Wanted to Commit Genocide, It Would Have Taken Exactly One Afternoon,'" *Times of Israel*, 11 August 2025, https://www.timesofisrael.

com/netanyahu-if-we-wanted-to-commit-genocide-it-would-have-taken-exactly-one-afternoon/.

18 See Robert van Krieken, "Rethinking Cultural Genocide: Aboriginal Child Removal and Settler-Colonial State Formation," *Oceania* 75 (2004): 125–51.

19 Champion, "From Katyn to Kamloops."

20 Nina Green, "Two-Thirds Did Not Attend Residential School," *Dorchester Review*, 13 July 2022.

21 Bruce Dowbiggin, "The PM Who Tells 'Made-Up' Stories to the World," *Todayville*, 26 August 2021.

22 DeWolf, "Myth Versus Evidence."

23 Green, "Two-Thirds Did Not Attend."

24 DeWolf, "Myth Versus Evidence."

25 Tom Flanagan and Brian Giesbrecht, "The False Narrative of Residential School Burials," *Dorchester Review*, 1 March 2022.

26 Miller, *Shingwauk's Vision*. The terms *scanty* and *sanitized* come from Scott Riney's review of Miller's work: "Review of Education by Hardship: Native American Boarding Schools in the U.S. and Canada, by K. Tsianina Lomawaima, Clyde Ellis, and J.R. Miller," *Oral History Review* 24, no. 2 (1997): 117–23.

27 C.P. Champion and Tom Flanagan, *Grave Error: How the Media Misled Us (and the Truth about Residential Schools)* (True North, 2023), 9.

28 Tadeusz Kugler, "The Demography of Genocide," in *Economic Aspects of Genocides, Other Mass Atrocities, and Their Preventions*, eds. Charles H. Anderton, and Jurgen Brauer (Oxford, 2016).

29 Conrad Black, "The Truth about Truth and Reconciliation," *National Post*, 20 March 2021.

30 Hymie Rubenstein, "Cultural Genocide and the Indian Residential Schools," *C2C Journal*, 9 November 2015.

31 Green, "Two-Thirds Did Not Attend."

32 Milloy, *A National Crime*.

33 Daschuk, *Clearing the Plains*.

34 My grandfather was one of the poor children scooped off the streets of London by Barnardo's orphanage and sent to Uxbridge, Ontario, to work on a farm.

35 Giesbrecht and Holle, "Kamloops Cemetery."

36 Gillian Wagner, *Children of the Empire* (Weidenfeld and Nicolson, 1982); Joy Parr, *Labouring Children: British Immigrant Apprentices to Canada, 1869–1924* (University of Toronto Press, 1994, originally 1980); Kenneth Bagnell, *The Little Immigrants: The Orphans Who Came to Canada* (Dundurn Press, 2001, originally 1980); Roy Parker, *Uprooted: The Shipment of Poor Children to Canada, 1867–1917* (UBC Press, 2008).

37 Champion, "From Katyn to Kamloops."

38 Champion, "From Katyn to Kamloops."

39 Though the word has been in circulation since at least the sixteenth century, its use to describe those who live on despite having experienced targeted violence can be traced to American psychoanalyst William Guglielmo Niederland's concept of "survivor syndrome," referring to the mental condition exhibited by Holocaust Survivors. But it quickly thereafter began to be applied to varied forms of suffering, such as from incest, rape, child abuse, genocide, and Hiroshima, among others. See

Shani Orgad, "The Survivor in Contemporary Culture and Public Discourse: A Genealogy," *Communication Review* 12, no. 2 (2009): 132–61.

40 Champion, "From Katyn to Kamloops."

41 John Torpey, *Making Whole What Has Been Smashed: On Reparations Politics* (Harvard, 2006).

42 Woolford and Wolejszo, "Collecting on Moral Debts."

43 Christopher Dummitt, "Genocide 'Concept Creep' More Likely to Harm Reconciliation," *National Post*, 29 October 2022.

44 Dummitt, "Genocide 'Concept Creep.'"

45 Flanagan and Giesbrecht, "False Narrative."

46 Peter Novick, *The Holocaust in American Life* (Mariner, 1999).

47 Dowbiggin, "PM Who Tells 'Made-Up' Stories."

48 This is the maximalist position held by Stephen T. Katz, "The 'Unique' Intentionality of the Holocaust," *Modern Judaism* 1, no. 2 (1981): 161–83.

49 DeWolf, "Myth Versus Evidence."

50 On the idea of an imaginary and its connection to nationalism, see Benedict Anderson, *Imagined Communities: Reflections on the Origin and Spread of Nationalism* (Verso, 1991). More generally, see Jean-Paul Sartre, *L'Imaginaire: Psychologie phénoménologique de l'imagination* (Gallimard, 1941); John Brookshire Thompson, *Studies in the Theory of Ideology* (Blackwell, 1984); Charles Taylor, *A Secular Age* (Belknap Press of Harvard University Press, 2007).

51 Flanagan and Giesbrecht, "False Narrative."

52 Miller, "Genocide, Macdonald and Canadian History."

53 Gregory Stanton, "The Ten Stages of Genocide," Genocide Watch (1995), https://www.genocidewatch.com/tenstages; Israel Charny, "A Classification of Denials of the Holocaust and Other Genocides," *Journal of Genocide Research* 5, no. 1 (2003): 11–34.

54 See "Decriminalizing Settler Colonialism in Canada: Entryways to Genocide Accusation and Erasure," in *Entryways to Criminal Justice: Accusation and Criminalization in Canada*, ed. George Pavlich and Matthew Unger (University of Alberta Press, 2019).

55 Rubenstein, "Cultural Genocide"; Rubenstein, "Digging for the Truth about Canada's Residential School Graves: Part 1," *C2C Journal*, 7 August 2021.

56 Raphaël Lemkin, *Totally Unofficial: The Autobiography of Raphaël Lemkin*, ed. Donna Lee Frieze (Yale University Press, 2013).

57 In 1996, well after Lemkin's passing, and in a move he surely would have opposed, the International Law Commission declared that genocide concerns only matters related to physical and biological destruction and excludes matters of culture. However, this interpretation bumps up against the fact that the language of the UNGC's Article II is most concerned with persistence of the group. See Kurt Mundorff, *A Cultural Interpretation of the Genocide Convention* (Routledge, 2020).

58 See Tolimir trial judgment, International Tribunal for the Former Yugoslavia, 12 December 2012, Case No.: IT-05088/2-T, para 746, https://www.icty.org/x/cases/tolimir/tjug/en/121212.pdf.

59 National Inquiry into Missing and Murdered Women and Girls, *A Legal Analysis of Genocide* (Canada, Privy Council Office, 2019); Tamara Starblanket, *Suffer the Little Children: Genocide, Indigenous Nations and the Canadian State* (Clarity Press, 2021);

David Macdonald, *The Sleeping Giant Awakens: Genocide, Indian Residential Schools, and the Challenge of Conciliation* (University of Toronto Press, 2019).

60 Meghan Grant, "International Criminal Court Called on to Investigate Kamloops Residential School Findings," *CBC News*, 3 June 2021, https://www.cbc.ca/news/canada/calgary/calgary-canadian-lawyers-icc-residential-school-investigation-1.6052054.

61 See, for example, *The Gambia v. Myanmar*, https://www.icj-cij.org/case/178, and *South Africa v. Israel*, https://www.icj-cij.org/case/192.

62 Michael Melanson and Nina Green, "Canada's Genocide—Case Closed?" *Dorchester Review*, 27 October 2022.

63 Lowman and Barker, *Settler: Identity and Colonialism in the 21st Century Canada*; Regan, *Unsettling the Settler Within*.

CHAPTER 9

RESIDENTIAL SCHOOL DENIALISM IS A CRIME
(In My Humble Opinion)

by Michelle Good

In 2022, Member of Parliament Leah Gazan put forward a motion before Parliament to recognize Canada's Indian Residential School (IRS) system as genocide as defined in Article II of the United Nations Convention on Genocide (UNCG). The motion was passed unanimously by all parties. In 2024, Gazan put a private member's bill before Parliament that would, if passed, criminalize residential school denialism. In her submission, Gazan—who is Lakota-Chinese on her mother's side and Jewish on her father's side—stated that to "downplay, deny, or justify" the impact of residential schools "is cruel, harmful and hateful." Sadly, like most private member's bills, it did not pass. However, analysis of existing Canadian law demonstrates that regardless of whether it is specifically articulated in the Criminal Code, residential school denialism meets the criteria for criminalization and is no less a crime than Holocaust denialism and should be recognized as such. As a member of the Red Pheasant Cree Nation, a former lawyer, and now a bestselling author of books such as *Five Little Indians* and *Truth Telling*, I offer in this chapter a breakdown of what makes Holocaust denialism a crime, how those same factors form the foundation of residential school denialism, and why that should not be ignored by lawmakers when it comes to considered changes to the Criminal Code to make residential school denialism a crime.

In 2022, a number of sections of the Criminal Code of Canada were added through Bill C-19. One of those additions specifically established that Holocaust denialism constitutes a crime. Part 5, Division 21, of the Bill became the basis for the creation of section 319(2.1) of the Criminal Code, which provides as follows:

> **Wilful promotion of antisemitism**
>
> 319(2.1) Everyone who by communicating statements other than in private conversation wilfully promotes antisemitism by condoning, denying or downplaying the Holocaust
>
> a) is guilty of an indictable offence and liable to imprisonment for a term not exceeding two years, or
>
> b) is guilty of an offence punishable on summary conviction.

What, we must ask, distinguishes between the genocide of World War II and the genocide that occurred in Canada during the years of operation of the IRS system? The answer, of course, is that there is little distinction other than means and magnitude. Destruction of the group, in whole or in part, defines both genocides. However, even that distinction is questionable when one factors in the intergenerational impacts of the harms done at Indian Residential Schools. And, most importantly, the definition for what constitutes genocide makes no mention of scale or the necessity of a certain degree of impact. The IRS system meets the definition of genocide, as the 2022 motion recognized. As Andrew Woolford's chapter already explained, denialists are known for downplaying or trying to neutralize the genocidal nature of residential schools by comparing it to the scale of the Jewish Holocaust. This argument is completely without merit.

The presence of genocide in the Jewish Holocaust is what created the foundation and necessity for recognition of Holocaust denialism as a crime, in Canada and elsewhere. In this country, prior to the criminalization of Holocaust denialism the only recourse for those experiencing antisemitism was by way of the hate crime provisions in the Criminal Code. Successful prosecution under these provisions of the Code were few and the weaknesses of the provisions are demonstrated by the paucity of convictions under those sections despite the documented rise of antisemitism and Holocaust denialism in Canada.

There is no question that the Holocaust was an act of genocide. In fact, it was the existence of this genocide that created the foundation for the development of the United Nations Convention on the Prevention and Punishment of the Crime of Genocide, or the Genocide Convention. The term *genocide* did not even exist until after World War II when it was coined by Raphaël Lemkin in the 1940s. Lemkin coined the term *genocide* from two words: *genos* (Greek: γένος, "family, clan, tribe, race, stock, kin") and *-cide* (Latin: *-cidium*, "killing"). Subsequent to the identification and international condemnation of genocide, the United Nations established the criteria for what constitutes genocide. These are as follows:

- killing members of the group;
- causing serious bodily or mental harm to members of the group;
- deliberately inflicting on the group conditions of life calculated to bring about its physical destruction in whole or in part;
- imposing measures intended to prevent births within the group; and
- forcibly transferring children of the group to another group.

Even a superficial analysis of the Indian Residential School System (IRSS) demonstrates that each of these criteria applies, though the proponents of denialism downplay the evidence in support of such a conclusion, as Woolford has shown. In this chapter, I will show how an analysis of each of the above criteria does in fact apply to residential schooling.

Perhaps the most controversial criterion with respect to Indian Residential Schools is the first, "killing members of the group." However, the testimony of IRS Survivors has been consistent, regardless of geographic location, with respect to stories of students digging graves for their classmates, of unmarked burials on school grounds, and of children disappearing under suspicious circumstances. Many of these stories were heard by the Truth and Reconciliation Commission of Canada (TRC), which was formed in 2008 and collected testimonies from over 6,000 Survivors. The TRC's 2015 *Final Report* made it quite clear that further recoveries of unmarked graves at the schools were inevitable. This was recently borne out, for example, by the findings of an Ontario's coroner's investigation that has identified an additional 220 deaths linked to residential schools in the province.[1]

Further, the TRC reported, relying not only on testimony but also Church and State records, that a primary contributor to the high death rate of Indigenous children at residential schools was the abominable conditions these children were forced to endure.

It is well documented that the conditions in the schools themselves were the leading contributor to the often-shocking death rates among the students. The Department of Indian Affairs' own medical officer, Peter Henderson Bryce, reported to his supervisor, Duncan Campbell Scott, in a 1907 report several deeply disturbing findings. He visited and inspected thirty-five government-funded schools in Western Canada. Bryce reported that 25 percent of all children who had attended these schools had died; at one school, the number was 69 percent. Bryce reported that "the almost invariable cause of death given is tuberculosis." Denialists pounce on this to support their argument that the majority of children who died in the schools died from natural causes. However, Bryce was explicit that the death rate from tuberculosis he witnessed was not natural or inevitable. To the contrary, Bryce attributed responsibility for these appalling death rates to the schools themselves. The schools were poorly constructed and lacked proper ventilation, and the staff frequently housed sick students in the dormitories alongside healthy students, therefore encouraging the transference of tuberculosis from one student to another. Bryce's report paints a clear picture of a profound negligence and disregard for the well-being and safety of the students under the care of the government in the schools. As Bryce explained, "doing nothing to obviate the preventable causes of death" in residential schools "brings the Department within unpleasant nearness to the charge of manslaughter."[2] Negligence causing death is a criminal act, and the negligence in the residential schools that nurtured tuberculosis epidemics and the resulting colossal death rate among the children must no longer be dismissed with the deaths being attributed to natural causes. This negligence must be considered as reaching the level of criminality that is obvious upon careful consideration of the evidence.

Further, the testimony of Survivors with respect to the other causes of student deaths must not be rejected out of hand. The evidence is incontrovertible that some schools were desperately violent places. Children were subjected to all manner of physical abuses, and it is not outside the realm of possibility, especially in light of Survivor testimony, that these abuses resulted in deaths. The testimony of Survivors cannot be impeached. There is nothing for them to gain in giving their evidence with respect to the deaths of children resulting from abuses, and the trauma they often suffer as a result of reliving these terrible memories is one that few would choose but for the larger motivation of truth telling and speaking out for those children who died in the schools.

Denial of the Holocaust is not limited to the denial of the Holocaust in its entirety but also to the specifics, such as the number of individuals killed. This is often the focus of Holocaust denialism—the claim that six million Jews did not die in the camps. Likewise with residential school denialism, one of the issues focused on is the number of deaths of children in the schools, and, as noted above, the cause of death.

The second criterion of genocide is "causing serious bodily or mental harm." The existence of serious bodily *and* mental harm is well established as it pertains to the intentional treatment of children in Indian Residential Schools. The question of bodily harm is addressed above and this fully meets the definition, given that it is articulated as bodily or mental harm. However, we must address the question of mental harms inflicted on these children, as this has created deeply damaging intergenerational harms that continue to injure and damage Indigenous Peoples.

It is critical to look at the intent of Indian Residential Schools, as this provides context for the nature of mental harms children experienced in the schools. Canada followed the example of Richard Henry Pratt, the founder of the Indian Boarding School System in the United States, who intentionally set out to deconstruct Indigenous children and reconstruct them in the image of white men. This view was brought to Canada through the 1879 report of Nicholas Flood Davin, who had been commissioned by Sir John A. Macdonald to visit the Carlisle Indian Industrial School in Pennsylvania, created and run by Pratt. It was on the strength of this report that Canada initiated its "contract" approach to residential schools by way of entering into arrangements with various Church denominations to operate the schools with partial federal funding. The Christian approach to fulfilling the federal mandate can be described only as mentally harmful in the most insidious ways. Children were often punished for speaking their own languages, usually the only language they knew. They were forced to dress in the style of non-Indigenous people, and any reference to their spiritual beliefs was strongly punished. As Bishop Vital Grandin, a strong advocate of residential schools and mandatory attendance at them, stated: "We instil in them a pronounced distaste for the native life so that they will be humiliated when reminded of their origins. When they graduate from our institutions, the children have lost everything Native except their blood."[3]

One would be hard-pressed to find any action more harmful than those designed to destroy a child's identity and self-confidence. To intentionally disparage a child's heritage for the purpose of disinheriting them can be described only as nothing short of a kind of death. This deconstruction of Indigenous identity was a stated purpose of the Canadian government and was zealously embraced by its Church partners, who also saw these children as fodder for their Christian proselytizing.

It is well established that sexual abuse was rampant in Indian Residential Schools, with supervising adults taking advantage of a lack of oversight to exploit these vulnerable children at will. It is equally well established that childhood sexual assault creates psychological harms that lasts a lifetime, particularly in cases where no therapeutic intervention is made available to the victim. The following are common impacts of childhood sexual abuse, and it is not controversial in the least that the Indigenous community suffers a much higher incidence of such harms than the non-Indigenous community.

- anxiety[4]
- behavioural disorders, impulsivity, and risk-taking behaviour[5]
- body image dissatisfaction[6]
- depression[7]
- eating disorders, borderline or anti-social personality disorders, schizophrenia[8]
- emotional, affective, and psychological distress and difficulties (for example, distress, despair, anger, attachment difficulties, identity disturbances)[9]
- feelings of shame and guilt[10]
- lower self-esteem[11]
- post-traumatic stress (for example, dissociation, flashbacks, avoidance of risky situations, intrusive thoughts, nightmares, hypervigilance, irritability)[12]

- problems with gambling[13]
- self-harm[14]
- suicidal ideation and behaviour[15]
- use of psychoactive substances, including abuse of or dependence on these substances (for example, alcohol, cannabis, tobacco, cocaine, opioids, other drugs)[16]

While these effects most obviously impact the lives of Survivors, they also have a significant intergenerational effect as they negatively impact the Survivor's ability to parent effectively. When the impacts of physical, sexual, and psychological abuse are combined, this definition of genocidal conduct is easily met with respect to the widespread ill-treatment of residential school students.

Legislation was passed in British Columbia in 1933 and Alberta in 1928 that permitted the sterilization of any person detained in a mental or penal institution. While it is well established that the notorious Indian hospitals that were often associated with particular Indian Residential Schools performed countless sterilizations on Indigenous women without their consent, the link between children from residential schools being sterilized is not adequately researched. However, the legislation noted above gave eugenics boards wide powers in determining who should be sterilized, and it would not be a surprise to discover that the definition of "institutions" in the Act was broadened to include residential schools. We have no doubt that countless IRS Survivors were ultimately sterilized.

And, lastly, the forcible transfer of children from one group to another is possibly the most blatant example of genocide inflicted on the inmates of Indian Residential Schools. Even before attendance at residential schools was made legally mandatory, it was treated as though it was so. Children taken from their families and communities, often by force, were required to attend residential school long before it was made mandatory by law. Again, clearly the purpose of this was to cut ties between the child and their family and community and thus their culture, language, and traditions. As so clearly stated to the House of Commons in 1883 by Sir John A. Macdonald:

> When the school is on the reserve the child lives with its parents, who are savages; he is surrounded by savages, and

> though he may learn to read and write his habits, and training and mode of thought are Indian. He is simply a savage who can read and write. It has been strongly pressed on myself, as the head of the Department, that Indian children should be withdrawn as much as possible from the parental influence, and the only way to do that would be to put them in central training industrial schools where they will acquire the habits and modes of thought of white men.[17]

This and other statements by Macdonald are a clear indication of the *intent* to remove children from their families and communities for the purpose of erasing their culture and assimilating them into white society.

And, thus, we see that all five criteria of genocide apply to the IRS system designed and implemented by the Canadian government and administered by various Churches.

The inclusion of Holocaust denialism in the Criminal Code is obviously to prevent the denial of the Jewish genocide of World War II. Therefore, after clearly illustrating that the IRS system was genocidal in nature and intent, it is difficult to find any reason whatsoever that residential school denialism should not also be criminalized, especially in light of the fact that all parties are united in the position that the schools were genocidal in nature and intent, according to the definitions of genocide as articulated in the United Nations Genocide Convention (UNGC). This leads to the bleak conclusion that it is further discrimination against Indigenous Peoples that is the cause of the resistance to recognize residential school denialism as a crime. This silence about speaking out in favour of criminalizing residential school denialism incites all forms of violence against Indigenous Peoples and must, in my view, be corrected.

Canada cannot continue to speak out of both sides of its mouth. It cannot declare publicly that the schools were genocidal and still refuse to criminalize conduct that claims it was not. If the country truly stands behind its commitment to reconciliation, it must establish that residential school denialism is a crime just as Holocaust denialism is a crime. If it does not, then it irrefutably gives the lie to its stated reconciliation objectives.

Notes

1 Brett Forester, "Coroner's Probe Finds 220 Additional Deaths at Ontario Residential Schools," *CBC News*, 2 December 2024, https://www.cbc.ca/news/indigenous/coroner-ontario-residential-schools-investigation-1.7396884.

2 Bryce as quoted in Milloy, *A National Crime*, 77.

3 LAC, RG10, vol. 3708, file 19502, part 1, *Northwest Territories and Manitoba—Correspondence and Reports Regarding Roman Catholic Missions, Farms on Reserves, and Destitute Indians*, Grandin to Macdonald, 27 September 1880, Online MIKAN no. 2061654 (online pages 57–58).

4 See, for example, the following: Ashley B. Woolweaver, Nadin Abu Khalaf, and Dorothy L. Espelage, et al., "Outcomes Associated with Adolescent Dating and Sexual Violence Victimization: A Systematic Review of School-Based Literature," *Trauma, Violence & Abuse* 25, no. 4 (2024): 2781–96, https://doi.org/10.1177/15248380241226; Erin C. Dunn, Kristen Nishimi, Alexander Neumann, et al., "Time-Dependent Effects of Exposure to Physical and Sexual Violence on Psychopathology Symptoms in Late Childhood: In Search of Sensitive Periods in Development," *Journal of the American Academy of Child and Adolescent Psychiatry* 59, no. 2 (2020): 283–95, doi: 10.1016/j.jaac.2019.02.022; Xavier Barsalou-Verge, Mélanie M. Gagnon, Renée Séguin, and Christian Dagenais, "Current Knowledge on Child Sexual Abuse in Indigenous Populations of Canada and the United States: A Literature Review," *American Indian Culture and Research Journal* 39, no. 3 (2015): 65–82, https://doi.org/10.17953/aicrj.39.3.barsalou-verge; Zhao Hu, Atipatsa Chiwanda Kaminga, Jun Yang, Jiefeng Liu, and Huilan Xu, "Adverse Childhood Experiences and Risk of Cancer During Adulthood: A Systematic Review and Meta-Analysis," *Child Abuse and Neglect* 117 (2021): 105088, https://doi.org/10.1016/j.chiabu.2021.105088; Kirsten E. MacGregor, Laia Villalta, Venetia Clarke, Russell Viner, Tami Kramer, and Sophie N. Khadr, "A Systematic Review of Short and Medium-Term Mental Health Outcomes in Young People Following Sexual Assault," *Journal of Child and Adolescent Mental Health* 31, no. 3 (2019): 161–81, https://doi.org/10.2989/17280583.2019.1665533.

5 L. Maaike Helmus and Ashley Kyne, "Prevalence, Correlates, and Sequelae of Child Sexual Abuse (CSA) among Indigenous Canadians: Intersections of Ethnicity, Gender, and Socioeconomic Status," *International Journal of Environmental Research and Public Health* 20, no. 9 (2023): 5727, https://doi.org/10.3390/ijerph20095727.

6 I. Denis, M. Brennstuhl, and C. Tarquinio, "The Consequences of Sexual Trauma on the Sexuality of Victims: A Systematic Review of the Literature," *Sexologies: European Journal of Sexology and Sexual Health/Revue européenne de sexologie et de santé sexuelle* 29, no. 4 (2020): 198–217, https://doi.org/10.1016/j.sexol.2020.05.001.

7 Helen P. Hailes, Rongqin Yu, Andrea Danese, and Seena Fazel, "Long-Term Outcomes of Childhood Sexual Abuse: An Umbrella Review," *The Lancet Psychiatry* 6, no. 10 (2019): 830–39, http://dx.doi.org/10.1016/S2215-0366(19)30286-X.

8 S. Tasharrofi and J. Barnes, "Carrying the Misery to Adulthood: The Impact of Childhood Sexual Abuse on Adulthood Impulse Control through Depression and Suicidal Thoughts," *Criminal Justice Studies* 32, no. 3 (2019): 239–63.

9 See, for example, the following: G. Kouvelis and M. Kangas, "Evaluating the Association Between Interpersonal Trauma and Self-Identity: A Systematic Review," *Traumatology* 27, no. 2 (2021): 118–48; K. Fletcher, "A Systematic Review of the Relationship Between Child Sexual Abuse and Substance Use Issues," *Journal*

of Child Sexual Abuse: Research, Treatment, & Program Innovations for Victims, Survivors, & Offenders 30, no. 3 (2021): 258–77; Jennie G. Noll, "Child Sexual Abuse as a Unique Risk Factor for the Development of Psychopathology: The Compounded Convergence of Mechanisms," *Annual Review of Clinical Psychology* 17 (2021): 439–64, doi: 10.1146/annurev-clinpsy-081219-112621.

10 Denis, et al., "Consequences of Sexual Trauma."

11 Olusolami B. Okunlola, Jonathan A. Odukoya, and Abiodun M. Gesinde, "Outcomes of Sexual Abuse on Self-Esteem Among Adolescents: A Systematic Review," *Cogent Social Sciences* 7, no. 1 (2021): 1–16, doi:10.1080/23311886.2020.1856296.

12 Lauren Bochicchio, Mariah Xu, Cindy B. Veldhuis, Charles McTavish, and Tonda L. Hughes, "Mental Health and Substance Use Among Sexual Minority Women Who Report Childhood Sexual Abuse: A Systematic Literature Review," *Psychological Trauma: Theory, Research, Practice, and Policy* 16, Suppl. 1 (2024): S163–S180, doi: 10.1037/tra0001476.

13 Jacinthe Dion, Michael Cantinotti, Amélie Ross, and Delphine Collin-Vézina, "Sexual Abuse, Residential Schooling and Probable Pathological Gambling Among Indigenous Peoples," *Child Abuse & Neglect* 44 (2015): 56–65, https://doi.org/10.1016/j.chiabu.2015.03.004.

14 Woolweaver et al., "Outcomes Associated with Adolescent Dating."

15 Helmus and Kyne, "Prevalence, Correlates, and Sequelae."

16 See, for example, the following: Kara Fletcher, "A Systematic Review of the Relationship Between Child Sexual Abuse and Substance Use Issues," *Journal of Child Sexual Abuse: Research, Treatment, & Program Innovations for Victims, Survivors, & Offenders* 30, no. 3 (2021): 258–77, doi: 10.1080/10538712.2020.1801937; Barsalou-Verge et al., "Current Knowledge on Child Sexual Abuse."

17 *Honouring the Truth*, 2.

CHAPTER 10

PROTECTING SURVIVORS

an Interview with Leah Gazan

SEAN CARLETON AND NIIGAAN SINCLAIR (EDITORS): We know that as a sitting Member of Parliament (MP) for Winnipeg Centre, you're very busy. We appreciate you taking time to talk about your recent work in Parliament and how you think we can best protect Survivors and confront residential school denialism. For those not familiar with your background and your story, could you explain more about why you've become such an active defender of Indigenous Peoples generally and residential school Survivors specifically, both personally and politically?

LEAH GAZAN: I have a very interesting background. My family has been impacted by multiple genocides. This is something that has deeply affected me. On one side, my father was a Holocaust Survivor. On the other, my mom was from Wood Mountain Lakota First Nation and grew up in child welfare. She, like many other Indigenous folks, was impacted by institutional violence and the intergenerational effects of colonization and residential schools. She ended up in child welfare after my grandmother left her and my uncle alone in a hotel room at five years of age.

Looking back at my history, and trying to come to grips with my own understanding of my grandmother—it's hard. I once asked my mom—because my mom had taken my grandmother into our house when she was dying at the end of her life—"How can you take her in? She abandoned you." I loved my mom. She was very instrumental in my life. She was an award-winning social worker, award-winning psychiatric nurse. She said, "My mother did the very best she could with what she had. She gave me all the things I needed in life—a healthy mind and a healthy body. For that, I will always love her." Like many people who have been struggling with colonization, my grandmother dealt with it through addiction. She was an alcoholic, and there were no supports for single parents at the time. There was no discussion of systemic racism.

One thing I know is that we will never be able to reconcile in this country unless we have truth about the harm the system has done for many Indigenous Peoples.

When you come from genocides from different parts of the world, with Holocaust and residential school, the '60s Scoop, and child welfare Survivors in my family, it gives me that different perspective. One of the things that I have from my father's side, thank goodness, is the fact that Holocaust denialism is now a part of the Criminal Code as a form of inciting hate. There's that kind of protection firmly in place. That gives you peace, not having that genocide up for debate. But that's not the case for Indigenous Peoples here in Canada, certainly not for Survivors, and I think that is unjust. That's not right. From a personal perspective, I see that as an injustice.

The very core of truth and reconciliation work must be centred on Survivors; I actually call them residential school warriors. We need to honour residential school warriors by not having their experience up for debate. I can't think of anything more violent than having your genocide disputed and disrespected, especially because denialism often comes from people who've grown up believing in the great Canadian myth—that this was an empty land, void of people. It's an erasure of our ways of life, our cultures, governance, educational systems. It's racism plain and simple. If we can't show respect to the Survivors who shared their stories about the residential school experience as a gift to contribute to reconciliation in this country, if we can't respect Survivors and their truth, we will never reconcile in Canada. You can't reconcile without first understanding and protecting the truth. You can't reconcile when you continue to ignore the ongoing violence that's being perpetrated against Survivors.

EDITORS: As you say, both sides of your family are impacted by genocides. The way in which Holocaust denialism has been dealt with is well known. Yet, there isn't very much being done about residential school denialism. But, before we talk about your private member's bill to address denialism, can you share more about your long-standing work as an MP to create awareness about residential schooling generally? In particular, you recently introduced in the House of Commons a motion to recognize the Indian Residential School System as genocide, which Michelle Good referenced in the previous chapter.[1] As well, perhaps you can share some of the pushback, hate, or anti-Indigenous racism you have experienced as part of your work on this issue.

LEAH: I think it's important to centre my work on community. People often look at elected officials and give us credit for making things happen. But we are powerless outside of the movement. We are representatives of the people. It takes a movement working together to make anything happen in the House of Commons. The idea of a motion, and the will for that to happen, really started with the Survivors who asked me to push for recognition of what happened in residential schools as genocide.

There's no question what happened in residential school is an act of genocide according to the criteria of Article II of the UN Genocide Convention.

EDITORS: Yes, the previous chapters make that very argument.

LEAH: Well, what I did in the House, as I read the UN Genocide Convention out loud, is that I asked the different Members of Parliament, "Is what happened in residential school an act of genocide?" I kept doing this over and over again.

An act of genocide, according to the UN, is:

a) killing members of the group;
b) causing serious bodily or mental harm to members of the group;
c) deliberately inflicting on the group conditions of life calculated to bring about its physical destruction in whole or in part;
d) imposing measures intended to prevent births within the group; and
e) forcibly transferring children of the group to another group.

Canada's treatment of Indigenous Peoples meets all five criteria, I would argue, certainly Article II(e) of the Convention—forcibly transferring children of the group to another group. It's undeniable. Regarding criterion (d), remember we still have ongoing forced sterilization of Indigenous women in Canada.

I know that during the Truth and Reconciliation Commission's investigation, the commissioners had put forward the notion of a cultural genocide, as the TRC's mandate prevented commissioners from examining the legal question of genocide to keep things out of court.[2] But, under the UN Genocide Convention, it's either genocide or it's not genocide. Residential schooling was clearly genocide.

The first time I put the motion forward, which needed unanimous consent in the House of Commons, two Conservative Members of Parliament voted against it. This was in 2021. I usually try to keep focused on the task at hand, but in this case, I actually posted their pictures on social media so that everybody could see who voted against the motion. I wanted people to see who was denying this genocide.

And it's not just Conservatives who downplay the severity of what happened in residential schools. Let me be clear: That kind of minimization comes in all political stripes, from all political parties. The minimization of the genocide of Indigenous Peoples is a non-partisan issue in this country, unfortunately.

If we cannot recognize our own genocide, here in Canada, who are we to be pointing fingers around the globe about human rights abuses and other serious crimes? How can we be an international leader on human rights if we have political leaders promoting genocide denialism? And for what? Greed, resource extraction, more capitalist profit? We see this in real time with parties of all different political stripes perpetuating the violent dispossession of lands away from Indigenous Peoples.

When my motion was ignored, I decided I wouldn't quit standing up for residential school Survivors. I launched a targeted social media campaign to raise more awareness. This is not an issue that should be ignored. I organized, and I let people know when I was going to put the motion forward again.

I kept asking ministers, and some of them just looked full of shame because they were instructed not to support the motion. I would read out the UN Genocide Convention, Article II, and I would say, "Is what happened in residential school an act of genocide? Yes or no?" Then I put forward the motion again in 2022, after a long campaign of pressure, and the motion received unanimous consent. This was a significant legal shift in Canada—the fact that Members of Parliament unanimously recognized what happened in residential school as genocide.[3]

However, there was still backlash, like Conservative Members of Parliament asking me if I "support the burning of churches?" This has been recorded in *Hansard*. They regurgitate far-right conspiracy theories to distract from truth and reconciliation. They don't ask non-Indigenous MPs this question. I've received a lot of racism inside and outside of the House of Commons like this. I don't let it deter me, though. When you tell the truth and you push for change, I call that "good troublemaking."

What concerns me is that these kinds of hurtful comments are really triggering for Survivors. I have blocked hateful people and their messages. Having people question your genocide, constantly—that's violent. Having people who are living in a fairy-tale world where their racism and hatred of Indigenous Peoples are so ingrained that they literally try to dig up potential burial sites, like what happened at Kamloops, is dangerous. Do I care what residential school denialists think of me? No. The fact that they don't appreciate me and my work is a compliment. I would be quite insulted if I had their support with the kind of hatred they spew. I am flattered by their dislike of me.

EDITORS: Thinking from a grassroots perspective, of being a people's representative and someone who is standing up for Survivors, can you talk more about why you think denialism is so harmful?

LEAH: I'll talk about it from an MP's perspective first. As Members of Parliament, we take an oath to uphold the rule of law, to uphold our Constitution, and to uphold all the conventions we've signed on to internationally. But there has been a normalization of genocide against Indigenous Peoples to the point that people flippantly deny the genocide that has been perpetrated against us—residential schooling being one among many genocides. The case of missing and murdered Indigenous women, girls, and 2SLGBTQQIA+ has also been recognized as an ongoing genocide, one genocide out of many that have been perpetrated against Indigenous Peoples. Questioning somebody's experience with genocide, questioning the intergenerational impacts that genocide has on families and children, is so harmful. Why should Indigenous Peoples have to put up with this hate? Genocide against Indigenous Peoples has been so normalized. As a result, people are able to question it, put forward disinformation, and even publish books for profit without any consequences. We need to do a better job protecting Survivors from residential school denialism.

In 2015, the Truth and Reconciliation Commission's *Final Report* was released and it highlighted Survivor truths. That was ten years ago. Where are we now? We're backsliding on our progress with truth and reconciliation. Why? Because we continue to minimize any sort of violence that is perpetrated against Indigenous Peoples, including the downplaying of the harms of residential school denialism and the impacts that it has on individuals and families. I hear arguments like, "Oh well, some people really benefited from residential schooling," or some people say, "Well, you wouldn't be where you are today if you didn't go to residential school." I don't know what kind of public school has a graveyard. The fact that many residential schools had cemeteries and nobody questioned that is a problem to me. And this whole move toward intellectualizing the experiences of residential school like it's a study—it's not. It's a lived experience that has reverberating impacts in our blood memory as Indigenous Peoples. There has been devastating disruption that continues, and will continue to be perpetuated, especially if we allow denialism to take root and face no consequences.

I think of Jim Keegstra from rural Alberta. He was a schoolteacher in the 1980s who was teaching students that the Holocaust never happened, downplaying and minimizing the genocide that occurred. How can you deny that the Holocaust happened? How can you deny the harms and abuses in residential school? There is so much documentation. This is not an educational exercise. Fortunately, Keegstra was charged under the Criminal Code for the wilful promotion of hatred against an identifiable group, the Jewish people, in 1984. I just want to see the same kind of justice for the Indigenous side of my family.

EDITORS: That's a good transition into thinking about the need for your bill to challenge residential school denialism. You mentioned that we can't have reconciliation without truth in this country. Yet, people who are disputing, downplaying, or twisting the truth about residential schooling are facing zero consequences for their actions. In terms of how to protect Survivors and advance reconciliation, there are, of course, many different tools. As educators, we have mostly focused on education as a solution. But as a legislator, you're working to create a legal tool, adding to Canada's Criminal Code, to make it a criminal offence to wilfully condone, deny, downplay or justify the damage caused by residential schools. Can you explain why you think a legislative tool is necessary?

LEAH: On the point about education before I talk about the bill: some denialists are actually educators. Like Jim Keegstra, a schoolteacher in Alberta charged in 1984 with wilful promotion of hate against Jews, they are spreading disinformation in classrooms. It's not just a kitchen table discussion, or informal hate; denialists are publishing books and writing articles that are being consumed by thousands of people and making money from the wilful promotion of hate. We need to take that more seriously.

My bill adds to Section 319 of the Criminal Code the wilful promotion of hate against Indigenous Peoples. Using the same language as Holocaust denialism, this bill aims to address the wilful promotion of hatred against Indigenous Peoples, for persons who communicate statements, other than in private conversation, that deny, downplay, or justify the Indian Residential School system in Canada or misrepresent facts related to it. I am not talking about a conversation at a Christmas dinner gathering.

I would say that people publishing books that promote, and having—although Members of Parliament are protected in the House—national leaders who promote, residential school denialism outside of the House of Commons is a serious problem. I am not talking about freedom of speech. That is not what my bill is about—it is about stopping the incitement of hate. There's a difference. I put forward the bill and it died on the Order Paper, because we went into the election. But this is something that Canada needs to consider moving forward. It's long overdue.

EDITORS: In terms of the way forward, can you inform readers a little bit more about the process? Will you reintroduce the bill? Are you working with different parties to try to get support as with your motion on recognizing residential schooling as a genocide?

LEAH: Well, a motion has legal impact, which is important, but a bill becomes part of our legislation. I did try to work with the former attorney general of the Liberal Party. I discussed this issue with him, without success. He brushed it off, which was terribly disappointing.

First Session, Forty-fourth Parliament,
70-71 Elizabeth II – 1-2-3 Charles III, 2021-2022-2023-2024

HOUSE OF COMMONS OF CANADA

BILL C-413

An Act to amend the Criminal Code (promotion of hatred against Indigenous peoples)

FIRST READING, SEPTEMBER 26, 2024

1st Session, 44th Parliament,
70-71 Elizabeth II – 1-2-3 Charles III, 2021-2022-2023-2024

HOUSE OF COMMONS OF CANADA

BILL C-413

An Act to amend the Criminal Code (promotion of hatred against Indigenous peoples)

His Majesty, by and with the advice and consent of the Senate and House of Commons of Canada, enacts as follows:

R.S., c. C-46

Criminal Code

1 (1) Section 319 of the *Criminal Code* is amended by adding the following after subsection (2.1):

Wilful promotion of hatred — Indigenous peoples

(2.2) Everyone who, by communicating statements, other than in private conversation, wilfully promotes hatred against Indigenous peoples by condoning, denying, downplaying or justifying the Indian residential school system in Canada or by misrepresenting facts relating to it

(a) is guilty of an indictable offence and liable to imprisonment for a term not exceeding two years; or

(b) is guilty of an offence punishable on summary conviction.

(2) Subsections 319(4) to (6) of the Act are replaced by the following:

Defences — subsection (2.2)

(3.2) No person shall be convicted of an offence under subsection (2.2)

(a) if they establish that the statements communicated were true;

(b) if, in good faith, they expressed or attempted to establish by an argument an opinion on a religious subject or an opinion based on a belief in a religious text;

Première session, quarante-quatrième législature,
70-71 Elizabeth II – 1-2-3 Charles III, 2021-2022-2023-2024

CHAMBRE DES COMMUNES DU CANADA

PROJET DE LOI C-413

Loi modifiant le Code criminel (fomentation de la haine contre les peuples autochtones)

PREMIÈRE LECTURE LE 26 SEPTEMBRE 2024

1re session, 44e législature,
70-71 Elizabeth II – 1-2-3 Charles III, 2021-2022-2023-2024

CHAMBRE DES COMMUNES DU CANADA

PROJET DE LOI C-413

Loi modifiant le Code criminel (fomentation de la haine contre les peuples autochtones)

Sa Majesté, sur l'avis et avec le consentement du Sénat et de la Chambre des communes du Canada, édicte :

L.R., ch. C-46

Code criminel

1 (1) L'article 319 du *Code criminel* est modifié par adjonction, après le paragraphe (2.1), de ce qui suit :

Fomenter volontairement la haine contre les peuples autochtones

(2.2) Quiconque, par la communication de déclarations autrement que dans une conversation privée, fomente volontairement la haine contre les peuples autochtones en cautionnant, en niant, en minimisant ou en justifiant le système des pensionnats indiens au Canada ou en dénaturant les faits à son sujet est coupable :

a) soit d'un acte criminel et passible d'un emprisonnement maximal de deux ans;

b) soit d'une infraction punissable sur déclaration de culpabilité par procédure sommaire.

(2) Les paragraphes 319(4) à (6) de la même loi sont remplacés par ce qui suit :

Défenses — paragraphe (2.2)

(3.2) Nul ne peut être déclaré coupable d'une infraction prévue au paragraphe (2.2) dans les cas suivants :

a) il établit que les déclarations communiquées étaient vraies;

b) il a, de bonne foi, exprimé une opinion sur un sujet religieux ou une opinion fondée sur un texte religieux auquel il croit, ou a tenté d'en établir le bien-fondé par argument;

Figure 10.1. Bill C-413. An Act to amend the Criminal Code (promotion of hatred against Indigenous Peoples). Courtesy of Leah Gazan.

I'm hoping to reintroduce the bill again and work with people in all political parties to push it forward. But it will require support from other Members of Parliament. I can't do it on my own. Unfortunately, we have residential school denialists among us in Parliament, which makes it hard to change the colonial status quo.

I'm committed to making residential school denialism something we talk about and confront. We have a lot of work to do in this country if we're going to implement the Truth and Reconciliation Commission's (TRC) 94 Calls to Action. There's still a lot of stalling. Justice delayed is justice denied.

But I'll speak plainly: I think Indigenous Peoples, and Survivors in particular, need protection under the law. I think we also need protection sometimes from people who get elected, who become legislators, who are, quite frankly, harmful. Denialism sometimes comes from within. Remember Senator Lynn Beyak? She was a legislator.

EDITORS: Yes, she was actually a member of the Standing Senate Committee for Aboriginal Peoples when she defended residential schooling as being "well-intentioned."

LEAH: That's exactly what I've been talking about. That's violent. There should have been consequences for that, but instead she doubled down and incited more hatred toward Indigenous Peoples. She kept her Senate seat for years and spewed hatred. It was wilful, just like other denialists. They know what they are doing and how hurtful it is; that's why they do it. There need to be consequences for those who make these choices.

EDITORS: Related to this—since proposing the bill, you've encountered a lot of negative attention on the political right and from denialists who, like Beyak, say that cracking down on residential school denialism would be an infringement on their right to free speech, et cetera.[4] Can you share a little bit about that response and why, in some ways, this only confirms the need to move forward with this piece of legislation, from your perspective?

LEAH: Well, there's an important distinction to be made first. There are people in positions of power and influence, in media or academia, and they are the ones wilfully creating this hateful denialist content. Then there are other people who are consuming this material and sharing, and thinking it's truthful and legitimate. This matters because it's the wilful promotion of hate that's the target of my bill. If the country can't do everything in its power to protect the dignity and human rights of the very Survivors who shared their stories by ensuring their safety in all circumstances, we're not ready to reconcile. Full stop.

If we can't come to grips with how this country was built—which has been built on the violent genocide and wrongful and violent dispossession of lands from Indigenous Peoples—we will never be able to reach what we could be as a country.

Taking a stand against residential school denialism is also my contribution to nation building, of building a better future.

EDITORS: We're grateful for all your hard work standing up for Survivors and keeping this conversation about confronting residential school denialism front and centre. In an earlier chapter, we were speaking with Phyllis Webstad, the founder of Orange Shirt Day, and she made the point that Survivors are not going to live forever and so now is the time to do this work.

LEAH: That's right. There's an urgency to do this work now.

EDITORS: For our final question, we always want to end with hope. There are a lot of negative things going on in the world today, but the optimism for change is really important. It has now been ten years since the TRC released its *Final Report* and 94 Calls to Action. We've made a lot of progress but clearly not enough. There are many things that continue to hold us back. Given the rise of denialism, and some of the backlash that we are seeing, what gives you hope for the future? What inspires you to keep up the fight and put truth before reconciliation?

LEAH: I was part of promoting the first Bill C-262 introduced by Romeo Saganash to affirm the application of the United Nations Declaration on the Rights of Indigenous Peoples (UNDRIP) in Canadian law. Unfortunately, his bill died on the Order Paper as a result of five Conservative senators stalling the process. The government decided to reintroduce his bill and it was passed in the following Parliament. It took a lot of effort but we got it passed! This was a result of a movement of thousands and thousands and thousands—hundreds of thousands—of people across the country who marched together, walked together, wrote together, spoke together. Bill C-15 was the result of a movement of people; it was a human rights movement.

I believe that people are inherently good. As I said earlier, when I was talking about my grandmother, my mother said, "She did the very best with what she could at the time." Then adding, "When people know better, they do better." We need to protect residential school truth so that people can know better and do better on a continuing basis in this country.

I've gotten a lot of pushback against my bill, but I've also got a lot of support, especially from Survivors, because although there are a lot of people who still deny, condone, or downplay, there's also a lot of people who want the truth to be told and protected. We must not lose sight of that fact. Particularly, people want residential school warriors, their family members, and communities to be respected. This is bigger than me. That's bigger than a bill. Putting truth before reconciliation will happen when people mobilize and it becomes a movement for justice—and this book is an important part of the process, of naming the problem and thinking of solutions. I've always been part of the movement, and I believe in the movement. I'm a representative. I hope this bill will be a gift that allows and inspires people to move forward toward real truth.

Notes

1 Richard Raycraft, "MPs Back Motion Calling on Government to Recognize Residential Schools Program as Genocide," *CBC News*, 27 October 2022, https://www.cbc.ca/news/politics/house-motion-recognize-genocide-1.6632450.

2 For more on the definition of genocide and its applicability to Canada, see Carleton and Woolford, "Ignore Debaters and Denialists, Canada's Treatment of Indigenous Peoples Fits the Definition of Genocide."

3 Temitayo Olarewaju, "Residential School System Recognized as Genocide in Canada's House of Commons: A Harbinger of Change," *The Conversation*, 11 January 2023, https://theconversation.com/residential-school-system-recognized-as-genocide-in-canadas-house-of-commons-a-harbinger-of-change-196774.

4 Jamie Sarkonak, "The Slipperly Slope Reality of Criminalizing Residential School 'Denialism,'" *National Post*, 29 September 2024, https://nationalpost.com/opinion/jamie-sarkonak-the-slippery-slope-reality-of-criminalizing-residential-school-denialism.

CHAPTER 11

SITES OF REMEMBRANCE:

The Role of Public History and Commemoration in Challenging Denialism

an Interview with Krista McCracken, Jackson Pind, Skylee-Storm Hogan-Stacey, and Erin Millions

> ***"Families go to museums together; they don't go to school together."***
>
> —The Honourable Murray Sinclair[1]

SEAN CARLETON AND NIIGAAN SINCLAIR (EDITORS): Kimberly Murray, in her *Final Report*, stressed that memorialization and commemoration for residential schooling, as "acts of resistance, acts of reparation," are key to the work of putting truth before reconciliation. Specifically, she argues that sites of remembrance can help counteract denialism. We're excited to bring you all into conversation to share more about your important work, what you have learned, and why you think public history and commemoration can play a role in challenging residential school denialism. To start, can each of you briefly introduce yourself and explain how you've come to truth and reconciliation work?

KRISTA MCCRACKEN: I'm a settler public historian and archivist who lives and works in Baawaating, also known as Sault Ste. Marie, Ontario, in Robinson Huron Treaty Territory. I come to this work through my work at the Shingwauk Residential Schools Centre, where I've worked since 2010. The Shingwauk Residential Schools Centre is one of the longest-running community archives dedicated to residential schools. It was set up by the Children of Shingwauk Alumni Association and operates on the site of the former Shingwauk Indian Residential School. I'm extremely grateful to have spent the last fifteen years of my career working alongside Survivors and intergenerational Survivors of Shingwauk, specifically, to advance the narrative around the Shingwauk Residential School and to help with some of that truth-telling work locally and nationally connected to residential schools.

JACKSON PIND: Thanks, Krista. I'm a historian of Indian Day Schools and Indigenous education generally. My background is of mixed ancestry, of Anishinaabe ancestry from Alderville First Nation and then some European nations as well. I teach at the Chanie Wenjack School for Indigenous Studies at Trent University in Peterborough, Ontario. I usually teach the Indigenous Content Requirement, which was introduced in response to the Truth and Reconciliation Commission's (TRC) Calls to Action to increase education and awareness.

I came to this work through my undergraduate degree at Laurentian University. When I was in undergrad, the TRC *Final Report* came out and I remember reading the first few pages and finding that Alderville played a role at the beginning of the Indian Residential School System (IRSS). That was not taught to me growing up and launched me on a journey of trying to understand why we never talked about the Alderville Indian Day School and my own family's history of enfranchisement. That led to me wanting to pursue my PhD at Queen's University, focusing on day school history.

Then I got connected to Kevin Lamoureux at the University of Winnipeg. He was doing a public history talk about the TRC Calls to Action and how schools could respond. I went to the lecture. I was pretty nervous; I didn't want to introduce myself, but one of the professors dragged me down there and introduced me. I asked Kevin why he didn't talk about day schools. He said that the story hadn't been written yet, and to call this Elder from Peguis, whose name was Raymond Mason. He gave me the number, and I called him. That call changed my life in many ways. Connecting with Raymond introduced me to the work of day school Survivors who were advocating for, at that time, the Indian Day School Settlement Agreement, but Ray had also worked on the Indian Residential Schools Settlement Agreement (IRSSA). Raymond and Garry McLean, along with other Survivors, launched the lawsuit that led to the day school agreement. We started working together closely to tell his history. He really wanted to write a historical book.

In the book we created, *Spirit of the Grassroots People*, Raymond talked about his experiences. But there is so much more to learn and understand. That was my entry point, and I have more recently been doing work with Curve Lake First Nation and their Indian Day School.

SKYLEE-STORM HOGAN-STACEY: I've been in different roles throughout the public history world for the past ten years. I started off as an archival assistant and a site interpreter when I was with the Shingwauk Residential Schools Centre with Krista from 2015 to 2018. Then I completed my master's degree in history and studied public history at Western University. From there, I worked with various museums, public history consultancies, and the Special Interlocutor for Missing Children and Unmarked Graves and Burial Sites associated with Indian Residential Schools. Everything, I feel, is interconnected. Throughout all of my work, while I've had different employers and worked for different groups, my personal accountability and motivation has been to residential school Survivors and the awareness of what happened in residential schools. My family is of my mixed ancestry. My dad lives in the Mohawk Nation of Kahnawà:ke. His family is Kanyen'kehà:ka, so they are Mohawk. My mom's family are settlers with European ancestry. Most of them live in the Toronto area and in what is now known as Newfoundland. I've had an upbringing with urban and Indigenous experiences. I think public history is an avenue that speaks well to those different identities.

ERIN MILLIONS: I'm an assistant professor in the Department of History at the University of Winnipeg, in Treaty 1 Territory and the National Homeland of the Red River Métis. I'm from Treaty 6 Territory in Saskatchewan and came to Winnipeg to complete my PhD at the University of Manitoba. My interest in Indigenous history is rooted in growing up in what was effectively a racially segregated small town in Saskatchewan in the 1980s and 1990s. Anti-Indigenous racism was rampant and the social and economic disparities between Indigenous people and non-Indigenous people were front and centre every day, but they weren't discussed in a meaningful way by non-Indigenous community members. We certainly were not taught anything useful about Indigenous histories in school. I wanted to find out the "why"

Figure 11.1. Shingwauk Hall, now a central part of the Algoma University campus, was first established in 1873 as part of the Shingwauk Indian Residential School in Sault Ste. Marie, Ontario. The Children of Shingwauk Alumni Association and Algoma University have collaborated to create the Shingwauk Residential Schools Centre, an archival repository and cross-cultural education centre on campus, to raise public awareness about the history and legacy of residential schooling. Visitors to Algoma are welcomed by *Reclaiming Shingwauk Hall*, a permanent display that transforms the former Shingwauk Hall into an exhibition space. Photo by Sean Carleton.

behind the racism and segregation that surrounded me growing up so I ended up studying western Canadian and Indigenous histories in university. I aimed (and still aim) to share those histories with broad audiences to help bridge that gap of knowledge and understanding that I grew up with.

I came to commemoration work on residential schools through my general interest in Indigenous histories of western Canada, but more specifically as a contract historical researcher after completing my PhD. I did work for organizations like the Canadian Museum for Human Rights, the BBC, and *Canadian Geographic*, and then worked as a historian for Parks Canada, where I was hired to work with community stakeholders to commemorate Indian Residential Schools

Figure 11.2. The "Cubby Hole," as part of *Reclaiming Shingwauk Hall*, shows visitors where children were confined as punishment at the Shingwauk Indian Residential School. Some students also sought out the "hole" to hide from discipline. Photo by Sean Carleton.

and Indigenous histories. I've carried this background into my current faculty role, where I continue to prioritize publicly engaged work in various ways.

EDITORS: You all touched on this a bit, but can you expand and share more about some of the public history or commemoration projects you've worked on and how they have raised awareness about residential schooling and its adjacent systems, like day schools and tuberculosis hospitals?

KRISTA: I think one of the largest public history projects that I have had the opportunity to work on with the Children of Shingwauk Alumni Association is the *Reclaiming Shingwauk Hall* exhibition. That is now a permanent exhibition in the halls of the former Shingwauk Indian Residential School, which is now Algoma University. This exhibition lines some of the main administration hallways, as well as a large auditorium space. It talks about the history of residential schools, specific to Sault Ste. Marie but also across Canada. It also addresses colonialism and decolonization in a much broader way. The exhibition space supports the need for raising awareness and ongoing conversations and dialogue about what actually happened at the Shingwauk Residential School and residential schools similar to it across the country.

The *Reclaiming Shingwauk Hall* exhibition represents over forty years of work by the Children of Shingwauk Alumni Association. They started coming together in the 1980s to begin to talk about their experiences at the Shingwauk Residential School. That is also when they started what would become the Shingwauk Residential Schools Centre Archive. As soon as they started gathering on the Shingwauk site, they began advocating for monuments to be put up, for new signage to be installed on the site, and for displays to be lining the hallways of the university. Visibility was important. That work has always been connected to their mission of sharing, healing, and learning, and this goal of making sure that their experiences are never forgotten. That truth-telling work is so important, and I'm really grateful that I have been able to be a part of that work.

One of the most impactful panels in the exhibition is called "Missing Evidence." Throughout the exhibition you are looking at photographs and archival documents, but what you are seeing in those images isn't necessarily the whole truth. It's only part of what happened at residential school, and many of those photos were staged. We know from Survivors and intergenerational Survivors that their experiences weren't always captured in archival documents and things like photographs. That's why I think public history has a really important role to play in interpreting the evidence of residential schools and helping raise awareness about how to critically look at historical documents and understand the past.

JACKSON: Two projects that I've been involved with that are trying to bring awareness to residential schooling and to the day school system in particular was the website (indiandayschools.org) I helped create with Elder Raymond Mason, along with another programmer named Benjamin Farmer Lacombe.[2] The website brings together data that were being used at the time of the class action Indian Day School Settlement Agreement. The material, largely archival documents, was hard to access and located in different places. This inaccessibility was a barrier. Ray really wanted a website that could compile these records and challenge some of the doubters of day school experiences. He wanted to create something that could be used for education. So we started developing this Indian Day School map, and started mapping out all of the locations of the Indian day schools. Sean and I worked on a GIS (or Geographic Information System) project, mapping Indian Day Schools, which showed the development and spread of day schools across Canada over time.[3] Once the locations were mapped roughly to their location, we started adding in archival data that was available in the RG10 archive about day schools from Library and Archives Canada. They gave us permission to download those archives, redigitize them, use some OCR (Optimal Character Recognition) scanning processes to make them easily searchable, and then tie them to the schools themselves on the digital map.

If you go to the website, you can look up in the top left corner for the closest Indian Day School to where you live or where your family attended and then find those records much more easily. The goal was to help day school Survivors apply for their own claims at that time. To get the highest levels of compensation, during the class action lawsuit, you had to have historical evidence or proof of what happened in the schools, and Survivors were left on their own to do that, especially during the pandemic. Accessibility was important, and the website made this easier for many.

One of the communities I worked with was Kettle & Stony Point First Nation, which was doing their own research at that time. One of their councillors, Jordan George, was researching his own family history. During that search, and using our website, he started piecing together some stories. He started connecting some of the dots and went to the day school site in the community. Then, in the backyard there was a mini-cemetery. One of his aunts was actually buried in that day school cemetery. I think this has really been overlooked in a lot of research. Aboriginal Peoples Television Network (APTN) has done a very brief overview. They requested about 800 documents, just a small sample size, and found forty day school deaths.

The website has been quite successful. It has over 25,000 views and a lot of files have been downloaded and used for research, including my own research with Curve Lake First Nation. Those files were also returned back to the community.

A new project I've been working on is the Indigenous Plaques Project with Ontario Heritage Trust, which has been redesigning a lot of historical plaques. They just redid the one at Shingwauk Hall recently, which maybe Krista or Skylee-Storm can talk more about. I think that spurred a lot of conversations about what is actually happening with plaques in the province. The trust has something like 1,200 plaques, and very few have Indigenous content or Indigenous people being a part of those conversations.

At Trent we've asked students to get engaged, find a plaque in their hometown that is outdated or that does not have Indigenous stories, and reimagine what that plaque would look like with Indigenous perspectives. There is a website now called indigenousplaquesproject.org, which is slowly building a database of these new plaques. We are hoping the trust will pick one or two of them to add. Then, we are also trying to show the trust that, right now, there are no plaques for Indian Day Schools. That's something I'm hoping to rectify. I know from some of the work that has been done in Curve Lake, they are now working on their own monument in their community, designed by themselves by the school. I am hoping more commemoration efforts like this will happen down that road as well.

SKYLEE-STORM: As I noted earlier, I worked with the Children of Shingwauk Alumni Association. I assisted them with the different types of Survivor and intergenerational Survivor gatherings they held in the summers. I also assisted with regular exhibitions and displays about residential school history in a local context—particularly about the Shingwauk Residential School, the Spanish Residential School, and, occasionally, the Wikwemikong Residential School, St. Joseph's. More of my work was focused on the actual site and raising awareness within the community because, similar to what Erin had mentioned about being in a very segregated town, Sault Ste. Marie is a lot like that. There are a lot of people who maybe went to school with people who were a part of the integration era or knew about the Shingwauk Residential School but thought of it more or less as an orphanage or a place where Indigenous children without parents lived—they did not recognize the full magnitude of the institution. Like Krista mentioned, it was really important to raise awareness amongst students who attend Algoma that the building was previously a residential school. That's where things like the *Reclaiming Shingwauk Hall* exhibition come in too. Being a part of some of that work—in a small way because I was an undergraduate student at the time—and understanding that piece of history was a big part of how I started off in public history.

Then, for me, I really wanted to focus on working for Survivors in other capacities. That involved gathering information and trying to organize it into a database and preparing reports based on what I found in those records—so really internal-facing stuff. This work gave Survivors and communities their own agency to share what they want to share in the way that they want to share it. Because of the work I was doing, I was introduced to Kimberly Murray, when she was still the lead of the Survivors' Secretariat. On a personal level, I learned that some of my family members had actually gone to the Mohawk Institute, so I became personally invested. That led to me going with Kimberly Murray when she became the Special Interlocutor. That process involved more research connected to actual requests from families to find missing loved ones. I was also involved in the *Canadian Geographic* Pathways to Reconciliation Map in a small capacity. I tried to fix some of the information for the schools that I was most knowledgeable about in Ontario.

In 2023, I actually worked on the new Ontario Heritage Trust plaque for the Shingwauk Hall site that Jackson mentioned. The original plaque was installed in the 1970s, and it was quite dated. It was written by the Anglican Historical Society and was very sympathetic to the intentions of the Anglican-run Shingwauk Hall. It placed a lot of emphasis on the school's first principal and his relationship with teaching. It said they were training students to become functioning members of society. When everything happened with the announcement at Kamloops, it was vandalized. The Heritage Trust finally listened to Krista and myself and decided they should replace the plaque. I worked on that for about a year, mostly with the Children of Shingwauk Alumni Association and the folks at the Shingwauk Residential Schools Centre. That plaque ended up being translated into four languages—there was

Figure 11.3. On 30 September 2022, the Ontario Heritage Trust unveiled an updated plaque to Shingwauk Hall on the grounds of Algoma University. The plaque's text appears in Anishinaabemowin, Swampy Cree, English, and French. Image courtesy of Ontario Heritage Trust.

English, French, Swampy Cree, and Anishinaabemowin. While there were many other languages and dialects at that school, those were the ones that really impact the local communities of Survivors who still live in the area.

ERIN: My work on residential school histories and commemoration spans a wide range of projects and engages the idea of commemoration in several different ways. The Manitoba Indigenous Tuberculosis History Project (MITHP) website and the MITHP *Missing Patients Research Guide* are co-authored by myself and Anne Lindsay with Mary Jane Logan McCallum.[4] Mary Jane and I launched what became the MITHP in fall 2019 as a way to share previously inaccessible and unrestricted historical health records from Manitoba tuberculosis (TB) sanatoriums and Indian hospitals with former Indigenous patients, descendants, and communities. The community demand for our outreach work meant that the project quickly grew into a five-year project funded by the Canadian Institute for Health Research (concluded in March 2025), but the onset of the pandemic in 2020 required us to shift from a focus on in-person community events to digital spaces, including the MITHP website.

Part of the community demand, like Skylee-Storm encountered, involved people asking us to help them find their loved ones who went away to the hospitals and never came home. I partnered with Anne Lindsay, who is both a historian and an archivist who specializes in residential school archival records, to research the administration of death and burial of Indigenous patients at the TB hospitals. The outcome of that work was the MITHP *Missing Patients Research Guide*, which provides step-by-step instructions for families or communities searching for Indigenous patients who never returned from Manitoba TB hospitals.[5] Anne and I were both aware, of course, of the interrelationship between TB hospitals and residential schools that is highlighted in the TRC *Final Report*. Our microstudy approach of working through patient case studies allowed us to better understand the criss-crossing municipal, provincial, and federal systems at play in treating Indigenous TB patients in Manitoba. Our work delineated both the higher-level patterns of administration and the locally specific information that were necessary to locate patients' burial sites. The case studies, along with Mary Jane Logan McCallum's broader research on Indigenous TB history, also point to hospital schools as part of the larger system of Indigenous education removal and the disappearing of residential school students who were transferred to hospitals. Hospital schools are generally not part of the scholarly discourse about Indigenous education removal, but the schools located in the federal Indian hospitals were administered by the Department of Indian Affairs alongside the residential schools and day schools. The records from some of those hospital schools are available on Jackson's Indian Day Schools website. The MITHP engaged with commemoration in ways that we don't often consider commemoration. We leveraged digital spaces, advocacy work, and community training to help people find their missing loved ones. Some of those newly found gravesites do or will feature new grave markers installed by their families.

I've also worked on physical site commemoration of Indian Residential School (IRS) histories through a few different roles. One aspect of my job at Parks Canada was working with community representatives to write the text that appears on the Historic Sites and Monuments Board of Canada (HSMBC) plaques commemorating individual residentials schools. In August 2025, I attended the unveiling of the HSMBC plaques commemorating the former Portage la Prairie Indian Residential School, which now houses the National Indigenous Residential School Museum of Canada outside of Portage la Prairie, Manitoba.[6] I was part of the team that worked with Portage la Prairie IRS survivors and Long Plain First Nation community members to produce the plaque text, which is recorded on the plaques in English, French, Anishinaabemowin, Anishinaabemowin syllabics, and Dakota. Although plaques are inherently colonial forms of commemoration, they are also physical, tangible, and long-lasting historical records that reach many, many people. Former Long Plain First Nation Chief and Survivor Elder Ernie Daniels noted at the unveiling ceremony that the school site had been rehabilitated from "a place of hurt to a place of healing." Part of that healing included witnessing the national and public recognition of their histories, told in their own way and in their own languages, on the HSMBC plaques.

I've also been involved in commemorating IRS histories locally, in Winnipeg. I've been a member of the Welcoming Winnipeg Initiative Committee of Community Members (CCM) since August 2020. The Welcoming Winnipeg Initiative is a municipal policy with a mandate to increase the commemoration of Indigenous histories and peoples in Winnipeg's municipal spaces. The Indigenous-led CCM is a group of volunteers with relevant experience who make recommendations to the mayor and city council related to Indigenous histories, naming, and commemoration of municipal assets.[7] Two of our projects have been directly related to residential schooling commemoration. We were involved in the renaming of two streets and one public trail in Winnipeg that were named after Bishop Vital-Justin Grandin, a nineteenth-century architect of the residential school system.[8] We supported the installation of a memorial commemorating a devastating 1972 plane crash, in collaboration with Bunibonibee Cree Nation and the Royal Aviation Museum of Western Canada. A plane carrying eight students from Bunibonibee Cree Nation—including students from Portage la Prairie IRS—was taking students home for summer vacation. The plane crashed in vacant lot shortly after takeoff from Winnipeg International Airport, killing all eight students and the pilot.[9]

I'm also involved in projects to commemorate the residential schools that were located in Winnipeg. Of the four local IRS schools, only

Figure 11.4. The Historic Sites and Monuments Board of Canada plaques commemorating the Former Portage la Prairie Indian Residential School (Long Plain First Nation near Portage la Prairie).

one has been commemorated so far, the Assiniboia Indian Residential School in the River Heights neighbourhood.[10] Progress is slow, however, because funding is unstable and operates on relatively short timelines, community capacity for commemoration work is limited, and commemorating schools that do not have a clear lead stakeholder community is complex.

EDITORS: Thank you all for your important work. Our way into talking about denialism is actually to go back to Shingwauk quickly—since many of you mentioned it—and the importance of representation. In the *Final Report* of the Office of the Independent Special Interlocutor for Missing Children and Unmarked Graves associated with Indian Residential Schools, there is a whole section on Bernice Logan and the Association of Former Indian Residential School Workers. As Skylee-Storm was mentioning, the Children of Shingwauk Alumni Association were holding their reunions and gatherings, and former employees—led by Logan—thought they were being unfairly criticized, so they created their own association and published materials defending themselves. It's in small ways that denialism manifests in the local context that Krista and Skylee-Storm have worked in. In shifting, then, to discussing denialism, we'd like to know more about how you have experienced residential school denialism in the work you've done. And why, since you're involved in truth-telling work in public-facing ways, you think denialism is so harmful?

KRISTA: In my work, some of the ways that residential school denialism appears, particularly on the archival front, is in getting requests from researchers who are doing residential school denialist publishing and looking for documents or photographs that they can then republish, repurpose, and reinterpret in ways that are not historically accurate.

EDITORS: Raymond Frogner's chapter talks all about this, and we know your work has further examined the use and misuse of residential school photographs specifically.[11]

KRISTA: Part of the challenge is that we do not always know how people are going to use images when they reach out to the archives. For that reason, we are working to create a framework that explicitly centres the Children of Shingwauk Alumni Association and the reasons why they created the Shingwauk Residential Schools Centre. We are making sure that people understand that the purpose of the archives is part of the educational work we are doing. We are also trying to put policies in place so that it is very clear we are not granting permission for hate speech or the use of our images associated with hate speech.

EDITORS: That's great to hear. The BC Museums Association has produced a guide titled, "How Museums Can Respond to Residential School Denialism," so this is certainly an emerging and important conversation.[12]

KRISTA: Beyond that, I've also had people who engage in our education and outreach programming who are openly residential school denialists. It can be very disruptive for other learners who are in that space. It can also be really harmful for Indigenous folks who are also on our tours. Sometimes intergenerational Survivors or Survivors themselves are coming back to the Shingwauk site for the first time and engaging in our outreach programming. The trauma and harm that can be done in that space are really intense.

EDITORS: Are you talking about people who are showing up to in-person events and trying to disrupt the tour with denialism?

KRISTA: Yes.

EDITORS: That's very troubling.

KRISTA: From my perspective, as someone who does education work connected to the Shingwauk site, there are websites out there that are sharing documents connected to the Shingwauk Residential School and reinterpreting them in ways that are denying the harms that we know happened. Those websites look really legitimate, and I think if you're not aware of the historical context or how archival documents are created, it can be really hard to determine whether or not what you are reading is true. I think more emphasis needs to be placed on historical literacy, not just historical facts. People need to learn how to detect disinformation and the twisting of evidence to defend residential schooling. I think that's something that as archivists and public historians we're just beginning to talk about. I think that no one has come up with a solution as to how to deal with archival requests that may be tied to denialism because there are so many unknowns. Also, as an archivist, it's not my place to know what everybody is researching and there's a level of privacy we want to be able to grant users of the archives. There is a balance there that I think is really tricky.

JACKSON: I want to echo what Krista said. Especially when we made the day school website, I don't think we fully realized that there would be a lot of people who would download and reinterpret documents to try to defend the Indian Day School System. Because we made the records easier to access, we also made it easier to access for denialists on those same websites that Krista mentioned. Some people want to cherry-pick and go through and find examples to say, "See, look how much we were doing to try to make education better in all of these different communities." There have been a lot of unfortunate ramifications of that, as a result—particularly once the settlement was announced. Whenever there is money involved, it feels like that is when there are waves of hatred directed toward Indigenous Peoples. Any time I have written about it or talked about it, there are always a few people who come forward and say, "Day schools weren't that bad."

A couple of weeks ago at graduation here at Trent—which you think would be a pretty progressive place as we have the first Indigenous Studies program—I was getting gowned up for convocation and someone—a high-ranking person in the community—came up and asked me about my research. I started to tell him about day schooling and my work. He had experience in the North. He said, "Oh, there is not that much research; they weren't that bad, right? They helped kids get educated and go to university." It was awkward, but I had to challenge him and we got into a back-and-forth about how bad day schools were versus residential schools. That is a very uncomfortable conversation to have, especially with someone who already had their mind made up about what they thought it was and had experience working in the North. They thought their experience, and their view of the experience, was the whole story. A lot of residential school denialists think the same way.

I also see denialism a lot on social media, and it's starting to bleed into other areas as well. I do some work on archaeology in the Anishinaabe area, especially public history and archaeology, and how we don't really talk about ancient sites here in Ontario through our curriculum and classrooms. We're trying to bring that into teaching to show that Anishinaabe people have historical sites all over, particularly in this region of the "land between" in southern Ontario, or what is known as today as Bon Echo, Petroglyphs, and Serpent Mounds Provincial Parks.

Recently, four Anishinaabe Nations came forward and were really upset that Ontario Power Generation (OPG) was digging up a parking lot right beside a plaque called the Scugog Carrying Place Plaque, which talks about how Anishinaabe people travelled from the north shore of Lake Ontario to Lake Scugog. It was an old portage route. They dug it up without any archaeology work, which you are supposed to do before you do any digs in this region or anywhere in the country. They dug up human remains in that site, which, again, was damaging—to basically say you're not going to use Indigenous people as cultural liaisons throughout this process. They made a statement apologizing, and then Curve Lake, Alderville, Scugog, and one other community came forward very upset, making a public statement saying that Ontario is not following their own laws. When news of this became public, you could really see the racism come alive in the comments online. There were actually a lot of comments about residential schools. I took some screenshots—I won't read them because I think they are all really depressing and upsetting—but they were basically parroting the same comments about residential schools. "Oh, show me the bodies; I don't believe you"; or, "Oh, Indigenous people are just asking for more money again"—those exact comments that you see about residential school burial sites and graves were then applied to an ancient burial ground. It was really frustrating to see that denialism has spread into all of these areas that Indigenous Peoples are grappling with right now.

There are also always anonymous emails and stuff I deal with, as do others. I think anyone who does public-facing work gets these types of emails about why you're lying or why you're trying to shape the narrative. There's a lot of hate and racism, and it can be really difficult and discouraging.

SKYLEE-STORM: I've experienced denialism on many levels. Personally, when I was working at Shingwauk—when I was in my twenties, still learning and not used to a lot of confrontation—I experienced residential school denialism quite often, as Krista alluded to. People sometimes got in my physical space to try to speak or yell over me or challenge me with, "I was here in 1966, and I didn't see anything wrong," and a lot of that kind of stuff. Did it get worse with the internet? Absolutely. I've left a lot of social media platforms. I've had colleagues be doxed. I've had colleagues threatened and followed. I'm thankful I've had some pretty awesome leaders in my life, who've shielded me a lot from that as a young First Nations researcher. I'm incredibly thankful for people like Kim Murray who recognized that I and the other young First Nations people I was working with were not ready to face some of the vitriol that came from the old-school historians and lay researchers who have dedicated their lives to spreading misinformation and harm. But as somebody who monitored the emails for the Pathways to Reconciliation Map and as someone who monitored some of the emails received by the Special Interlocutor's office, I can say that a lot of it was from the usual suspects—so a lot of the names that we recognize, who have authored a lot of the denialism content that is on the internet today. Most of what they had to say was nothing new, but there were some new people—private citizens—who would say absolutely terrible things, make actual threats against people, and accuse them of being a part of some type of grand conspiracy.

I've seen really prominent, strong researchers and historians leave the field or slowly start distancing themselves, myself included, because of threats like, "We know where you live," or "You better stop talking before someone makes you stop talking." When you're young, live on your own, and you're a female-identifying person, that kind of intimidation can be really scary.

ERIN: I referenced the renaming of Bishop Grandin Boulevard earlier. Its new name is Abinojii Mikanah, which means "Children's Way" in Anishinaabemowin. The renaming was a legacy project of outgoing Mayor Brian Bowman and was triggered by the announcement of the 215 potential unmarked graves at Kamloops in May 2021 and the public attention that followed. The project was completed in stages over three years, with the final installation of signs and unveiling in June 2024. That's three years of regular media attention to residential school history commemoration. What the Welcoming Winnipeg team has witnessed since that renaming project got underway is a decrease in support for Indigenous naming and commemoration overall from the mayor and city council, and an increase in public vitriol directed at the CCM's work. It's not residential school denialism specifically, because our projects are not always related to residential schools, but an overall backlash. The public feedback that we received on applications and particularly social media commentary often featured denialist rhetoric. Committee members have also been targeted with anti-Indigenous rhetoric on social media, by email, and in news editorials. There's that bleeding, or slow creep, that Jackson noted.

I'm also increasingly encountering denialist rhetoric in the classroom. I teach primarily Indigenous Course Requirement (ICR) courses at the University of Winnipeg. Prior to 2021, students who were learning about residential schools in my classes were often learning about the IRS system for the first time or came in with a basic understanding that the schools existed but didn't know the details. Their response to my class content was generally angry, both about the schools themselves and that the education system had failed to teach them about the IRS system. Increasingly there is less of this total lack of knowledge among students who graduated from Canadian high schools, but I have noticed a shift in the questions that students ask. I was away from teaching for two years, and since my return in 2023 students now specifically ask, "Did students really die in residential schools?" That's not a question students had ever asked me before 2021. Students are often asking these questions out of genuine curiosity, but it also means that denialist rhetoric is making its way into my classroom by way of students encountering it out in the world.

On a more practical level, the political will to prioritize Indigenous histories and residential school commemoration at various levels of government is waning. The CCM has been in conflict with city council for two years, and for the past year our work has effectively been shut down by "policy review." The mayor and city council used this time to push through naming and commemoration initiatives that the CCM previously advised against. Federal funding for residential school commemoration has also been decimated. I was hired at Parks Canada under special funding to support Parks Canada's implementation of the TRC's Call to Action 79.[13] That funding, which in part provided dedicated resources for IRS commemoration, expired in March 2025 and was not renewed.

EDITORS: It's interesting that all of you are doing very public-facing, important work and are experiencing or witnessing denialism in different forms. Yet, you keep doing it, which is why we wanted to speak with you. How do you think continuing to do public history and commemoration work can play a role not just in truth telling about residential schooling but also play a role in challenging denialism?

KRISTA: One of the biggest strengths of public history is its ability to communicate information in a range of media and formats and provide education in an accessible way to the general public. I think that's a really strong way to combat denialism—through education that is accessible. Part of it is flat-out naming denialism when it comes up, particularly in the field of archives and public history. When it's there, calling it out professionally is something that needs to be done. But I think the general public also needs to have that education piece. If we are talking about residential schools in an exhibition space, are we also talking about denialism in that exhibition space? I think they need to go side-by-side, so people understand that this is out there and this is happening—the more you know, kind of thing.

JACKSON: Yeah, that's something we really think about at Trent. We take it to heart. We are proud of our legacy of Indigenous Studies, being the first in the country to have that type of program and always trying to push the boundaries. Trent has gone through this controversy over Samuel De Champlain and trying to change the name of Champlain College on campus. There was a big report that was launched, and it ultimately didn't change the name. I think, in some ways, that damaged the relationship with local First Nations here. I think the community has moved forward by saying, "If you are going to keep Champlain, then we are going to make a cornerstone that talks about the Michi Saagiig Anishinaabeg Nations in this area in a prominent part of campus with both languages." This is to say, we were here first. You can say Champlain was the most important person and name a building after him, but we were the first people here. A new college is going to be named Gidigaa Migizi for Doug Williams, who recently passed away. He was a really well-respected Elder from Curve Lake. That is being built as we speak. There are always going to be people who want to commemorate Champlain, people like John A. Macdonald, and those colonial figures. But, if we keep making stronger commemorations with Indigenous backing, at a certain point it is going to tip in favour of these more authentic stories about the past and this place.

We've also been trying to think about how to challenge students in ways that aren't uncomfortable for them, especially first-year students who might be coming into this knowledge for the first time, or Indigenous students who have already experienced this.

But I think it's always something that is going to be hard to actually confront because I do think it hides a lot of the time. It is very rare that you'll see someone confront you. I haven't experienced what Krista or Skylee-Storm have experienced, of someone coming up and denying in person. I think that's why it is so prevalent online, because it's easier to hide behind a keyboard rather than to come up to someone and say, "I don't believe your story," or "I'm not going to agree with this new plaque that's going to be placed here in the centre of campus." I think it's hard and I don't really have an answer on the ways to challenge it that feel like a silver bullet and will ensure they will never have a denialist come forward and confront a student or a person of the community. I think public history and commemoration have important roles, though, as I think most people don't learn history through universities or reading, to be honest, anymore. They just find a plaque, a museum like Shingwauk Hall, another museum in their town, or even a Facebook post to learn. I think the more we can get into these different spaces and tell authentic stories from Indigenous perspectives, the more chance we have of reaching people with the truth.

SKYLEE-STORM: I think history as an interpretive practice has gotten lost in some ways; that's the historical literacy piece Krista was mentioning. A lot of people who are outside of the field of history, in particular, and outside of the subject area, see history as a factual, impartial, set of events that you can't dispute because there's archival evidence and people remember it. But I think that public history shows that history is actually a set of relationships and interpretations—that there are many realities, as with the quote by Shawn Wilson about research as ceremony and understanding, that there are multiple realities and experiences.[14] Even when we're talking about Indigenous ways of knowing, the ontologies and epistemologies of Indigenous Peoples and cultures across this country are so vast. It's hard to really talk about it generally. Yet, there's this understanding from a colonial, Western, European standpoint that history needs to be impartial and you can't have any relationship to it. But with that approach, people don't realize that there is inherently a relationship there. They just made a conscious choice to interpret that history and analyze their documents and primary sources in a particular way. When people go back and reanalyze those things, a lot of people from that era get very upset and feel as though they're being told they're wrong. That's another thing—I think public history has a role to provoke the public and other folks who interact with it to maybe question their learned narratives. There are people who will never admit they're wrong or accept another perspective or interpretation. But I think that's the role of public history and commemoration: to create that space.

When we talk about historical or archival silences, things are really interpreted from both points of view. I think that these projects and initiatives focused on reconciliation, healing, and giving a voice to Survivors and their families are important, giving an opportunity for different voices to be heard. I think there's a lot more of those voices than there are denialists and it drowns them out. A really good example—one that I've held on to for many years and was fortunate enough that it got to be used in the Interlocutor's *Final Report*, as was mentioned earlier—was the case of Bernice Logan, who used to be known as Bernice Mason. She worked at a variety of Anglican residential schools and was a vocal proponent of denialism quite early on. She started speaking out against residential school Survivors in the late 1970s and early 1980s. So, it's something that has been going on for a really long time. I think showing her efforts also shows that this hatred stems from a very particular place—she didn't even recognize it as hatred; she took Survivor truth as a personal attack. I think it's necessary to show that history to the public and highlight her letters, what she had to say and her responses. I think sharing stories like that also shows that there is power in Survivors organizing in communities and telling their own stories. A lot of the Survivors of the Children of Shingwauk Alumni Association are leaving us; they're passing on. They empowered their children and grandchildren to continue that advocacy work. Their words and legacy live on much longer than the words and legacy of people like Bernice Logan. I think that's the real power of public history to fight denialism.

ERIN: Public history and commemoration related to residential schools are important both as education and as healing. Both, I think, fight IRS denialism. I find that there's a spectrum of knowledge and understanding about residential schools in Canada. At one end, there are people who know a lot, like Survivors, advocates, scholars, and others. At the other end of the spectrum are hard-core denialists. But most people exist in the space in the middle. They might know something, but they don't know a lot. Many of this group are interested in learning more about residential schools but aren't necessarily keen on reading an academic book or even watching a documentary. But they will click on a website, or stop and read a plaque, or visit a historical site to learn more. These are the people whom public history and commemoration has the opportunity to reach and impact. That includes settlers but also a lot of Indigenous people who haven't necessarily had the opportunity to learn about these things for a variety of reasons. Community-led IRS commemoration also has an important role to play in Survivor and community healing, which in turn opens up more space for conversations and learning.

Plaques and memorial sites are important but so is preserving the buildings as physical testaments to the IRS system. All of us who engage with IRS denialism understand the parallels with Holocaust denialism. World War II concentration camps in Europe that have been preserved as physical spaces and function as public historic sites have stood as important counterpoints to Holocaust denialism. That experience of physically being in the same space—whether a concentration camp or a former IRS building—has a far greater impact than any book or plaque or podcast. In general in Canada, we are failing at preserving former Indian Residential Schools as public historic sites. Only a handful of former IRS buildings are still standing. Some of the structures that remain, like Shingwauk or the Mohawk Industrial Residential School or the Kootenay Indian Residential School in British Columbia, have been repurposed for other uses, and that repurposing sometimes includes on-site interpretation of IRS histories. But it's not the same as visiting a site that specifically reflects the IRS experience. The National Indigenous Residential School Museum in Portage la Prairie is attempting to do this work with what have been inconsistent and insufficient resources. Canada is missing an opportunity to preserve former IRS buildings as sites of public education that could stand against IRS denialism, in the way that concentration camp sites have stood against Holocaust denialism.

EDITORS: Yes, we remember when the Birtle Indian Residential School in Manitoba was for sale on Kijiji for $79,000. There was a tremendous opportunity there for public history, but it's not being invested in.

You can look at it one of two ways—the glass is half empty or half full. What we're trying to do in this collection is accentuate some hope. We think that if you read the TRC report, there's a lot of hope that things can be better—that knowledge will spark action, and action will lead to healing, justice, and reconciliation. On that note, our final question is about hope. It's now been ten years since the TRC released its *Final Report* and its Calls to Action. Given the rise of denialism and the backlash that we're seeing and have talked about today, what gives you hope for the future? What inspires you to keep up your public history and commemoration work to help put truth before reconciliation and challenge denialism?

KRISTA: I have a lot of hope for the future. Partially, it's the youth who give me hope. Working with youth through the Shingwauk Residential

Schools Centre—they get it. School groups come into the Shingwauk Residential Schools Centre on a regular basis, and often that involves doing a guided truth walk, spending time in the *Reclaiming Shingwauk Hall* exhibition, and spending time with a Survivor. The impact of that visit on youth and their response to that visit give me a tremendous amount of hope for the future—the fact that we can make change and that we can push back against denialism.

Beyond youth, I think the other thing that keeps me doing this work and keeps me inspired is the strength of the Children of Shingwauk Alumni Association and the Survivors I work with. Some of these folks have been fighting denialism for over forty or fifty years at this point. They're in their seventies and eighties and they're still doing this work. It's hard work, but that strength is something that gives me a lot of hope and is an inspiration.

JACKSON: The youth are getting smarter, stronger, and more articulate, especially at the university level. I've had a lot of discussions with my colleague David Newhouse, who used to teach the ICR when it first started. Trent, I think, was the second after the University of Winnipeg to start the Indigenous Course Requirement. There was a bunch of pushback at that time, and if you asked students if they'd heard of residential schools, it would maybe be 20 percent of the class. Now, if you asked that on the very first day, it's almost 100 percent of the class has heard of residential schools. I think that the number of 20 percent is about the day schools now. We're trying to get that up a bit more through some of the initiatives I mentioned earlier. But students are coming into the classroom with more knowledge about Indigenous Peoples than ever before. I think if you just extrapolate that over several generations—those kids have kids and those kids have kids—the vast awareness of people is drastically increasing. I think that spreads throughout all sectors of society. That gives me a lot of hope.

SKYLEE-STORM: I think, for me, what instills hope is seeing what communities have done themselves. That includes communities like formal First Nations or Rights-holding identity communities, but also communities of interest, Survivor organizations, and people who might be all from very different places but come together under this common experience to support each other—seeing them fighting that fight for fifty or more years and really sticking to their convictions because they don't want to see this happen to more children. As you know, the backlash years have come, and the United States and other countries are doing those things actively. I was fortunate enough to work with Paulette Regan for a couple of years. Her concept of restorying history, creating spaces for other narratives, and building a story that reflects the real truth of people's experiences is still what gives me hope.

As loud as the backlash has been, it has not eclipsed the truth of First Nations, Inuit, and Métis peoples who have been through the residential school system or have lost their families in other assimilationist systems. I think a lot of people are starting to wake up to how interconnected a lot of these systems are. A lot of the backlash and denialism is starting to look desperate, and many people ignore it now. That gives me hope. What also gives me hope is that there are a lot of conservative people I've known in my life who now think denialism is nonsense. That's hopeful for me because that's not something that I was seeing ten years ago when this was really growing. Before, people did not accept that it's proven and there are records and documented systems of people going through hell in these systems.

What also gives me hope is that there are still people who are willing to be on the front lines of that. As much as I would like to see a lot more Indigenous people in the field of history, I understand the importance of settler advocates—people like Paulette Regan, who are saying, "Hey, we've done something here and it's our responsibility to interrogate that narrative and establish the truth." As long as those people remain, that gives me hope. When those people stop speaking or they're no longer in that space, that's when I'm probably going to start to get worried. For now, I have a lot of hope.

ERIN: I draw hope from a couple of main sources. One is connected to what Skylee-Storm said about Survivors. They have been leading this work for decades. Jennifer Wood is one of the Survivors carrying on this work, and she has worked on community-led IRS commemorations through the National Centre for Truth and Reconciliation. She told me that when she talks to people about residential school history she always ends on hope, with the implication being that hope is what will carry things forward. I carry that with me as a reminder to keep moving forward. If the Survivors who have been doing this work for so much longer and with much greater barriers can continue on with hope, then so can I. And in turn I can try to share the same message with my students.

The other source of hope for me is my kids. My kids are both in middle school and as long as they have been in school, their schools have marked Orange Shirt Day and now National Day of Truth and Reconciliation. Their school curriculum integrates Indigenous languages and knowledge. Their schoolyards feature Indigenous art murals on the walls, and ceremony, including smudging, is conducted throughout the year. They've learned more about residential schools by middle school than I did by the third year of my undergraduate degree. They know so much more about residential schools and Indigenous histories in general compared to previous generations. As a wise friend says regularly, "The kids are all right." They give me hope.

Notes

1 The Honourable Murray Sinclair, Canadian Museums, Association Conference, Ottawa, April 2017, as quoted by, The Honourable Patricia Bovey, Truth and Reconciliation Day Assiniboia Residential School Historic Sites and Monuments Board of Canada Designation, 30 September 2025.

2 Lacombe and Pind, "Digitally Mapping the Indian Day Schools and the RG10 School Files Series in Canada."

3 Pind and Carleton, "Raising Awareness about Canada's Indian Day Schools with Digital History."

4 Manitoba Indigenous Tuberculosis History Project, accessed 17 February 2026, https://indigenoustbhistory.ca/.

5 Manitoba Indigenous Tuberculosis History Project, *Missing Patients Research Guide*, accessed 17 February 2026, https://indigenoustbhistory.ca/files/MITHP-Missing-Patients-Research-Guide_Final_2024.pdf. Kathryn Boshmann supported the conversion of the *Guide* from web content to hard-copy publication.

6 Former Portage la Prairie Indian Residential School National Historic Site, Parks Canada, accessed 17 February 2026, https://parks.canada.ca/culture/designation/lieu-site/pensionnat-portage-residential-school; National Indigenous Residential School Museum of Canada, https://nirsmuseum.ca/.

7 "Welcoming Winnipeg: Reconciling Our History," Indigenous Relations Division, City of Winnipeg, accessed 17 February 2026, https://legacy.winnipeg.ca/indigenous/welcomingwinnipeg/default.stm.

8 Bishop Grandin Boulevard was renamed Abinojii Mikanah, Bishop Grandin Trail was changed to Awasisak Mēskanôw, and Grandin Street was changed to Taapweewin Way. "Abinojii Mikanah," Welcoming Winnipeg, Indigenous Relations Division, City of Winnipeg, accessed 17 February 2026, https://legacy.winnipeg.ca/indigenous/welcomingwinnipeg/abinojii-mikanah/default.stm.

9 "Historical Marker Commemorating Victims of 1972 Plane Crash in Winnipeg Unveiled," City of Winnipeg, 25 September 2024, https://www.winnipeg.ca/news/2024-09-25-historical-marker-commemorating-victims-1972-plane-crash-winnipeg-unveiled.

10 Assiniboia Residential School Legacy Group, accessed 17 February 2026, https://assiniboiaresidentialschool.com/. The other three schools are the Red River Indian Mission School, the Rupert's Land Indian Industrial School, and the St. Boniface Indian Industrial School.

11 McCracken, "Archival Photographs in Perspective."

12 BC Museums Association, "How Museums Can Respond to Residential School Denialism," 12 October 2023, https://museum.bc.ca/brain/how-museums-can-respond-to-residential-school-denialism/.

13 "Residential Schools in Canada – Parks Canada and Call to Action #79," Parks Canada, accessed 17 February 2026, https://parks.canada.ca/culture/designation/pensionnat-residential.

14 "It is important to recognize that the [Indigenous] epistemology includes entire systems of knowledge and relationships. These relationships are with the cosmos around us, as well as with concepts. They thus include interpersonal, intrapersonal, environmental and spiritual relationships, and relationships with ideas. Indigenous epistemology is our cultures, our worldviews, our times, our languages, our histories, our spiritualities, and our places in the cosmos. Indigenous epistemology is our systems of knowledge in their context, or relationship." Shawn Wilson, *Research Is Ceremony: Indigenous Research Methods* (Fernwood Publishing, 2008), 74.

CHAPTER 12

TAKING CARE OF COMMUNITY

an Interview with Neegaunibinessikwe, Crystal Gail Fraser, and Kisha Supernant

SEAN CARLETON AND NIIGAAN SINCLAIR (EDITORS): It's an honour to be able to sit down with you all and have you share your experiences and expertise in taking care of community and challenging residential school denialism. To start, can you introduce yourselves and explain your relationship to truth and reconciliation work?

NEEGAUNIBINESSIKWE: Boozhoo. My spirit name is Neegaunibinessikwe. My clan is Maiingan, Wolf. I've stood before the Midewiwin Door four times. I'm a Matriarch to many children, grandchildren, and great-grandchildren already.

I'm Anishinaabe Kwe from Long Plain First Nation, originally from the Myerion line. I'm a third-generation residential school Survivor. My grandmother, my mother, my generation, and my young sons are all residential school Survivors. That truth lives across generations in my family. It's not only something that happened in the past. It's continued on in the lives we lived afterward.

Today, I sit as one of the National Centre for Truth and Reconciliation's Survivors Circle members, and I take great honour in participating in this work. It's careful work. It's sacred work. And there's no template for it. We're not following some finished model. We're guided by one another—by our peers, our colleagues, and by the responsibilities we carry to our communities. More recently, I've also been involved with the Missing Children and Unmarked Burials

Initiative at the NCTR. That work has brought us into conversation with communities about the search for missing children and unmarked burials, and about the development of a national residential school student death registry. These are painful responsibilities, but they're necessary ones. They're part of what it means to take care of community.

This work matters even more because we're living in a time when some people are trying to deny, diminish, or distort the truth about residential schools. That denialism is very painful for Survivors and for our communities. It's harmful because it asks us to question what we know, what we lived, and what's already been told with great courage. It's harmful because it tries to push truth back into silence. For many of us, that silence is not new. It's something we've already lived through. So, when people deny the history or try to soften it, they're not only arguing about the past. They're continuing the harm in the present.

The path that brought me into this work began many years ago, in a way that felt both ordinary and profound. I was with the Three Fires Midewiwin Society, and we were constructing our spring initiation lodge, which is like our degree-conferring system. The Midewiwin Society is very old. It's been practiced and carried forward through generations. While I was helping to build that lodge, Murray Sinclair—who was already a member of the society—came up to me and said, "I have a question to ask you. I've been asked to sit as chair of a commission ... it has to do with establishing the truth about residential schools." I remember feeling happy when he said that, because nothing like it had ever been done before. It wasn't even on anybody's radar. It was unheard of at the time. I said to him, "Yes, take it."

That was the beginning, for me, of being involved in the work that became the Truth and Reconciliation Commission. But even before that, there had already been another moment—one of those moments that changes something deep inside you, even before you fully know what's happened.

My partner and I used to watch CBC's *The National* every night at home. In October 1990, Phil Fontaine was interviewed about residential schooling. We were surprised by what we were hearing. Phil said that he and others had been sexually abused at residential school in Sagkeeng, at the Fort Alexander Indian Residential School. I don't know exactly what happened in that moment between my partner and me, but we both looked at each other and said, "Whoa, yeah, that's right, isn't it?" We just woke up. We woke up to the realization that both my partner and I had been in residential school, too.

Where we had put all of that memory before then, I don't know. I don't know how we had suppressed or stored it all those years. But in that moment, something came back. And in my opinion, Phil Fontaine woke up our collective memory as a people and the whole of Canada, too. That was when the public conversation about residential schools began to change. That was when people began to remember, "Yeah, me too. Me too. I was there. That happened to me."

That's why denialism is so dangerous. It goes against that remembering. It goes against the truth that Survivors brought forward, often at great personal cost. It goes against the years of courage it took for people to speak at all. For me, Phil Fontaine and Murray Sinclair are both deeply important in this work. One helped wake us up collectively, and the other helped lead us toward the courage of truth and action. There was no template for any of it. We simply began the work and knew that our truth would guide us.

When I started with the TRC, I came on board as one of the original Statement Gatherers. I carried my equipment in a toolbox from Canadian Tire. I can still picture it. I put the audio system on one shelf, a recorder on another, the DVD equipment where it fit, and all my lighting and documents alongside it—everything people needed in order to give permission and share their statements with me. I didn't so much as care about what I was using, although I did get those kinds of looks in public spaces. By day, I gathered statements from Survivors across Canada. We went to places you would never dream of going to on your own. By night, my colleague would transfer what I had collected onto files. After a while, I was enlisted to assist in training other Statement Gatherers when National Events were being planned and conducted. Each province would select its own team, and I'd come in to help train and manage. I stayed with the TRC for quite a while.

I loved being a Statement Gatherer. I loved helping to create space for people to share their truths and experiences, especially our people, and especially when they were speaking about what had happened to them. There is something very important in that moment when a person is able to speak what they've carried for so long. And there is something just as important in how they are received. To be met with care, kindness, and respect matters. To be listened to properly matters.

To have your truth handled gently matters. That, to me, is also part of taking care of community.

This work was never just professional for me. It was also deeply personal. While I was helping other people tell their truths, I was also trying to understand myself as a Survivor. That wasn't easy. It was very difficult trying to make sense of the Western world and my Anishinaabe world. Sometimes I couldn't separate the two. They were so intertwined. In some ways, the Western part had overtaken the Anishinaabe part. That kind of impact is part of what residential school did. It did not only harm children in the moment. It carried itself forward into the rest of our lives—in the way we understood ourselves, in the way we moved through institutions, in the way we tried to make sense of the world.

That is one of the things I want people to understand when we speak about residential schools: The experience did not end when a child left the building. It kept going. It moved through families, through communities, through language, through identity, through memory. It shaped how people carried pain, how they carried silence, and how they tried to survive. When Survivors speak, they're not only speaking about something historical. They're speaking about a living reality and about its long shadow. Denialism tries to sever that connection. It tries to turn something lived and ongoing into something distant, doubtful, or debatable. But for us, it's not abstract. It's our lives.

I saw that long shadow in other systems too. As part of the Survivors Circle, we look at many issues, including research—how it is conducted in institutions, and how different that can be from what we would want to see. I've seen real problems and internal struggles to address fairness and equity in those processes. I saw it especially when we launched our lawsuits for settlements. I was called in from time to time to be an interpreter. I would sit between the adjudicator and the claimant, and that whole process was so messed up. At first, sitting there, I did not fully understand what I was seeing and hearing. But then the adjudicator accused me of leading the claimant on, and that was when I realized just how deeply Western that system was, and how little it understood us as Anishinaabe people. In our language, when we speak, we set the context first before we ask the question. That is how meaning is carried. That is how understanding is built. But in that system, our way of speaking was treated almost like a problem instead of being recognized as a valid and respectful way of communicating.

Experiences like that taught me something important. They showed me that telling the truth is not enough on its own. The truth also has to be received in ways that honours who people are. If the systems hearing Survivors are still shaped by assumptions that do not understand us, then harm can continue even inside processes that are supposed to bring justice and healing. The same is true with denialism. It's not only a disagreement over facts. It's a refusal to receive the truth in a good way. It's a refusal to honour the lives and words of those who've already spoken.

That's why taking care of community means more than documenting the truth. It also means protecting that truth. It means refusing the return of silence. It means standing with Survivors when their memories and experiences are questioned, minimized, or denied. It means creating conditions where our people can be heard, respected, and supported, and speaking out when truth is being diminished.

For me, that's what this work has come to mean. It's about truth. It's about history. But it's also about the present. It's about how we support one another. It's about whether we know how to sit with people's pain without doing more damage. It's about whether we can build processes that do not erase us again. It's about whether healing is something we only talk about, or something we actually achieve.

There was no template for this work when we began, and in many ways there still isn't one. We've had to learn by doing, by listening, by making mistakes, by returning to one another, and by staying grounded in community. What's kept me going are the experiences that made the need to do this work so clear. Working with other Survivors gave me strength, and they deepened my understanding of what our people are up against. They reminded me that this work is not only about bringing truth forward. It's also about protecting it from being buried again.

For me, that's part of healing. And that's taking care of community. Miigwech.

EDITORS: Thank you for all of your work. It's really great to have your expertise as part of this conversation. What about you, Crystal?

CRYSTAL GAIL FRASER: My name is Crystal Gail Fraser. I'm Gwichyà Gwich'in and of Scottish and English ancestry, originally from Inuuvik (Inuvik) and Dachan Choo Gę̀hnjik, my fish camp in the Northwest Territories. My grandmother, Marka Bullock, was institutionalized at Immaculate Conception Residential School in Akłarvik (Aklavik).

My grandmother did not share extensively about her residential schooling story, and did so only with select people. From what I've read, she was one of the students in charge of carrying the spittoon buckets at the residential school. There was a big hospital next door to the residential school, with many tuberculosis patients. I believe she was exposed to many illnesses because of her job there, as a child, and so she was quite often sick. That was her way out of residential school. Because she was so sick, she was sent home. It was a relief that she was sent home and lived, given the living conditions at many of these institutions.

My mother, Juliet, was institutionalized at Grollier Hall. This was one of the most notorious "modern" residential schools in Canada; it closed in 1996. My mother's early life was shaped by a household affected by alcohol abuse and interpersonal violence. This was not uncommon in Inuuvik. The federal government built Inuuvik in the late 1950s. Homes for relatively well-to-do Indigenous families were called 512s, which were little boxes—512 square feet. The poor Indigenous families lived in Tent Town. The white people (government workers, RCMP [Royal Canadian Mounted Police], and teachers) lived in the fancy homes on the other side of town. Inuuvik was racially segregated. But my mom grew up in a 512 with nine siblings, her mom, and her dad. There were some children in Inuuvik who perceived residential school as a way to improve their lives, to meet their basic needs of housing and food, my mother included. Most found that residential schools were not what they thought and created other severe problems. I write about the history of Akłarvik and Inuuvik's Indian Residential Schools in my book, *By Strength, We Are Still Here: Indigenous Peoples and Indian Residential Schooling in Inuvik, Northwest Territories*.

Both my grandmother and mother had painful experiences, and so did others. For Survivors, their pain is often layered and complex. Some children were forcibly removed from their homes and sent thousands of kilometres away for years at a time. There was no going home during the summer, or at Christmas and Easter. That was a common experience in the North, particularly for Inuit children from the Eastern Arctic. Others may have been geographically closer to their families and Indigenous Lands but were severely abused. In the North, residential schools were also a tool of the justice and child welfare systems. If an Indigenous child was in trouble with the law, they could be sentenced to a residential school. Indigenous children who were removed from their parents because of "unsatisfactory" living conditions, or if a child did not have a legal guardian, went to the residential school. Others are Survivors of several residential schools. In the Beaufort Delta, for example, it was not uncommon for a child to have started at an Akłarvik residential school, then be moved to Grollier or Stringer Hall in Inuuvik, and then to Akaitcho Hall in Sǫǫ̀mbak'è (Yellowknife). Some even went further and were sent to southern Canada for vocational schooling.

This is a part of the history of my family, of Dinjii Zhuh, and other northern Indigenous Peoples. But we also have rich histories of being on the Land, practising our cultures and speaking our languages, and welcoming the first newcomers in the North. My great-grandmother Julienne The'dahcha (who sometimes also used the surnames Jerome and/or Andre) was born in 1887 and raised many children on the Land with her husband, John Tsell.[1] This was a time when an increasing number of fur traders and missionaries were arriving in the North. Many newcomers would not have lived through the long Arctic winters without the expertise and help of our people. My grandmother Marka was born in 1926 and also welcomed non-Indigenous newcomers to the North. In 1944, Marka lost her first husband, Francois Coyen, after only eight days of marriage, to influenza. She went on to meet my grandfather Richard Bullock. With his family, he emigrated to Toronto from England when he was an infant. His job as the first Indian Day School teacher in Tsiigehtshik (Tsiigehtchic) brought him north. I'm sharing this because we all have complex histories and we're all connected to colonialism in different ways. I encourage everyone to learn more about their family histories and heritage.

As a child, I made many observations in my community—addiction, incarceration, untimely deaths, ongoing operations of Grollier Hall—and I started to quietly ask questions. I didn't find answers to those questions until I was in early adulthood. In many ways, I was very much caught in the cycle of family upheaval. My own immediate family fell apart when I was eight years old. Then, when I was a teenager, my family left Inuuvik for Lethbridge, which was extremely disruptive. I did not know how to live down south. I missed my grandmother and fish camp immensely. I left high school early and was homeless for a short time. I fought my way out of that life, somehow. Today, I sometimes reflect on how my life could have gone very differently.

Like many other people in my generation, I didn't learn about residential schools until I was older, despite this being a very personal family history. Around 2008, a non-Indigenous professor mentioned residential schooling. It was never something taught or talked about directly in my home community, or at least I was not a part of those conversations. And although a few Survivors had publicly shared their experiences and a few historians had written about the Indian Residential School system, it was not yet a common part of Canadian national dialogue.

When I began my PhD, some of my Elders asked me to undertake research into the history of what happened to our people at Indian Residential Schools. At the time, the Truth and Reconciliation Commission of Canada was already underway, and they even hosted a National Event in Inuuvik. At the same time, I was aware of my privileged position and my desire to help myself and my community. I was worried about causing harm, and that there wouldn't be the right supports available. I had to rely on community members and Elders to mentor and guide me. My cousins Alestine Andre and Agnes Mitchell were and are my biggest supporters when it comes to this work. They are champions every step of the way.

I learned that I needed to be patient and understanding, and that this process was bigger than me. It needs to unfold in a certain way that benefits community at every step. I practised patience and empathy, while also trying to learn how to be a new parent. My daughter was born during my PhD program, which prompted new questions as I thought through student experiences at Indian Residential Schools and my own family's history. It was difficult on multiple levels: being disconnected from some family members, living away from Gwich'in homelands, not having regular access to Elders or language speakers, and being at an institution and in an academic discipline where there were very few Indigenous leaders. It was not easy, but I knew learning the truth would help benefit my community and me, so I pressed on with my research on the histories of residential schooling in Inuuvik. And I persisted and succeeded.

Currently, I'm an associate professor cross-appointed in history and Indigenous Studies at the University of Alberta. Four years ago, I was also welcomed into the Governing Circle at the National Centre for Truth and Reconciliation, and then I became a founding member of the

National Advisory Committee on Residential Schools Missing Children and Unmarked Burials (NAC) to help guide this important work.

EDITORS: What about you, Kisha?

KISHA SUPERNANT: Thank you for sharing those stories. I'm Kisha Supernant. I'm a citizen of the Otipemisiwak Métis Government. On my dad's side, I have a lot of connections to Métis communities in Alberta as well as back to Red River. I'm related to Cree and Mohawk ancestors who came west with the fur trade as well. On my mom's side, I'm descended from second- and third-generation British settlers.

I have a somewhat different story, but I think it's all interconnected. Like Neegaunibinessikwe and Crystal, my personal experience has motivated me to help care for community as a core part of my work, and this now also includes challenging residential school denialism.

My father was raised in the child welfare system. He was born in Edmonton, where I'm currently located as a professor of archaeology at the University of Alberta. My father was born in 1953. Pretty much as soon as he was born, as far as we can tell, he was taken from his unwed, teenage Métis mother. He spent a couple of years in an orphanage and then moved into the foster care system. He was never adopted. He bounced around when he was young and then landed with one family but was never really part of that family on a permanent basis.

As a result, I grew up very disconnected from that part of my heritage and who I am as a Métis woman. I was always very curious about learning more about who we were, and have spent a lot of my adult life coming home to my community. Being disconnected affected my family in a whole bunch of different ways that I've come to really understand only now later in life. I had a very itinerant and unsettled childhood, which I very much tie to my father's experience growing up. He was never part of a family, so it's not surprising that he wasn't able to be very present as a father.

I entered university knowing vaguely that we were Métis but not really having a sense of what that meant. I was very interested in studying archaeology and understanding the past. Reflecting on that interest today makes me realize it was because I was partly seeking who I was and feeling that sense of disconnection.

My educational journey also took me into learning more about who I was and starting to figure out who our family members were, who our relatives were, and what it really meant to be Métis. There remain many widespread misconceptions about who is Métis, but I learned we were part of the historic Métis Nation and that my family has been Métis for generations.

My academic journey was part of that work of learning and reflection. I was raised mostly in British Columbia, away from my ancestral homeland. I didn't spend much time in those homelands until I got offered a job at the University of Alberta in 2010, as I was finishing up my PhD.

By that time, I had already been working with Indigenous communities as part of my research. During my PhD, I worked alongside the Stó:lō Nation and Yale First Nation in British Columbia and was doing archaeology in a way that was attentive to the interests and needs of Indigenous communities, or at least attempting to do so, not always successfully.[2] I had been in community in different kinds of ways but not in my own.

When I came back to Alberta, it was a very interesting experience for me because being in my ancestral homelands and then finding out more and more that my close relatives are here in this place made a big difference for me.

I started developing a research program where I was working with my community about what archaeology can do for them. In a roundabout way, my reconnecting journey took me into community. And then community started asking for me to help them with various kinds of things.

My expertise as an archaeologist is actually in the application of digital technology and less invasive methods to understanding the past through mapping and landscape-level work. What started happening is that the people I was talking to in my community and in related communities were asking: Can you help us find unmarked burials on the grounds of former residential schools? This was well before the 2021 announcement by Tk'emlúps te Secwépemc. Many communities already knew about additional deaths and the potential for unmarked burials on school grounds. This knowing is why the TRC included a whole volume on the subject—Volume 4, *Missing Children and Unmarked Burials*—calling for more research to be done.

When communities began asking, I immediately began working on how to approach the ground-search process. What are the techniques that we can use? We started exploring what the options were from other archaeologists who had been using various techniques to find unmarked graves. It was those relationships that led to the first time I was asked to do a search for unmarked burials associated with an Indian Residential School. That was in the Muskowekwan First Nation in 2018.

Getting involved in this work was very much an outcome from a lot of the other relationships that I had built over the years. Based on those relationships, community trusted me to help with this sensitive work. They wanted to know whether or not there were burials behind the building that they still have, which was the residential school.

This was also after the Truth and Reconciliation Commission's 94 Calls to Action, of which number 71 through number 76 are specifically about the missing children, as I just mentioned. I started to see a potential role that I could play if communities needed and wanted help to address some of those Calls to Action with the skills I have been privileged to learn.

From 2018 onward, I've been working with different Nations to do searches of historic burial grounds, not necessarily only at residential schools. But I have been learning more about the techniques, the landscapes, the challenges, and the possibilities.

In 2021, when Tk'emlúps made their announcement about the preliminary results from the ground-penetrating radar (GPR) survey, I immediately started getting emails and phone calls and inquiries from communities who were now interested in thinking about applying these types of technologies to the landscapes around the schools on their territory and where their children had been stolen.

As someone who had experience, is Indigenous, and had long-standing relationships with community, I became overwhelmed with the demand to undertake what is a very complex and overwhelming large question: Where are potential burials of children associated with residential schools across the entire country?

Early on, after the announcement from Tk'emlúps, I started talking to communities from across Canada about what they might consider, what ground-penetrating radar is, what it can and cannot do, and how they might think about applying it to the landscapes that they wanted to search. At the same time, I was doing a ton of media about clarifying what role the technology plays in the truth-telling process. There was a lot of misunderstanding at first, such as the persistent idea that ground-penetrating radar can easily and quickly find bodies, which is not the case. We already know about deaths in residential schools, so the process of ground searching is not to prove children died. That truth is already established; it's already been told. What we're trying to do is help figure out where these children might be buried. Trying to raise awareness about the technology, what was possible, what isn't possible, and what was needed, became important. As part of that work, I have been continually supporting a number of communities to do this—the ground search, which is just one part of the whole research process.

Like Crystal, I was asked to join as a founding member of the National Advisory Committee on Residential Schools Missing Children and Unmarked Burials as a technical expert in 2022. I was there as someone who understood the technology that can be applied in these places, what some of the challenges and complexities of using it are, and how to do it in a way that is supportive of community, respectful of Survivors and their knowledge, and in a way that also doesn't overstate what these technologies can bring to the table.

That's really what's brought me into the realm of truth and reconciliation. I'm focused on the telling of the truth, not so much on the reconciliation part because, as Crystal mentioned, this is an event, this is a crime, and this is something that is ongoing. Until the truth is told, there is no chance at any form of reconciliation.

EDITORS: It's interesting that truth determination is a key part of all of your work, in different ways. Concerning the issue of missing children and unmarked burials, there has been a lot of pushback on this part of the work, especially relating to searches for unmarked burials and the use of GPR technology, as we discussed in Chapter 4 with archaeologist Andrew Martindale.

We have seen since the Truth and Reconciliation Commission *Final Report* released in 2015, and increasingly after the Kamloops announcement, a rise in the number of people who are seeking to undermine the truth, to obscure the truth, to shake public confidence in that truth as a form of anti-Indigenous backlash and racism and hate, a way of undermining the truth of Survivors, the credibility of communities, and the people who work in alliance with communities to establish that truth. This is residential school denialism. Why do you see this kind of attack as being so harmful?

NEEGAUNIBINESSIKWE: I understand this denialism to be like a secondary wounding to residential school Survivors, and all of my ancestors.

Growing up, I used to play around graves, too, but being a child, you don't pay attention to this kind of stuff. Those concepts aren't there yet, like Crystal was saying. But it's there and harmful. For non-Indigenous people, denialism shows their limitations; they are uneducated about what really happened. They've not ever come to me, to talk to me, or to talk to us as Survivors or to anybody who's ever gone to a residential school. I've never seen them come and step on the reserve and say, "Let's sit down and talk, you know, just have a good talk." I haven't seen it.

There is just this constant attack, attack, attack while we are busy trying to do our work, and trying to understand where we fit in all this, and trying to heal. We're still being attacked. And so, where on Earth are other people having to live this way, having to live with that every day and still maintain our strength? It's a very difficult place to be. For me to pay attention constantly to what the denialists are saying, which I have no control over, I can't do that. I can't do that to my children, my grandchildren. I can't do that for my ancestors. It hurts too much. I need to be focused and keep moving forward. We have work to do. We have a lot of work to do, which hasn't even begun in some instances.

We are consulting; we are meeting with our communities. Give us the time; let us do our work; let us do our relationship building. A community like ours, where there's a lot of conflict trying to make sense of the world around us, there's a lot of lateral violence, there's a whole lot of issues, and we're all still struggling to find our way to healing. Some of us are only coming to terms with how many people were taken out of our reserves, especially in September for residential school, and the damage and disruption that it caused and still causes.

But I've always loved the land. Growing up, before I went to residential school, it was the land that took care of me as a child when I had to run out the door when my uncle would be drinking, as a result of his traumas. They'd start drinking, and I knew when he would first slap my hand. I knew that was my chance to get out, and I'd be out on the land all night, if you can think of this, as a five-year-old. I'd be out on the land all night with rabbits, owls, squirrels, and the moon. I had no fear whatsoever. I was not afraid of anything. It was only in residential school where I learned what fear was. And even today, I know that I will come back home to that land again because it's the land that will take care of me. When my work is done here on Earth, that land will lovingly take me again. And just as it has done with the uncovering of our graves, the land has taken care of our loved ones and still is until such time as families determine what they want to do. That's their right, it's our people's right, to determine what they want to do with their loved ones, and that's the work that we're undertaking. We're doing this work for us, not to prove anything to Canadians. That's why I see denialism as a secondary wounding. It affects us all in different ways, and for some of us it hits deeper.

Never did I ever believe you'd have all these negative people putting additional pressure on Indigenous communities trying to learn the truth. You have this expectation, this demand. We're coming into ourselves, where we're starting to talk. Now we're starting to realize where we come from and appreciate where we come from. We are starting to find our way. Our path, our road. We're working with each other, and it's so very, very difficult to walk this road.

I want to say to those denialists—come and sit with us and listen and learn. We will not hurt you. We will talk. Let's have some food and talk about the truth together.

CRYSTAL: Thanks, Neegaunibinessikwe, for answering in that way.

The denial of Indigenous Knowledge systems, and our experiences, has long characterized and defined colonialism on these Lands now called Canada. There's always been some form of violence or disbelief or undermining of our world views, the way we experience things, the way we practise our cultures. Residential school denialism is not about denying that the schools existed.[3] Instead, it involves downplaying the harm they caused, exaggerating "positive" experiences, questioning oral histories, or demanding ever-increasing levels of "evidence." It's a tactic that undermines Survivors and protects settler innocence.[4] In my public writing, I've described denialism as a refusal to accept Canada's genocidal past—and present—and a deflection from Indigenous truths and justice.[5]

But as Neegaunibinessikwe mentioned, residential school denialism is like being hurt all over again. You have people who were removed from their families and their Traditional Lands, sometimes violently, and then institutionalized. They were victims in many ways, and of course some didn't survive—which is why we're here today talking about the work we do to locate and honour them. Calling all of that into question or downplaying facts is a direct attack on our truths. We need to be able to offer supports to Survivors who are going through this because it's not just in the past. Denialism is harmful because it eats away at us.

It's also a distraction from the work that we're trying to do with and for communities to facilitate healing and justice. Cree political scientist Matthew Wildcat calls us, as Indigenous Peoples, nation builders because we have the task of trying to pick up all of the little pieces and rebuild something that once existed. That process can be painful, and then to have it challenged by deniers—who benefit from our oppression—makes that much harder. What I've come to see in this work is that denialism isn't just ignorance—it's a defence of the colonial status quo. It's an attempt to shift attention away from Survivors and communities doing the hard work of healing and truth telling.

As a public educator, I have two primary ways of seeing the harm of denialism. On the one hand, it hurts on a personal level; Survivors have attested to that. On the other, the amount of work, at the post-secondary level, that is required to constantly be teaching and unteaching about residential schools is exhausting and unique to this field. I have come to understand that I have overestimated the nature of reconciliation in this country, and also to understand how easy it is for many Canadians to dismiss the TRC's 94 Calls to Action. The year 2025 is the tenth anniversary of the TRC's *Final Report*. Some people have not even read Call to Action number 1, let alone read the *Final Report*.

Like Kisha said, residential school deaths and unmarked burials have never been a secret. We've known that children died and disappeared. We do not yet have an accurate estimate of those deaths and disappearances because the TRC was working with limited archival materials during their research process. I am hopeful that the NCTR, working with Indigenous communities, will add to our understanding of these genocidal systems. For me, the solution lies in education. This is how we counter different forms of denialism related to residential schools.

Most of the time, I need to believe that people engage in residential school denialism because they are ignorant, and they do not intend to hurt Indigenous Peoples. Murray Sinclair says that education is the solution. I teach hundreds of students every single year, and they all learn something new about the histories of residential schools. I teach them the truth. I believe that they are good humans, and they will share what they've learned with their friends and relatives, and maybe I'll inspire them to take another course and learn more. I have to continue believing in my role as a teacher who centres the truth. In that sense, education is not just about awareness—it's a form of resistance. Every time a student learns from a Survivor story, examines archival photographs, or engages in critical discussion, they are rejecting the idea that these histories are debatable. Teaching becomes a way of confronting denialism not through debate but through clarity, compassion, and truth. That's how we build resilience against misinformation.

Now, there is a small percentage of people who are mean-spirited, often looking for a social media platform and to profit from these false narratives. They want to make big and bold statements to boost their stature and profiles. These people are dangerous. These are the people who can sometimes sway political leaders to make uninformed statements that have severe consequences. I don't engage with these people in the same way. My energy is better spent focusing on the people who are teachable but also my community, Elders, and relatives. Still, some of it is alarming. The hateful posts on social media or the emails that we all receive are ugly. In this work, we need to protect our own spirits, time, and energy if we are going to be useful for our communities. I'm just so grateful that we're in a space where—even though denialism is certainly on the rise—we have networks of support. We have resources, connections, and colleagues who are interested in the same questions. We're not alone. We can share this burden.

KISHA: I think Crystal made a really important distinction between the people who are spreading denialism deliberately and then those who are allured by it or are susceptible to it because of ignorance and because they don't necessarily have access to good information.

For me, that 10 percent of people who are creating and spreading misinformation regarding residential schools—and it's probably a lot less than 10 percent, honestly—they are just people who are unwilling to accept the truth that Canada is built on genocide.

There is a fundamental disconnect between how they understand Canada and the reality of Canada that they are unable or unwilling to resolve. Therefore, they cling to what they see as positive aspects of residential schooling because they are so invested in the project of settler colonialism and the erasure of Indigenous Peoples. These are people who want that project to continue. I don't think they are people who will ever change their minds, and I don't want to spend time trying, because as I've said and will continue to say, they will always move the bar of evidence.

First, these kinds of people insisted that residential schools were "positive" and "well-intentioned"; now they say "no bodies" have been found, which is not actually true, but that's also not the point.[6] It wouldn't matter if we find remains; they will still find some way to downplay the genocide that was at the heart of residential schools. They don't care about us or our communities. They do their work to cause harm.

I think what's important is to have that focus on taking care of community, Survivors, and intergenerational Survivors first. We can also focus on the folks who are maybe listening or susceptible to those narratives and who come out of that 10 percent, and equip them to be able to recognize the major talking points and rhetorical devices that the denialists use. People need to be prepared to challenge the common talking points that denialists use to shake confidence in the truth. We need to empower people to use the actual truth to talk to friends, family, and their own networks to help to clarify and get people to counter that denialist narrative.

I would also love to see denialism deplatformed. That's not something that's necessarily in our control. Still, I think that's one of the tensions in the university environment at a time where conversations about the intersection between academic freedom, tenure, and freedom of expression are creating a ripe environment for a lot of really harmful misinformation to be platformed and spread as legitimate even when it's not actually grounded in good scholarship.

We're in an interesting environment that way, and universities, I think, are perhaps reluctant to take stands about things for fear of reprisal. There needs to be more courage from our leadership around these issues so that we can deplatform the people who are spreading these untruths.

Denialists are afraid of the truth. What I find sometimes ironic is that they say we are the ones who are afraid of the truth when it's clear to me they're the ones who don't want to accept their own genocidal history, or admit to the ongoing impacts of that genocide in the lands that we call Canada today. I see that as the truth becomes known by more people, we see this rise in hate and backlash to try to turn the tide. I think this is what happened after Tk'emlúps. Like Crystal, I sometimes overestimate the amount of awareness that the average non-Indigenous Canadian person had, as evidenced by the shock and horror after Tk'emlúps. Clearly many hadn't been paying enough attention to the TRC findings in 2015, because in 2021 people were shocked by what we knew years ago.

I think that because there are more non-Indigenous Canadians listening, paying attention, and seeking that truth, we are seeing a rise in the backlash, because the more truth that is told, the harder it is to deny those other findings and realities. Denialists feel like they are losing control. The status quo is changing, and they don't like that.

I completely agree that we cannot focus on that small percentage of people who want to keep their heads in the sand or deliberately cause harm, because they're never going to change. They don't want change. What we need to do is deplatform hate and spread good information and resources on how to recognize and counter denialism for the average non-Indigenous Canadian who might be reading those hateful articles or seeing those debates on social media.

EDITORS: We've all had personal experiences with denialism, and we think it's important to name these and shine a light on what often happens to people doing this work. Personally, we've received death threats and hate mail for the work we've done speaking out against denialism. If you feel comfortable, could you share some of your own experiences to help people really understand the extreme forms that denialism often takes?

CRYSTAL: There's just so many examples of denialism that we encounter in this work. You become immune to it at a certain point. Also, a part of resiliency and strength is finding the humour in the things that we cannot necessarily change, so let's not leave humour behind either. I did, however, receive a letter at my home once. It was a handwritten letter from a Christian missionary in Germany who defended Canadian Indian Residential Schools. That was unsettling. Then, I experienced a threat on campus and had to work with campus police and university administration. These incidents were a stark reminder that we need to look out for each other, and also report every incident to our employers so they are aware of what we experience in our jobs and the need to further think through our safety.

Speaking more broadly about the discipline of Canadian history, I see a lot of denialist rhetoric. Thinking about even the title of a book is important; for example, J.R. Miller's book *Shingwauk's Vision* has always caused some confusion for me.[7] That's one example, but other historians have ended the residential school story in the 1960s or 1970s, failing to note that the last residential schools didn't close until 1997. This treatment presents these histories as historic. They're clearly not.

We're not perfect people when we come to this work, but, even so, I find many of my colleagues fail to listen or even make room for these conversations. This contributes to the problem. This can promote denialism willingly or unwillingly. Not everyone should do community-engaged research, but academics should never work in isolation and should be in relationship with Indigenous Peoples wherever they live. This fosters dialogue, ongoing education, and accountability for scholars at all ranks. As Allyson Stevenson and I have argued elsewhere, truth and reconciliation is "a practice, and, like other activities worth practising, it takes commitment and work."[8]

KISHA: Echoing what's already been shared—the nasty and regular emails are a little bit easier to navigate because I create a filter and they all go into my archive. Where this is also challenging is when it intersects more directly with my academic work. There have been now two talks, related to my community and academic work, that I've given in public spaces where we have had to be very deliberate about the kind of spaces that are created. In one of them, I actually had a security detail because there was concern about reactions from the audience. In both cases, we were very clear that we did not do an open "question and answer" with the audience. It was a significant concern that it would be creating a platform, which again gets framed, and Crystal mentioned this, as genocide being open to debate. It gives denialists the opportunity to spread hate as "debate," as "just asking questions." We don't debate fundamental human rights. It's not a debate. This is the truth.

But that's how residential school knowledge sometimes gets framed in these spaces when there's an open mic and someone says, "Oh, just in the interest of asking questions, you know, or seeking clarification," but then it quickly becomes a "show me the bodies" gotcha moment. I can handle the response to that, of course, but it doesn't feel safe. I can manage it, but it's still part of that hurt we have been talking about.

My big issue in those public forums is everyone else in the audience. Often, they are Survivors and intergenerational Survivors, students, and people genuinely wanting to learn. The truth is that they are all there, and they're listening and they're experiencing that denialist attack. I'm also very careful about the kinds of spaces that I'm in and have some role in creating so that we don't create spaces of harm. The places where I've encountered the need to navigate around that and try to diminish the impact of denialists are when they show up in person to talks to try to disrupt and platform hate. Actually, at one of the talks that I gave, individuals from the institution did not feel comfortable or safe coming to hear me talk because they knew well-known denialists would be in the audience. They just couldn't even be present, which makes me sad. That's how bad it has become. Even though what I was saying probably would have been very supportive for them, I couldn't even create that space because that person was in the audience. I find academia a harder space sometimes to navigate, when denialism is so present in the academic world and it's often protected by the same reasons that we need protection, through things like tenure and academic freedom. Denialists are often protected by those same systems.

EDITORS: Thanks for being vulnerable and sharing some of those experiences. It's clear that these kinds of attacks are about undermining the truths of Survivors, of course, but also anyone working with community to establish the truth. Denialism is about causing harm and intimidating those telling the truth in an effort to protect the colonial status quo. Part of the idea of bringing us all together was, yes, to talk about the harm of denialism, to be clear about the hurt being caused. But the goal, really, was to also bring us together to talk about how we can take care of one another and community as we continue to do our work. Despite the denialism we frequently encounter, how can we continue to support Survivors and those still affected by the residential schooling system?

Based on your perspective and expertise, what kinds of supports are needed from a community perspective so that we can continue to do the work of telling the truth? Whether it's from your work with the National Advisory Council or the communities you work with and for, what are the kinds of supports that we need to put in place to help ensure that new generations will want to continue to do that work? To us, that seems to be one of the key issues in this, not getting distracted or discouraged from the task at hand: supporting community.

NEEGAUNIBINESSIKWE: To move forward, I think that this discussion we're having needs to be bigger. We need to have more Survivors around the table. It needs to get a bit bigger so it becomes a whole lot of our voices, and not just some voices.

It also needs to be in a safe space, like what Kisha said. Safety is very important to me. We need to have someone who is really, really skilled at being able to facilitate what we are doing. You need people who are really skilled at being able to facilitate and read what is going on to provide support that way. Kisha also talked about security. We have our own security. We have our own Anishinaabe warriors. And in the communities, we haven't even gotten to that point yet to have sharing circles amongst us as Survivors, amongst us as families. We're not there yet. We're on the periphery. We're starting, but we need more time. We need to be respected and given our privacy to do that with our people, with kindness.

Many different forms of support are required to help us in this work. We need health supports. Some of the damage to the health supports has come from academia—counsellors and social workers who have a really ingrained, academic way of understanding how you counsel and how you provide support. It feels very colonial—disrespectful, sometimes. We really need to screen out even our own people who don't understand what being Anishinaabe—who want to build relationships rather than intervene—is all about and how you do community work with our people.

I like this forum that we're in today. I feel safe with you. I think this is exactly the kind of forums that needs to happen more, and maybe on a bigger scale. Bring us in. Bring us Survivors in while we're alive. Bring us in to do sharing circles in your classrooms. Let us be the ones conducting the sharing circle and talking because we are the last generation of Survivors who have lived experience with the residential school system. Use us as much as you can. Work with us.

CRYSTAL: People in communities are trying to live good lives, and surviving, raising families, relearning language, and they're having people deny, downplay, or minimize their lived experiences and histories. Recently, I was in conversation with Gwich'in Survivors about how to best commemorate our history of residential schooling. I was told that a great deal of healing still needs to take place. There are people struggling with addiction and mental illness who need help. There are people who have such a great desire to connect with the land, waterways, and animals. What could that sort of healing look like? Perhaps language programs, spending time on the land or waters, learning how to cut fish, or training community midwives so women can birth locally. There are many different healing initiatives that aren't directly linked to residential schools but have the potential to reverse the damage of those systems. Providing a good education—ideally from Survivors and Elders using an intergenerational approach—about our people's histories has the potential to heal our people.

KISHA: In my experience, working with a number of different communities, there are people at all different stages in this process with specific kinds of needs. I think there are two big areas.

One is focused on healing. That healing means coming together, doing nation building, and gathering the pieces of our communities. Survivors are still here, many of them. We're losing more all the time, but they're here. Gathering and renewing those relations to each other, to place, to culture—all of those things are important. Healing is definitely what's needed. There needs to be holistic, ongoing, and sustainable support for healing, whether that be Survivor circles, language revitalization, or bringing home belongings that have been taken away to far-off places, so people can relearn how to do the sewing and the making that are done. All of that is really important, and it's something that needs to be sustainable and long-term.

The other piece is accountability. Who has been held accountable for what happened to Survivors and those who did not survive? The accountability and justice pieces are crucial moving forward. There needs to be ongoing support for those initiatives. First, Canada needs to address all forty-two obligations that the Office of the Special Interlocutor, Kimberly Murray, laid out because those include mechanisms that can be used for things such as denialism and hate speech.

Finding ways to get that justice, whether through national or international mechanisms, is a necessary next step. Having a process where, if there are communities and people in communities who want to bring the physical remains of their children home, that is possible with the right structure and support. This is an extremely complicated and difficult thing to do, but there are ways to make more of that possible.

There also needs to be a structure that doesn't have to involve the Royal Canadian Mounted Police, so it doesn't have to involve the existing legal systems, and can better support Survivors and families. They need people they can go to whom they can trust to tell them what's possible, what's not, and to provide that advice when they are seeking it.

This is why groups like the National Advisory Committee are important, because we're Indigenous, and we know, and we get it. It's like talking to an Indigenous reporter. People need to talk to the Indigenous GPR operator; they need to talk to me because they don't have to start with explaining themselves. I come in with my ribbon skirt and my Protocol, and I know what the ceremonies are where I go, and I can be respectful of community need. Unfortunately, the mandate of the National Advisory Council was ended in March 2025, meaning we no longer have the platform or support to gather with Survivors and search teams, provide advice through a Survivor-led process, or advocate for meaningful change.

Now, more than ever, we need allies to continue to do the work that the community shouldn't have to do. We need to focus on healing, justice, and accountability as communities see fit. They don't need to encounter denialism all the time. I've been in situations where I've heard Elders say that we have to dig up our children so we can prove the denialists wrong. That should *never* be the reason for the choice that communities are making. That should never be the reason to undertake a very difficult and emotional process. If they want to find that child for their own reasons to return them home, that's one thing. However, to do it because of the demands of denialists for a truth we already know seems so wrong to me. We need more of these spaces to say, this is the truth, this is what denialism looks and sounds like, and here is how you counter it, so the Elders in the communities I go in are not feeling worried that they are going to have to do something they don't want to do just to counter denialism.

This is a decades-long project that is going to take a lot of time and resources. I don't know if there will ever be enough investment without a settlement or some sort of legal action. I'm not convinced that there'll ever be enough. But there needs to be way more than there is now. The year-by-year approach can't continue. It's also very hard on Survivors.

The heart of this work, when I'm in community, is those Survivor Gatherings. When people come together, many Survivors share their experiences for the first time, and they need all kinds of support in that. All of that has to be at the heart of it for Survivors and intergenerational Survivors if you have any hope of building, rebuilding those Nations, and renewing those relations before it's too late.

EDITORS: Speaking of hope, that's where we'd like to end our conversation. What gives you hope? In spite of the hate and hostility, what gets you out of bed in the morning and gives you the energy to continue to do this work—to take care of community and push for the truth about residential schooling?

NEEGAUNIBINESSIKWE: Thanks for this question. What gives me hope? My hope is that we can all take responsibility for the truth. We talk about seven generations. We have to continue to do that work so that people know the truth and they still carry the truth when we are gone.

What gives me hope is our ceremonies and our young ones. We have young kids starting to lead now, and we adults are sitting back, and they're running things. That's what gives me hope. They know how to do it, and they're solid in what they do.

My spirit name, as I said earlier, is Neegaunibinessikwe. When I first asked Gweemeh why she gave me that name, she said it was because I have a job while I'm here on Earth. She said, "Your name means that you're the female leader of the Thunderbirds; you have a responsibility to lead and facilitate a path for others to follow." And I said, "Why?" I said, "What am I going to do with that name?" I will demonstrate to you what she did. Think of this as an axe, because back in the day, we were still cutting wood. She had her skirt, and she raised it, and she had this axe she took from the woodpile. She says, "This is you." She put one foot forward and she cut. She said, "You are building a path that has never been made before. Nobody has ever been there before." For years, I resisted, but I came into my own. That is my work here on

Earth: To do what we are doing here. To clear a path. There's no template. I've never had a template in my life to follow. That gives me hope and reassures me that I'm where I'm supposed to be. That's what gets me up early in the morning and gives me the fighting spirit and gives me the hope for the future.

CRYSTAL: It's important to define your goals and priorities in all aspects of your life, and, in my experience, that is not something that society necessarily teaches us. I had to seek education on how to do that. The most important thing, for me, is to be a good parent. Residential schools fractured my immediate family, so the best way for me to cultivate a healthy family is to be a present, substance-free, and loving parent. This requires balance. We are asked to do a million things all the time. Indeed, our expertise is needed and collectively we can make meaningful change. But at what cost? Unreasonable work expectations, chasing that next promotion, or adopting a demanding publication schedule should not put our families in jeopardy. My family comes first. Our children, our happiness and our healing, are what give me hope. I don't wake up and think about the work. I wake up and think about my kids because I didn't have what they have. My mom didn't have what they have. Her mom didn't have what they have. My children's futures give me hope.

KISHA: Honestly, Neegaunibinessikwe gives me hope. The strength of Survivors gives me a lot of hope. I'm also very grateful for those who have kept Traditional Knowledge and the fires of that knowledge burning even when there are attempts to put the fires out. They still find a way. So, the Survivors and intergenerational Survivors who are doing the hard work of reclaiming, reconnecting, and healing give me a lot of hope.

But, like Crystal, what really gives me hope is my daughter. This work is hard, and it does take a lot, but it has also brought a lot into my life. It's brought me into the ceremony in my relatives' communities in a number of ways. My daughter was able to attend her first-ever Pipe Ceremony when she was seven. It was part of the residential school work we were doing. We were invited in, and she was able to come and sit in the teepee and experience the Pipe Ceremony. I was thirty-three when I first sat in a Pipe Ceremony. To me, that's the motivation for this. She knows who she is, she's proud of who she is, and she's connected to her relatives. That's one of the ways we can build a brighter future for her and for the generations to come after her. Fighting for the truth now can play an important role in creating that future.

Notes

1 For more about Julienne and how I understand her legacy, see Crystal Gail Fraser, "Visiting Julienne The'dahcha: A Reflection on Memory, Land, and Dinjii Zhuh Knowledge," *NiCHE, Network in Canadian History and Environment*, 8 July 2025, https://niche-canada.org/2025/07/08/visiting-julienne-thedahcha-a-reflection-on-memory-land-and-dinjii-zhuh-knowledge/.

2 Supernant and Warrick, "Challenges to Critical Community-Based Archaeological Practice."

3 See Heath Justice and Carleton, "Truth Before Reconciliation."

4 Tuck and Yang, "Decolonization Is Not a Metaphor."

5 Crystal Gail Fraser, "Residential School Denialism Is an Attack on the Truth," *The Conversation*, 3 July 2024, https://theconversation.com/residential-school-denialism-is-an-attack-on-the-truth-233318.

6 See, for example, Tammy Rollie, "Horrors of Residential Schools Existed Not Far from Okotoks," *Western Wheel,* 8 June 2021, https://www.westernwheel.ca/local-news/horrors-of-residential-schools-existed-not-far-from-okotoks-3849354.

7 Miller, *Shingwauk's Vision.*

8 Fraser and Stevenson, "Reflecting on the Foundations," 29.

CHAPTER 13

STANDING UP FOR THE TRUTH

an Interview with Kimberly Murray

SEAN CARLETON AND NIIGAAN SINCLAIR (EDITORS): Thank you for making time to talk more about your important work. Can you introduce yourself, explain how you've come to truth and reconciliation work generally, and your role as the Independent Special Interlocutor for Missing Children and Unmarked Graves and Burial Sites associated with Indian Residential Schools (OSI) in particular?

KIMBERLY MURRAY: I'm Mohawk and a member of Kanehsatà:ke Mohawk Nation. I'm a lawyer. I started my legal career off at Aboriginal Legal Services of Toronto, where I worked for fifteen years. While I was with Aboriginal Legal Services, I was asked to come and work at the Truth and Reconciliation Commission of Canada (TRC). I was the executive director of the TRC for five years. I had the great honour and privilege of working with the commissioners as they implemented their mandate and wrote their *Final Report*. In that capacity, I oversaw the research that was being done and the work of putting the chapters together, including Volume 4 of the TRC's *Final Report* on *Missing Children and Unmarked Burials*. I think that experience led Canada and some individuals to put my name forward to be the Special Interlocutor for Missing Children and Unmarked Graves and Burial Sites. I accepted that role and served from June 2022 until December 2024.

EDITORS: As we prepare for another Orange Shirt Day and National Day for Truth and Reconciliation, we're wondering if you can reflect on the past year (2025), as a lot has happened in this work. Your office released its *Final Report* in October 2024. Many residential school teams, such as Williams Lake and Penelakut, have made interim announcements confirming additional deaths. The Fort Resolution team announced they've exhumed burials of five children as part of their investigation. But government support for search teams has also dried up and denialism and anti-Indigenous racism seems to be growing. As an expert and someone who's been doing this work for a long time, where do you think we're at with the important work of truth and reconciliation a decade after the TRC's *Final Report*?

KIMBERLY: It's very troubling to me that communities are being left hanging and wondering whether they're going to continue to receive funding from the federal government to do the investigations that are, and have been, happening across the country. Some are far along in their investigations and others are at the early stages. To be cut off at whatever stage they're at is a big problem. I did have some hope when the recent federal election was happening (2025) because in the platform of the Liberal government, they said that they would continue to support the investigations for missing children and unmarked burials. But, as of today, we do not know what that's going to look like in the near future. As I said in my *Final Report*, I feel that Canada has legal, ethical, and moral obligations to continue supporting communities as they search for the missing and disappeared children. Until we get that commitment, I think that Canada, as a government, is just causing more trauma to Survivors and communities, and that is certainly not good for reconciliation.

Regarding the second part of the question, about where we are with truth and reconciliation, I find it very difficult to understand where we are as a country—federally, provincially, and institutionally—with the implementation of the Calls to Action. I blame that on the fact that Canada dragged its heels on implementing the National Council for Reconciliation Call to Action (Call to Action 53). It's now implementing it. But here we are, ten, almost eleven, years later, and we still don't have the entity created; only the inaugural board has been selected. We're waiting for the entity to be created so that they can be the oversight to the 94—or the other 93—Calls to Action. I feel that if that was the first Call to Action that was implemented about ten years ago, we would have a better understanding. From what we can see, when we look at the Indigenous Watchdog or CBC, we're very slow at implementation. But I don't want to take away from the progress that has been made—I think that there's been implementation on the ground at local levels that isn't being captured by some of these oversight watchdog agencies or organizations. I'm looking forward to this new National Council for Reconciliation and seeing what they're going to be able to accomplish through gathering information on all the Calls, issuing reports, and calling on Canada and the provinces to respond to them and issue their own reports.

EDITORS: When reflecting on a decade since the Calls to Action, it's quite easy to look at many of the measuring sticks—like the Beyond 94 website, which we use often with students—and see fifteen Calls to Action completed, depending on how you count, in ten years, and it doesn't look very good. Especially since many of the Calls that have been completed are more on the symbolic or performative level. That's not to say that those aren't important; they were included for important reasons. But there hasn't been much progress on the big Calls addressing systemic issues. At the same time, Murray Sinclair used to say that the damage was done over generations, and so the solution will take generations too. We feel that there has been a lot of awareness created. We remember a time when most people we'd talk to had little to no knowledge of residential schools. Now, we think there is a lot of awareness and knowledge, but we're lacking on the action piece. We've done a lot of truth telling, but there is still a lot of healing, justice, and reconciliation left to do.

It's interesting that you bring up the election—that might be a good way to transition to denialism. In one of the last budgets that Prime Minister Justin Trudeau tabled, there was funding specifically allocated to challenging residential school denialism. Now, like any budget, it was a promise down the road when his political future was far from certain. But it was put into the budget and identified as an issue that was harming the progress of truth and reconciliation. When Mark Carney took over as prime minister, he was being questioned on the campaign trail in the 2025 election about whether he was going to continue to make progress on these issues. He didn't sit down with Aboriginal Peoples Television Network (APTN), and he was dodging the issue for quite a while. Eventually, he did say that he and the Liberal Party were going to continue to make progress on truth and reconciliation. We're now well into his term and those promises are being questioned. Will his government actually take action on truth and reconciliation? What about the commitment to challenge residential school denialism like the previous government? Will that continue? We think that hesitation, in this moment, is harmful because it's allowing denialism to take root, as Michelle Good and Leah Gazan argued in their chapters.

From your perspective, why is denialism so harmful? Why do you think people, specifically non-Indigenous people, should take responsibility to challenge denialism?

KIMBERLY: We first raised the issue of denialism in our *Interim Report*. In that report, I didn't have recommendations; it was a key finding based on what I was hearing on the ground from communities. We had a small section on denialism and identified that it was something I kept hearing—about how upsetting it was to Survivors. I was actually quite surprised by the attention that the media gave to that one and only issue following our *Interim Report*. I released the *Interim Report* in Cowessess and Minister Lametti received it— he didn't come to the community; he Zoomed in. He gave his speaking notes after I released the report. The only question that came from the media was about denialism, which was shocking to me. That seemed to snowball. Every time I did an interview, it was about denialism and adding to the Criminal Code. I tried so many times to get reporters to look at the other important issues identified in the *Interim* and *Final Reports*.

I did meet with the attorney general and the minister of Crown Indigenous Relations after I released my *Final Report* and before my mandate ended. It was a very interesting meeting because I questioned them about whether they would add to the Criminal Code and their response was about whether I could get the New Democratic Party on board with their Online Harms Act, which we also write about in the same chapter where I mentioned denialism. They seemed to indicate that that's where they thought the solution was—that they could respond to denialism through that piece of legislation and that we didn't need to add to the Criminal Code and potentially infringe on people's freedom of expression. I reminded them that we already have a similar provision in the Criminal Code against Holocaust denialism. I found that response interesting and disappointing.

Time and time again in communities, Survivors were so emotional talking about the fact that people don't believe them. It hasn't just started now in relation to the unmarked burials. It was an ongoing issue during the Truth and Reconciliation Commission process about whether abuses happened, whether people were sexually assaulted in the institutions, whether they were apprehended and taken to the institutions, or whether their parents put them there—you both know how denialists operate. It was so upsetting to Survivors because of the way the settlement agreement was created through the Independent Assessment Process (IAP). The IAP was a closed-door process—no one gets to read the decisions and there is no testimony that's public. The TRC process was there, and people shared their experiences. But a number of Survivors just didn't feel that they were acknowledged or that their harms were acknowledged in the way that they needed. To have these "high profile," if you will, Canadians denying and putting out misinformation and disinformation is really harmful to individuals. It's trying to silence Survivors, call them liars and cheaters, and claim that they're stealing money and are only trying to get people to burn down churches. It just goes from one ridiculous statement to another. It's retraumatizing Survivors and makes them afraid to come forward and speak the truth. Our gatherings had to be so guarded about who was allowed to attend. When I did my closing, we had to ban someone from coming in because they were harassing all the youth on my Youth Council. They had also harassed a number of Survivors and Elders. It just wasn't a safe environment for people to come together to share their experiences. We heard a lot from Kúkpi7 Rosanne Casimir about how she was targeted after Tk'emlúps made their announcement. So many communities are now saying they don't want to speak to the media, release information, or do interviews because it will get twisted, and then the bots and the people who are sending emails to everyone will come.

When I was doing my *Final Report* and the chapter on denialism, we got such hurtful, angry, and hateful emails from all kinds of people, one person in particular, if it was even a real person. Early on, I decided to keep those emails, write about them, and put examples of them in the OSI *Final Report* so that people could see how hateful and hurtful it is. We decided we were going to use the emails to make our argument that additions be made to the Criminal Code to address denialism. We noticed that every time there was a National Gathering, or a community made an announcement about their investigation, there was an increase in the emails coming to our info line, directly to me, or on my social media. Since I'm not in that job anymore, I actually just block everybody. I didn't block them when I was Special Interlocutor because I thought it was better for them to direct their hate at me than to Survivors and communities. But now, I just block them. I don't want to read or hear them anymore, so that's what I do.

At one of the TRC's hearings, I remember former National Chief Shawn A-in-chut Atleo became very emotional when he was speaking about his grandmother who had passed away. He was talking about how on the day the apology was issued by Stephen Harper, 11 June 2008, she turned to him and said, "Grandson, they're just starting to see us." I feel like the denialists know that, right? Canadians are starting to see and understand the harm that has been perpetrated against Indigenous Peoples, and so denialists are trying to make sure Indigenous Peoples continue to be unseen. They want to take away the progress that has happened as a result of the Settlement Agreement, apology, TRC, and all the things that have happened since the initial lawsuits were filed in relation to residential schooling.

EDITORS: We think a lot of people who don't have direct experience in community don't realize how difficult it was, has been, and continues to be for Survivors to even talk about their experience. People here in Manitoba, like the late Ted Fontaine, often talked about how difficult it was to break the culture of silence about these issues, and Survivor Neegaunibinessikwe confirmed this in the previous chapter. It's interesting that you're saying that now a lot of people are questioning if they want to continue to do this work, if they are not being believed. That's exactly what denialists want; it's about reinforcing that culture of silence and intimidating Survivors.

Can you talk more about the denialism you experienced prior to your work as Special Interlocutor?

KIMBERLY: With the work that we were doing and the emails we were getting, there were a lot of intimidation tactics. Maybe because I'm a woman as well, there was a lot of "shut your fat, ugly mouth up" and "if you don't, things are not going to end well for you." There were intimidation and threats made toward me, claiming that I'm committing treason or that I shouldn't be conversing with the United Nations Rapporteur or any United Nations body because it's not my job. They even wrote articles about me, challenging my Indigenous identity and trying to say I'm lying and that my mother is not born in Ireland—just stupid stuff to try to come at me from every angle and shut me up, basically.

They were starting to follow me around and pop into the many public speaking events I did outside of Survivor Gatherings. It came to the point where I would always have to ask about security and warn people that this was happening to me, especially on the online platforms.

I'll give you an example. I did a National Day for Truth and Reconciliation event for the Law Society of Ontario. That's the governing body of thousands of lawyers in the province of Ontario. It was on Zoom, and there were close to 1,000 people signed up. I had sent a warning to the Society beforehand because it was a public event. I said not to do a Q&A where it's open to everyone to read and, instead, shut down the comments. I told them that there were a lot of denialists following me around and putting really hurtful, harmful things in chats. For me, I was more worried about the other Indigenous people on the platform who aren't used to getting this in their inbox or on social media every day. They shut down the chat and had a moderator. The moderator was the one who got the questions. But the moderator was an Indigenous person. You could actually see the impact it was having on her reading the chat. She had to go through them and figure out which ones to ask in the public domain and you could see how emotional she was getting because she was now being subjected to these hateful comments that people from the legal profession were putting into the chat. I asked the Law Society to save the Zoom chat and send it to me, so I do have that.

Of course, the thing is, individuals hide behind a screen. We don't know who they are. They don't put their real identity. I always say I can take on a denialist. I'm okay—I could be in any room and someone could challenge me. I've seen the evidence. I know what's out there; I know what's in the archives. I know what Survivors have told me, and I've been on the grounds of the burial sites. I'm able to respond to the denialists. But it shouldn't be on Survivors to have to provide the proof. I think that was part of what we wanted to do with the *Sites of Truth,*

Sites of Conscience report. A lot of the report was made up of what the TRC wrote in Volume 4 of the *Final Report, Missing Children and Unmarked Burials*. But it was footnoted—we quoted from documents, included it in the footnotes, and someone would have to go to Library Archives Canada or the National Centre for Truth and Reconciliation to look at the document themselves. The idea of putting in the images of the letters, burials, cemeteries, and funerals was to make it easier for Canadians to learn the truth rather than be swayed by the lies of the denialists.

EDITORS: Now that it has been ten years since the TRC's *Final Report* was released, and given the rise in denialism and backlash that we've been talking about, we wonder: What gives you hope for the future? What inspires you to keep doing the work that you do to put truth before reconciliation and confront denialism?

KIMBERLY: When I get asked that question—What gives you hope?—I always respond as Murray did: Young people give me hope. Where I live in Toronto, I walk my dog every day past the elementary school that has orange ribbons on the fence. I think, yeah, that could be performative or seen as symbolic. But they're being taught something about why those orange ribbons are on the fence—and that's junior kindergarten to grade six. When we reflect on the ten years, I can see it. Now I'm working at a university, and I can see that people now were those kids who were learning about the TRC's Calls to Action in high school. Even before the Calls to Action came out, Murray Sinclair, Marie Wilson, and Wilton Littlechild met with the ministers of education from coast to coast to coast and challenged them to implement mandatory curriculum about Indian Residential Schools and the history of Indigenous Peoples. We saw some good progress before the end of the TRC. But with everything, there are two steps forward and one step back. Changing government and changing curriculum—we saw that happen in Ontario when Doug Ford got elected. I think we are further ahead today on young people's understanding of the history of Canada, colonialism, genocide, and crimes against humanity. We just have to keep focused and not let denialists detract from our important work.

Also, what keeps me going are those stories of resistance that Indigenous Peoples, Survivors, and communities have and continue to have. One of the Survivors at our gathering called it defiance—the defiance of those kids to fight those institutions and fight against what was happening to them. I feel we don't do enough to enhance and show those stories. They're buried in the history chapters of the TRC. I would love for people to write about the defiance that happened, and how the community, leadership, and parents fought for us to be where we are now, for Indigenous Peoples to be here today, and that Church and State failed in their attempts to exterminate Indigenous Peoples and culture. I get to hear about that defiance and resistance all the time and I see it every day. That gives me hope that people are doing everything they can to make their ancestors proud and that will continue. Denialists aren't going to stop that.

I think the thing that's troubling about denialists and people accepting what the denialists say—and we wrote about this in the report—is that it's an easy way out for Canadians because they don't have to do anything. We need to ensure people aren't those bystanders to reconciliation. That's why I get so angry when Canada and the Churches don't speak up. They have the evidence. They have everything to counter what the denialists are saying, and they just remain silent. They leave it for people like you, me, Survivors, and communities to have to fight. I think that if Church and State would speak up, that could help us a lot moving forward.

EDITORS: We hope that continuing to have conversations like these will mean that denialists will have a diminishing population of people who will believe their ideas.

KIMBERLY: I feel like there's the key players, the prominent denialists—they know the truth; they just don't want others to know the truth. You've probably heard this—it's what Murray always used to say, and he used to say it to me a lot. I remember having a conversation with him one day because I flew into Winnipeg and was complaining about how I was on the plane—this was back when they had newspapers on planes—and people would open their newspapers, and if there was a piece on Indigenous people, realities, or a case, they just flipped the page. They weren't reading it. I remember saying to Murray that I find it so frustrating. There would be a piece on the TRC, and people wouldn't want to read it. We would have these conversations about—and the TRC wrote a lot about it—how to get people from their head to their heart. Murray always used to say that there are three kinds of people

Figure 13.1. The National Day for Truth and Reconciliation Healing Walk in Winnipeg, Manitoba, 2025. Photo by Sean Carleton.

out there—those who are never going to be on our side, those who are already on our side, and we have to focus on the middle, which is the majority of the Canadians. They just don't know enough to decide where they want to be. I feel like those prominent denialists are never going to be on our side. They know the truth. They don't like the truth. They don't want people to have any kind of care for or solidarity with Indigenous People. They want the land. They want to develop. They want to do fear mongering, like saying that Indians are coming to take your homes and we have to put a stop to it and all this reconciliation stuff. You both have written about this a lot—it's purposeful; they have a plan, and they're following it. We just need to challenge those key players and create opportunities for everyone else to learn the truth. We can't let denialism distract us from putting truth before reconciliation.

CONCLUSION

by Sean Carleton and Niigaan Sinclair

The Truth and Reconciliation Commission (TRC) of Canada released its *Final Report* ten years ago, in 2015, and it changed Canada forever. On the one hand, we have witnessed a lot of progress in the last decade.[1] In 2019, the Government of Canada passed the Indigenous Languages Act to protect, revitalize, and promote Indigenous languages, directly addressing Calls to Action 13, 14, and 15. In 2021, responding to Call to Action 80, 30 September (originally, Orange Shirt Day) was established as the National Day for Truth and Reconciliation, and the Residential Schools Missing Children Community Support Fund was created to help communities search for unmarked burials and missing children. Also in 2021, responding to Calls to Action 43 and 44, Canada adopted the United Nations Declaration on the Rights of Indigenous Peoples. In 2022, the House of Commons recognized the Indian Residential School System as genocide. As well, responding to Call to Action 58, Pope Francis came to Canada to apologize to Survivors and recognized the Indian Residential School System as genocide. In 2025, the National Council for Reconciliation was established to track and guide future progress on the TRC's Calls to Action. These are all positive steps toward reconciliation.

On the other hand, not enough has changed in the past decade, and that has led to a lot of frustration.[2] As of 2026, Canada has only completed 15 of the 94 Calls to Action. Clearly, much remains to be done.

Before his passing in 2024, Murray Sinclair (Mazina Giizhik-iban) shared his concern that Canada was rushing reconciliation and leaving the truth behind.[3] Currently, the Government of Canada is stalling on its commitment to reconciliation and increasingly—as evidenced by Bill C-5 and the attempt to sidestep free, prior, and informed consent—adopting a more aggressive approach to its relationship with Indigenous Nations.[4] This change in tact is happening against the backdrop of a rise in anti-Indigenous racism generally and residential school denialism specifically, all as part of a backlash to truth and reconciliation. These are concerning developments that, as the chapters of this collection have outlined, put meaningful reconciliation at risk. We need to take these attacks on truth and reconciliation seriously and work hard to establish a coordinated, dynamic, and multi-faceted strategy to stand up for Survivors and defend the truth. Confronting residential school denialism is an ethical and shared responsibility.[5]

In looking for guidance, we return to the TRC's *Final Report* and Murray Sinclair's contention that education is the key to reconciliation. In the sixth volume of the *Final Report*, *Canada's Residential Schools: Reconciliation*, the TRC highlights the following comment made by Rory Shead, an Indigenous youth, at the Vancouver gathering:

> We cannot progress as a society until we learn from the mistakes made in the past. . . . Knowledge is power and knowledge should be shared. The history and impacts of the residential school system must be taught because to *deny* a part of our history simply because it is unpleasant or controversial means to *deny* ourselves the chance to grow as a society. . . . Reconciliation is the process of accepting what happened and growing from it. . . . We must listen to the testimonies of those who survived such events. . . . We must learn to live together, and to do that, we must first reconcile with our past.[6]

The spread of residential school denialism thus does more than harm Survivors. It also damages the relationship between Indigenous Peoples and Canadians and risks our collective future together in these lands.

In the end, the TRC's formula for reconciliation was clear: learning the truth about residential schooling will lead to the healing and justice that is necessary for reconciliation. The problem is that denialists understand this formula and are trying hard to undermine public confidence in the truth by isolating it, decontextualizing it, and questioning it to plant seeds of doubt. This is being done as part of a willful strategy to create chaos and confusion about the truth so as to block the path to healing, justice, and reconciliation. This, however, will only keep Canada and Canadians stuck in a colonial cul-de-sac. Denialism only offers a false refuge. It forecloses the future for us all.

We must, then, take heed from Cree artist Kent Monkman's message in A Steady Brightness of Being: "Do not let chaos distract you, keep focused on the world that should be, and make it our future."[7]

Without truth we cannot learn to live together and build a better world for future generations. This is why education is so important. Indeed, Murray Sinclair famously said that "education is what got us into this mess and education is what will get us out."[8] As this collection has made clear, such education—broadly understood—must include both learning the truth about the history of Indian Residential Schools and taking action in the present. ReconciliACTION must include defending that truth *and* confronting denialism, alongside the work of revitalizing relationships, demanding restitution, and pushing for peace and justice for all. For this reason, we must continue to put truth before reconciliation.

Notes

1 See Niigaan Sinclair, "What Reconciliation Looks Like 10 Years After TRC's Final Report," interview by Adrienne Arsenault, 30 September 2025, *CBC News*, https://www.cbc.ca/player/play/video/9.6922597.

2 Dennis Ward, "Lack of Action on TRC's Calls to Action 'Frustrating' says Professor and Author Niigaan Sinclair," *APTN News*, 25 November 2025, https://www.aptnnews.ca/facetoface/lack-of-action-on-trcs-calls-to-action-frustrating-says-professor-and-author-niigaan-sinclair/.

3 Forester, "Residential school deniers, white supremacists biggest barrier to reconciliation says Murray Sinclair."

4 See, for example, Katsi'tsakwas Ellen Gabriel, "Regression: Bill C-5–An Act to Enact the Free Trade and Labour Mobility in Canada Act and the Building Canada Act," David Suzuki Foundation, 23 February 2026, https://davidsuzuki.org/story/regression-bill-c-5/; Pamela Palmater, "National Interest Should Include the Rights of Indigenous Women," *The Hill Times*, 29 September 2025, https://www.hilltimes.com/2025/09/29/national-interest-should-include-the-rights-of-indigenous-women/474487/; and Sean Carleton and Katsi'tsakwas Ellen Gabriel,

"Resisting Canada's 'Elbow's Up' Colonialism," *Canadian Dimension*, 18 September 2025, https://canadiandimension.com/articles/view/resisting-canadas-elbows-up-colonialism.

5 Sean Carleton and Benjamin Kucher, "Confronting Residential School Denialism is an Ethical and Shared Canadian Responsibility," *The Conversation*, 23 September 2025, https://theconversation.com/confronting-residential-schools-denialism-is-an-ethical-and-shared-canadian-responsibility-265127.

6 Truth and Reconciliation Commission of Canada, *Canada's Residential Schools: Reconciliation*, 130 (emphasis added).

7 Kent Monkman in Sara Sinclair and Stephanie Sinclair, eds., *A Steady Brightness of Being: Truth Wisdom, and Love from Celebrated Indigenous Voices* (Penguin Random House), 109.

8 Murray Sinclair as quoted in "Reconciliation Through Education," National Centre for Truth and Reconciliation, https://nctr.ca/education/.

SELECTED BIBLIOGRAPHY

Ahenakew, Edward. "Little Pine: An Indian Day School." *Saskatchewan History* 18, no. 2 (1965): 55–62.

Akhavan, Payam. "Cultural Genocide: Legal Label or Mourning Metaphor?" *McGill Law Journal* 62, no. 1 (2016): 243–70. https://lawjournal.mcgill.ca/article/cultural-genocide-legal-label-or-mourning-metaphor/.

Anderson, Kjell. *Perpetrating Genocide: A Criminological Account.* Routledge, 2018.

Armitage, David. "In Defence of Presentism." In *History and Human Flourishing*, edited by Darren M. McMahon. Oxford University Press, 2023. https://scholar.harvard.edu/armitage/publications/defense-presentism.

Asch, Michael, John Borrows, and James Tully, eds. *Resurgence and Reconciliation: Indigenous-Settler Relations and Earth Teachings.* University of Toronto Press, 2018.

Bandura, Albert. "Mechanisms of Moral Disengagement." In *Insurgent Terrorism*, edited by Gerald Cromer. Routledge, 2006.

Bandura, Albert. "Moral Disengagement." In *The Encyclopedia of Peace Psychology.* John Wiley and Sons, 2011. https://doi.org/10.1002/9780470672532.wbepp165.

Banner, James M. *The Ever-Changing Past: Why All History Is Revisionist History*, 1st ed. Yale University Press, 2021. https://doi.org/10.2307/j.ctv1g2496z.

Bazyler, Michael. *Holocaust, Genocide, and the Law: A Quest for Justice in a Post-Holocaust World.* Oxford Academic, 2016.

Beauvais, Edana, and Mark Williamson. "The Prevalence and Correlates of Residential School Denialism in Canada." *Canadian Journal of Political Science/Revue canadienne de science politique* (2025): 1-32.

Berkhofer Jr., Robert. *The White Man's Indian: Images of the American Indian from Columbus to the Present.* Vintage, 1978.

Betke, Tyla. "'Not a Shred of Evidence': Settler Colonial Networks of Concealment and the Birtle Indian Residential School." *Canadian Historical Review* 104, no. 4 (December 2023): 519–544. https://doi.org/10.3138/chr-2023-0001.

Bevernage, Berber. "Denial in the Age of Apology: Some Reflections on Recent Trends in Historical Denialism." *South Central Review* 39, nos. 2–3 (2022): 44–59. https://doi.org/10.1353/scr.2022.0020.

Capitaine, Brieg, and Karine Vanthuyne, eds. *Power Through Testimony: Reframing Residential Schools in the Age of Reconciliation.* UBC Press, 2017.

Carleton, Sean. "'I Don't Need Any More Education': Senator Lynn Beyak, Residential School Denialism and Attacks on Truth and Reconciliation in Canada." *Settler Colonial Studies* 11, no. 4 (2021): 466–486. https://doi.org/10.1080/2201473X.2021.1935574.

Carleton, Sean. *Lessons in Legitimacy: Colonialism, Capitalism, and the Rise of State Schooling.* UBC Press, 2022.

Carleton, Sean. "Settler Anxiety and State Support for Missionary Schooling in Colonial British Columbia, 1849–1871." *Historical Studies in Education* 29 (Spring 2017): 57–76.

Carleton, Sean, and Andrew Woolford. "Ignore Debaters and Denialists, Canada's Treatment of Indigenous Peoples Fits the Definition of Genocide." *The Conversation*, 25 October 2021, https://theconversation.com/ignore-debaters-and-denialists-canadas-treatment-of-indigenous-peoples-fits-the-definition-of-genocide-170242.

Césaire, Aimé. *Discourse on Colonialism.* Monthly Review Press, 1972.

Coulthard, Glen Sean. *Red Skin, White Masks: Rejecting the Colonial Politics of Recognition.* University of Minnesota, 2014.

Curthoys, Ann. "Expulsion, Exodus and Exile in White Australian Historical Mythology," *Journal of Australian Studies* 23, no. 61 (1999): 1–19. https://doi.org/10.1080/14443059909387469.

Daschuk, James. *Clearing the Plains: Disease, Politics of Starvation, and the Loss of Aboriginal Life.* University of Regina Press, 2013.

Di Cesare, Donatella. *If Auschwitz Is Nothing: Against Denialism.* Polity Press, 2023.

Draper, Nicholas. *The Price of Emancipation: Slave-Ownership, Compensation and British Society at the End of Slavery.* Cambridge University Press, 2010.

Elliott, Alicia. "Foreword." In *This Place: 150 Years Retold*, edited by Alicia Elliott, Kateri Akiwenzie-Damn, Sonny Assu, et al. Portage and Main Press, 2019.

Evans, Richard J. *Lying about Hitler: History, Holocaust, and the David Irving Trial.* Basic Books, 2001.

Fanon, Frantz. *Black Skin, White Masks.* Grove Press, 2008.

Fanon, Frantz. *The Wretched of the Earth.* Grove Press, 2004.

Fontaine, Theodore. *Broken Circle: The Dark Legacy of Indian Residential Schools.* Heritage, 2010.

Francis, Daniel. *The Imaginary Indian: The Image of the Indian in Canadian Culture.* Arsenal Pulp Press, 1992.

Fraser, Crystal Gail. *By Strength, We Are Still Here: Indian Residential Schooling in Inuvik, Northwest Territories.* University of Manitoba Press, 2024.

Fraser, Crystal Gail, and Allyson Stevenson, "Reflecting on the Foundations of Our Discipline Inspired by the TRC: A Duty to Respond during This Age of Reconciliation." *Canadian Historical Review* 103, no. 1 (2022). https://doi.org/10.3138/chr-2020-003.

Furniss, Elizabeth. *The Burden of History: Colonialism and the Frontier Myth in a Rural Canadian Community.* UBC Press, 1999.

Gallie, W.B. "Essentially Contested Concepts." *Proceedings of the Aristotelian Society* 56, (1956): 167–198. https://www.jstor.org/stable/4544562.

Gaudry, Adam, and Danielle Lorenz, "Indigenization as Inclusion, Reconciliation, and Decolonization: Navigating the Different Visions for Indigenizing the Canadian Academy." *AlterNative: An International Journal of Indigenous Peoples* 14, no. 3 (2018): 218–27. https://doi.org/10.1177/1177180118785382.

Gerbrandt, Reid, and Sean Carleton. *Debunking the 'Mass Grave Hoax': A Report on Media Coverage and Residential School Denialism in Canada.* Centre for Human Rights Research, 2023.

Giancarlo, Alexandra, Janice Forsyth, and Braden Te Hiwi, with Kelly Bull, Chris Chromarty and David Wesley. *Beyond the Rink: Behind the Images of Residential School Hockey.* University of Manitoba Press, 2025.

Gibney, Mark. *The Age of Apology: Facing Up to the Past.* University of Pennsylvania Press, 2008.

Gudonis, Marius, and Benjamin T. Jones, eds. *History in a Post-Truth World: Theory and Praxis.* Routledge, 2021. https://doi.org/10.4324/9780429319204.

Gudonis, Marius, and Benjamin T. Jones. "Who Controls the Past?" In *History in a Post-Truth World: Theory and Praxis*, edited by Marius Gudonis and Benjamin T. Jones. Routledge, 2021. https://doi.org/10.4324/9780429319204.

Hall, Catherine. *Lucky Valley: Edward Long and the History of Racial Capitalism.* Cambridge University Press, 2024.

Harris, Jillian, Alexandra Maass, and Andrew Martindale. "Practicing Reconciliation." In *Reflections of Canada: Illuminating our Biggest Opportunities and Challenges at 150 Years,* edited by Phillipe Tortell, Margot Young, and Peter Nemetz. Peter Wall Institute for Advanced Studies, 2017.

Hess, Diana E. *Controversy in the Classroom: The Democratic Power of Discussion.* Routledge, 2009.

Hier, Sean P. "Moral Panics, Conservative Contrarianism, and the Polarizing Debate about Missing Children, Unmarked Burials, and Residential School Denialism in Canada." *Crime, Media, Culture: An International Journal* (2026), https://doi.org/10.1177/17416590251407986

Hill, Richard W., Alison Norman, Thomas Peace, and Jennifer Petit, eds. *Behind the Bricks: The Life and Times of the Mohawk Institute, Canada's Longest-Running Residential School.* University of Calgary Press, 2025.

Howell, Lisa, and Nicholas Ng-A-Fook. "A Case of Senator Lynn Beyak and Anti-Indigenous Systemic Racism in Canada." *Canadian Journal of Education* 45, no. 1 (2022): 1–34, https://doi.org/10.53967/cje-rce.v45i1.4787.

Johnston, Basil. *Indian School Days.* Key Porter Books, 1988.

Jones, Adam. *Genocide: A Comprehensive Introduction.* Routledge, 2006.

Justice, Daniel Heath, and Sean Carleton. "Truth before Reconciliation: Eight Ways to Identify and Confront Residential School Denialism." *The Conversation*, 5 August

2021. https://theconversation.com/truth-before-reconciliation-8- ways-to-identify-and-confront-residential-school-denialism-164692.

Lacombe, Benjamin Farmer, and Jackson Pind. "Digitally Mapping the Indian Day Schools and the RG10 School Files Series in Canada." *Historical Studies in Education* 35, no. 2 (Fall 2023): 55–68.

LaRocque, Emma. *When the Other is Me: Native Resistance Discourse, 1850–1990.* University of Manitoba Press, 2010.

Latour, Bruno. *We Have Never Been Modern.* Harvard University Press, 1993.

Lee, Peter. "Putting Principles into Practice: Understanding History." In *How Students Learn: History, Mathematics and Science in the Classroom*, edited by M. Suzanne Donovan and John D. Bransford. National Academies Press, 2005.

Lester, Alan. "The British Empire in the Culture War: Nigel Biggar's *Colonialism: A Moral Reckoning*." *Journal of Imperial and Commonwealth History* 51, no. 4 (2024): 763–95. https://doi.org/10.1080/03086534.2023.2209947.

Lester, Alan. "British Settler Discourse and the Circuits of Empire." *History Workshop Journal* 54, no. 1 (Autumn 2002): 24–48. https://doi.org/10.1093/hwj/54.1.24.

Lester, Alan. *Deny and Disavow: Distancing the Imperial Past in the Culture War.* SunRise, 2023.

Lester, Alan, ed. *The Truth About Empire: Real Histories of British Colonialism.* Hurst, 2024.

Linstrum, Eric. "Escape From Empire: Decolonisation as Disentanglement, Erasure and Evasion." In *The Truth About Empire: Real Histories of British Colonialism*, edited by Alan Lester. Hurst, 2024.

Lowman, Emma Battell, and Adam J. Barker, *Settler: Identity and Colonialism in the 21st Century Canada.* Fernwood Publishing, 2015.

MacDonald, David B. *The Sleeping Giant Awakens: Genocide, Indian Residential Schools, and the Challenge of Conciliation.* University of Toronto Press, 2019.

Maracle, Lee. *My Conversations with Canadians.* BookThug, 2017.

Martell, Christopher C., and Kaylene M. Stevens. *Teaching History for Justice: Centering Activism in Students' Study of the Past.* Teachers College Press, 2021.

Mason, Raymond, edited by Jackson Pind and Theodore Michael Christou. *Spirit of the Grassroots People: Seeking Justice for Indigenous Survivors of Canada's Colonial Education System.* McGill-Queen's University Press, 2020.

McCallum, Mary Jane Logan. "'I Would Like the Girls at Home': Domestic Labour and the Age of Discharge at Canadian Indian Residential Schools." In *Colonization and Domestic Service: Historical and Contemporary Perspectives,* edited by Victoria Haskins and Claire Lowry. Routledge, 2014.

McCallum, Mary Jane Logan. *Nii Ndahlohke: Boys' and Girls' Work at Mount Elgin Industrial School, 1890–1915.* FriesenPress, 2022.

McCracken, Krista. "Archival Photographs in Perspective: Indian Residential School Images of Health." *British Journal of Canadian Studies* 30, no. 2 (2017): 163–182.

McNally, Mary, and Debbie Martin. "First Nations, Inuit, and Métis Health: Considerations for Canadian Health Leaders in the Wake of the Truth and Reconciliation Commission of Canada Report." *Healthcare Management Forum* 30, no. 2 (2017): 117–122. http:/doi: 10.1177/0840470416680445.

Mackey, Eva. *Unsettled Expectations: Uncertainty, Land, and Settler Decolonization.* Fernwood Publishing, 2016.

Memmi, Albert. *The Colonizer and the Colonized.* Beacon, 1991.

Miles, James, and Lindsay Gibson, "Rethinking Presentism in History Education." *Theory and Research in Social Education* 50, no. 4 (2022): 509–29. https://doi.org/10.1080/00933104.2022.2115959

Miles, James, and Lindsay Gibson. "Truth Telling in History Classrooms: Pedagogical Responses to Denialism and Pseudohistory." *Globalisation, Societies and Education* (2026): 1–14. http://doi.org/10.1080/14767724.2025.2608674

Miller, J.R. *Residential Schools and Reconciliation.* University of Toronto Press, 2017.

Miller, J.R. *Shingwauk's Vision: A History of Native Residential School.* University of Toronto Press, 1996.

Milloy, John S. *A National Crime: The Canadian Government and the Residential School System.* 2nd edition. University of Manitoba Press, 1999.

Moine, Louise. *My Life in a Residential School.* Provincial Chapter I.O.D.E., Saskatchewan, in cooperation with the Provincial Library of Saskatchewan, 1975.

Montano, John Patrick. *The Roots of English Colonialism in Ireland.* Cambridge University Press, 2011.

Moreton-Robinson, Aileen. *The White Possessive: Property, Power and Indigenous Sovereignty.* University of Minnesota Press, 2015.

Mosby, Ian. "Administering Colonial Science: Nutrition Research and Human Biomedical Experimentation in Aboriginal Communities and Residential Schools, 1942–1954." *Histoire sociale/Social History* 46, no. 91 (May 2013): 145–172. Doi:10.1353/his.2013.0015.

Niezen, Ronald. *Truth and Indignation: Canada's Truth and Reconciliation Commission on Indian Residential Schools.* University of Toronto Press, 2017.

O'Brien, Jean M. *Firsting and Lasting: Writing Indians out of Existence in New England.* University of Minnesota Press, 2010.

Ohlmeyer, Jane. *Making Empire: Ireland, Imperialism and the Early Modern World.* Oxford University Press, 2023.

Perry, Adele, Sean Carleton, and Omeasoo Wahpasiw, "The Misuse of Indigenous and Canadian History in *Colonialism.*" In *The Truth About Empire: Real Histories of British Colonialism,* edited by Alan Lester. Hurst, 2024.

Pind, Jackson, and Sean Carleton. "Raising Awareness about Canada's Indian Day Schools with Digital History." *Active History.* 29 November 2022. https://activehistory.ca/blog/2022/11/29/raising-awareness-about-canadas-indian-day-schools-with-digital-history-and-gis-mapping/.

Powell, Christopher. "What Do Genocides Kill? A Relational Conception of Genocide." *Journal of Genocide Research* 9, no. 4 (2007): 527–47.

Regan, Paulette. *Unsettling the Settler Within: Indian Residential Schools, Truth Telling and Reconciliation in Canada.* UBC Press, 2010.

Reid, Darren. "'Compound Dispossession' in Southern Ontario: Converging Trajectories of Colonial Dispossession in Inter-Indigenous Conflict, 1886–1900," *Journal of Canadian Studies* 57 (Winter 2023).

Ricoeur, Paul. *Memory, History, Forgetting*. Translated by Kathleen Blamey and David Pellauer. University of Chicago Press, 2004.

Rifkin, Mark. "Settler States of Feeling: National Belonging and the Erasure of Native American Presence." In *A Companion to American Literary Studies*, edited by Caroline F. Levander and Robert S. Levine. Wiley-Blackwell, 2011.

Rosenberg, Sheri P. "Genocide Is a Process, Not an Event." *Genocide Studies and Prevention: An International Journal* 7, no. 1 (2012): Article 4. https://digitalcommons.usf.edu/gsp/vol7/iss1/4.

Russell, Bill. "Probing a Dark Decade: Recordkeeping in the Indian Affairs Branch, 1937–1947." *Archivaria* 96 (Fall 2023): 98–135. https://archivaria.ca/index.php/archivaria/article/view/13933.

Said, Edward. *Culture and Imperialism*. Chatto and Windus, 1993.

Said, Edward. *Orientalism*. Pantheon, 1978.

Schissel, Barnard, and Terry Wotherspoon. *The Legacy of School for Aboriginal People: Education, Oppression, and Emancipation*. Oxford University Press, 2003.

Sellars, Bev. *They Called Me Number One: Secrets and Survival at an Indian Residential School*. Talonbooks, 2013.

Sennett, Richard. *The Uses of Disorder: Personal Identity and City Life*. Verso, 1970.

Simon, Roger I. "The Pedagogy of Remembrance and the Counter-Commemoration of the Columbus Quincentenary." In *Touch of the Past: Remembrance, Learning, and Ethics*, edited by Roger I. Simon. Palgrave Macmillan, 2005.

Simon, Roger I. "The Touch of the Past: The Pedagogical Significance of a Transactional Sphere of Public Memory." In *The Touch of the Past: Remembrance, Learning, and Ethics*, edited by Roger I. Simon. Palgrave Macmillan, 2005.

Simpson, Leanne Betasamosake. *As We Have Always Been: Indigenous Freedom Through Radical Resistance*. University of Minnesota Press, 2017.

Sinclair, Niigaan. "Where Hate Foments." In *Wînipêk: Visions of Canada from an Indigenous Centre*. McClelland and Stewart, 2024.

Starblanket, Gina, and Dallas Hunt. *Storying Violence: Unravelling Colonial Narratives in the Stanley Trial*. ARP Books, 2020.

Supernant, Kisha, and Gary Warrick. "Challenges to Critical Community-Based Archaeological Practice in Canada." *Canadian Journal of Archaeology* 38, no. 2 (2014): 563–591. https://www.jstor.org/stable/43487314.

Survivors of the Assiniboia Indian Residential School and Andrew Woolford. *Did You See Us? Reunion, Remembrance, and Reclamation at an Urban Indian Residential School*. University of Manitoba Press, 2021.

Sykes, Gresham M., and David Matza. "Techniques of Neutralization: A Theory of Delinquency." *American Sociological Review* 22, no. 6 (1957): 664–670. https://doi.org/10.2307/2089195.

Truth and Reconciliation Commission of Canada. *Canada's Residential Schools: Reconciliation*. Vol. 6 of *The Final Report of the Truth and Reconciliation Commission of Canada*. McGill-Queen's University Press, 2015.

Truth and Reconciliation Commission of Canada. *Honouring the Truth, Reconciling for the Future: Summary of the Final Report of the Truth and Reconciliation Commission of Canada*. McGill-Queen's University Press, 2015.

Tuck, Eve, and K. Wayne Yang. "Decolonization Is Not a Metaphor." *Decolonization: Indigeneity, Education and Society* 1, no. 1 (2012): 1–40. https://jps.library.utoronto.ca/index.php/des/article/view/18630.

Ward, Stuart. "No End of a Reckoning." In *The Truth About Empire: Real Histories of British Colonialism,* edited by Alan Lester. Hurst, 2024.

Webstad, Phyllis, Allison Parker, and Brock Nicol, *Phyllis's Orange Shirt.* Medicine Wheel Publishing, 2019.

Webstad, Phyllis, and Kewageshig Emily. *With Our Orange Hearts.* Medicine Wheel Publishing, 2023.

Webstad, Phyllis, and Kristy McLeod. *Decolonization and Me: Conversations about Healing a Nation and Ourselves.* Medicine Wheel Publishing, 2025.

Wilson, Shawn. *Research Is Ceremony: Indigenous Research Methods.* Fernwood Publishing, 2008.

Wineburg, Samuel S. *Why Learn History (When It's Already on Your Phone).* University of Chicago Press, 2018.

Woods, Eric Taylor. "On the Making of a National Tragedy: The Transformation of the Meaning of the Indian Residential Schools." In *Power Through Testimony: Reframing Residential Schools in the Age of Reconciliation*, edited by Brieg Capitaine and Karine Vanthuyne. UBC Press, 2017.

Woolford, Andrew. *This Benevolent Experiment: Indigenous Boarding Schools, Genocide, and Redress in Canada and the United States.* University of Nebraska Press and University of Manitoba Press, 2015.

Woolford, Andrew. "Ontological Destruction: Genocide and Canadian Aboriginal Peoples." *Genocide Studies and Prevention* 4, no. 1 (2009): 81–97. https://digitalcommons.usf.edu/gsp/vol4/iss1/6.

Woolford, Andrew, and Stefan Wolejszo, "Collecting on Moral Debts: Reparations for the Holocaust and Pořajmos." *Law and Society Review* 40, no. 4 (2006): 871–901. https://doi.org/10.1111/j.1540-5893.2006.00284.x.

Yerushalmi, Yosef. *Assassins of Memory: Essays on the Denial of the Holocaust.* Columbia University Press, 1993.

Zimmerman, Jonathan, and Emily Robertson. *The Case for Contention: Teaching Controversial Issues in American Schools.* University of Chicago Press, 2017.